JOB DIMENSIONS AND EDUCATIONAL NEEDS IN LIBRARIANSHIP

JAMES J. KORTENDICK
AND
ELIZABETH W. STONE

The Catholic University of America

American Library Association
Chicago 1971

The research reported herein was performed pursuant to a grant with the Office of Education, U.S. Department of Health, Education, and Welfare. Contractors undertaking such projects under Government sponsorship are encouraged to express freely their professional judgment in the conduct of the project. Points of view or opinions stated do not, therefore, necessarily represent official Office of Education position or policy.

International Standard Book Number 0-8389-3126-X (1971)

Library of Congress Catalog Card Number 70-157141

Printed in the United States of America

Contents

Acknowledgments	v
1. Objectives of the Study	**1**
Goals	1
Focus on Practicing Librarians	3
Focus on Federal Librarians	4
Problems	9
Related Research	20
2. Design of the Study	**33**
The Questionnaire	33
The Sample	43
The Interview	50
3. Background Information about Federal Librarians	**61**
Personal and Job-Related Variables	62
Work Variables	77
Educational Variables	80
Federal Librarians Compared with Other Librarians	86
Summary of Background Characteristics	91
4. Job Dimensions of the Federal Librarian	**96**
Analysis of the Job Inventory	96
Qualitative Analysis of Job Activities	116
Summary and Conclusions	124
5. Course Demand and Employee Characteristics	**128**
Demand for Courses and Workshops	129
Relationship between Demand for Courses and Two Job-Related Variables	144
Attainment of Objectives	152
6. Additional Data about Building a Post-Master's Program in Library Science	**158**
Interest in Formal Post-Master's Programs	158
Self-Perceived Deficiencies in Professional Training	173
Knowledge, Abilities, and/or Skills for Replacement	177
Suggestions about a Post-MLS Program	180
Summary and Conclusions	195
7. Interviews with Top-Level Library Administrators	**205**
Course Needs at the Post-MLS Level	206
Most-Needed Skills and Competencies at the Post-Master's Level	223

CONTENTS

    Additional Data about Building a Post-Master's Program   245
    Summary and Conclusions   272
8. **Conclusions and Recommendations**   276
    Professional Problems Reflected in Study   277
    Library Education Needs at the Post-Master's Level   281
    Recommendations for Further Study and Research   308

Appendixes

A Questionnaire and Cover Letter Sent to Professional
    Federal Librarians   315
B Outline of Interview Schedule with Top-Level
    Library Administrators   342
C Questionnaire to Determine Interviewees' Attitudes
    toward Post-MLS Programs   344
D Directions for the Card Sort and Card-Sort
    Reporting Form   345
E Appendix Tables   347

Bibliography   405

Acknowledgments

This study is possible only because of the cooperation and assistance of many people to whom the principal investigators are deeply grateful. First we want to acknowledge our indebtedness to Mr. Paul Howard, Executive Secretary of the Federal Library Committee. From the very beginning, his interest and wise counsel as a consultant were most helpful in the development of the project, in identifying the population to be surveyed, and in seeking the cooperation of federal libraries and librarians.

After discussion with library educators and federal librarians, the project was defined and the proposal was submitted to the Bureau of Research of the United States Office of Education. Dr. Quincy Mumford, Librarian of Congress and Chairman of the Federal Library Committee, graciously wrote in support of the project to the Office of Education. Grateful acknowledgment is made to the staff of the Bureau of Research of the Office of Education for its continuing interest and cooperation during the project since funding on June 23, 1968.

We are indebted to the other consultants: Dr. Russell Shank, Director of the Smithsonian Institution's Libraries and Chairman of the Education Task Force of the Federal Library Committee; Dr. Charles H. Goodman, Associate Dean of the School of Government and Public Administration of American University, who had been a participant in another library research project and leader in library workshops; Dr. Harlan Mills, Manager of the Computer Mathematics Department, Center of Exploratory Studies, Federal Systems Development of

ACKNOWLEDGMENTS

International Business Machines; Mr. Joseph Becker, Adjunct Associate Professor in the Department of Library Science of Catholic University and a Director of EDUCOM (Interuniversity Communications Council). Consultants brought in during special phases of the project were: Dean Sarah Rebecca Reed of the Library School of the University of Alberta; Dr. Robert Landau, Scientific Advisor, the Office of Science and Technology in the Executive Office of the President; and Major Eldon Mills, formerly Chief, Systems Integration Branch of the Personnel Headquarters of the U.S. Air Force. The last served as programmer of the data for computer tabulation.

Within Catholic University, Mr. Dhirendra Ghosh, of the Mathematics Department, from the first stages of the study has been a member of the research team and has given wise counsel, developing the sampling design used and assisting in the interpretation of the statistical data. Carol Henderson, Micki Jo Young, and Carolyn Leopold served as valuable research assistants at various stages of the project. Sandra J. Beeson has served as secretary during most of the study, typing all the official reports and providing expertise in the design of tables and charts. Mary Feldman, Barbara Koopmann, Barbara Ruthven, Barbara Sabbia, and Amy Lee have our thanks for their help in the clerical phases of the project and in checking the statistical and bibliographical work.

We are especially indebted to the 365 federal librarians, around the world, who contributed their time in answering the mail questionnaire. Without their initial cooperation the study would not have been possible. The many additional comments that they offered so freely in the open-end sections of the questionnaire provided substantive material for the study.

Grateful acknowledgment is also expressed to the faculty of the Library Science Department of Catholic University, who advised on the job inventory; to the federal librarians in the area who participated in pretesting the questionnaire, including the Education Task Force of the Federal Library Committee; and to the members of the Panel on Education of the Committee on Scientific and Technical Information, who demonstrated interest and encouragement in the project. Finally, our special gratitude goes to the twenty library administrators who gave so generously and helpfully of their time in the interviews.

1
Objectives of the Study

This study was undertaken to meet more fully the demands for improved and expanded training of library personnel, especially at the middle and upper levels, occasioned by the rapidly changing roles and functions of libraries as they try to adapt to the vast social, economic, and technological changes currently in progress. The rise to a higher level of required skills and competencies—often new—has brought about an urgent need for improved training beyond the first professional degree at the post-master's level. The basic purpose of this research is curriculum development at the post-master's level that will equip the middle- and upper-level personnel in libraries for the changes confronting them. Although it would be possible to restructure the master's program and add the courses that this study shows a need for, that alternative has not been pursued for two reasons: a fairly stable master's curriculum is widely accepted and institutionalized and, more important, the new courses are designed for a different group of students—experienced librarians.

GOALS

Before discussing the design of the project, it is worthwhile to note a few of the demands being placed on librarians which necessitate increased competence to be obtained primarily from education beyond the master's degree in library science. The adoption of a scientific method of research for solutions to social, scientific, and industrial problems has, over the years, enlarged the research establishment, or knowledge industry.

OBJECTIVES OF THE STUDY

As knowledge in every discipline advances, the public, aware of the social and economic role of information, has a right to expect library service to be performed in the most efficient manner possible. However, Bundy and Wasserman (5:9—10) maintain that most librarians resist the idea that the most important commodity of modern times is information in myriad forms, and their continuing reliance on the book combined with their lack of specialized knowledge in subject areas have resulted in their failure to satisfy the newly emerging demands from their clients. Klempner (40:729) believes a major factor contributing to this inability of the librarians to meet newly emerging user demands is the lack of continuing education for librarians.

One of the major conclusions in a recently completed study by Dolby, Forsyth, and Resnikoff (14:2) states: "Exponential growth of library holdings will persist for the foreseeable future. To maintain current growth rates, *automation of the production of portions of the intellectual content*, as well as the production of the physical books and equivalent forms of stored information, will increase." The question arises, Are librarians, especially those in middle- and upper-level positions, with only the basic qualification of a master's degree in librarianship, properly equipped to handle this changing situation?

For the management personnel of the library this change has meant new problems in understanding, planning, staffing, communication, and coordination. The library administrator and his staff now have to use new sophisticated and complex management tools. The need for training in management was also singled out by Ginzberg (31:59), who emphasized that the library schools must make a place for administrative concepts and skills in their curriculum in light of recent changes:

> As libraries make more use of supporting personnel, it becomes important that senior librarians have some understanding of personnel management. Similarly, as libraries are grouped into larger systems, the leadership needs some understanding of the science and art of management of large organizations. If graduate schools are to educate leaders rather than technicians, they must stress many hitherto neglected aspects of management.

Today, not only are the traditional academic and scientific disciplines in an active state of cross-fertilization, but also they feel the impact of new disciplines. The National Advisory Commission on Libraries

---

Citations given in parentheses refer—by item and page numbers—to the numbered list of references at the end of the chapter.

(60:16), while noting that library personnel need a broader range of competence than has ever been required before, lists as one of the dilemmas of the profession the need for "enlisting more fully the aid of the various disciplines of the social, behavioral, and applied sciences in preparing library science students for the changing requirements of library management and the evolving role of the library in our society."

The seeming shortage of manpower in librarianship could be much better attacked if the existing manpower could be better directed and utilized, since there is evidence to support the premise that the profession is a long way from realizing the potential represented by the personnel already recruited. To correct this situation, additional training for middle- and upper-level personnel beyond the first professional degree is necessary, for it is training, as pointed out by Hall (33:1), that must precede and will determine to a large extent how effectively manpower *can* be used.

The rapidity of the technological, societal, and behavioral changes soon overwhelms a librarian who does not develop a continuous sytem of self-education. It has become increasingly difficult for the individual library practitioner to keep up with the literature unless he has correspondingly advanced his background training. The need in continuing education is both for overcoming obsolescence in areas covered in one's basic training and for enabling the individual advancing in the hierarchy of the library to equip himself with a broader and deeper, and often newer, base of knowledge than that he received in the fifth-year master's program. Simultaneously, as Corson (10:144—61) points out, the rising manager or administrator must develop competencies which include a solid grasp of administrative and executive skills and processes, especially the capacity for directing others, as well as a familiarity with the internal and external environment. The needs of librarians in positions of responsibility today would seem to demand immediate attention as it is they (as pointed out by Drennan [15] and by Bundy and Wasserman [5]) who will determine whether librarianship will be able to institute changes and transform itself in a manner demanded by current pressures in society.

FOCUS ON PRACTICING LIBRARIANS

Before delineating the specific objectives of the study, it is necessary to pause and clearly specify the audience for whom the proposed postmaster's program is being developed as a result of this study. Library education is at the crossroads today so far as the sixth-year programs

OBJECTIVES OF THE STUDY

are concerned. On the one hand, there are the needs of future library educators to consider, and on the other hand, there are the needs of the practicing librarians. Traditionally, the fifth-year master's program makes no such distinction — nor is it necessary at that level — but the distinction, asserted by Swank (75), needs to be made at the sixth-year level. The sixth-year programs in existence today, according to Swank, aim primarily at education for the practicing librarians, but the Fryden study (23:16—19) of post-master's programs in librarianship show that some schools try to do both. Danton (13) has perceived this problem. He makes as one of his eleven specific recommendations for post-MLS programs that, "The schools spell out clearly and in detail, and put into print, the nature of their programs, what they entail, what a student may expect to secure by enrolling, and what will be expected of him" (13:81).

Even as Swank suggests in the field of librarianship, Culbertson (12) recommends in the discipline of education a differentiated training program at the postgraduate level for those preparing for administration and for positions as teachers or researchers. Culbertson bases his argument for differentiation on the assumption that the skills and values, as well as the setting in which skills and values are to be applied by these two groups of personnel, are substantially different. Further, Culbertson contends that it is no longer possible for one given individual to acquire effectiveness in all aspects of knowledge utilization, and so he proposes a program for administrators and practitioners that is specifically different in regard to skills, values, and knowledge required from the program he recommends for the preparation and improvement of teachers and researchers. It is advocated here that the training for administrators and practitioners returning for post-master's training should refer to the existing organizational setting while the problems prescribed for teachers and researchers would be derived from a more theoretical context.

FOCUS ON FEDERAL LIBRARIANS

In a statistical study such as this one, it is always judicious to concentrate on one sector of a large population because of its internal homogeneity. The search for such a sector within librarianship ended with the selection of federal librarians. The federal libraries form such a homogeneous sector and seemed to satisfy all the necessary criteria for choosing a sector:

1. In federal libraries there is a uniformity in the definition of middle- and upper-level personnel which makes the task of analysis easier.
2. Federal libraries are distributed geographically all over the United States and the world. Also, among them every type of library service — special, academic, public, and school — is represented. This variety automatically suggests the hypothesis that federal librarians are representative of all types of librarians (which is verified in the study).
3. Federal libraries have, in some cases, progressed farther than other types of libraries in the use of current technological innovations, in the development of new concepts—such as those involved in automation, selective dissemination of information, use of systems analysis, and development of communication networks—and in the use of new management concepts—such as program planning and budgeting. Therefore, it was premised that some of the newer technological and management advances would be adequately represented in the federal library complex.
4. The existence of library complexes, with regional branches scattered all over the country, makes the federal libraries especially interesting from the point of view of future utilization of automation and the future development of information network communications systems, such as the one now being developed at the National Agricultural Library called the Agricultural Science Information Network Development Plan (51).
5. Since the Federal Library Committee was interested in the study and cooperated in the project in many ways, it was felt that the nonresponse rate would be low.
6. The Federal Library Committee made available a list of all federal libraries, so that the population could be identified.
7. Although federal librarians are all over the world, the heaviest concentration of middle- and upper-level personnel is in the greater Washington area, which has meant that the Department of Library Science of the Catholic University of America has been in an excellent position to interview and make direct contacts with the personnel in all the types of federal libraries. Thus the human and material resources essential to the study have been close at hand, making for convenience and economy in conducting the research.

OBJECTIVES OF THE STUDY

Furthermore, an examination of data presented in studies by Drennan (15), Schick (63), and Schiller (65) indicates that if a profile of the average federal library were made for the Stratum II libraries in this study (which would include all types of libraries, but exclude the Library of Congress), it would show that in terms of service characteristics, size, and structural patterns, federal libraries are similar to all other libraries. However, because the unit for which data were collected for this study was the *librarian* rather than the *library*, it is not possible to give for the library the extensive comparative statistics that have been presented relative to the profile of the federal librarian.

Concerning special nongovernmental libraries, Schick (63:2, 11, 12) presents data which lead him to conclude that federal libraries: (1) in their regulations concerning use "follow policies similar to those of special non-governmental libraries" (with the exception of classified materials); (2) perform "traditional library activities"* in relation to their clientele; (3) serve two publics — the primary group consisting of the personnel of the agency and the secondary group of outside users who are permitted access to the library's materials on the premises or through interlibrary loan; (4) frequently administer a general reading collection in addition to their own special library collection; and (5) "extend their services directly or indirectly to all segments of the population."

There are also indications that it is not only in relation to the nongovernment special library that similarities in tasks performed and services rendered exist. For example, Drennan (15) published a statistical report on public libraries, one phase of which covered the tasks in which public librarians engage. The most frequently occurring tasks of public librarians bear great similarity to the tasks performed by the federal librarians in this survey. Comparative statistics are presented to show this similarity (table 1). It should be noted that where differences do occur, they are due possibly more to the way tasks are listed in the survey instructions than to basic difference in kinds of activity performed. Looking ahead to some other findings presented in chapter 3, it is noted that supervising the work of others was listed in studies of

---

*The "traditional library activities" that Schick (63:17) found most frequently performed by the reporting federal libraries were, in rank order: (1) reference and/or information services; (2) circulation of library materials; (3) interlibrary loan transactions; (4) compilation of bibliographies upon request; (5) preparation of acquisition lists; (6) routing of new journals; (7) cataloging and classification of collection; (8) regularly issuing publications for distributing to the public or library clientele; and (9) administering a general reading collection in addition to their own special library collection.

TABLE 1

MOST FREQUENTLY OCCURRING TASKS PERFORMED BY PUBLIC LIBRARIANS BY PER CENT AS COMPARED TO FEDERAL LIBRARIANS

KIND OF ACTIVITY [6] (As worded in the Public Library Survey)	PERCENTAGE OF RESPONDENTS PERFORMING TASKS	
	Public	Federal
Supervise the work of others	78.4	62.7
Compile and annotate bibliographies, search and select literature	71.4	75.1[1]
Keep records	71.2	----[2]
Public relations, publicity work, speeches	54.3	45.5[3]
Recruit, train people in the organization	50.7	52.5
Briefing superiors on my work [4]	44.2	34.5[4]
Counseling clients, students	37.6	37.5
Budgeting, costing, controlling, allocating expenditures [5]	33.4	27.4[5]
Writing, technical and general reports or projects	25.0	23.3
Consult or advise clients or customers on technical matters	24.0	33.7
Coordinate activities of professionals at same level	19.0	22.2
Statistical analyses	14.9	15.6
Engage in basic research	12.5	11.2

[1] For the Federal library study, this represents a composite figure as the heading used in the Public Library study was much broader than the wording in the present study which was "Compile bibliographies" (30%); "Search literature" (13.1%); "Select literature" (32%).

[2] No comparable heading in Federal questionnaire, as record keeping was listed under several headings.

[3] Public relations for the Federal libraries is broken down into several categories so in actuality a comparable figure might be assumed to be nearer to the 54.3%.

[4] As "Brief superiors on my work" is a more general wording than that used in the Federal survey (which was "Report progress to higher management") it would be expected to elicit more responses.

[5] This heading covers specifics broken down in the Federal survey.

[6] Four other items mentioned which received small percentage responses on the Drennan study and were not listed in the Federal questionnaire were "Teach courses" (11.3%), "Exploration or field work" (—), "Supervise construction" (—), "Travel" (10.3%).

OBJECTIVES OF THE STUDY

both men and women and, as Drennan (15:12) comments, "should have relevance for their training."

Of course there are special services performed by public libraries (such as services to the disadvantaged) not performed by federal libraries, even as there are services performed by federal libraries (such as preparing translations) which are not generally handled by public or academic libraries. However, it would seem justifiable to state that federal libraries generally engage in a large number of activities quite similar to those performed in public libraries.

Concerning the characteristics of present positions as they exist in the academic library, Schiller (65:45) has pointed out that one out of seven academic librarians is a chief librarian and that "roughly half of all academic libraries have professional staffs of less than three," which indicates a large number of very small academic libraries. That a similar situation exists with the federal libraries is evidenced by the large proportion of head librarians among respondents, the substantial proportion of librarians in one- to three-man libraries, and the overall average of 1.09 professional librarians per federal library in Stratum II.

In regard to library budgets, Schick (63) points out that the budget of the federal special library varies from agency to agency, but that most library budgets consist of basic items of operating expenditures: salaries (or personnel costs), library materials, and binding and rebinding. Table 2 shows a comparison between federal libraries, public libraries, and

TABLE 2

SELECTED LIBRARY EXPENDITURE DATA (IN %)
BY TYPE OF LIBRARY AND CATEGORY

Item	Public libraries serving 25,000 population and over	College and University libraries	Special Federal Libraries	
			Civilian National Agencies	Defense Agencies
Total operating expenditures	100.0	100.0	100.0	100.0	100.0
Salaries	65.6	49.2	70.3	66.5	61.0
Library Materials	17.0	33.4	8.6	27.9	24.5
Binding and rebinding	1.2	3.8	1.6	2.4	2.0
Other	16.2	13.6	19.5	3.2	12.0

Source: Schick (Ref. 63:22)

college and university libraries. The national libraries in the federal group show a particularly low percentage of funds spent for materials due to extensive exchange programs and to their ability to secure free copies of materials through the provision of United States copyright legislation.

To summarize: From the total population of librarians, a sample was chosen proportionately from one type of librarianship that had representatives of all kinds of libraries — special, public, academic, and school. It was assumed that this sample population would have certain basic needs which would reflect the needs of the total population of librarians. Although it was recognized that no sample of librarians would be completely homogeneous with the total population of librarians, it was shown that within the scope of the federal library sample, the librarians have broadly the same personal characteristics and do the same kinds of work as does the larger total population as found in data from other surveys. Hence, it was postulated that the continuing education needs of the total population would be similar to those of the federal librarians. (A report of the outcome of this study in relation to others regarding course demand is given in chapter 8.)

PROBLEMS

Basic Assumptions

This study started with the premise that to establish a sound base for curriculum development, it was necessary first to determine what concepts, knowledge, and techniques are required for middle- and upper-level library personnel to perform at an optimum level of efficiency. Explicitly, it was felt that for the development of useful curricula and courses at the post-MLS level, a prime source of knowledge should be functional behaviors that are necessary in the job situation.

To determine specifically what these terminal performance behaviors should be so that learning experiences provided could be rooted in reality, the decision was reached, after an extensive review of related research and literature,* to use a systems approach to curriculum development. The general systems approach to educational planning

---

*See Bibliography, especially the section Educational Planning: Multi-Media and Systems Approaches.

that has been used in this study has been defined by Lange (42) as representing an attempt to break the mold of traditional concepts and to approach interaction from an open, innovative, and product-oriented perspective. "In evaluating the status of available knowledge, the systems orientation pays attention to how what is known might be used and to what new knowledge is needed to develop useful products" (42:113).

The general philosophy used in this study also embraces general characteristics which Cook (7:3) has suggested as helpful concepts to employ when applying systems approaches to education planning. These concepts include: (1) considering the problem at hand in its broadest context; (2) placing emphasis on the functional relationships between the variables in the system; (3) investigating the interactions between the variables along with their main effects; and (4) studying and developing flow-diagram models (as distinct from mathematical models), which are used to represent the actual system.

More specifically, the systems approach to curriculum and course development has been conceived by Ofiesh (54:763) as involving "the specification of behavioral objectives, the assessment of student repertories, the development of instructional strategies, testing and revising instructional units (validation), and finally the packaging and *administering a validated learning system.*" Such an approach results in the development of learning experiences which are adjusted to students' needs and learning modes. The learning experiences are designed to produce the behaviors specified for each course. In other words, the specified behavioral objectives, or terminal functional behaviors, would be, as explained by Ofiesh, the constants of the system. To develop effectively the final packaged courses proposed, it is recognized that the system approach suggested must be sensitive to various stimuli and include elements for appropriate response, feedback, and adjustment.

A review of educational research and literature related to curriculum construction and educational planning revealed increasing evidence of educators not only talking about but also utilizing systems concepts in their work. Cook (8) has pointed out that systems theory is not the exclusive domain of management since it pervades almost all fields of human endeavor as well as natural phenomena. The advantages of using this approach to educational planning and development are: (1) clearer statements of project objectives and goals are achieved; (2) the means by which objectives will be reached are explicit; (3) clearer definitions are formulated for each task to be done; (4) trouble spots can be identified in advance; (5) areas that call for replanning are identified early in the project; and (6) the communication processes are clearly understood as they are portrayed graphically for all involved to see (9).

As early as 1962, Glaser (32), director of the Learning Research and Development Center at the University of Pittsburgh, edited a book, *Training for Research and Education*, designed "to provide an account of training research and to examine the implication for education in general." Preparation of that volume was stimulated by recognition of the relevance to civilian education of research and development in problems of military training and of the underlying phenomena of learning. The chapters in the Glaser compilation are organized around a general conception of an instructional system that includes the following elements: (1) instructional goals—the system objectives; (2) entering behavior—the system input; (3) instructional procedures—the system operator; (4) performance assessment—the output monitor; and (5) research and development. The first four represent the main flow of the instructional system. The research and development efforts are oriented toward producing results that can be put to practical use.

Since Glaser's work, various research attempts have been made to apply the system approach to educational problems. Well-known examples are Crawford's "Concepts of Training" in Gagné's *Psychological Principles in Systems Development* (11); studies by Robert G. Smith of the Human Resources Research Office of George Washington University (67—69); and a cluster of works by Gagné (24—30). It is also encouraging to note new emphasis upon experimental work within the field of curriculum. "By manipulating variables in school practice and noting consequences, curriculum knowledge is gained, and at the same time the objectives, content, and methods of instruction are changed" (46:313). As long as curriculum studies were purely descriptive, it was difficult for curricular knowledge to be a force in changing what was taught and how it was taught.

Further examples of this concern with the systems approach in education is shown in the publication of a small paperback entitled *New Look at Education*, by John Pfeiffer, which carried as its subtitle "Systems Analysis in Our Schools and Colleges" (56). In engineering education Taft (76) has taken the position that techniques developed in systems technology are applicable to the field of education, both in administration and curriculum development, and that it is only a question of securing multidisciplinary cooperation to put them into practice. There are also efforts underway, as noted through an increasing number of studies reported in ERIC (Educational Resources Information Center), to provide educators with some substantive knowledge and competence in actually using the systems approach. One

OBJECTIVES OF THE STUDY

example is the work of Donald Miller (48) with Operation PEP in a statewide project to prepare educational planners in the state of California for using the systems approach in solving a wide range of problems.

Elements in the Data Base

To investigate the interactions between variables, an important concept in developing a systems orientation, the decision was made to use a multifaceted approach in gathering information for the data base on which to build curricula and courses. Four main elements, or types of information, were sought for this study. They are listed on the following pages, and for each a rationale is presented indicating the need and usefulness of obtaining this type of data to develop the end product designed for this research project, namely packaged courses for a post-MLS curriculum for middle- and upper-level library personnel.

The first type of information comprises the kinds of job activities in which middle- and upper-level professional staff members of libraries are actually engaged. The answer to the deceptively simple question What do people do in their jobs? provides a more precise knowledge base on which to build courses and curriculum than has been available before. It is necessary to know what talents and skills and concepts are required for middle- and upper-level professional posts in the evolving library both now and in the future and what terminal behavior patterns following a post-MLS program are most needed to staff and manage a library effectively.

The objective in going to the librarians to find out what they are doing in their jobs is one aspect of establishing the need for continuing education based on objective study rather than on subjective opinion. In their study, *Men Near the Top*, Corson and Paul (10) emphasize the importance of finding out what work activities are engaged in by the upper-level employees who constituted the population in their study. They stated that no improvement could be brought about in training programs until this information is obtained. Questions of training can be satisfactorily answered only when "one knows in detail just what people do in their jobs." This question is a familiar one in business and in industry. It was first raised in an organized and analytical fashion more than fifty years ago by Frederick W. Taylor (78), the father of scientific management. To the degree that it was scientific, the movement developed guidelines based on careful observation of what people do, their behavior, and relationships to others in the job. In business since the days of Taylor, there has been a tremendous amount of research based on continuous study and research, but there is no counterpart to this body of information in libraries.

Positions grow and change with the impact of the individual holding them and often bear little resemblance to the sterile job description provided for a given position. The questionnaire for the present study was designed to find out the librarian's view concerning the importance of his job activities and the relative amount of time he spent on them. The process of going directly to the librarian who is performing the job rests on some basic assumptions. First, although it is assumed that a substantial portion of the variance in work at the middle and upper levels is due to the demands or requirements of the position, at least as much is attributable to the personality and style of the performance of the incumbent. The research of Stogdill and others (71, 72) indicates that this is a reasonable assumption. A second assumption is that the incumbent of a middle- or upper-level library position is the best-qualified informant concerning the nature of his work and is capable of rating on appropriate scales a number of job activities in terms of time and importance. Based on research findings, others have considered this a reasonable assumption. Hemphill concluded that comparative studies "provide no evidence which would suggest that incumbents tend to distort the descriptions of their positions in a favorable direction" (34:27—28). Similarly, McLennan stated that the incumbent seemed the most reliable source for the data: "In view of the fact that the respondents were the most qualified persons for evaluating the skill make-up of their jobs and also because there was no evidence of bias, it can be assumed that these data were relatively reliable" (44:237). In the same regard, Corson and Paul (10) feel one of the most important aspects of their study is that their chief conclusions about career development and training needs are based on data obtained from incumbents in the grade levels they were studying. Finally, it was assumed that the job-activity items represent an adequate sampling of the work undertaken in common by the librarians. This assumption points to the importance of the construction of the questionnaire and the rationale for the method used in this regard is dealt with in the section on the first data-gathering instrument, The Questionnaire, in chapter 2.

The aspect of course development that should receive primary attention is the development of well-defined, job-relevant objectives. When objectives are appropriately developed, they provide clear guidance that permits an orderly presentation of course content. Out of data obtained about work activities by the incumbents, it is possible to determine competencies required, and these can be stated in behavioral

OBJECTIVES OF THE STUDY

terms. Peterson (55) also emphasized that the needs on the job must be found out before any objectives can be set and that determination of subject matter to be covered should be based on the actual job, the work activities performed, and the competencies required. It is also significant to note that the School Library Manpower Project (53:7) established for its Phase I a task analysis survey "to identify the multiplicity of tasks performed in school libraries today and the types of staff personnel performing each of these tasks. . . . and the tasks performed will be analyzed to determine the preparation, knowledge, and skills necessary to perform them. These results will be studied for two implications: (a) implications for training programs . . . and (b) implications for the certification of school librarians."

It should be emphasized that there is still another important reason for finding out directly from the librarian the work activities in which he is engaged—and that is motivation for continuing education. It was discovered in a recent study of librarians (74) that the primary reasons that librarians become involved in continuing education activities are related to the content of the programs offered—whether or not the content of the educational opportunity offered is directly related to the work processes in which the librarian is engaged at the time the opportunity is offered. The design of this study was based partially on the findings of Herzberg (35, 36) that motivating factors at work are achievement, recognition, the work itself, responsibility, and advancement. As Crawford (11:329) has pointed out, the Herzberg studies point to the importance of the work itself and indicate the importance of taking work factors into account in building continuing-education programs. This is to say that if courses are not offered which the librarians feel will fill their job-related needs, they will not take them. Indeed, this was the reason given by some respondents in the Stone survey (74) for not having taken any courses since receiving the MLS degree.

The second element is the self-perceived educational needs of the federal librarian respondents and the courses for which there is the greatest demand. For curriculum construction a listing of possible courses that might meet the needs of librarians as they planned for their individual career development was essential. The federal librarians indicated on the questionnaire their educational needs in several ways: (1) the areas in which they would be interested in taking courses; (2) the areas in which they would be interested in taking workshops or short-term courses; (3) whether or not they would enroll for a one-year post-MLS program (as distinguished from single courses) in library science; (4) whether or not they would enroll for a doctoral program in library science; (5) whether or not they would enroll for a graduate program in non-library science subject areas at a predoctoral or doctoral level; (6) what type of formal study they had engaged in since receiving their MLS degree; (7) whether or not there were any formal scientific, technical, or professional courses they lacked which they felt would have been especially helpful to them in their present position; (8) whether or not there are activities that they felt they should be engaged in for which their previous training had not prepared them; and, finally, (9) their general suggestions for courses and curricula at the post-MLS level were solicited.

In developing an on-going collegiate curriculum the college should accumulate evidence over a period of years about what the graduates are doing, what parts of the curriculum they feel benefit them most, and what changes they would recommend. The college should also maintain closer relationships with its supporting public so that it will reflect the real wants and needs of society at a given point in time. The college which asks future employers of its graduates what they expect of college-educated men and women is illustrating this technique. "Such a process is time consuming and one which colleges are tempted to bypass. However, if one wishes to develop a rational curriculum, there can be no substitute for it" (47:30). Some may object to such an approach on the ground that the college ought to lead rather than follow. "Such an objection overlooks the fact that basically the college is a norming institution. It is not intended to create people who reject the prevailing cultural values. Rather it prepares people to enter the mainstream of life in that society. . . . The college should identify the most important knowledge, skills, and attitudes which enable people to survive in the American context and make them the substance of the curriculum" (47:31). If this is true of undergraduate curricula, how much more true is it for a graduate curriculum, particularly a post-MLS curriculum in library science which is not required for any kind of certification or advancement, but which the student engages in solely on the basis of his own individual motivation. Strong personal motivation is required for a librarian to keep up to date.

The reasons for seeking the self-perceived needs of librarians who have completed the MLS degree and are now working in libraries—as well as for discovering their attitude toward continuing education needs as related to their jobs—are based on the systems approach to contemporary curriculum design in which faculty preference gives way to learner needs. The learner and his needs are placed at the center of educative process at the post-MLS level. Rogers (61:199) bases his model for graduate education, for example, on a basic assumption:

OBJECTIVES OF THE STUDY

"Most significantly the plan is built on the hypothesis that *the student has the potentiality and the desire to learn*, providing that a suitable environment can be established." He believes that the focus at the graduate level should be providing a psychological climate suitable for self-directed and significant learning. Also assumed by Rogers (62:38) is that significant learning takes place where the subject matter is perceived by the student as having relevance for his own purposes—where it is relevant to the goals he is trying to achieve. The research staff found that the data requested pertaining to the librarians' self-perceived needs were directly related to this basic assumption.

Other assumptions made by Rogers (61) also seem pertinent to the building of a post-MLS program and constitute a partial justification of why the librarian, as potential learner, was asked for his opinions: (1) learning is facilitated when the student participates responsibly in the learning process—when he chooses his own directions, decides his own course of action; self-initiated learning, involving the whole person, is the most persuasive and lasting; (2) creativity in learning is best facilitated when self-criticism and self-evaluation are of primary importance and evaluation by others is secondary; and (3) the most socially useful learning in the modern world is the learning of the process of learning—a continuing openness to experience, an incorporation into oneself of the process of change.

In summing up the views of contemporary theories in a compilation of essays entitled *Instruction: Some Contemporary Viewpoints*, Siegel (66:329) states, "The most exciting and far-reaching generalization emerging for me from this sample of contemporary formulations is that to be most effective, instruction must be tailored to the needs, capabilities, and histories of the individual learners." Siegel predicts that in spite of increasing enrollments instruction will be custom-tailored to the needs and capabilities of the learner. Determining the student's demand for courses is certainly one aspect of making post-MLS education relative to the needs of the students.

In the development of curriculum, the use of data indicating the continuing education needs from the librarians in the field is, of course, but one means of implementing experimental learning, but it is a step in meeting the elements of such learning described by Rogers (62:38) as: (1) personally involved; (2) self-initiated; (3) pervasive—makes a difference in his behavior and attitudes; (4) evaluated by the learner in terms of what he wants to know—in this instance relative to his job situation; and (5) meaningful to the learner because it is built into the whole learning experience.

In other professions the research-based method of asking the practitioner what his self-perceived continuing education needs are in relation to his job is frequently used. One excellent and comprehensive series of examples of this approach is provided by Dubin (17—22) and his colleagues at Pennsylvania State University. Typically, each of these studies would have as its stated objectives: (1) to determine the self-perceived education needs of the professional who has been out in the field for a number of years; (2) to determine the attitudes of the professional group toward continuing education needs as related to their job, supervision, and employer; and (3) to recommend methods for providing continuing education programs to update the professional group being studied. Also, typically, the methods used would be: (1) a written questionnaire asking for background information about the respondent, including his education and lists of courses which the respondent would check off on a three-point scale (such as: "should have," "could use," "don't really need"); and (2) group interviews or questionnaires used to obtain the opinion of supervisors regarding the continuing education needs of those they supervise. Typically, also, recommendations, based on the survey, would be made to relevant groups: the university, the employing organization, the professional society, the state government, and the individual practitioner.

The studies of Schill and Arnold (64) and of Arnold (2), leading to the development of curricula for six kinds of technical education, have used a listing of courses (using card-sort format) in which individual course descriptions were rated according to a weighted scale in order to define curriculum content functionally related to the occupational needs in a variety of technologies. Schill and Arnold (64:22) state that this method of developing curriculum remains valid. Their research design called for the use of the card sort with both the technicians and their supervisors, and from this experience the team reached one of the basic tenets of its research: "To find out what a technician does and what knowledges are related to the job, the place to go is to the employed technicians." These studies serve as another example in which an important item in curriculum development was based on the self-perceived needs of those currently holding positions in areas for which courses were being developed.

The third class of findings is the comparison of assessments made by administrators with those made by questionnaire respondents. It also includes those courses and competencies for which, in the eyes of the administrators, continuing education at the post-MLS level has the greatest need. To the project staff a necessary part of the research was to find out the extent of agreement between what the librarians

OBJECTIVES OF THE STUDY

expressed as their needs for courses and programs at the post-MLS level and what their supervisors thought would be the most important elements to be added to the base knowledge which the MLS provides. How should the employee best receive training in these additional competencies? Answers to these questions will give an indication of how much support, in finances and time, the administrative personnel will be willing to give in promoting the program or programs developed.

In a project that had as its ultimate aim the development of courses and curricula, there were many reasons which led to the decision to include interviews with top library administrators as one of the data-gathering instruments. Informal discussions with library administrators about the study showed that they were interested in the kinds of courses that might be developed at the post-MLS level for their employees. A common reaction was that they had ideas that they would like to give about such continuing education. Also, it was felt by the project's consultants that information should be obtained from interviews with top-level administrators to add to the data base. The premise was that the decision is not which research method to use, but rather which set of methods should be combined to reflect the total situation (79). Thus the information obtained in the questionnaire was cross-validated through the use of interviews with twenty library administrators.

Assuming that top-level personnel are hired or promoted because they understand broad relationships and have the knowledge of—and concern for—improving library service, the research staff and consultants reasoned that those same people know what libraries need and desire at the middle and upper levels. Any success that educational planners of post-MLS programs may have in producing librarians who can adapt to future as well as current job requirements is contingent upon satisfying the personnel needs of libraries—more specifically, of those administrators (designated in this study as interviewees) who hire and promote librarians at lower levels.

Schill and Arnold (64:8), in their study of curricula content for six technologies, point out that various groups and individuals have been assumed by our democratic society to have legitimate concern for, and understanding of, curricular problems for the different areas of education. Three groups logically concerned with the education of librarians are: (1) the librarians themselves, (2) the administrators and teachers in the library schools and the administrative staffs of their parent universities, and (3) the libraries employing middle- and upper-level professional personnel, or, more specifically, the administrators of these libraries, who are familiar with the tasks being performed by librarians.

In our society specialization of work is a condition encouraging the growth of professional groupings. Organized associations today occupy a much more significant place than they did years ago. Because men in their working hours live differently from one another, they think differently. The position of occupational groups in the economic processes of society fosters common attitude patterns (70:7). Thus management personnel will display a community of purpose. Arnold (2:16) indicates that the views of managers regarding educational curricula are different from those held by the employees whom they supervise.

If the three groups described above are considered as groups in the sense that Stanley considers them, then all should be given a voice in library curriculum matters. Stanley (70:7) says, in this regard, "Members of these groups typically conceive their purposes, not in terms of private advantage, but in terms of their conceptions of the common weal." It would seem that the three groups all qualify as segments of society and, at the same time, have unique qualifications for making curricular decisions. These same groups might typically be identified as potential members for advisory committees in the formulation of curricular and administrative educational policies at local, state, and national levels. As a matter of fact, the Vocational Education Act of 1963 provided for the formation and use of such committees in the making of recommendations for revisions and additions to vocational programs and facilities.

The purpose of this discussion has been to give background for the assumption made in the study that the top-level library administrators might be expected to exhibit different views toward courses and curriculum development at the post-MLS level than the librarians they supervise. Smith (67—69) makes a strong case for getting information from supervisors in deciding what to teach in course development. He outlines the rationale for determining what is to be taught in a given course, including the importance of the activity in determining the success or failure of the unit mission and the suitability of the job situation itself for learning the task. Smith states that in these areas the supervisor is the best person from whom to obtain the information. Based on data obtained from the job incumbent and the supervisor, Smith suggests the use of decision rules to decide the level at which training should be given within a given course.

The fourth element in the data base is the analysis of variables pertaining to the individual librarian (age, education, time in position,

OBJECTIVES OF THE STUDY

etc.) their relationships to job structures and course demand. In keeping with the systems approach, it was deemed necessary to obtain this type of data in order to discover the interrelationships and correlations between individual variables and continuing education needs. This type of data makes possible a meaningful, coherent picture of the respondents and shows patterned relationships between variables rather than a mass of meaningless data.

The input into the system is the individual librarian who seeks professional growth through formal courses in a university environment. These data, therefore, indicate some of the constraints that the individual learner places upon the instructional system. Because the heterogeneity of the prospective students places particular burdens on the training program, it must be assessed—through an analysis of variables—if the training provided is to be maximally effective. Candidates for admission to the post-MLS program will have various sets of knowledge, skills, and attitudes based on their environment, educational achievement level, experience (for some it is a first career choice; for some, a third), all of which provide the curriculum planner with facts about patterns of student repertories and suggest elements that might be considered in developing criteria of admissions to the post-MLS program. One requirement already fixed by the nature of the project would be the possession of a graduate degree in library science; another to be decided upon would be level of experience; and another would be prerequisite courses required for admission to a given course.

Regardless of the standards set for admission, it is expected that there will be differences in individual needs and backgrounds and that adjustment to these individual differences should be an overriding concern of those teaching the courses. However, the analysis of selected variables will facilitate the development of a curriculum in accordance with student background and orientation.

RELATED RESEARCH

Throughout the project, a review of relevant literature was carried on concurrently with other activities. Depending upon the needs of the project at different periods of time, this literature search concentrated on such areas as: investigation of current related projects; survey of current trends in library science education and curriculum development; continuing education; the methodology of constructing job inventories; techniques of questionnaire construction; interview techniques and techniques of constructing an interview schedule; systems approach to educational planning and curriculum building; preliminary identification of instructional techniques and methods that would seem to be of value in developing and packaging new library science courses. The literature in these areas which would seem to be the most valuable to others planning post-MLS educational programs is listed in the Bibliography by major subject areas.

Courses and Programs at Post-MLS Level

In the specific area of post-master's programs in library science or a sixth-year program, the chief sources of information on the programs are a survey by Fryden (23), an article by Swank (75), and a study by Danton (13).

In Williamson's (80) report of 1923 to the Carnegie Corporation, the weaknesses of library education in this country were forcefully presented. One of his recommendations was that all library schools be attached to institutions of higher learning. This change gradually took place. In 1926 the Board of Education for Librarianship of the American Library Association, after consultation with the Association of American Universities, determined that a student who had completed a year's work in librarianship after four years of college work would receive a second bachelor's degree (BS, BSLS, etc.) rather than a professional master's degree. It was decided that advanced training could be obtained through the sixth-year programs at the Type I library schools and, after 1928, the doctoral program at the University of Chicago.

In the early 1950s this pattern began to change. The BLS was converted into a fifth-year master's degree, the sixth-year master's rapidly disappeared, and the doctorate was offered at more than one library school. The point to be emphasized in this study is that the sixth-year master's degree almost completely disappeared. That degree was intended to provide advanced training needed by the profession, but to be less demanding than the work needed to obtain a doctorate. Although many library schools have allowed interested persons who have had training in librarianship to take additional course work on an informal basis, the degree program per se has virtually disappeared. In the last few years, however, several library schools have inaugurated formal programs of instruction at the post-master's degree level which are distinct from the doctoral programs.

These programs, most generally designated as "post-master's programs" were examined by Fryden (23) in 1968, at which time he found that there were eleven such programs in American library schools accredited by the American Library Association's Committee on Accreditation. References to these programs are few, and there never seems to have been a printed list of schools offering such programs until Fryden made his listing early in 1968. He included: the University of California at Los Angeles, Columbia University, Emory University, Florida State University, the University of Illinois, Louisiana State University, the University of Maryland, the University of Minnesota, the University of Pittsburgh, Western Michigan University, and the University of Wisconsin. In addition to the eleven schools cited by Fryden, the research staff found that in the fall of 1969, eight other schools stated in their most recent catalogs that some kind of advanced certificate or degree was offered for completion of a sixth-year program. Those listing such programs were: Drexel, Kent State, Michigan, North Texas State, Peabody (which had some type of program until 1965, when it was discontinued until the fall of 1968), Texas, and Texas Women's University—a total of sixteen in all.

After his study of the programs in operation at the time of his report, Fryden (23:26) raised some pertinent and troubling questions about the present status and future prospects of these programs. One of them was, "On what base do these programs build?" Fryden found that the requirements varied widely from school to school. He also found that there was not a clear relationship between the post-master's programs and the doctoral programs.

Fryden gave particular attention to the coincidence between the availability of governmental funds and (1) the dates when the programs began and (2) the number of students. He raised the pertinent questions: "What would happen if the funds were severely cut or dropped completely? To what extent would the universities then fund the programs themselves? Indeed, what would have happened if no outside money had been available?" In fact, at least one of the programs listed by Fryden has been dropped because of the lack of federal support. He further queries about whether other schools will start post-master's programs and whether they will depend on outside sources of money, and asks if the programs will eventually require some sort of evaluation and accreditation. He asks:

> To what extent is it proper that the Office of Education be the agency which so strongly controls the destiny of the programs? In short, by relying so heavily on outside funds which are subject (1) to Congressional vagaries, (2) to competition from the requests from other library schools, and (3) to an extramural committee

and the Commissioner of Education; do the schools surrender a part of their autonomy? [23:29]

Fryden concludes with the general, but practical, suggestion that other occupational groups be examined to see what they do to promote continuing education beyond the first professional degree.

In writing about these programs in library science in 1967, Swank (75:17) asserts that "sixth-year programs of specialization are desirable and may indeed soon be necessary." He emphasized, as noted earlier in this chapter, however, the necessity of distinguishing education for service from education for teaching or research. Swank candidly sums up the library profession's provision for post-master's programs in one short sentence: "We are all mixed up."

In addition to giving a history of the development of the twenty programs that have been offered (three were inoperative as of 1968–69), Danton (13) analyzes the student attrition rate (665 total enrollees vs. 196 total graduates), the support received by the schools from the Department of Health, Education and Welfare (for at least two-thirds of the schools this support had been "determinant and perhaps crucial"), the graduates and their evaluation of the programs in which they participated, as well as assessments from employers of 64 percent of the graduates of these programs. The male-female ratio of graduates was almost 1:2.5; 80 percent of the females and more than 60 percent of the males were over thirty-five. In spite of the weaknesses indicated in these programs, Danton concludes that:

(1) the basic concept of the sixth-year program is sound, and the idea should be supported and encouraged;
(2) a large majority of the programs are viable, will continue, and will probably improve qualitatively and expand quantitatively;
(3) a majority, probably a strong majority of the programs are functioning reasonably well to excellently;
(4) most programs can be, and a few need to be, improved in one or more respects [13:79].

Unfortunately, Danton's excellent survey was not available to the researchers of the present study until their survey was completed. Danton's status quo study provides important added perspective for the findings of the study which focuses attention on the future development of content and form for such programs.

A recent study by E. W. Stone (74) provided some evidence that graduate librarians do not rate formal course work at the post-master's

OBJECTIVES OF THE STUDY

level as truly important to their career development when weighed against other professional activities. In this study the librarians were asked to indicate the relative importance of 37 opportunities for professional development. Of them a sixth-year program in library science received the lowest possible rank. Other types of formal course work also received low rankings from the respondents, who were 1956 and 1961 graduates of accredited American library schools. Formal course work beyond the MLS for certification purposes was rank 36. Formal course work toward getting a second master's in a subject specialty was 28. Formal course work toward getting a doctorate was 25. In this same study the librarians were also asked to indicate their own degree of involvement in the 37 opportunities. In the amount of involvement in relation to the other opportunities, formal course work again received uniformly low rankings. Rank 37 was formal course work in sixth-year post-master's programs; rank 34 was formal course work for certification purposes; rank 31 was formal course work toward a second master's degree in a subject specialty; and rank 30 was formal course work toward a doctoral degree.

It was also found that only 5.8 percent of the entire sample of 138 librarians had obtained an additional advanced degree following the MLS. However, 38.4 percent had taken some courses for credit after the fifth-year master's degree in library science. Apparently the respondents recognized the importance of knowledge in the area of automation since it was a substantial favorite of the workshops and short courses that they took. Of these short courses in automation, however, 19 percent were evaluated as being of little or no help to them in their jobs.

Further, the Stone study found that the three forces that most strongly influence librarians to enroll in formal course work were: (1) the opportunity to use new knowledge on the job, (2) the high quality of course work itself, and (3) the opportunity to be exposed to new and creative ideas. The major deterrents to taking such work were: (1) the lack of available time and the difficulty of scheduling; (2) the inconvenience of formal course work; and (3) the lack of encouragement from the respondent's supervisor, administration, or board. These findings and others within that study point to the need for library schools to weigh properly the importance of motivation in encouraging librarians to study at the post-master's level. They also point up the dilemma that the profession faces, as concluded in that study, of reevaluating the type of activities that the librarian considers most important for his professional development in order to meet the felt needs of society today in terms of improved service.

Also relevant to the present study was a survey in 1968 by Phillips (57) which identified the most pressing training needs among federal librarians then. Based on replies from ninety-five respondents with an average 9.5 grade level and 10 3/4 years in the federal service, the top five training needs listed by the respondents were: (1) keeping up to date with developments in library science; (2) staff development and motivation; (3) application of automatic data processing to library activities; (4) management practices and problems in federal libraries; and (5) human relations and supervisory practices.

The Professional Education of Media Service Personnel (73), a report on one of the projects of the Center for Library and Educational Media Studies at the University of Pittsburgh, addresses itself through a series of papers by specialists to the problems involved in developing a curriculum on three graduate levels for the professional training of media specialists in schools and colleges. It defines the various competencies, skills, and knowledges required by the specialist; it points out the interdisciplinary nature of media service and the need to draw upon the sources of such areas as educational psychology, communications, sociology, and computer sciences; and it further indicates the need to identify and evaluate new instructional techniques to be used in the training programs.

Continuing Education in Related Disciplines

In his work on the professional school, McGlothlin (43:29) stated that a qualified professional should have "competence in practice of the profession, social understanding, ethical behavior, and scholarly concern." He placed responsibility for this accomplishment on the professional school when he added: "These aims are not reached, therefore, at a single point in time. The school must judge itself and be judged on its influence over the full careers of its graduates. Nothing less than endless growth can be considered success."

In recent years professional schools have become increasingly aware of the necessity for being concerned about continuing education. Speaking at the 1967 Midwinter Meeting of the American Library Association, Houle (39:261) expressed the importance of continuing education to professions:

> While continuing education will not cure all the problems of the professions, without it no cure is possible. The task for this generation is to work, amid all the distractions and complexities of practice, to aid the individual, either alone or in his natural work

OBJECTIVES OF THE STUDY

emphasized in certain types of public library activities and analyzed them in relation to course offerings at the master's level in library schools. Another study, by Clayton (4), appraises the personality characteristics among library students. The School Library Manpower Project mentioned earlier, in some ways parallels for school librarians this study on federal librarians. The first published report of the study was entitled *School Library Personnel Task Analysis Survey* (53). Two other major phases of this five-year program center attention on education for school librarianship and recruitment.

Appropriate material from all of these studies, as well as many others cited in the Bibliography in relation to specific phases of the project, has been drawn upon in its design and accomplishment. But this study focuses its attention principally on a matter of primary concern to the profession, and one which was emphasized by Asheim (3) in his report to the National Advisory Commission on Libraries, namely, education tailored to the demands of the field.

REFERENCES IN CHAPTER 1

1. Alvarez, Robert S. "Qualifications of Heads of Libraries in Cities of over 10,000 Population in the Seven North-Central States." Doctor's dissertation, Univ. of Chicago, Graduate Library School, Chicago, 1939.
2. Arnold, Joseph P. "Technical Education Curricular Recommendations by Management Representatives of Manufacturing Establishments in Illinois." Doctor's dissertation, Univ. of Illinois, Urbana, 1965.
3. Asheim, Lester. "Statement of Dr. Lester Asheim, Director, Office of Library Education, American Library Association." Paper read to the National Advisory Commission on Libraries, New York City, Mar. 6, 1967.
4. Bryan, Alice I. *The Public Librarian: A Report of the Public Library Inquiry.* New York: Columbia Univ. Pr., 1952.
5. Bundy, Mary Lee, and Paul Wasserman. "Professionalism Reconsidered," *College and Research Libraries* 29:5—26 (Jan. 1968).
6. Clayton, Howard. *An Investigation of Personality Characteristics among Library Students at One Midwestern University.* Final Report. Brockport: State Univ. of New York, 1968 (ED 024 422).
7. Cook, Desmond. *The Impact of Systems Analysis on Education.* Columbus: Educational Research Management Center, Ohio State Univ., 1968 (ED 024 145).
8. ——— "An Overview of Management Science in Educational Research." Paper presented as part of a symposium on Management Science in Educational Research, 15th international meeting of the Institute of Management Science, Cleveland, Ohio, Sept. 1968 (ED 025 002).
9. ———*PERT Applications in Educational Planning.* Columbus: School of Education, Ohio State Univ., 1966 (ED 019 751).

REFERENCES

10. Corson, John J., and R. Shale Paul. *Men Near the Top: Filling Key Posts in the Federal Service.* Baltimore: Johns Hopkins Pr., 1966.
11. Crawford, Meredith P. "Concepts of Training," in Robert M. Gagné, ed., *Psychological Principles in System Development,* p.301—41. New York: Holt, 1962.
12. Culbertson, Jack. "Differentiated Training for Professors and Educational Administrators." Paper read to annual meeting of the American Educational Research Association, Chicago, Feb. 8—10, 1968 (ED 021 309).
13. Danton, J. Periam. *Between M.L.S. and Ph.D: A Study of Sixth-Year Specialist Programs in Accredited Library Schools.* Chicago: American Library Assn., 1970.
14. Dolby, J. L., V. J. Forsyth, and H. L. Resnikoff. *The Cost of Maintaining and Updating Library Card Catalogs.* Final Report. Los Altos, Calif.: R & D Consultants Co., 1969.
15. Drennan, Henry T., and Richard L. Darling. *Library Manpower: Occupational Characteristics of Public and School Librarians.* Washington, D. C.: Gov. Print. Off., 1966 (ED 017 299).
16. Dryer, Bernard V., ed. "Lifetime Learning for Physicians: Principles, Practices, Proposals," *Journal of Medical Education* 37:1—134 (June 1962).
17. Dubin, Samuel S., and others. *The Determination of Supervisory Training Needs of Hospital Personnel: A Survey of Pennsylvania Hospitals.* University Park: Pennsylvania State Univ., 1965.
18. ———*Research Report of Managerial and Supervisory Educational Needs of Business and Industry in Pennsylvania.* University Park: Pennsylvania State Univ., 1967.
19. ———*Survey Report of Managerial and Supervisory Needs of Business and Industry in Pennsylvania.* University Park: Pennsylvania State Univ., 1967.
20. ———, Everett Alderman, and H. LeRoy Marlow. *Educational Needs of Managers and Supervisors in Cities, Boroughs and Townships in Pennsylvania.* University Park: Pennsylvania State Univ., 1968.
21. ———*Highlights of a Study on Managerial and Supervisory Educational Needs of Business and Industry in Pennsylvania.* University Park: Pennsylvania State Univ., 1968.
22. ———, and H. LeRoy Marlow. *Highlights: A Survey of Continuing Professional Education for Engineers in Pennsylvania.* University Park: Pennsylvania State Univ., 1968.
23. Fryden, Floyd N. "Post-Master's Degree Programs in Some American Library Schools." Research paper, Graduate Library School, Univ. of Chicago, 1968.
24. Gagné, Robert M. "A Systems Approach to Adult Learning," in K. M. Wientge and others, eds., *Psychological Research in Classroom Learning,* p.6—21. St. Louis: School of Continuing Education, Washington Univ., 1967 (ED 017 703).
25. ———"The Analysis of Instructional Objectives for the Design of Instruction," in *Teaching Machines and Programmed Learning II.* Washington, D. C.: National Education Assn., 1965.
26. ———*The Conditions of Learning.* New York: Holt, 1965.
27. ———, ed. *Psychological Principles in Systems Development.* New York: Holt, 1962.

28. —— and others. "Factors in Acquiring Knowledge of a Mathematical Task," *Psychological Monographs: General and Applied* 76:7. Washington, D.C.: American Psychological Assn., 1962.
29. ——, and R. C. Bolles. "A Review of Factors in Learning Efficiency," in E. Galanter, ed., *Automated Teaching.* New York: Wiley, 1959.
30. ——, and Noel E. Paradise. "Abilities and Learning Sets in Knowledge Acquisition," *Psychological Monographs: General and Applied* 75:14. Washington, D.C.: American Psychological Assn., 1961.
31. Ginzberg, Eli, and Carol A. Brown, *Manpower for Library Services.* New York: Conservation of Human Resources Project, Columbia Univ., 1967 (ED 023 408).
32. Glaser, Robert, ed. *Training for Research and Education.* Pittsburgh: Univ. of Pittsburgh Pr., 1962.
33. Hall, Anna C. *Selected Educational Objectives for Public Service Librarians: A Taxonomic Approach.* Pittsburgh: Univ. of Pittsburgh, 1968.
34. Hemphill, John. *Dimensions of Executive Positions.* Research Monograph no.98. Columbus: Bureau of Business Research, Ohio State Univ., 1960.
35. Herzberg, Frederick. "One More Time: How Do You Motivate Employees?" *Harvard Business Review* 46:53—62 (Jan.-Feb., 1968).
36. ——, Bernard Mausner, and Barbara Synderman. *The Motivation to Work.* 2d ed. New York: Wiley, 1959.
37. Hewitt, Gordon B. *Continuing Education in Pharmacy: A Report.* British Columbia: Pharmaceutical Assn., 1965 (ED 019 545).
38. Honey, John C. "A Report: Higher Education for Public Service," *Public Administration Review* 27:294—321 (Nov. 1967).
39. Houle, Cyril O. "The Role of Continuing Education in Current Professional Development," *ALA Bulletin* 61:259—67 (Mar. 1967).
40. Klempner, Irving M. "Information Centers and Continuing Education for Librarianship," *Special Libraries* 59:729—32 (Nov. 1968).
41. Knox, Alan B. "Continuing Legal Education of Nebraska Lawyers." Nondegree study, Nebraska State Bar Assn., Lincoln, 1964.
42. Lange, Carl J. *Developing Programs for Teachers.* Professional Paper 20-69. Alexandria, Va.: Human Resources Office, George Washington Univ., 1969 (ED 033 902).
43. McGlothlin, William J. *The Professional Schools.* New York: Center for Applied Research in Education, 1964.
44. McLennan, Kenneth. "The Manager and His Job Skills," *Academy of Management Journal* 10:235—45 (Sept. 1967).
45. McMahon, Ernest E., Robert H. Coates, and Alan B. Knox. "Common Concerns: The Position of the Adult Education Association of the U.S.A.," *Adult Education Journal* 18:197—213 (Spring 1968).
46. McNeil, John D. "Forces Influencing Curriculum," *Review of Educational Research* 39:293—318 (June 1969).
47. Mayhew, Lewis B. *The Collegiate Curriculum: An Approach to Analysis.* Atlanta, Ga.: Southern Regional Education Board, 1966 (ED 014 790).
48. Miller, Donald. "The Role of Educational Leadership in Implementing Educational Change," in *Operation PEP Symposium on the Application of Systems Analysis and Management Techniques to Educational Planning in California,* p.32—41. Washington, D. C.: U.S. Office of Education, 1967 (ED 020 584).

REFERENCES

49. Morrison, Perry David. *The Career of the Academic Librarian: A Study of the Social Origins, Educational Attainments, Vocational Experience, and Personality Characteristics of a Group of American Academic Librarians.* ACRL Monograph no.29. Chicago: American Library Assn., 1968.
50. Mosher, Frederick. *Professional Education and the Public Service: An Exploratory Study.* Final Report. Berkeley: Center for Research and Development in Higher Education, Univ. of California, 1968 (ED 025 220).
51. "NAL/Land-Grant Network Plan Completed," *Educom Bulletin* 4:1—3 (Oct. 1969).
52. National Education Association. National Commission on Teacher Education and Professional Standards. *The Development of the Career Teacher: Professional Responsibility for Continuing Education.* Washington, D.C.: The Association, 1964.
53. ——Research Division. School Library Manpower Project. *School Library Personnel Task Analysis Survey.* Chicago: American Library Assn., 1969.
54. Ofiesh, Gabriel D. "The New Education and the Learning Industry," *Educational Leadership* 26:760—63 (May 1969).
55. Peterson, Clarence E. *Electronic Data Processing in Engineering, Science, and Business: Suggested Techniques for Determining Courses of Study in Vocational and Technical Education Programs.* Washington, D.C.: U.S. Office of Education, 1964 (ED 013 325).
56. Pfeiffer, John. *New Look at Education: Systems Analysis in Our Schools and Colleges.* Poughkeepsie, N.Y.:Odyssey Pr., 1968.
57. Phillips, Kathleen. "Training for Federal Librarians," *Federal Library Committee Newsletter* 22:7—13 (June 1968).
58. Randall, Raymond L., and Dick W. Simpson. *Science Administration Education and Career Mobility.* Summary of proceedings and working papers of the University Federal Agency Conference, November 7—9, 1965. Bloomington: Institute of Public Administration, Indiana Univ., 1966 (ED 019 563).
59. Reisman, Arnold, ed. *Engineering: A Look Inward and a Reach Outward.* Proceedings of the Symposium. Milwaukee: Univ. of Wisconsin-Milwaukee, 1967.
60. "Report of the National Advisory Commission on Libraries," *Congressional Record* (Oct. 14, 1968), p.16.
61. Rogers, Carl B. *Freedom to Learn.* Columbus, Ohio: Merrill, 1969.
62. ——"The Facilitation of Significant Learning," in Laurence Siegel, ed., *Instruction: Some Contemporary Viewpoints.* p.37—54. San Francisco: Chandler, 1967.
63. Schick, Frank L. *Survey of Special Libraries Serving the Federal Government.* Washington, D.C.: National Center for Educational Statistics, U.S. Dept. of Health, Education and Welfare, 1968.
64. Schill, William J., and Joseph P. Arnold. *Curricula Content for Six Technologies.* Report of the Bureau of Educational Research and the Dept. of Vocation and Technical Education. Urbana: Univ. of Illinois, 1965.
65. Schiller, Anita R. *Characteristics of Professional Personnel in College and University Libraries.* Urbana: Library Research Center, Univ. of Illinois, 1968 (ED 020 766).
66. Siegel, Laurence, ed. *Instruction: Some Contemporary Viewpoints.* San Francisco: Chandler, 1967.

67. Smith, Robert G., Jr. *Controlling the Quality of Training.* Technical Report 65-6. Alexandria, Va.: Human Resources Research Office, George Washington Univ., 1965.
68. ——— *The Design of Instructional Systems.* Technical Report 66-18. Alexandria, Va.: Human Resources Research Office, George Washington Univ., 1966.
69. ———*The Development of Training Objectives.* Alexandria, Va.: Human Resources Research Office, George Washington Univ., 1964.
70. Stanley, W. C. *Education and Social Integration.* New York: Teachers College, Columbia Univ., 1953.
71. Stogdill, Ralph, and others. *Patterns of Administrative Performance.* Columbus: Ohio State Univ., 1956.
72. ———*A Predictive Study of Administrative Work Patterns.* Columbus: Ohio State Univ., 1956.
73. Stone, C. Walter, ed. *The Professional Education of Media Service Personnel: Recommendations for Training Media Service Personnel for Schools and Colleges.* Preliminary edition. Pittsburgh: Center for Media Studies, Univ. of Pittsburgh, 1964.
74. Stone, Elizabeth W. *Factors Related to the Professional Development of Librarians.* Metuchen, N.J.: Scarecrow, 1969.
75. Swank, Raynard C. "Sixth-Year Curricula and the Education of Library School Faculties," *Journal of Education for Librarianship* 8:14—19 (Summer 1967).
76. Taft, Martin I. "Design for Education: A Systems Approach," in Arnold Reisman, ed., *Engineering: A Look Inward and a Reach Outward: Proceedings of the Symposium,* p.41—60. Milwaukee: Univ. of Wisconsin-Milwaukee, 1967.
77. Taylor, Edward B. "Relationship between the Career Changes of Lawyers and Their Participation in Continuing Legal Education." Doctor's dissertation, Univ. of Nebraska, Lincoln, 1967.
78. Taylor, Frederick W. *The Principles of Scientific Management.* New York and London: Harper, 1919.
79. Webb, Eugene J. *Unobtrusive Measures: Nonreactive Research in the Social Sciences.* Chicago: Rand McNally, 1966.
80. Williamson, Charles C. *Training for Library Service: A Report Prepared for the Carnegie Corporation of New York.* New York: Carnegie Corp., 1923.

2
Design of the Study

Before separating the procedures and methods into individual parcels for explanation, the presentation of an overview of the total design may make the methodology more meaningful to the reader. The first data-gathering instrument for the study, a questionnaire containing 392 items,* was sent to a randomly selected sample of federal librarians, grades 9 through 14, holding a master's degree in library science. The questionnaire is appendix A. Three hundred and sixty-five federal librarians completed and returned the questionnaire. The second data-gathering instrument was an interview with twenty top-level library administrators, which was designed to (1) supplement and combine the data gathered through the questionnaire, and (2) compare the assessments made by the librarian respondents with those made by the administrators concerning courses, curricula, and programs at the post-master's level. Details concerning the interviews are presented in the last section of this chapter.

THE QUESTIONNAIRE

The questionnaire as mailed to the librarians in the sample was entitled "A Study of Job Dimensions and Educational Needs: Post-MLS Education for Middle and Upper-Level Personnel in Libraries and Information Centers." The arrangement was logical and at the same

---

*There are 430 numbered items in the questionnaire, but 38 of these are labeled "other" to be filled in by the respondent if needed to specify something not on the basic list.

DESIGN OF THE STUDY

time was designed with the intent of sustaining the respondent's interest. The wording, especially the headings, was deliberately made personal. The covering letter attached to each questionnaire identified the project director and the associate project director. It also explained the benefits of the study to the individual respondent and to the profession as a whole. It assured the anonymity of the replies.

The final structure of the questionnaire is shown by its headings:

Part I: Evaluating Job Activities You Perform in Relation to Time and Importance

Part II: Your Educational Needs

Part III: Some Information about Yourself and Your Career

Part IV: Lastly, Your Ideas and Comments

Part I: Job Inventory

The primary purpose of the job inventory is to answer three important questions: In what kind of job activities are the middle- and upper-level professional staff members of libraries engaged? How much time do they devote to these activities? How important are these activities at the level of the individual position?

It is the current view, supported by considerable research evidence, that the development of well-defined, job-relevant objectives based on the individual's needs for effective job performance is the aspect of curriculum development that should receive primary emphasis. Smith (25) has stated that job-related objectives, appropriately developed, provide clear guidance for a systematic development of the course content. It was found in a recent study by Stone (26) that application of knowledge in the actual job situation was the primary motivation for engaging in formal course work at the post-master's level. This supports the premise that curriculum development at the post-master's level must start with an accurate assessment of the librarian's job activities.

There have been many surveys to identify what the individual actually does on the job. Before deciding that the job inventory was the method best suited to gather information on what the federal librarian does in his job, the researchers studied the other surveys carefully and noted the advantages of the different methods.

One of the most common approaches to the study of job activities is the use of a self-recording system in which the respondent records how he utilizes his time on an analysis sheet provided by the investigator.

Three important studies using this method were: Carlson's (8) influential work on the behavior of Swedish executives; Corson and Paul's (9) recent study of top-level federal employees; and Underwood's (28) administrative profile for the director of a hospital. After a review of studies using self-recording techniques, it appears that these techniques have not yet produced any one generally reliable instrument for measuring duties performed by managers and administrators. Some of the studies, such as the one by Corson and Paul, do not fully analyze all the data obtained from the detailed diaries that were submitted. A known weakness in this method is that the very act of recording behavior influences the individual's performance during the time that the diary is kept, thus affecting the validity of the results. The technique of the detailed daily observations of employees is subject to this same criticism of observer affecting observation.

The open-end questionnaire is the common means for obtaining job-related information through a mail survey. The questionnaire usually asks for certain identifying information about a job and provides space for the respondents to write in additional personally descriptive information. Morsh (19) points out that this method tends to produce data which are invalid in content and amount.

The individual interview is another method by which the analyst records data on a standardized form. This method usually combines responses from several interviews on a specific type of position. The interview, like the questionnaire, depends to a large degree on recall. Its value is largely dependent upon the competence of the interviewer, and it cannot be used for large samples.

The job inventory might really be considered as a special kind of questionnaire which utilizes a list of descriptive task or activity statements. In its simplest form the incumbent is asked to check the tasks he does in the course of his work and to rate each item according to scales for amount of time, degree of importance, and necessary knowledge or experience. Examples of the use of the job inventory are legion; a few will illustrate the scope and possibilities of this method. The classic study was one conducted by Hemphill (14) involving 93 business executive positions. Each of the executives completed a questionnaire containing 575 position elements and described his position on an eight-point response scale in terms of the degree to which each element was a significant part of his position. Later Hemphill constructed a shortened version of the questionnaire, containing 191 items, which has been very influential in the development of other job inventories and was the basis on which the Educational Testing Service (11) developed

DESIGN OF THE STUDY

their Job Dimensions Project. Another significant study based largely on Hemphill's method, which has particular relevance to this study was the study by Curnow (10) of federal executive positions.

The chief problem inherent in the job-inventory method is that there is no information provided about the sequence in which activities are performed. This is a disadvantage in comparison to other methods mentioned in this section. However, the sequence is not important in the building of courses, which was the main use for which data from this part of the questionnaire was used.

The job inventory has many advantages which are responsible for the decision to use it to determine what an individual actually does in his job. One such advantage is that it is amenable to statistical analysis. The uniformity of the data collected' makes meaningful statistical statements possible with a minimal loss of reported information. Using a questionnaire form for the inventory permits a broad sample to be queried.

A further advantage is that the procedure is simple for the respondents. Instead of trying to recall all duties and tasks, it is much easier for the respondent to check the items listed and give an evaluation of the time and importance of each item. Since all the information is gathered on a single standardized form, it permits simple, rapid quantification by hand or by machine tabulation. Information about the job items—such as frequency and time of performance, importance of task difficulty, and supervision required—can be easily built into the inventory. The process provides a practical and economical method for obtaining job information from any number of respondents and makes possible the gathering of such information at each of the grade levels included. Also, the standardized form used in the inventory greatly facilitates comparison of work performed across jobs within a specialty or among specialties.

Some basic assumptions underlie the use of the job inventory. First, it is assumed that the incumbent of a position is the best-qualified informant concerning the nature of his work. Other researchers using this method have considered this a reasonable assumption. Hemphill (14), after performing tests in this area, concluded, "These comparisons provide no evidence which would suggest that incumbents tend to distort the descriptions of their positions in a favorable direction." Secondly, it also assumes that the incumbent is capable of rating on appropriate scales the time required for a number of job activities relative to other activities, and, further, the importance to performance of each task. Finally, it is assumed that the job-inventory items represented the actual work undertaken in common by federal librarians. This assumption is verified in the questionnaire under the heading Applicability of the Questionnaire.

The first research effort for the job inventory involved making an extended list (about 400 cards with one activity per card) of job activities undertaken by federal librarians. For the section on administration and management functions, the published questionnaires of Curnow (10), Hemphill (14), McLennan (17), Morsh (19), Saunders (21), and Teller and Camm (27) provided a large percentage of items for the first draft which were necessarily modified to fit the federal library setting. Studies of descriptions of executive work, such as Bernstein (4), Carlson (8), Corson and Paul (9), and Underwood (28) suggested other items, as did standard works on public administration and management, such as Koontz (15). Useful sources of activity items for Part I-A of the questionnaire, Specialized Library Functions, were the U.S. Civil Service Standards for the 1410 and 1412 series (29, 30), published job descriptions, library science course syllabi, and works describing job functions in libraries and information centers, such as Meltzer (18) and Wallace (31). Finally, criticisms and comments from three pretest pilot groups, representing a wide range of grades, positions, and types of federal libraries, and from both faculty and master's candidates (with a wide variety of work experience) in the Library Science Department at the Catholic University of America proved very helpful in reducing the list to the 223 items actually used in the questionnaire, Part I.

Each respondent was asked to consider statements relating to his job activities in two dimensions — time and importance. For those statements applicable to a given position, a rating was to be made on two separate scales. Each scale had four degrees of applicability from which the respondent could choose regarding a given job-activity item. The four levels from which ratings were to be made were: (1) "one of the most time-consuming (important) activities of the position"; (2) "consumes a substantial part of the time" (a substantial part of the position); (3) "is one of the least time-consuming (important) activities of the position"; and (4) "the factor is not present at all in the activities of your position now."

The job inventory is divided into two sections: Performing Specialized Library Functions (items numbered 1 through 127), and Performing General Administrative and Management Functions (items numbered 128 through 244). It should be noted that in the section Performing Specialized Library Functions, there are thirteen areas of job activities listed: abstracting, acquisitions, bibliography, cataloging and classification, circulation, clientele services, indexing, literature searching, maintenance of holdings, reference, research, selection, and translation. Each of these areas has a group of activity items listed under it. Similarly, under the section Performing General Administrative and Management Functions, there are eight areas of activity listed: planning, organizing, staffing, directing, coordinating, controlling, representing, and housing. It should also be noted that the section B items apply to the administrative and management functions that the respondent performs in his job, whether it be for the whole library, a department, a branch, or a specialized library function, such as cataloging or reference service.

In selecting the items for inclusion in the final edition of the questionnaire, certain criteria were used:

1. Avoidance of statements which were so general that they would apply equally to all executive positions

2. Avoidance of items so specific that they would be restricted merely to one or two positions

3. Each item must differ in some way from all the others

4. Each statement must lend itself to a rating on the dimensions of both time and importance

5. Each item must represent what the individual actually does in his job.

Part II: Educational Needs

Established curricular guidelines for library education at the post-master's level are still lacking; but, as Fryden (12) points out, the demand for librarians with some training beyond the fifth-year master's degree is greater now than ever before. In Fryden's report on the eleven ALA-accredited American library schools which offered a sixth-year post-master's program in 1968, there is abundant evidence that differing philosophies, objectives, standards, content, and requirements of these programs have produced as many variations as there are schools offering them. The question asked by Fryden (12:26) is quite logical and worthy of an attempt to answer, "On what base do these programs build?"

In this study it is deemed important to know the dimensions of the demand for post-master's education as perceived by the middle- and upper-level librarians themselves. Practically, it must always be remembered that whether students enroll or not at the post-master's level is strictly a matter of personal choice. The choice of courses at this level is largely determined by the practicing librarians. Hence, to build courses in a vacuum without relationship to the actual demand of practicing librarians would constitute merely an intellectual exercise rather than a genuine contribution toward the continuing education of librarians.

This part of the questionnaire was designed:

1. To identify those subject areas which practicing federal librarians are most interested in studying at the post-master's level

2. To identify three types of interest in the listed courses: (a) interest in a workshop or institute, (b) interest in the course now, and (c) interest in the course later (identified in the questionnaire as three to five years from now); and to rank the different courses according to the type of interest or combinations thereof

3. To examine critically this interest in relation to other variables analyzed in other parts of this study; for example, to determine whether the respondents are chiefly interested in studying in areas that are related to their present positions or in new areas

4. To determine the interest of the respondents in further education in library science or a graduate program in another subject area.

Part II, entitled Your Educational Needs, contains two sections. The first section lists 78 courses,* grouped under 17 broad course areas.** It was developed with the intent of representing essentially all areas of library science which could be considered of possible value to the practicing librarians.

Course listings from catalogs of all ALA-accredited library schools, of

---

*Under each of the 17 broad course areas, there is a numbered item labeled "other" to be filled in by the respondent if needed to specify something not on titles are listed.

**The 17 course areas are: acquisitions and selection; administration and general management of libraries; administration of special types of library services; automation; bibliography; cataloging and classification; circulation; clientele services; housing and equipment; indexing and abstracting; information science; libraries, government, and society; publication; reference; research; specialized information sources; and systems analysis.

DESIGN OF THE STUDY

a few nonaccredited library schools offering graduate programs, of a selected group of schools offering graduate programs in information science, and of a few of the leading schools of business and public administration in various sections of the country, as well as courses listed by Shilling and Berman (24) in their suggested science information-specialist training program, provided the basic list of courses with which the research team started. On the basis of these procedures, reasonable coverage of ongoing library science and related programs was assumed. Each course title with its description from the sources examined was placed on a separate card. This curriculum deck was then arranged by major course areas and then by individual courses. From these courses, those that are usually taught at the master's level as part of the core or required degree program were eliminated. The remaining cards with their descriptions provided the master list of courses.

Next a group of specialists went over the master list, combining, regrouping, eliminating, and renaming courses; always keeping in mind the following guidelines:

1. The final checklist of courses should be as exhaustive as possible, including all those courses that might be appropriately offered at the post-MLS level.
2. There should be very little overlapping between the contents of the courses.
3. The courses should be, in so far as possible, of equal length.
4. The courses should be given the title most appropriate to describe the content.

A new list established by these procedures was formulated, in which the courses were listed by title only, except in those instances in which the scope left doubt about possible content, when a brief description was included. This new list was submitted to three pilot groups, and after their recommendations for additions, deletions, and regrouping were received, it was further modified by the research staff. The result is the listing of 78 courses presented in the first section of Part II of the questionnaire.

To those not familiar with recent curricular development at the post-MLS level, some of these courses might seem to have insufficient content to sustain a semester's work. Most of the current MLS offerings only touch on these new areas of professional activity. However, at the post-master's level they stand independently as full courses to be studied in much greater depth and scope—commensurate with the new technological, behavioral, and societal advances—and to provide a great deal more information and greater conceptual understanding than possible at the master's level.

Each respondent was asked to check his interest in taking these 78 courses according to the following categories (questionnaire, Part II, p.6):

WORKSHOP:	If you are interested in spending time in a short-term (few days to four weeks) workshop or institute;
COURSE NOW:	If you are interested in taking a post-MLS course for credit at the present time;
COURSE LATER:	If you are interested in taking a post-MLS course for credit at a later time (three to five years from now). If you are not interested in formal study in a given course, please leave the boxes that pertain to it blank.

The second section of Part II asks if the respondents would:

1. Enroll for a one-year post-MLS program in library science
2. Enroll for a graduate program in some other subject area
3. Enroll for a doctoral program in library science
4. Enroll for a doctoral program in another subject area

The respondent was also asked what conditions would be necessary for him to enroll.

The final question in this section is, "In addition to offering courses, institutes, and workshops, in what other ways do you see that the library school could help you in your professional development?"

Part III. Background Characteristics

The objective in gathering background information about the federal librarians was to provide a basis for realistic planning of potential course and curricula offerings at the post-master's level. Educational planning for librarians will be haphazard, at best, without definite knowledge of the qualifications and characteristics of those for whom continuing education programs are planned. To study in depth the demand for further training, it was necessary to study these character-

DESIGN OF THE STUDY

istics to determine whether or not patterns existed between them, the job structure, and the educational needs. To understand fully the demand structure for courses, it is necessary to see what characteristics typify those expressing interest in courses and in engaging in a postmasters program.

It was also necessary to learn of the background and personal characteristics of the federal librarians to verify the premise that federal librarians are representative of the large population of librarians in general. This type of data permits an assessment of whether the respondents are typical of other types of librarians.

In this part of the questionnaire there are a total of 80 questions. They make it possible to isolate and analyze variables relative to the respondents' professional experience and present position, and they provide valuable clues with which to examine the job structure and course demands in depth. The questions fall into two groups: personal background variables, which include age, sex, position title, GS (General Schedule) grade level, educational level, degrees held, experience in occupations other than librarianship, and length of time in present position and in the federal service; and position variables, which include occupational series code; major responsibility of the position; location of the position in an agency headquarters office, or in a regional, field, or branch library; size of library; and number of people supervised.

Other information that is asked for, which it is felt will give valuable background data for curriculum building, includes: (1) Is there any formal scientific, technical, or professional training you lack which you feel would have been especially helpful in your position? (2) What minimum experience in library or information center assignments is required to perform your job? (3) How well does your job utilize your talents? (4) How many hours per week are you required to do avoidable detail work that you feel should not be part of your job? (5) Are you involved at an administrative or supervisory level in applying electronic data-processing procedures? (6) Which activities in your library are automated? (7) What is the nature of your past experience in an occupation other than librarianship? (8) What knowledge, abilities, or skills would you recommend for your replacement?

Part IV. Reactions to the Research Project

In the last part of the questionnaire there are three open-end questions. The first asks for the respondents' comments on the job inventory; the second seeks their suggestions regarding courses and curricula; and the third asks for their reaction to the study as a whole.

Three pretests of the questionnaire were carried out with groups of federal librarians. Details of the pretest samples are summarized in table 3. These three pretest groups were of great help in determining the final

TABLE 3
PRE-TEST SAMPLES: 1968

Group Number	Number in the Group	Number of Federal Departments and Agencies Represented	Source of Sample
I	12	11	Judgment sample designed to pick representatives from various grade levels, library schools and types of positions.
II	4	4	Judgment sample of top-level Federal library administrators.
III	10	10	Judgment sample designed to cover higher percentage in GS 9 level than in Group I and to cover agencies and types of positions not covered in Group I
Total	26	25	

form of the questionnaire, which was systematically studied item by item to ensure the inclusion of all of their suggestions which seemed valid to the research team. The final version of the questionnaire was printed on yellow paper to attract attention on a full desk top.

THE SAMPLE

Defining the Population

The ultimate objective for this study was to build curricula at the post-master's level, hence the research team logically concluded that the population for this study should be librarians with a graduate degree in library science. On page 11 of the questionnaire, where questions are

DESIGN OF THE STUDY

asked about professional and preprofessional experience, this definitional note was inserted:

> In this study, the term "professional librarian" includes all librarians, administrators, and other specialists with responsibility in the field of librarianship or information science who have received a Master's degree in Library Science, or, before the early 1950's, a Bachelor's degree in Library Science at the graduate level.

How to define the "middle and upper level" was a problem that had to be decided early in the study. Earlier researchers, facing a similar problem, decided that within the federal complex, rank is the most appropriate of possible differentiae. As Warner, Van Riper, and others (32:289) state, "In the civil service ... rank ... reflects level of work, responsibility, and official status, all on a fairly uniform basis throughout the service." However, all the experts differ in their decisions about the grades that should be included in the "upper" demarcation, as distinguished from "lower" grades.

The situation was further complicated by the fact that at the very time this decision was being made the U.S. Civil Service Commission ruled that in the fall of 1968, the entering level for the MLS graduate would be grade 9, replacing the entry level of grade 7 previously in effect. However, in consultation with the Federal Library Committee, individual federal librarians, and government executives, it was realized that to exclude the GS 9 category from the population would eliminate the directors and administrators of a large number of federal libraries outside the greater Washington area. It had been found in the Schick survey (22:20) of special libraries serving the federal government that more than half (56 percent) of the chief librarians in federal agencies were grades GS 9 to GS 11. Curnow (10:38) has pointed out in his study that field positions tend to be classified somewhat lower than positions of similar responsibility in the greater Washington area. Therefore it was necessary to include GS 9 personnel to get the directors of many libraries in federal field installations. It was the belief that these librarians, in some cases supervising a considerable number of persons and sizable collections, were involved in duties of a caliber that would be considered "middle" or "upper level" by almost any definition. It was also believed that the GS 9 level might contain many librarians who would want to come back for post-master's studies. Weighing all these factors the research staff decided to include GS 9 in the study.

The upper demarcation line was also a problem. It centered around grade 15 which had thirty-five librarians. The main reason that they were excluded was that part of the research design for the study included interviews with twenty top-level library administrators and grades 16 to 18 together had only eleven librarians according to data provided by the U.S. Civil Service Commission in June 1968.* Hence, the thirty-five librarians in grade 15 were needed for inclusion in the interview group.

In summary, the following operational definitions were established for the librarians in this study:

GS 9   Lower-middle level
GS 10—11   Upper-middle level
GS 12—14   Upper level
GS 15—18   Top-level administrators

A limitation which this study shares in common with other studies undertaken within the federal complex is that security organizations, such as the Central Intelligence Agency and the Federal Bureau of Investigation, are excluded from this study.

The information for librarians employed at the Library of Congress had to be secured in a different manner from that of the other federal libraries. There were at the time of the questionnaire 832 librarians employed at the Library of Congress in grades GS 9 through GS 14, but no record was easily accessible for determining whether or not they had graduate degrees in library science. Further, contrary to the procedure followed by all other types of federal libraries, the Library of Congress does not identify individuals by GS ratings. This list of 832 positions, arranged by departments and then by position titles, was carefully examined and reduced to 614. The research team was reasonably confident that these 614 would include all the people in the Library of Congress with a degree in library science.

Table 4 gives separately for the Library of Congress and other federal libraries the breakdown of the total population of librarians, GS 9 through 14, with a graduate degree in library science, by agency.

The Sampling Frame

To identify the population of the federal librarians for the study, the research team was fortunate to have a mailing list of federal libraries

*A subsequent release of the U.S. Civil Service Commission increased the figure to twenty-one after the survey to the federal libraries to determine the number in the population from GS 9 through 14 was already in progress.

TABLE 4
BREAKDOWN OF THE TOTAL POPULATION OF PROFESSIONAL FEDERAL LIBRARIANS[1]
BY AGENCY OR DEPARTMENT AND GRADE AS OF FEBRUARY 3, 1969.

Agency or Department	Code	Grade Level						No CSC		Total	Percentage of Total
		9	10	11	12	13	14	Grade			
Library of Congress	0000	196	3	STRATUM I 200	115	60	40	0		614[2]	
Percentage of Total		31.92%	0.49%	32.58%	18.73%	9.77%	6.51%	0.00%		100.00%	
				STRATUM II							
Army	1000	84	17	86	34	12	2	0		235	17.44%
Navy	2000	53	0	34	18	7	2	0		114	8.46%
Air Force	3000	188	19	97	32	8	3	0		347	25.76%
Veterans Administration	4000	55	38	33	6	2	1	0		135	10.02%
D.C. Public Library	5000	27	3	33	9	3	0	0		75	5.57%
Health, Education, and Welfare	6000	16	0	37	9	11	2	0		75	5.57%
Agriculture	7000	10	0	29	7	5	1	0		52	3.86%
Other Agencies	8000	74	1	93	58	33	12	0		271	20.12%
Non GS Category	9000	0	0	0	0	0	0	43		43	3.19%
Total		507	78	442	173	81	23	43		1347	100.00%[3]
Percentage of Total		37.64%	5.79%	32.81%	12.84%	6.01%	1.71%	3.19%		100.00%	

[1] In this study, the term "professional librarian" includes all librarians who have received a master's degree in library science, or, before the early 1950's, a bachelor's degree in library science at the graduate level. Therefore, this represents a smaller, more select universe than in the total 1410 series, as reported by the U.S. Civil Service Commission.
[2] The total number of librarians (professional and nonprofessional, GS 9-14) in the Library of Congress is 832. Of these, 218 were eliminated at the initial stage (due to lack of a master's degree) leaving 614.
[3] The percentages in the tables, although showing a total of 100, do not always equal 100 because the figures have been rounded off to the nearest one-tenth of one per cent.

compiled and supplied by the Federal Library Committee. To it were added the names of a few information centers provided by COSATI (Committee on Scientific and Technical Information). Eliminating duplication, the figure of federal libraries (and information centers) stood at 652 (excluding army libraries, air force libraries, and the Library of Congress).

A covering letter telling of the study and a form requesting a list of librarians in the 1410 and 1412 series, grades GS 9 through GS 14 with a graduate degree in library science, were sent to all federal libraries and information centers. To increase the percentage of returns, a follow-up letter was sent three weeks later to those libraries from which returns had not yet been received.

Of the 652 federal libraries, 529 libraries replied, listing a total of 765 professional librarians. The research team got the complete list of army and air force professional librarians (totaling 582) from their respective services. Thus the total number of names of professional librarians received, who according to the data supplied fell within the criteria of limitation, was 1,347 (except for the Library of Congress). Only six of them were in the 1412 series.

It is further statistically estimated on the basis of these returns that at most 60 professional librarians are missing from the final list of 1,347. However, the actual figure is assumed to be smaller since the research team logically concluded from returns that came late that a large majority of those libraries that did not send any reply had no professional librarians.

The Sample Design

It was decided to treat the librarians of the Library of Congress as one separate stratum and all the other federal librarians as another stratum.* These two strata then comprised our whole population. A 50 percent systematic sample for each stratum was decided upon.

It was found from the pretesting that the applicable job-inventory items were often quite limited for an individual with a narrow specialization, and, hence, a large sample was necessary to obtain a valid estimate even for the whole population. Further, it was anticipated that in spite of the care taken to have only those with a graduate degree in library science included in the population, it would nevertheless contain many librarians without such a degree. This, in turn, would reduce the

*The word *stratum* in this study has been used in the accepted statistical sense, meaning a group, and does not convey any type of hierarchical meaning.

DESIGN OF THE STUDY

absolute size of the effective sample. Lastly, it was estimated that the nonresponse rate would be about 50 percent. These three considerations prompted such a seemingly large sample.

The final list of the 614 librarians from the Library of Congress was grouped by sections and by grades within a section. A systematic sample of 307 was drawn from this list and was sent back to the Library of Congress for checking. It was found that 147 of these 307 librarians did possess a graduate degree in library science. Thus, these 147 librarians formed our sample from the first stratum.

For the second stratum consisting of all federal librarians other than those employed at the Library of Congress, the individual cards for each librarian in the population were arranged first by grade level, second by agency or department within each grade, third by geographical location within each agency, and lastly by the number of personnel of the library in each geographical location. This ensured the representativeness of the sample. After the cards were arranged in this order, a systematic sample of 677 librarians was drawn for Stratum II. The grade distribution of the sample for Stratum II is:

GS 9	257
GS 10	39
GS 11	223
GS 12	87
GS 13	39
GS 14	11
Non GS	21
	677 Total for Stratum II

Return of Questionnaires

The questionnaire, together with a covering letter and reply-paid envelope, was mailed to the library address of each of the 147 librarians in Stratum I and to each of the 677 librarians in Stratum II, a total of 824 mailings. At the end of the fourth week, when only 30 percent in Stratum II had responded, a letter of reminder was mailed to 473 librarians along with a second copy of the questionnaire (see appendix C).

By the cutoff date, 421 of the 824 questionnaires mailed had been returned, or 51.1 percent. The returned questionnaires were examined for completeness; responses were scrutinized to ascertain if the librarians held the MLS degree and to check the respondents' adherence to instructions. Based on this check, it was found that of the 421 returned, 56 were not usable. Thirty-six were not usable because, in spite of every effort at prior screening, the individuals did not hold a master's degree in library science and therefore did not fall within the scope of this study. Twenty were not usable because these respondents no longer worked, or because they omitted large sections of the questionnaire. This left 365 questionnaires which met all criteria and could be analyzed. It is interesting to note that the response rate falls about in the middle of the response rates for two prior surveys of federal employees, which also used a job-inventory approach in a questionnaire format (9:13—14; 10:49—50).

Other Studies	Percentage of Return
Corson and Paul	54.0
Curnow	43.0

It is worthwhile to examine whether the nonrespondents differed from the respondents in regard to any significant variables. One variable to be considered in this connection is grade level, which is broken down in table 5. Only Stratum II is considered since this information for Stratum I was not available to the research group. There is some indication that the response rate increases with the grade level. However, this rate of increase is very small; hence, it can be safely assumed that the representativeness of the sample is not vitiated. A distribution of returns by department and agency was also tabulated.

TABLE 5
DISTRIBUTION OF RETURNS BY GRADE LEVEL
IN STRATUM II: 1968

Grade Level	Number in Population	Number of Usable Returns	Percentage of Usable Returns
GS 9	507	91	18.0
GS 10	78	16	20.5
GS 11	442	101	22.8
GS 12	173	43	24.8
GS 13	81	25	30.9
GS 14	23	7	30.4
Non GS[1]	43	9	20.9
Total	1347	292	21.7

[1] The few respondent who reported they were outside the Civil Service grade classification system were assigned equivalent GS grades.

DESIGN OF THE STUDY

The variability of percentage of returns between the different departments and agencies was found to be quite small. The foregoing analysis then suggests that, in general, the final sample is representative of those occupying library positions in grades GS 9 through 14 in federal libraries.

THE INTERVIEW

The objectives of the interviews of top-level administrators were:

1. To study the attitude of administrators toward post-master's education. This study would provide a level of interpretation different from that of the middle- and upper-level librarians concerning needs in the area of continuing professional education.
2. To identify courses which administrators think are essential for inclusion in a program of continuing education for librarians at the post-master's level. Their suggestions would supplement the information obtained through the questionnaire from the librarians (GS 9 through 14) themselves.
3. To determine the skills, competencies, and knowledge that the administrators feel can be imparted better on the job than in a university setting.

The rationale for conducting the interviews is the belief that the judgment of both the librarians and supervisory and administrative personnel should be taken into account in building courses at the post-master's level. The implicit assumption is that any plan for training for any job can best be based on the combined judgments of those performing the job and the supervisors responsible for the job. It was assumed by the investigators that the overall reason for initiating post-MLS curricula is to help librarians adapt to current and future job requirements and that, therefore, the attitudes of top-level administrative personnel toward post-MLS curricula could be advantageously explored. It was further assumed that administrators might tend to show some similarity of views toward curricula which are different from the views of the librarian respondents (GS 9 through 14).

Following these assumptions, the interview was included as part of the research design because of the:

1. Realization that the demands as expressed by the librarians themselves (respondents in this study to the questionnaire) might often be restricted or qualified by the attitudes and judgments of their supervisors. It was found in the Stone (26) study, for example, that librarians were deterred from taking formal course work when they felt that their supervisors and administrators were opposed to it.
2. Value of knowing how much financial support and time supervisory and administrative personnel are willing to seek for librarians wishing to engage in post-master's education. For, as was expected, the respondents to the questionnaire stressed the necessity of having financial aid if they were to engage in post-master's programs.
3. Belief that the administrative personnel would be able to give a projection or picture of the future knowledge and skill requirements based on a realistic estimate of the impact of new technology on future facilities, procedures, and library positions and tasks to be performed.
4. Necessity of learning the supervisor's interpretation of the importance in accomplishing the library's mission of tasks in which the librarian is lacking or deficient.
5. Importance of knowing whether the supervisors would be apt to give support to librarians seeking post-master's education through courses given as part of a longer sixth-year program.

In more general terms, it is assumed by the research staff that the overall reason for the initiation of a post-master's program is to better prepare professional librarians for their current and future job requirements. Library administrators who select, employ, and promote professional librarians should have some voice and responsibility for the development of appropriate curricula to meet perceived needs for new competencies, knowledge, and skills. They therefore can effectively serve as partners with library educators and prospective post-MLS students in the enterprise.

Review of Related Literature

The literature reviewed for this section of the study was selected and classified as: (1) materials on the collection of data by interviewing, and

DESIGN OF THE STUDY

(2) samples of interview schedules used in other research projects. As both of these categories of materials are included in the Bibliography in the section on interviewing, only the works that were found to be most helpful are mentioned here.

After a review of the literature on the interview as a method of data collection, it was decided by the research staff that the semistructured interview would probably provide the maximum return on the research investment for this study. Of all the materials reviewed on this type of interviewing, the detailed discussion on the semistructured research interview by Argyris (2) proved to be the most helpful.

Argyris not only gives a full sample of a typical interview of the type that he conducted, but he describes basic principles with emphasis on the fact that "questions are tools with which to explore unknown territory" (2:43). Particularly applicable to the present study is his belief that one can not only vary the way questions are phrased, but that, depending on the informant, one can also vary somewhat the questions themselves. The type of items to be covered in explaining the research project to each respondent is also dealt with in some depth, as is the administration of the interview. Another factor that he emphasizes is the importance of knowing the biases both of the interviewer and of the interviewee in analyzing the data. Argyris reported that, with upper-level executives, especially those who are quite verbal, he had found the tape recorder most helpful. (It was the method of recording the data used in this project.) Finally, he presents detailed information on the use and importance of internal validity checks and a chapter on the analysis of the data following its collection through the semistructured interview.

Of the works devoted entirely to interviewing, *Interviewing: Its Forms and Functions* by Richardson and others (20) was found to be the most helpful. The authors make a clear and specific distinction between the schedule interview and the nonschedule standardized interview in which the interviewer is taught exactly what information is required of each respondent, but is allowed to vary the wording and the sequence of questions for maximal effectiveness with individual respondents. One of the especially helpful features of this work is the criteria set for a good interview. These criteria of satisfactory respondent participation, validity, relevance, specificity, clarity, and completeness of coverage were used to design an evaluation sheet which was filled out on each of the interviews held in connection with the present study (appendix C).

Cannell and Kahn (7) stress the necessity of structuring the interview so as to create an instrument which will serve to translate the research objectives without bias into terms understandable to the respondent and, at the same time, assist rather than retard the interviewer in motivating the respondent to communicate. The specific aspects of interview construction are presented, including frame of reference, information level, language, and question sequence. It is emphasized that questions should be phrased so that they contain no suggestions of the most appropriate response. Another key point made is that the only accurate way to reproduce responses is to record them during the time of the interview, either by taking notes or by some mechanical method.

In conjunction with Axelrod, Cannell (6) made another study to determine how respondents react to being interviewed. This is important because it related to the respondent's motivation to communicate accurate responses to the questions being asked. It was found that a major element in achieving favorable reaction to interviews was the pleasure and rapport developed in the relationship with the interviewer, which was sufficient to make even questions on delicate subjects possible.

Among the model interviews that were particularly helpful, the first to deserve mention is the study by Arnold (3), which includes a complete sample of an interview schedule and one that was very helpful in designing the schedule for this study. Interviews were held with both management respondents and technicians as a basis for developing a core curriculum for technicians in six technologies. Details for the administration of the interview were also included. One special feature of this study was a card sort of a curriculum deck which served as a model for administering the card sort for the present study.

A related curricular study by Schill and Arnold (23) gives helpful details on how to select a management sample to be interviewed concerning lower-level technicians. For each technician in the study, management interviews were planned so that three levels of supervision for the technicians performing the job were represented. Contrary to the hypothesis with which the study was undertaken, it was found that the curricular views expressed by management respondents were not measurably different from those of the technicians they supervised.

Another detailed description of an interview guide was one by Hall (13:101--25). It was formulated for use in interviewing library school personnel regarding instruction in job activities in ongoing courses in library school. Many of the types of questions asked in this interview schedule were similar to those in the present study. The interview guide was designed to accomplish the following purposes: (1) bring out course content applicable to the list of job activities which had been formulated; (2) identify the level of knowledge, skills, and abilities which are currently being developed in the library school; and (3) determine if the educational objectives for library school courses had been identified specifically. The format of the interview guide, which is presented in full, is particularly helpful, as are also the thirty-six questions listed, each with a brief note of explanation. Details are given on the methodology for recording the data.

Several other interview guides also proved helpful in building the schedule and in suggesting ways of recording data. One was on the discovery and dissemination of scientific information among psychologists, as published by the American Psychological Association (1:105–6). Another was the University of Wisconsin's guide for a library materials project (16). Still another was the interview guide developed by Bunge (5:99) for a study of professional education and reference efficiency. Although none of these guides developed by others was on a subject directly related to the subject of this study, all were helpful in suggesting methodology.

General Methodology

Before a description and discussion of the separate techniques and procedures, a general outline of the interview design may be of value to the reader. Respondents were selected from among top-level administrators of federal libraries. Each interviewee was asked to respond to the queries in terms of a particular type of library position; they were not asked in any way to evaluate the employees who perform these jobs for them. A card-sorting procedure was completed by each respondent at the close of each interview. By the card sort, respondents identified courses which they considered to be most essential for development as a part of a post-master's sixth-year program based on the type of library position under discussion. Each interviewee also answered a group of specific questions concerning his reactions to the need for and the scope of a post-master's program.

Each of the administrative librarians to be interviewed was briefed by telephone on the purpose of the interview and the nature of the study. The data collection interviews were scheduled at a time and place where it would be possible to hold the interview without interruption. If there was no place suitable in the supervisor's office (or if preferred by the interviewee), the interview was conducted in the project director's office at Catholic University. Before starting the interview, each respondent was asked if he would object to the use of the tape recorder during the interview, and as none objected, it was used in all the interviews. The length of the interviews averaged one and one-half hours. Except in one instance (the one interview held outside the Washington area) the interviews were conducted by at least two members of the research staff. Those conducting the interviews were the project director, the associate director, and the project's statistician.

The semistructured research-interview format was used, as it was deemed best suited to this study. The basic items about which questions would be asked were determined after the analysis of data from the questionnaire had been made. That analysis provided an indication of where additional data were necessary to give a more comprehensive and precise view of the total problem. A card sort and a one-page checklist were also used in connection with the interview.

The interview opened with a five- to ten-minute orientation on the research project which included the following items:

1. Objectives of the research
2. Reasons for the research
3. An overview of what had been accomplished in the project to date
4. An explanation of the role of the supervisory or administrative respondent
5. An explanation of how the results would be reported, and assurance that the name of the interviewee would not be used in the report
6. A statement on the nature of the questions that would be asked.

Following the opening remarks of explanation, respondents were asked for replies to interview items listed in appendix C. The interview portion of the contact with the administrative respondents varied because of the conversation involved, but usually about forty minutes was used for covering the following areas: additional competencies needed for the position about which respondent was being interviewed; the best method of attaining these competencies; availability of funds and time for participating in a continuing education program; the comparative merits of the institute format in relation to the course format; the attitude toward post-master's programs in general; an estimation of the effect of automation on jobs and the implications of this for educational planning; and, finally, the administrator's opinion of the importance of personal characteristics in the job situation. Between fifteen and twenty minutes time was then taken for the card-sorting procedure. In the last five minutes of the interview, the respondent filled out a one-page sheet asking for reactions to the concept of a post-master's program (appendix D).

One means through which data were acquired by the research team was the card-sorting procedure. All the supervisory personnel were asked to sort the seventy-eight-card curriculum deck (which listed the same courses as had been used in the questionnaire to the librarians) into three stacks: courses judged to be most essential for performance of the library position in question; courses judged to be useful but not essential for performance of the position; and courses judged to be unnecessary for the performance of the job in question. Further, the supervisory personnel were asked to rank those cards in group 1 ("should have this course") in order, with the one they thought most essential on top, the second next, etc. Finally, the supervisory personnel were asked to toss the cards in group 3 ("don't really need this course") into two stacks: one which they felt was not at all needed for the position being discussed, and one which they felt was perhaps necessary, but could be better obtained through on-the-job training than through formal courses. Directions for the card sort as used by the interviewee during the sort are found in appendix D. No restrictions were placed on the number of cards to be assigned to any given category. Upon completing the task, respondents were asked to review their selections.

Following each interview, the results of the card sort were entered on a tally sheet (appendix D); a form evaluating the overall coverage of the interview was filled out; and eight summary charts concerning data covered were checked.

Identifying the Universe and the Sample

The universe for the administrative and supervisory personnel for the study consisted of federal librarians GS 15 and above. They were administrative and supervisory personnel who were from one to three steps of authority above the level of professional librarians in this study, and who were responsible for work for the particular type of library position about which the interview was conducted (figure 1).

The method used to obtain a sample from this universe was quota sampling based on a proportionate number of administrators for each main category of positions represented in the responses received from the practicing librarians. Table 6 gives the number of administrators interviewed for each type of position.

FIGURE 1
LEVELS OF SUPERVISION IN FEDERAL LIBRARIES FROM WHICH REPRESENTATIVE ADMINISTRATORS WERE SELECTED TO BE INTERVIEWED:1969

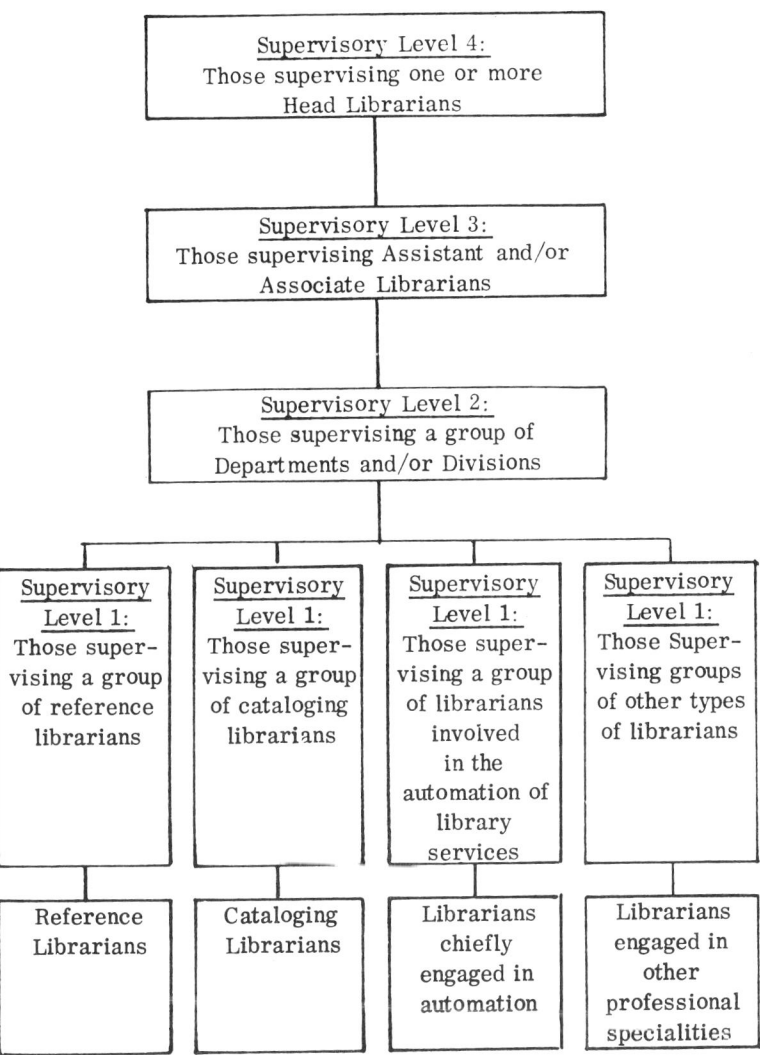

DESIGN OF THE STUDY

TABLE 6
NUMBER OF TOP-LEVEL ADMINISTRATORS INTERVIEWED FOR
MAJOR TYPES OF JOBS HELD BY FEDERAL LIBRARIAN
RESPONDENTS: 1969

Type of Position for which the Administrator Responded in Interview	Number of Top-Level Administrators Interviewed
ADMINISTRATIVE POSITIONS	
Head of library	5
Assistant Head of Library	1
Head of Department or Division	4
Head of Branch Library	2
NON-ADMINISTRATIVE POSITIONS	
Cataloger	3
Reference	3
Automation	1
Other/Non-Administrative:	
Readers' Services	1
	20

REFERENCES IN CHAPTER 2

1. American Psychological Association. *The American Psychological Association's Project on Scientific Information Exchange in Psychology.* v2. Washington, D.C.: The Association, 1965.
2. Argyris, Chris. *Understanding Organization Behavior.* Homewood, Ill.: Dorsey Pr., 1960.
3. Arnold, Joseph P. *A Study of Recommendations for Technical Education Curricula.* Final Report. West Lafayette, Ind.: Purdue Univ., 1965 (ED 016 064).
4. Bernstein, Marver H. *The Job of the Federal Executive.* Washington, D.C.: Brookings Institution, 1958.
5. Bunge, Charles A. *Professional Education and Reference Efficiency.* Research Series no.11. Urbana: Library Research Center, Univ. of Illinois, 1967 (ED 019 097).
6. Cannell, Charles F., and Morris Axelrod. "The Respondent Reports on the Interview," *"American Journal of Sociology* 62:177—81 (Sept. 1956).
7. ——— and R. L. Kahn. "The Collection of Data Interviewing," in L. Festinger and D. Katz, eds., *Research Methods in the Behavioral Sciences,* p.327—80. New York: Dryden Pr., 1953.

REFERENCES

8. Carlson, Sune. *Executive Behavior: A Study of the Work Load and the Working Methods of Managing Directors.* Stockholm: Stromberg Aktiebolag, 1951.
9. Corson, John J., and R. Shale Paul. *Men Near the Top: Filling Key Posts in the Federal Service.* Baltimore: Johns Hopkins Pr., 1966.
10. Curnow, Geoffrey Ross. "The Dimensions of Executive Work in the U.S. Federal Career Civil Service: A Factor Analytic Study." Doctor's dissertation, Cornell Univ., Ithaca, 1967.
11. Educational Testing Service. "Appendix B: Selected 'Job-Elements' from a Check List with the Job Dimensions Project," in *Assessing Managerial Potential: Report of a Seminar*, p.69—71. Ann Arbor, Mich.: Foundation for Research on Human Behavior, 1958.
12. Fryden, Floyd N. "Post-Master's Degree Programs in Some American Library Schools." Research paper, Graduate Library School, Univ. of Chicago, 1968.
13. Hall, Anna C. *Selected Educational Objectives for Public Service Librarians: A Taxonomic Approach.* Pittsburgh: Univ. of Pittsburgh, 1968.
14. Hemphill, John. *Dimensions of Executive Positions.* Research Monograph no. 98. Columbus: Bureau of Business Research, Ohio State Univ., 1960.
15. Koontz, Harold, and Cyril O'Donnell. *Principles of Management: An Analysis of Managerial Functions.* 4th ed. New York: McGraw-Hill, 1968.
16. Lyman, Helen. *The Library Materials Project.* Library School Project 348. Mimeographed. Madison: Library School, Univ. of Wisconsin, 1969.
17. McLennan, Kenneth. "The Manager and His Job Skills," *Academy of Management Journal* 10:235—45 (Sept. 1967).
18. Meltzer, Morton. *The Information Center: Management's Hidden Asset.* New York: American Management Assn., 1967.
19. Morsh, Joseph E., Raymond E. Christal, and Joseph M. Madden. *Job Analysis in the United States Air Force.* Lackland Air Force Base, Tex.: Personnel Laboratory, Air Research and Development Command, 1961.
20. Richardson, Stephen A., Barbara S. Dohrenwend, and David Klein. *Interviewing: Its Forms and Functions.* New York: Basic Books, 1965.
21. Saunders, David R. *Use of an Objective Method to Determine Engineering Job Families That Will Apply in Several Companies.* Princeton, N.J.: Educational Testing Service, 1954.
22. Schick, Frank. *Survey of Special Libraries Serving the Federal Government.* Washington, D.C.: National Center for Educational Statistics, U.S. Dept. of Health, Education, and Welfare, 1968.
23. Schill, William J., and Joseph P. Arnold. *Curricula Content for Six Technologies.* Report of the Bureau of Educational Research and the Dept. of Vocational and Technical Education. Urbana: Univ. of Illinois, 1965.
24. Shilling, Charles W., and Bruce Berman. *Science Information Specialist Training Program: A Progress Report.* Washington, D.C.: Biological Sciences Communication Project, George Washington Univ., 1968.
25. Smith, Robert G., Jr. *The Development of Training Objectives.* Alexandria, Va.: Human Resources Research Office, George Washington Univ., 1964.
26. Stone, Elizabeth W. *Factors Related to the Professional Development of Librarians.* Metuchen, N.J.: Scarecrow, 1969.
27. Teller, James D., and William B. Camm. *Studies of Air Force Executives: I, Development of an Experimental Task Inventory for Executives (TIE) of the USAF.* Washington, D.C.: U.S. Air Force, 1962.

DESIGN OF THE STUDY

28. Underwood, Willis O. "A Hospital Director's Administrative Profile," *Hospital Administration*, 8:6—24 (Fall 1963).
29. U.S. Civil Service Commission. *Position—Classification Standards, Transmittal Sheet No. 60*. Technical Information Services Series GS-1412. Washington, D.C.: The Commission, 1966.
30. ——*Civil Service Handbook X-118: Qualification Standards for White Collar Positions under the General Schedule, Transmittal Sheet No. 108*. Librarian Series GS-1410. Washington, D.C.: The Commission, 1967.
31. Wallace, Everett M., and others. *Planning for On-the-Job Training of Library Personnel*. Technical Memorandum 3762/000/00. Santa Monica, Calif.: System Development Corp., 1967.
32. Warner, W.L., Paul P. Van Riper, and others. *The American Federal Executive*. New Haven: Yale Univ. Pr., 1963.

3
Background Information about Federal Librarians

The request for background information was put in Part III in the questionnaire. However, when the analysis of the data was made, it became obvious that the reporting of the data gathered about the respondents should come early in this report as the material in later chapters would be more meaningful once the reader was aware of these characteristics. Within this chapter the information about the federal librarian respondents is grouped under four headings: (1) personal and job-related variables; (2) educational variables; (3) characteristics of federal librarians compared with those of other types of librarians; and (4) summary and implications.

Personal and job-related variables include: grade level of respondents, type of position, geographical distribution, sex ratio, age distribution, professional experience, years with the federal government, job mobility, absence from library work for six months or more, experience in occupations other than librarianship, relationship of position level to type of job activity, years in present position, number of employees supervised, location of library in agency (headquarters or field), number of people employed in library, estimated minimum experience required for present job, hours spent on avoidable details, and utilization of talents. Educational variables include library degrees and undergraduate major, and area of concentration of nonlibrary graduate degrees. The remainder of the chapter contains characteristics of federal librarians compared with those of other types of librarians and presents a summary profile of the background characteristics of the federal library respondents.

BACKGROUND INFORMATION

PERSONAL AND JOB-RELATED VARIABLES

At the outset of this discussion of background characteristics, it is necessary to discuss the grade level of the respondents and the two categories into which positions were divided. This information is of importance because the manner in which these categories were constituted is reflected in nearly all of the tables that are presented in this study.

Grade Level and Position

The statistical analysis for this project started with an examination of the grade structure of the 365 respondents. It has already been mentioned that the 9 respondents who belonged to non-GS categories were assigned equivalent GS grades. It was noticed that certain grades had too few respondents, and there was no justification for making these grades a separate category for the analysis of the data. Hence, the grades were combined into three groups, and throughout the study these groups were adhered to. Table 7 gives the grade level of federal

TABLE 7
GRADE LEVELS OF FEDERAL LIBRARIANS AND THE MANNER IN WHICH THEY WERE COMBINED FOR PURPOSES OF ANALYSIS: 1968

GS Level	Number of Respondents	Per Cent	Combined Grouping for Analysis	Number of Respondents	Per Cent
GS 9	115	31.51	GS 9	115	31.51
GS 10	16	4.38	GS 10, 11	140	38.36
GS 11	124	33.97			
GS 12	60	16.44			
GS 13	40	10.96	GS 12, 13, 14	110	30.14
GS 14	10	2.74			
Total	365	100.00		365	100.00

librarians and the manner in which they were combined into groups.

A major decision early in the study related to the manner in which respondents should be grouped for analysis regarding type of position. It was decided that only two major categories of positions, administrators and nonadministrators, would be used throughout the study. However, when the questionnaire was formulated, it was pointed out that the distinction between the administrator and nonadministrator was not very clear in a small library, and the decision could be arbitrary if it was left to the librarian in such a library. So it was decided that librarians working in one- to three-person libraries would report only the fact of working in such a library, and the research team would assign them to one of these two categories — administrative or nonadministrative — on the basis of the following factors: official title of position; GS-1410 series titles; GS grade level; location of present position; number of employees supervised; number of employees in library with a grade of GS 9 or higher; total number in the library system; and the kind of job activity items checked in Part I of the questionnaire.

The same problem arose for librarians who are supervisors. In these cases, too, arbitrariness was avoided and uniformity ensured by asking them to report only this fact, and the research team assigned them to the two categories — administrative and nonadministrative — on the basis of the factors mentioned above. Further, it may be pointed out that the number of people in the two groups (39 and 47 respectively) was not sufficient to treat them as separate categories for statistical analysis.

Thus there were four groups in the questionnaire for reporting the type of position: (1) administrators, (2) supervisors, (3) persons working in one- to three-man libraries, and (4) persons working in a professional specialty. Obviously group 1 was to be assigned to the administrators, and group 4 to the nonadministrators; groups 2 and 3 were to be treated in the manner mentioned above (table 8).

By far the heaviest concentration of respondents was, as expected, in the District of Columbia, with a total representation of 43.0 percent, which was almost equally divided between Stratum I (Library of Congress) and Stratum II (other federal agencies). In addition, there was representation from thirty-seven states, with California, Maryland, Colorado, and New York leading. APO (Army Post Office) addresses were given for the 7.4 percent of the responding librarians stationed overseas. The statewide distribution of respondents is presented in appendix table 1 (in appendix E).

TABLE 8
FREQUENCY OF ADMINISTRATORS AND NON-ADMINISTRATORS BY GRADE LEVEL: 1968

Type of Position and GS Grade Level	Number	Percentage in Stratum	Percentage of Total (N=365)
Stratum I (N=73)			
LIBRARY OF CONGRESS			
Administrators			
GS 9	0	0.00	0.00
GS 10, 11	0	0.00	0.00
GS 12-14	14	19.18	3.84
Subtotal	14	19.18	3.84
Non-Administrators			
GS 9	21	28.77	5.75
GS 10, 11	21	28.77	5.75
GS 12-14	17	23.29	4.66
Subtotal	59	80.83	16.16
TOTAL	73	100.00	20.00
Stratum II (N=292)			
OTHER AGENCIES			
Administrators			
GS 9	63	21.58	17.26
GS 10, 11	79	27.05	21.64
GS 12-14	74	25.34	20.27
Subtotal	216	73.97	59.17
Non-Administrators			
GS 9	31	10.62	8.49
GS 10, 11	40	13.70	10.96
GS 12-14	5	1.71	1.37
Subtotal	76	26.03	20.82
TOTAL	292	100.00	79.99
Total (N=365)			
ALL TOGETHER			
Administrators			
GS 9	63		17.26
GS 10, 11	79		21.64
GS 12-14	88		24.11
Subtotal	230		63.01
Non-Administrators			
GS 9	52		14.25
GS 10, 11	61		16.71
GS 12-14	22		6.03
Subtotal	135		36.99
TOTAL	365		100.00

Sex Ratio

In the present study 73.4 percent of the respondents were women. The data presented in table 9, column 3, which shows the relation of grade level to sex, would seem to warrant the conclusion that generally the higher the grade, the higher the percentage of men holding these federal library positions. Thus, 85.7 percent of the administrators at GS 9 are women, and 82.3 percent of the GS 10 and 11 administrators are women; but at the GS 12—14 level the percentage of women has dropped to 53.4 percent. A similar pattern is noted among the nonadministrators: at the GS 9 level, 84.6 percent are women; at the GS 10 and 11 level, 73.8 percent are women; while at the GS 12—14 level, only 59.1 percent are women. These statistics are given for the total number of respondents and cannot be related to any promotion policies. In examining the statistics it is interesting to note that there are two areas where there are fairly large variations or drops in the sex ratios. For the administrators the largest drop is in Stratum II (agencies other than the Library of Congress), where there is a drop of 34.3 between the 85.7 females per 100 respondents at the GS 9 level and the 51.4 ratio at the GS 12—14 level. For the nonadministrators there is a drop of 19.5 between the 71.4 women per 100 respondents at the GS 9 level and the 52.9 ratio of women per 100 respondents at the GS 12—14 level in Stratum I.

Of the 91 head librarians represented in this study — who are distributed almost equally in grades GS 9, GS 10—11, and GS 12—14 (table 10) — 72.5 percent are women. This is almost the identical ratio of women that obtains for all the respondents — 73.4 percent.

In contrasting the sex ratio in librarianship with other professions, Schiller (6) points out that when all professional and technical occupations are taken together, the ratio of women to men is almost exactly reversed from the ratio found in librarianship. Figures released in 1966 showed that 38 percent of all positions in professional and technical occupations were held by women. The comparison of sex ratio between academic librarians and faculty is striking: 64 percent of women as compared to only 20 percent, and a recent study shows that women constitute only 10 percent of all faculty in selected leading universities. It has also been found that women have only a small representation among scientists (8 percent), lawyers (3 percent), and engineers (1 percent).

TABLE 9
DESCRIPTIVE STATISTICS FOR THE RESPONDENTS IN ADMINISTRATIVE AND NON-ADMINISTRATIVE POSITIONS BY GRADE LEVEL AND STRATUM: 1968

Type of Position and GS Grade Level	Total Number in Group	Sex Ratio (No. of females per 100 respondents)	Average Age	Average Number of Professional[1] Years[2]	Average Number of Years Elapsed[1] since MLS[2]
		STRATUM I			
Library of Congress					
Administrators					
GS 9	0	--	--	--	--
GS 10, 11	0	--	--	--	--
GS 12-14	14	64.29	43.00	15.75	14.54
Sub-group	14	64.29	43.00	15.75	14.54
Non-Administrators					
GS 9	21	71.43	32.62	1.20	.60
GS 10, 11	21	61.90	34.71	5.72	5.05
GS 12-14	17	52.94	42.00	11.72	10.81
Sub-group	59	62.71	36.07	5.84	5.11
TOTAL Stratum I	73	63.01	37.40	7.74	6.74
		STRATUM II			
Other Agencies					
Administrators					
GS 9	63	85.71	45.10	13.60	13.65
GS 10, 11	79	82.28	47.09	17.99	18.69
GS 12-14	74	51.35	48.88	19.35	18.71
Sub-group	216	72.69	47.12	17.04	17.08
Non-Administrators					
GS 9	31	93.55	39.97	8.46	9.03
GS 10, 11	40	80.00	44.75	12.20	12.46
GS 12-14	5	80.00	53.20	23.00	23.20
Sub-group	76	85.53	43.36	11.41	11.74
TOTAL Stratum II	292	76.03	46.14	15.58	15.69

Table 9 (Continued)

Type of Position and GS Grade Level	Total Number in Group	Sex Ratio (No. of females per 100 respondents)	Average Age	Average Number of Professional[1] Years[2]	Average Number of Years Elapsed[1] since MLS[2]
		ALL TOGETHER			
Administrators					
GS 9	63	85.71	45.10	13.60	13.65
GS 10, 11	79	82.28	47.09	17.99	18.69
GS 12-14	88	53.41	47.94	18.76	18.09
Sub-group	230	72.17	46.87	16.96	16.94
Non-Administrators					
GS 9	52	84.62	37.00	5.47	5.73
GS 10, 11	61	73.77	41.30	9.93	9.78
GS 12-14	22	59.09	44.55	14.28	13.76
Sub-group	135	75.56	40.17	8.94	8.83
TOTAL	365	73.42	44.39	13.99	13.91

[1] These two averages are expected to be very close because of their definitions as stated in the questionnaire. The purpose of including both was to check the reliability of the data collected.

[2] Divisors used in obtaining the above percentages are widely varied as they correspond to the numbers of respondents answering each question rather than the totals of each respondent grouping. These divisors are given in Table 33.

Age Distribution

The mean age is 44.4 (table 9, column 4) for all respondents. As might be expected, the average age of the administrators is higher than that of the nonadministrators: 46.9 compared with 40.2. The single group with the highest average age was the nonadministrators in Stratum II (libraries other than the Library of Congress), the GS 12–14 group, with a mean age of 53.2. The single group with the lowest average age was the GS 9 nonadministrators at the Library of Congress.

BACKGROUND INFORMATION

The mean age for the women was 45.0 years as compared to 43.1 for the men. It should be noted in this connection that it is possible that the mean age of federal women librarians in this sample may actually be somewhat higher than the 45.0 listed, as 24 women did not fill in their age, and a search of *Who's Who in Library Service* and other directories did not reveal these missing ages. Only 6 of the men did not reveal their age.

Professional Experience

The mean number of years of professional experience for the 365 federal librarians in the study is 14.0, as indicated in table 9 which shows the mean number of years of professional experience by grade and by type of library position for all of the 365 respondents. One statistical figure to which special attention should be called is the mean of 13.6 years for the GS 9 administrators. This seems quite high, especially in view of the new civil service ruling, adopted in the fall of 1968, which places a new MLS-degree graduate in the same grade with persons of more than 13 years of experience. It is also significant to note that the average number of years of professional experience for the administrator is 17.0 as compared to 8.9 years for the non-administrator.

The average number of years that the respondents have held their present positions is 4.9. The GS 9 respondents have an average of 3.0 years in their present positions, which is 2.5 years less than the average of those in GS 10—14 positions. Also, the administrators, with 5.9 years, have averaged 2.5 more years in their present positions than have the nonadministrators (appendix table 2).

The greatest variations in number of years in present position is found when the respondents are divided according to agency. Those employed in the Veterans Administration, the District of Columbia Public Library, and the Navy have averaged the highest number of years in their present position: 10.6, 7.9, and 6.4 years respectively. The lowest average, regardless of how the respondents are categorized, is held by those employed at the Library of Congress—2.0 years.

When divided by sex, it is found that the women have been in their present positions 1.6 years more than the men — 5.4 years as compared to 3.8.

The average number of years that the respondents have worked for the federal government is 11.0. The women average 2.8 years more with the federal government than do the men — 11.7 years as compared to 8.9. The GS 9 respondents have worked an average of 7.1 years for the federal government, which is 5.2 less years than those in GS 10—11, with an average of 12.3. Between the GS 10—11 and GS 12—14, there is only a difference of 1.2 years — 12.3 as compared to 13.5. The administrators have an average of 5.7 years more than do the nonadministrators — 13.0 years as compared to 7.3 (appendix table 2).

The greatest variations appear when the respondents are divided by agency. The three agencies in which respondents have the greatest average number of years with the federal government are the Veterans Administration, the Navy, and the Army: 16.7, 15.0, and 13.9 respectively. The Library of Congress has the lowest average in this respect, 5.9 years.

Counting their present position, the respondents on an average have worked in two other libraries in the federal government and an average of 1.4 libraries outside the federal government. Overall, the respondents have worked in an average of 3.4 libraries (appendix table 2). One might expect that those in the higher grades would have moved considerably more than the lower ones, but they are very nearly the same, with the combined average for the GS 12—14 of 3.7 as compared to 3.3 for grades 9 through 11. Basically, there is very little difference in the number of libraries the different grades have worked in.

There is a slightly greater difference between the administrator and the nonadministrator. The administrator has worked in an average of 1.6 more libraries (taking both inside and outside the federal government together) than the nonadministrator: 4.0 as compared to 2.4 libraries for the nonadministrator. Of the respondents 37.8 percent have worked in no other library than the one in which they are now employed; 27.1 percent have worked in one library outside the federal government; and 19.0 percent have worked in three outside libraries.

In the present study 21.4 percent of the federal library respondents state that they had left library work for six months or more at some point after they had begun professional employment (appendix table 3). Proportionately more of the administrators had left than the nonadministrators (25.2 percent compared with 14.8 percent). By grade the GS 10—11 respondents had the highest percentage who had left — 24.3 percent.

The most frequent reason for leaving was for marriage or family reasons (28 respondents, or 35.9 percent, of the 78 who had left gave this as their reason). The other major reason for leaving was to obtain more education (20 respondents, or 25.6 percent, of those who left cited this as their reason). It is interesting to note that only 14 (18.0 percent of 78) had left for another occupation and then returned. These statistics, of course, give no indication of those who have left and

BACKGROUND INFORMATION

not returned to federal librarianship, as the present study only included those who are currently employed in federal libraries.

The findings indicate that nearly half of all the respondents (46.6 percent) had come to federal librarianship by way of experience at a professional, technical, or administrative level in other fields. Experience in teaching predominated and accounted for more than half (52.4 percent) of the respondents who listed an occupational experience prior to librarianship. The second largest category is writing, editing, and journalism, but this group is quite small in comparison to the teachers — only 10.6 percent of those reporting prior occupations.

The complete breakdown of the respondents who reported a first prior occupation is given by grade level in appendix table 4, but in summary:

GS 9	52.2 percent reported a first prior occupation
GS 10—11	41.4 percent reported a first prior occupation
GS 12—14	47.3 percent reported a first prior occupation

It was also found that 11.5 percent of the respondents had a second prior occupation at a professional, technical, or administrative level. Of the 42 respondents reporting a second prior occupation, 23.8 percent had this second occupation in teaching, while 76.2 percent had experience in a variety of 12 other occupations (appendix table 4). The different grades show very little variation in a second prior occupation.

The breakdown of respondents reporting prior occupations by type of position is shown in appendix table 4. There was no significant difference between the percentages of administrators and non-administrators. Of the administrators reporting a prior occupation, 57.7 percent were teachers, but only 42.4 percent of the nonadministrators had been teachers. Of 89 respondents having teaching as the first prior occupation, 64 were administrators (71.9 percent), while of 81 respondents having other occupations as the first prior experience, 47 were administrators (58.0 percent). Thus, there would seem to be a slight indication that librarians with teaching experience were more apt to become administrators than those whose experience was in other occupations.

These statistics reinforce the findings of previous studies, including the 1968 survey by Schiller (6), which have shown that librarianship is often a second occupational choice. It is difficult to evaluate the importance of this experience factor at this stage of the study, because the data will be more meaningful when related by further study to the length of time the respondents spent in those other occupations based on the amount of time between their BA and MLS degrees.

Schiller found in her study of academic librarians that more than half of all the respondents have nonlibrary experience at a professional, technical, or administrative level. In her study, education was also found to predominate overwhelmingly (855 individuals of 1,176 who reported a prior occupation) (6:24). Morrison (4) in his 1961 study found that more than half of his respondents had had experience in other occupations. Commenting on this situation, Schiller (6:24) states:

> The fact that a large proportion of librarians do not elect librarianship as a first occupational choice reflects very seriously upon the profession itself, and on its reputation as a challenging and rewarding career. Why this occurs is a crucial question which requires further examination. For the moment, however, we can simply note that late career decisions have an important bearing on the relatively high age levels among librarians.

It would seem that this condition would have important implications for recruitment for post-MLS and doctoral programs, but it is not possible to estimate the precise nature of these implications.

Type of Job Activity

One-fourth (24.9 percent) of the federal library respondents in the study reported that they are heads of libraries (table 10). One factor contributing to this high percentage is that so many of the federal libraries are small in size. For example, of the 91 heads of libraries in the study, 14 are heads of one- to three-man libraries. This fact partially explains why 67.0 percent of the head librarians in the study are grade GS 11 or less.*

The second largest category (18.1 percent of the respondents) is composed of those holding positions as heads of departments or divisions. By contrast with the head librarians, here the heaviest concentration is in GS 12—14, with 56.7 percent of these respondents in this grade level as compared to the 43.3 percent found in the GS 9—11 groups combined. This comparison seems to indicate that in libraries large enough to have department and division heads, the grade level tends to be higher than for head librarians in smaller libraries.

The third largest concentration is in the area of cataloging, which accounts for 11.8 percent of the total. Among the catalogers, 83.7 percent of the respondents fall in grades 9 and 10—11, with almost

---

*Another possible reason for the generally low grade level of head librarians is discussed in the section Avoidable Details, page 77.

TABLE 10
FREQUENCY DISTRIBUTION OF TYPES OF LIBRARY ACTIVITIES
IN WHICH THE RESPONDENTS ARE PRIMARILY ENGAGED
BY GRADE LEVEL:1968

Type of Position	Grade Level			All Respondents	
	9	10,11	12-14	No. (N=365)	%
Administrators					
Head of Library	28	33	30	91	24.93
Assistant or Associate Head	11	5	9	25	6.85
Head of Department or Division	11	21	34	66	18.08
Head of Branch	4	6	4	14	3.84
Head of Regional or Field Library	8	10	4	22	6.03
Head of Library System	1	4	7	12	3.29
Non-Administrators					
Abstracting	0	0	0	0	0.00
Acquisitions	2	1	0	3	.82
Analyzing Source Materials	0	0	0	0	0.00
Archives	0	0	0	0	0.00
Bibliography	2	10	1	13	3.56
Cataloging	19	17	7	43	11.78
Circulation	0	0	0	0	0.00
Classification	1	2	3	6	1.64
Clientele Services	0	1	0	1	.27
Coordinator	0	3	2	5	1.37
Data Processing	0	1	1	2	.55
Documents and/or Reports	2	1	0	3	.82
Editing and/or Writing	0	0	1	1	.27
Indexing	1	1	0	2	.55
Information Retrieval	0	0	0	0	0.00
Literature Searching	0	1	0	1	.27
Non-Print Materials	0	0	0	0	0.00
Personnel	0	1	0	1	.27
Public Relations	0	0	0	0	0.00
Reference	17	17	4	38	10.41
Research	0	0	0	0	0.00
Revision	0	1	0	1	.27
Selection of Materials	0	0	0	0	0.00
Serials	1	0	0	1	.27
Subject Speciality	2	1	0	3	.82
Systems Analysis	1	1	2	4	1.10
Technical Services	1	1	1	3	.82
Terminology Control	0	0	0	0	0.00
Translation	0	0	0	0	0.00
Other	3	1	0	4	1.10
TOTAL	115	140	110	365	100.00

equal numbers in both groups. The only other sizable concentration by type of activity is that of the reference librarians who comprise 10.4 percent of the total number of respondents. Of the reference librarians, 89.4 percent are found in the GS 9 and the GS 10—11 categories, with the same number falling within each of these groups. Only eleven catalogers and reference librarians come within the GS 12—14 bracket, and of these, all but three are employed at the Library of Congress. These statistics point up a condition which was reported by the respondents in the open-end questions, namely, that to advance in the civil service grade structure as a librarian, one usually has to be engaged in administrative activities.

It is interesting to note, in view of the demand expressed for courses in automation later in this report, that only 2 of the 365 respondents had data processing as their primary activity. One is in the GS 10—11 category; 1 in the GS 12—14 group. There are 4 respondents who list systems analysis as their primary activity: 1 is a GS 9, 1 is in the GS 10—11 category, and 2 are in the GS 12—14 group.

As both Hemphill (3) and Curnow (2) had found that not much precise information can be inferred about similarity of work performed by position titles alone, the respondent was asked for the official title of his position and his civil service category, as well as for the kind of library activity in which he was primarily engaged. It was found that the official title of position and the primary type of activity tend to run parallel with one another, but the civil service category is not useful in determining type of activity as it is too broad. (The official title of position is a fairly good indicator of primary responsibility, except for the title "librarian.") Grouped by the broad civil service categories, the distribution of the respondents is as follows:

Librarian	161 respondents	44.11%
Administrative librarian	120 respondents	32.88%
Supervisory librarian	64 respondents	17.53%
Library director	14 respondents	3.84%
Other	6 respondents	1.64%

Number of Employees Supervised

Few of the respondents supervised large numbers of people: 30.0 percent reported that they supervise no one; 31.1 percent supervise more than 5; 8.1 percent supervise 20 or more; and 1.7 percent supervise 50 or more. The overall mean is 6.4 people (table 11). The men are somewhat more likely to supervise larger staffs: 30.3 percent

TABLE 11

NUMBER OF EMPLOYEES SUPERVISED BY THE RESPONDENTS BY TYPE OF POSITION AND SEX: 1968

Number of People Supervised	Type of Position				Sex				Total	
	Administrative		Non-Administrative		Males		Females			
	No. (N=214)	%	No. (N=130)	%	No. (N=89)	%	No. (N=255)	%	No. (N=344)	%
0	17	7.94	87	66.92	28	31.46	76	29.80	104	30.23
1 - 2	38	17.76	21	16.15	10	11.24	49	19.21	59	17.15
3 - 5	55	25.70	19	14.62	15	16.85	59	23.14	74	21.51
6 - 9	38	17.76	3	2.31	9	10.11	32	12.55	41	11.92
10 - 19	38	17.76	0	0.00	17	19.10	21	8.24	38	11.05
20 - 49	22	10.28	0	0.00	7	7.87	15	5.88	22	6.40
50 and over	6	2.80	0	0.00	3	3.37	3	1.18	6	1.74
Total	214	100.00	130	100.00	89	100.00	255	100.00	344	100.00
Mean	9.7		0.9		9.0		5.5		6.4	

of the men as opposed to 15.3 percent of the women supervise more than 10 people. The mean number of employees supervised by the men is 9.0 as compared with a mean of 5.5 supervised by the women. However, 29.8 percent of the women (compared to 31.5 percent of the men) supervise no one.

For the administrators, who constitute 63.0 percent of the respondents, the average number of employees supervised is 9.7, while the mean for the nonadministrators is 0.9. The mean number of employees supervised varies from a high of 16.1, for administrator respondents in the GS 10—14 category, to 0.5, for the GS 9 nonadministrators. Of the administrators 30.8 percent, as compared with 0.0 percent of the nonadministrators, supervise more than 9 people. The average number of employees supervised by administrators is higher at the headquarters libraries than at the regional or field offices (12.1 as compared to 7.3), but this relationship does not exist when the mean is computed for the whole sample, including the nonadministrators. Then the number supervised is slightly higher in the field and regional offices than in the headquarters libraries (table 12).

Location of Library in Agency

The chief characteristic to be noted about the location of the libraries where the respondents are employed is that 52 percent of the respondents work in an agency headquarters library, as compared with 36.3 percent who work in regional or field offices. However, it should also be noted that there is a substantially greater number of nonadministrators who work at agency headquarters, 83.7 percent, than administrators, 32.7 percent (table 12).

Number of People Employed

The respondents were asked to report the number of employees in their libraries and also the proportion of them in GS 9 or higher. In Stratum II the average of the first figure was 36.7 and the average of the second was 14.4. It must be remembered that 36.7 does not stand for the average number of employees in a federal library per se, since the sampling unit in this study was a librarian rather than a library and as a consequence larger libraries had more librarians in the sample than smaller libraries.

TABLE 12

STATISTICS RELATING TO POSITION LOCATION WITHIN AGENCIES OF RESPONDENTS AND AVERAGE NUMBER OF EMPLOYEES SUPERVISED BY TYPE OF POSITION AND GRADE LEVEL: 1968

Type of Position and Grade Level	Location Within Agencies								TOTAL	
	Headquarters		Regional or Field		Branch or Post		Other			
	Number of Respondents	Average Number Supervised	Number of Respondents	Average Number Supervised	Number of Respondents	Average Number Supervised	Number of Respondents	Average Number Supervised	Number of Respondents	Average Number Supervised
Administrators										
GS 9	6	5.3	46	3.1	7	4.6	3	3.0	62	3.5
GS 10,11	21	6.7	39	6.1	6	6.0	4	31.0	70	7.7
GS 12-14	43	15.7	30	15.2	3	3.7	6	28.5	82	16.1
Subtotal	70	12.1	115	7.3	16	4.9	13	23.4	214	9.7
Non-Administrators										
GS 9	39	0.4	6	0.3	4	1.5	1	0.0	50	0.5
GS 10,11	50	0.8	4	3.0	2	1.5	4	3.0	60	1.2
GS 12-14	20	1.4	0	--	0	--	0	--	20	1.4
Subtotal	109	0.8	10	1.4	6	1.5	5	2.4	130	0.9
TOTAL	179	5.2	125	6.8	22	4.0	18	17.6	344	6.4

WORK VARIABLES

Experience Requirements

The respondents were asked to estimate the minimum experience in libraries and information centers required to perform their present jobs (Part III of questionnaire, item 32, p.10). The results are set forth by type of library activity in supplementary table 5. In all the job activities which contained the larger number of respondents, there was considerable difference in judgments about the minimum experience needed. The estimates varied from no experience to more than 7 years. The same number of respondents (32) thought no experience was required for their jobs as those who thought "over 7 years" was necessary. The highest concentration of those stating no experience is necessary is the catalogers. Two heads of libraries and two assistant heads thought no experience was necessary, as did three reference librarians. At the other end of the scale, ten heads of departments or divisions and nine heads of libraries thought more than 7 years of experience was necessary. It should be noted that only 5.3 percent of the nonadministrators answering this question (114) thought more than 5 years was necessary to perform their jobs. On the other hand, 24.0 percent of the administrators answering this question (192) estimated that more than 5 years experience was necessary to perform their jobs.

Avoidable Details

Of the 321 respondents who answered the question about hours spent on avoidable detail (Part III of the questionnaire, item 34, p.10), 90.3 percent report spending from 1 to 38 hours a week on avoidable detail work that they feel should not be a part of their jobs. Only 9.7 percent of those answering this question report no time spent in this manner. These results are in marked contrast to the 16.5 percent of the respondents who spend more than 16 hours a week on avoidable details (table 13). The chief differences between categories of respondents are found in the "21 and above" classification of table 13 in which 5.4 percent of the administrators indicated this category as compared with 0.8 percent of the nonadministrators. Also to be noted is the 16—20 hour span which shows that 14.3 percent of the administrators come in this group, while only 10.0 percent of the nonadministrators fall within it. Another difference is the 1—5 hour category, where the nonadministrators have a higher frequency — 37.0 percent as compared to 28.2

TABLE 13

DISTRIBUTION, BY TYPE OF POSITION AND GRADE LEVEL, OF HOURS PER WEEK SPENT ON AVOIDABLE DETAILS BY THE RESPONDENTS:1968[1]

Number of Hours	Administrators								Non-Administrators								Total	
	GS 9		GS 10,11		GS 12-14		All		GS 9		GS 10,11		GS 12-14		All			
	No. (N=63)	%	No. (N=79)	%	No. (N=88)	%	No. (N=230)	%	No. (N=52)	%	No. (N=61)	%	No. (N=22)	%	No. (N=135)	%	No. (N=365)	%
None	4	7.55	3	4.41	9	11.11	16	7.92	7	16.67	3	5.17	5	26.32	15	12.61	31	9.66
1- 5	9	16.98	22	32.35	26	32.10	57	28.22	13	30.95	25	43.11	6	31.58	44	36.97	101	31.46
6-10	14	26.42	25	36.77	29	35.80	68	33.66	12	28.57	16	27.59	5	26.32	33	27.73	101	31.46
11-15	5	9.43	7	10.29	9	11.11	21	10.40	5	11.91	8	13.79	1	5.26	14	11.77	35	10.90
16-20	14	26.42	9	13.24	6	7.41	29	14.36	4	9.52	6	10.34	2	10.53	12	10.08	41	12.78
21 and above [2]	7	13.20	2	2.91	2	2.47	11	5.44	1	2.38	0	0.00	0	0.00	1	.84	12	3.74
Total	53	100.00	68	100.00	81	100.00	202	100.00	42	100.00	58	100.00	19	100.00	119	100.00	321	100.00

[1] Percentages are based on the actual number of people in each category answering this question (321 out of 365 answered).

[2] The breakdown on the 12 respondents included in the "21 and above" category follows:

```
24 hours................1
25 hours................6 (one of these is the one non-administrator in the group)
27 hours................1
30 hours................2
37 hours................1
38 hours................1
```

percent for administrators. The mean number of hours spent by the 321 respondents answering this question is 9.1 a week.

In the analysis of the open-end questions, Part IV of the questionnaire, it was found that one of the chief factors that respondents complained about was the necessity of having to do work which they feel should be done by supportive staff. Even though no comments were called for in the instrument at the place this question about avoidable detail (question 34 in Part III) was asked, and no space was left for comments, nearly a dozen respondents wrote around the margins of the page or attached separate notes clipped to this question stating their dissatisfaction. The following two comments are typical:

> I want to give good service, but I do not have sufficient clerical staff to give efficient service unless I do many of the clerical-type tasks myself.

> I listed 37 hours per week, because I get paid a GS 9 salary to check in newspapers and route them.

The answers to this question would seem to have several implications for curriculum building. For one thing, the response to this question may be an important factor in the reason for the high demand for automation courses which is reported on in detail in a later section of this study. It may be that the respondents feel that automation might be a means of taking away some of their clerical work. Further, it would seem to indicate that course content in management or administration should include this problem of attempting to find ways and means for the administrator to make better use of the professional staff assigned to the library, with or without automated techniques. The full use of the talents that have been recruited to the profession is an important problem and one that is a part of the total library manpower issue.

These findings also have implications related to some areas of personnel work within the federal civil service system. These statistics would seem to point up a fact brought out in a recent survey of a selected group of federal librarians related to the new Civil Service Classification System for librarians (7) about the attitude of job classifiers toward libraries and library positions. The survey showed that many of the librarians sampled felt that the personnel office seemed to assume that librarians are glorified clerks, and it has a tendency to grade jobs that way. This assumption may be one of the reasons why 67.0 percent of the chief librarians in this study were found to be in grade 11 or less.

BACKGROUND INFORMATION

The question arises whether this amount of time spent on avoidable details that should be handled by supportive staff is typical of that found in surveys of other professions. One example is found in a study of research and development officers in the Air Force in 1965, which was made by Morsh and others (5:10). When this same question was asked of the 798 respondents in the Morsh study, it was found that the mean number of hours per respondent was considerably lower than for the library respondents in this study — 5.2 hours a week in the Air Force study, as compared to 9.1 hours a week in this study.

Utilization of Talents

Table 14 summarizes the responses of the respondents to the question "How well does your job utilize your talents?" Generally, the higher the grade, the better used are talents, but this condition has a tendency to be slightly more pronounced for the administrator than for the nonadministrator. Of all 365 respondents, 52.3 percent indicated that they thought their talents were being used "very well" or "excellently." Forty-three percent thought their talents were being used "very little" or only "fairly well." In the questionnaire there was an additional heading, "not used at all," but none of the respondents checked this category. The question was not answered at all by 4.7 percent of the respondents.

It was noted in the analysis of the replies to the open-end questions that in many cases the respondents felt that their talents were not being utilized properly. However, table 14 would seem to indicate that most of the people were fairly well satisfied. This seeming inconsistency needs further probing, especially in view of the fact that 90.3 percent of the respondents answering question 34 in Part III stated that they were engaged in avoidable details that should be handled by supportive staff.

EDUCATIONAL VARIABLES

Inasmuch as the data from this study are conceived as being one base on which to build courses for those who have already received the first professional degree, the master's in library science, only those who had received this degree or who had received a bachelor's degree in library science at the graduate level before the early 1950s were involved in the study.

TABLE 14

DISTRIBUTION OF RESPONSES TO "HOW WELL DOES YOUR JOB UTILIZE YOUR TALENTS?":1968[1]

Type of Position	Non-Response		Talents Utilized						Total	
			Excellently		Very Well		Fairly Well		Very Little	
	No.	%	No.	%	No.	%	No.	%	No.	%	No. (N=365)	%
Administrators												
GS 9	(3)	0.82	8	2.19	18	4.93	26	7.12	8	2.19	63	17.25
GS 10, 11	(5)	1.37	11	3.01	32	8.77	29	7.95	2	0.55	79	21.65
GS 12-14	(2)	0.55	15	4.11	43	11.78	25	6.85	3	0.82	88	24.11
Subtotal	(10)	2.74	34	9.31	93	25.48	80	21.92	13	3.56	230	63.01
Non-Administrators												
GS 9	(2)	0.55	4	1.10	17	4.66	19	5.21	10	2.74	52	14.26
GS 10, 11	(3)	0.82	8	2.19	21	5.75	25	6.85	4	1.10	61	16.71
GS 12-14	(2)	0.55	6	1.64	8	2.19	5	1.37	1	0.27	22	6.02
Subtotal	(7)	1.92	18	4.93	46	12.60	49	13.43	15	4.11	135	36.99
TOTAL	(17)	4.66	52	14.24	139	38.08	129	35.35	28	7.67	365	100.00

[1] Percentages are computed on a base of 365.

BACKGROUND INFORMATION

Library Degrees

It was found that a high percentage of the respondents had as their highest professional degree the graduate fifth-year BLS, which was granted before the early 1950s. In fact, of the total of 365 respondents, 29.9 percent hold this type of degree only; 2.7 percent hold both the fifth-year BLS and the MLS; and 67.4 percent hold the MLS degree. The distribution of these graduate degrees by agency is shown in table 15. In addition, four of the respondents stated that they have participated in a sixth-year post-MLS program in library science. Table 16 gives the frequency distribution of the years in which the respondents received their MLS (or graduate BLS) degrees, by grade. Percentages are based on the number giving exact year of degree (348).

TABLE 15
DISTRIBUTION OF TYPE OF GRADUATE LIBRARY SCIENCE PROFESSIONAL DEGREES HELD BY THE RESPONDENTS BY AGENCY-1968

Agency	Those Holding Only a Fifth-Year Graduate BLS Degree	Those Holding Both a Fifth-Year Graduate BLS and an MLS	Those Holding Only an MLS	Total
Library of Congress	6	4	63	73
Army[1]	20	1	31	52
Navy	8	1	19	28
Air Force	18	0	33	51
Veterans Administration	20	2	14	36
D.C. Public Library	6	0	8	14
Health, Education, and Welfare	6	0	15	21
Agriculture	4	1	10	15
Other Agencies	21	1	53	75
Total	109	10	246	365
Per Cent	29.86%	2.74%	67.40%	100.00%

[1] One respondent in this group also has a Ph.D. in library science.

TABLE 16
FREQUENCY DISTRIBUTION OF THE YEARS IN WHICH THE RESPONDENTS OBTAINED MLS (OR GRADUATE BLS) BY GRADE LEVEL: 1968

Years	Grade Level			Total	
	9	10, 11	12-14	No.	(N=348) %
Before 1950	20	48	38	106	30.49
1950-1954	13	18	23	54	15.52
1955-1959	8	21	19	48	13.79
1960-1964	25	26	13	64	18.39
1965-1969	45	21	10	76	21.84
Subtotal	111	134	103	348	100.00
No Date	4	6	7	17	–
TOTAL	115	140	110	365	–

Undergraduate Major

Analysis of table 17 reveals that the major fields of study reported most frequently by those respondents who specified their undergraduate major were English and journalism (23.3 percent of the 365 respondents), history (11.5 percent), foreign languages and literature (9.9 percent), and education (7.1 percent). These four subjects constitute 51.8 percent of all the subjects reported. When the courses are grouped by large areas, 41.4 percent fall in the humanities and 28.5 percent in the social and behavioral sciences. There is no apparent relationship between bachelor's major, type of job, or grade level, with the one exception that more nonadministrators than administrators proportionately have bachelor's degrees in social and behavorial sciences.

Nonlibrary Graduate Degrees

A summary of the graduate degrees held by the respondents in nonlibrary areas is given in table 18. As is the case with the bachelor's degree, the heaviest concentration is in the humanities and in the social and behavioral sciences. At the master's level, the subjects in which there is the heaviest concentration are foreign languages and literature (11 respondents), and the second highest grouping is in the fine and applied arts (9 respondents). Only one of the respondents has obtained an advanced degree in administration or management although administrators make up 63.0 percent of the 365 respondents. (Subject breakdown is not given in table 18.)

TABLE 17

BACCALAUREATE MAJOR BY TYPE OF POSITION AND GRADE LEVEL: 1968

Baccalaureate Major	Type of Position				Grade Level						Total Respondents	
	Administrative		Non-Administrative		9		10, 11		12-14			
	No. (N=230)	%	No. (N=135)	%	No. (N=115)	%	No. (N=140)	%	No. (N=110)	%	No. (N=365)	%
Humanities and Arts												
English and Journalism	56	24.35	29	21.48	27	23.48	31	22.15	27	24.55	85	23.29
Foreign Languages and Literature	25	10.87	11	8.15	9	7.83	10	7.14	17	15.45	36	9.86
Fine and Applied Arts	10	4.35	6	4.45	8	6.96	3	2.14	5	4.55	16	4.38
Other	9	3.91	5	3.70	5	4.35	3	2.14	6	5.45	14	3.84
Subtotal	100	43.48	51	37.78	49	42.62	47	33.57	55	50.00	151	41.37
Social and Behavioral Sciences												
Administration and Management	3	1.30	1	0.74	2	1.74	1	0.71	1	0.91	4	1.10
Psychology, Philosophy, and Religion	6	2.61	2	1.48	2	1.74	2	1.43	4	3.64	8	2.19
History	25	10.87	17	12.59	12	10.43	17	12.14	13	11.82	42	11.51
Other	24	10.43	26	19.26	14	12.17	20	14.29	16	14.54	50	13.70
Subtotal	58	25.21	46	34.07	30	26.08	40	28.57	34	30.91	104	28.50
Basic and Applied Sciences[1]	25	10.87	14	10.37	12	10.43	16	11.43	11	10.00	39	10.68
Education	18	7.83	8	5.93	11	9.57	12	8.57	3	2.73	26	7.12
Library Science	6	2.61	4	2.96	4	3.48	5	3.57	1	0.91	10	2.74
Not Specified	23	10.00	12	8.89	9	7.83	20	14.29	6	5.45	35	9.59
TOTAL	230	100.00	135	100.00	115	100.00	140	100.00	110	100.00	365[2]	100.00

[1] Applied sciences include such subjects as engineering, nursing, agriculture, pre-med., forestry, etc.

[2] Four respondents listed 2 bachelors degrees, or which only the first received was used in this table. The second bachelors listed by four individuals are: 2 in education, and one each in English and library science.

TABLE 18
AREA OF CONCENTRATION OF NON-LIBRARY GRADUATE DEGREES BY TYPE OF POSITION AND GRADE LEVEL: 1968

Descriptive Category	Grade Level			Type of Position		TOTAL	
	9	10,11	12-14	Administrative	Non-Administrative		
	(N=115)	(N=140)	(N=110)	(N=230)	(N=135)	No. (N=365)	%
GRADUATE: Masters							
Before MLS							
Humanities	5	4	8	13	4	17	4.66
Social and Behavioral Sciences	4	10	2	2	14	16	4.38
Basic and Applied Sciences	--	2	2	4	--	4	1.10
Education	2	2	2	4	2	6	1.64
Subtotal	11	18	14	23	20	43	11.78
GRADUATE: Masters							
After MLS							
Humanities	1	5	4	9	1	10	2.74
Social and Behavioral Sciences	--	1	3	3	1	4	1.10
Education	--	2	1	1	2	3	.82
Subtotal	1	8	8	13	4	17	4.66
Total Masters	12	26	22	36	24	60	16.44
GRADUATE: Ph.D.							
Before MLS							
Social Sciences	--	--	3	2	1	3	.82
GRADUATE: Ph.D.							
After MLS							
Social Sciences	--	--	1	1	0	1	.28
Total Ph.D.	--	--	4	3	1	4	1.10
TOTAL Graduate Degrees in Non-Library Science Areas	12	26	26	39	25	64	17.54

BACKGROUND INFORMATION

There does not seem to be any apparent relationship between type of position held and the possession of a master's degree in any particular subject area. Master's degrees in other subject areas seemed to be fairly equally distributed between administrators and nonadministrators. Some differences in grade level are noticeable, however. For example, there is a distinct difference between GS 12—14 and GS 9 in the number of respondents holding a master's in another subject area, with a noticeably larger number falling in the GS 12—14 category.

The sequence of training of those respondents who hold an advanced degree in another subject area in addition to the MLS is interesting to note. Of the 64 advanced degrees held in nonlibrary subjects (in addition to the MLS) 71.9 percent completed their degrees in the other subject areas before receiving the MLS. The fact that only 28.1 percent of the degrees were received after the MLS indicates a pattern of education that is also noted in the Schiller study of college and university librarians (6). In other words, those who are planning post-MLS programs for librarians should be aware that the pattern set by the librarians to date indicates a much heavier evidence of advanced degree study before the MLS rather than after.

FEDERAL LIBRARIANS COMPARED WITH OTHER LIBRARIANS

The question arises, Are the federal library respondents in this study unique in the personal and job-related variables presented about them in this survey, or are they very similar to librarians in general? In an attempt to answer this question partially, a profile of the respondents in this study and the respondents in two other 1968 surveys of other types of librarians is presented in table 19. The second column in the table reports profile data of the federal librarian respondents in this study. The third column reports data concerning college and university librarians as set forth in a survey by Schiller (6), and the fourth column summarizes data from a study of all types of librarians by Stone (8).

Examination of this profile chart reveals a close similarity between many of the personal and job-related characteristics covered by these three separate surveys. As background for examination of the table, certain characteristics of each study should be noted. Whereas the present study of federal librarians and the Stone study of all types of librarians included only those individuals with the fifth-year master's degree in library science, the Schiller study included all professional personnel employed in academic libraries; and of the respondents in the latter study, 16.5 percent did not hold a fifth-year graduate degree (6:39). There are certain other differences also to be noted in the populations from which the samples were drawn for each of these studies. The present study excluded the lowest level of professionals (GS 7) as well as the highest levels (GS 15 through 18). With these exclusions the population, based on statistics released by the Civil Service Commission, equals 2,677. Of this number it was found that just over 50 percent, or 1,347, held MLS degrees, and this number constituted the population used in this study. The population for the college and university study (6:23) comprised more than 13,000 persons employed either on a full-time or part-time basis in academic libraries; the population for the Stone study (8:14) consisted of 806 MLS graduates of the 1956 and 1961 classes of the library schools accredited by the American Library Association and whose names were listed in the 1966 edition of *Who's Who in Library Service*. The data from these different studies provide some comparisons that seem to be important to course and curriculum building.

Age

It is to be noted that the average age at the time of the survey was very similar in all three groups. Thus none of these three groups is so old that retirements will deplete its numbers in the near future, which implies that motivation toward post-MLS study should be of vital concern to all three groups when the profession needs to be transformed along the vastly different lines which technological, societal, and behavioral advances require.

Attention, too, should be drawn to the fact that in the Stone library survey (column 4 of table 19) the mean age is almost as much for those receiving their MLS in 1956 and 1961 as it is for the other groups which include many who received their MLS degrees much earlier. This would seem to be an indication that the average age of entrants to library school is rising. This is a factor which deserves the major concern of those involved in building post-MLS programs, for it is brought out in these studies that the older the entry level to the MLS-level program, the less likely persons are to engage in formal course work following their MLS degree. Basically, this is a problem to be faced by recruitment and admissions officers of the MLS program.

TABLE 19
A PROFILE OF FEDERAL LIBRARY RESPONDENTS
COMPARED WITH OTHER TYPES OF LIBRARIANS: 1968

Variable	Type of Librarian Respondents from Three Different Studies		
	Federal	College and University[1]	Academic, Public School, and Special[2]
	(N=365)	(N=2282)	(N=138)
Background Characteristics			
Average age at time of survey	44.4[3]	44.9(median)	42.6
Sex: Percentage female	73.4	64.0	58.0
Average age of female respondents	45.0	48.0(median)	44.0
Average age of male respondents	43.1	41.3(median)	44.0
Education			
Percentage with 5th-year graduate BLS	29.9	17.8	--
Percentage with MLS in library science	70.1	65.7	100.0
Percentage with Ph.D. in library science	0.3	0.8	--
Percentage with Ph.D. in subject area	1.1	1.7	1.4
Percentage with master's in subject field in addition to MLS or 5th-year BLS	16.4	17.6	23.2
Percentage with 6th-year post-MLS program	1.1	5.5	0.0
Baccalaureate Major:			
Percentage in humanities	41.4	49.3	40.6
Percentage in social and behavioral sciences	28.5	26.6	33.3
Percentage in education	7.1	7.9	13.0
Percentage in basic and applied sciences	10.7	6.8	10.9
Percentage in library science	2.7	4.9	2.2
Percentage not specified	9.6	4.5	--
Percentage having master's in addition to MLS	16.4	17.6	23.1
Percentage in humanities	7.4	--	10.9
Percentage in social and behavioral sciences	5.5	--	7.2
Percentage in education	2.5	--	3.6
Percentage in basic and applied sciences	0.8	--	1.4
Percentage of advanced non-library degrees received after the MLS	28.1	21.0	5.8

Table 19 (Continued)

Variable	Type of Librarian Respondents from Three Different Studies		
	Federal (N=365)	College and University[1] (N=2282)	Academic, Public School, and Special[2] (N=138)
Percentage of those who received their MLS before 1950	30.5[4]	25.0[5]	--
Percentage of those who received their MLS between 1950 and 1959	29.3[4]	29.0[5]	--
Percentage of those who received their MLS after 1960	40.2[4]	46.0[5]	--
Experience			
Average number years in present position	4.9	3.9	4.3
Percentage in administrative positions (Heads, Assoc./Asst. Librarian; Department or Division Heads)	60.3	61.7	73.1
Percentage who are heads	24.9	15.3	33.0
Percentage of men who are heads	26.0	21.6	37.9
Percentage of women who are heads	24.5	11.8	26.6
Supervision			
Percentage supervising no one	30.0	26.6	--
Percentage supervising more than 5 people	31.1	25.9	--
Percentage supervising 20 or more people	8.0	7.7	--
Percentage of men who supervise more than 10 people	28.1	25.9	--
Percentage of women who supervise more than 10 people	13.3	10.5	--
Percentage with non-library experience at a professional, technical or administrative level	46.6	51.1	53.6
Percentage who had left library work for 6 months or more	21.4	24.2	--
Percentage who had left for marriage or family	35.9	39.5	--
Percentage who had left for further education	25.6	28.2	--
Percentage who had left to work in another field	18.0	15.0	--
Percentage who had left for military service	12.8	11.2	--

[1] Schiller (Ref. 6)
[2] Stone (Ref. 8)
[3] Average given is the mean unless otherwise noted.
[4] Percentages based on 348 out of 365.
[5] Percentages based on 1792 respondents out of 2282.

BACKGROUND INFORMATION

Sex Ratio

In a profession that, as a whole, is typically thought of as an occupation made up of women, the fact that the federal librarians have a higher ratio of women than the other two groups represented deserves particular attention; for, as pointed out in each of these studies, there is a tendency for more men to return for formal education programs following the MLS degree than for women. Therefore, the fact that in the Stone library survey the ratio of men would seem to be increasing might mean that the demand for courses at the post-MLS level in the future would show an increase if the tendency to graduate more men with the MLS degree continues.

Education

There is a marked similarity between the three surveys relevant to the subject fields covered, both in undergraduate programs and in graduate degree work in addition to the MLS. This similarity in educational background of the three groups of librarians would seem to substantiate the argument that any curriculum built from the conclusions of this survey would also be acceptable and satisfactory to librarians other than federal librarians. It means that the post-MLS program can plan on a base of knowledge that is fairly uniform in its essential composition.

For curriculum builders, it would seem important to note that the established pattern, as borne out in all three of these surveys, is for the additional graduate work, in whatever field, to be taken before rather than after the MLS. In other words, up to this time there has been comparatively little degree-taking by MLS holders after that degree is received. In building a post-MLS program, it would seem that an awareness of this should be kept in mind, as lack of motivation to take work following the MLS may continue to be a barrier in building well-attended programs. This trend, as a matter of fact, is reflected in the exceedingly small number in any of the three groups who have availed themselves of the opportunity of participating in a sixth-year program in library science, programs which have been established now for several years. It might be noted here that one possible reason for the lack of participants in the post-MLS programs is the very name of the programs — sixth-year program in library science — which brings no objectives or purpose to mind. It would seem that a definite type of title with a degree involved might be more appealing and indicate a given school's type of specialty, such as Master of Library Administration.

Experience

Perhaps the most striking statistics among those in the "experience" category in table 19 is the high percentage of those in administrative positions, in spite of the fact that the college and university survey included 16.5 percent who do not hold a fifth-year degree, and that in the Stone librarian survey the earliest date for receiving the MLS degree was 1956. Even so, this group in the latter study has the highest percentage in the administrative group. With administrative tasks occupying this high percentage of practicing librarians—most of whom from their educational background have not been particularly trained for this type of position—one definite guideline for post-MLS curriculum builders would seem to be that there is a real need for advanced work in the area of administration and management — a fact which is, in reality, brought out in many sections of this survey. Concerning this high number of people in administration, it is also interesting to note that the average time in present position is very nearly equal for all groups, and that having been in their positions such a short time, but yet having these advanced posts, indicates something of the demand for people with expertise in library administration.

Another factor to note in all three studies is the high percentage who entered librarianship from other professions. Such a high proportion of second-career people admitted to the MLS program may cut down the potential available for post-MLS programs, for there seems to be a tendency for those who come from another profession to be less apt to engage in post-MLS formal study than for those who have librarianship as their first career choice.

The most interesting thing about the percentages for those who have left library work for six months or more and come back is the great similarity in each instance between the federal librarians and the college and university librarians.

SUMMARY OF BACKGROUND CHARACTERISTICS

Table 19 has been presented to visualize the fact that even though the federal librarians represent but one type of library service today, their personal characteristics, educational background, and experience are very similar to that of other types of librarians that have been surveyed. Therefore, it would seem safe to conclude that a post-master's program

BACKGROUND INFORMATION

that was sensitive to their needs and demands would, in all likelihood, also be able to meet the needs of other types of librarians.

Some of the background characteristics of federal librarians would seem to have special importance for interviewing supervisory personnel. They could be used to establish and assess relationships between management's concepts of post-MLS training and the views of the practicing federal librarians. Also, they are data which can be used in forecasting future patterns for post-MLS programs in library science.

1. The average age of the administrators in the study was 6.7 years higher than the age of the nonadministrator's.

2. The average age for the women in the study was slightly higher than that of the men.

3. The average number of years of professional experience for the administrators was 8.0 years higher than that of the non-administrators.

4. Administration was a major concern to 63 percent of the respondents. Twenty-five percent of the respondents were heads of libraries; 18 percent were heads of departments or divisions. It should be noted, however, that 14 of the heads (4 percent of all 365 respondents) were heads of one- to three-man libraries. At the present time, to advance in the civil service structure, the librarians almost necessarily have to leave subject specialties behind and go into administrative positions. This pattern raised questions for top-level library personnel being interviewed: Is this tendency to advance only through the medium of administration going to last? Is it further accentuated by the advent of automation, or will it be less accentuated? Did they believe those under them in a given category needed special training in administration to perform more effectively?

5. Among the nonadministrators the two largest job types were catalogers (12 percent of the respondents) and reference librarians (10 percent of the total). Eighty-four percent of the catalogers and 89 percent of the reference librarians fell within grades 9 to 11.

6. Ninety percent of the librarians report spending an average of 9.1 hours a week on avoidable detail, which is 4 hours more than research and development management officers in the air force spent (5:10).

7. Fifty-two percent of the librarians reporting in this survey are of the opinion that their talents are well used by their jobs.

8. Judgments differed with respect to the minimum experience needed to perform federal library jobs as represented in this survey. However, the librarians, in general, have considerably more experience than they judge to be minimal. The catalogers constitute the largest group indicating no experience is needed for their jobs.

9. It was found that administrators tended to have worked longer in their present positions than nonadministrators (2.5 years more) and that the number of years worked in present position tends to increase with the grade level. The average number of years in the present position for the respondents was 5 (4.9), and the average number of libraries in which the respondents had worked was 3.4.

10. The federal librarians have worked in more libraries within the federal government (average 2.04) than in libraries outside the government (average 1.4); all together they have worked in an average of 3.4 libraries. There is a tendency for the women to move less and to be in their present positions longer than the men, and to have worked for the federal government longer. The overall average of the respondents was 11.0 years with the federal government. There was a great deal of variation among the agencies in both years in the federal government and years in the present position. The Veterans Administration, District of Columbia Public Library, and the Navy employed those with the highest number of years in their present positions; the Veterans Administration, the Army, and Navy employ those with the most years in the federal government. The Library of Congress employees had the least time in their current position and the least time working for the federal government. It would seem that the bulk of tomorrow's federal library leaders will come from within the ranks of those already recruited. The questions arise, What is to be done about providing competence to those who reach the top posts? and What can be done about retaining them once they get there?

11. In the present study, one out of five federal librarians (21.4 percent) stated that he had left library work for six months or more at some point after he had begun professional

BACKGROUND INFORMATION

employment. Of those leaving temporarily, one out of four left to obtain further education (25.6 percent of the 78 who had left cited this reason).

12. Perhaps the most important finding about supervision as related to course building is that the average number of employees supervised by the administrators is 9.7, with a range from 2 to 93, and that the average for the nonadministrators is less than one person (0.9) and the range is only 1 to 9. Further, 37.9 percent of the nonadministrators supervise no one. This might imply that if administrators and nonadministrators were admitted into the same post-MLS program, a great deal of effort should be made to match the training to the individual needs and background of those enrolled. Another possibility might be a differentiated training program for administrators and nonadministrators, as suggested by Culbertson for educational administrators (1). The program for administrators would select its candidates only from those in administrative positions in libraries or from those who have displayed leadership abilities and wish to prepare to become administrators.

13. Fifty percent of the respondents were employed in headquarters libraries, as compared to 35 percent who worked in field offices; however, a higher number of the administrators were employed in regional or field libraries than in headquarters libraries.

REFERENCES IN CHAPTER 3

1. Culbertson, Jack. "Differentiated Training for Professors and Educational Administrators." Paper read to annual meeting of the American Educational Research Association, Chicago, Feb. 8—10, 1968 (ED 021 309).
2. Curnow, Geoffrey Ross. "The Dimensions of Executive Work in the U.S. Federal Career Civil Service: A Factor Analytic Study." Doctor's dissertation, Cornell Univ., Ithaca, 1967.
3. Hemphill, John. *Dimensions of Executive Positions*. Research Monograph no.98. Columbus: Bureau of Business Research, Ohio State Univ., 1960.
4. Morrison, Perry David. *The Career of the Academic Librarian: A Study of the Social Origins, Educational Attainments, Vocational Experience, and Personality Characteristics of a Group of American Academic Librarians.* ACRL Monograph no.29. Chicago: American Library Assoc., 1968.

REFERENCES

5. Morsh, Joseph E., M. Joyce Giorgia, and Joseph M. Madden. *A Job Analysis of a Complex Utilization Field: The R & D Management Officer.* Lackland Air Force Base, Tex.: Air Force Systems Co., 1965.
6. Schiller, Anita R. Characteristics of Professional Personnel in College and University Libraries. Urbana: Library Research Center, Univ. of Illinois, 1968 (ED 020 766).
7. Stone, Elizabeth W. "Evaluation of the Civil Service Qualification Standards and the Position Classification Standards: A Survey, June 26, 1968." Mimeographed. Library Administration Division, American Library Assoc., 1968.
8. ——— *Factors Related to the Professional Development of Librarians.* Metuchen, N.J.: Scarecrow, 1969.

4
Job Dimensions of the Federal Librarian

The primary purpose of the job-inventory survey was to identify and examine the specific job activities performed by federal librarians. The detailed quantitative analysis of the job inventory, the qualitative analysis of it—much smaller in scope, and the summary and conclusions of the research findings presented in this chapter were deemed necessary to understand the educational needs of the subjects. Thus, the design for this part of the study was based on the assumption, supported by considerable research evidence, that the aspect of course development that should receive primary attention is the development of well-defined, job-relevant objectives. Smith (4:5) emphasizes and demonstrates that when objectives are appropriately developed, they provide clear guidance that permits an orderly presentation of course content.

ANALYSIS OF THE JOB INVENTORY

The quantitative analysis of the job inventory has the following facets: (1) examination of the applicability of the job inventory used; (2) separate analyses of the activity items in the job inventory in two different dimensions, namely, time and importance; (3) analysis of the job activities when these two dimensions are combined; and (4) analysis

ANALYSIS OF JOB INVENTORY

of the thirteen major job functions or areas of major activity under which the job activities were grouped in the questionnaire.

Before embarking on a detailed analysis of the results obtained from the job inventory, it should be pointed out that up to this point in the presentation, the analysis has been related to variables for which it is possible to obtain and to report precise information, insofar as the questions were answered by the respondents. In dealing with the data from the job inventory, however, it needs to be emphasized that the statistics presented are based largely on data of a subjective nature. The respondent presumably gave an accurate indication of the job items he performs, but his estimate of the relative time and importance that he attaches to each job activity is subjective. Nevertheless, it was important to discover how the respondents view the activities that they perform in relation to time and importance, so that the job roles they actually perform could be determined—a necessary dimension in task analysis aimed at curriculum building.

Applicability of the Questionnaire

Each respondent was asked to consider statements relating to the job activities he performed in two dimensions — time and importance. For all of those statements applicable to a given position, a rating was to be made on two separate but parallel scales. Each scale had three degrees of applicability from which the respondent could choose regarding a given job activity item: (1) most, (2) substantial, and (3) least. It also needs to be remembered that the job activities were divided into two sections: Specialized Library Functions (114 job activities listed under 13 areas), and General Administrative and Management Functions (109 job activities under 8 areas). Scattered throughout the job activities at the end of each of the main areas there were 21 lines marked "other." Uniformly, there were very few items listed by the respondents under the "other" headings, and in almost every instance where something had been filled in, it was found to be an item which had been covered in the listings but somehow had been overlooked by the respondent.

Tables 20 and 21 give the means, medians, standard deviations, and ranges of the frequency of job-activity items checked according to type of position and grade. Examination of these tables shows that the respondents varied widely in the degree to which they found the questionnaire applicable to their positions (see also supplementary tables 6 and 7). Taking all the 365 respondents together, the mean number of items checked in the job inventory for specialized library functions is 17.99 with a standard deviation of 17.59 and a range of 0-105; the mean number of administrative items checked by all the

TABLE 20

APPLICABILITY OF JOB INVENTORY: FREQUENCY OF JOB ITEMS
CHECKED BY RESPONDENTS BY TYPE OF POSITION: 1968

Number of Job Items	Frequency by Respondent							
	Specialized Library Functions			Administrative Functions			All Functions Together		
	Administrative	Non-Administrative	Total	Administrative	Non-Administrative	Total	Administrative	Non-Administrative	Total
Mean	22.72	9.99	17.99	42.77	6.59	29.36	65.44	16.58	47.35
Median	18.00	8.00	13.00	41.00	3.00	20.00	59.00	14.00	38.00
Standard Deviation	19.41	9.65	17.59	26.78	9.56	28.10	39.95	15.48	41.15
Range	0-105	0-77	0-105	0-109	0-45	0-109	8-192	1-107	1-192

TABLE 21

APPLICABILITY OF JOB INVENTORY: FREQUENCY OF JOB ITEMS
CHECKED BY RESPONDENTS BY GRADE LEVEL. 1968

Number of Job Items	Frequency by Respondent											
	Specialized Library Functions				Administrative Functions				All Functions Together			
	Grade			Total	Grade			Total	Grade			Total
	9	10,11	12-14		9	10,11	12-14		9	10,11	12-14	
Mean	23.08	19.31	10.48	17.99	30.59	27.39	38.60	29.36	53.67	46.57	49.08	47.35
Median	15.00	15.00	8.00	13.00	7.00	17.00	38.00	20.00	24.00	37.00	51.00	38.00
Standard Deviation	21.69	15.72	10.67	17.59	18.56	27.02	23.85	28.10	47.59	40.65	32.61	41.15
Range	0-105	0-77	0-60	0-105	0-109	0-99	0-103	0-109	1-192	2-153	1-125	1-192

respondents is 29.36 with a standard deviation of 28.10, and a range of 0-109; taking all the job items together, the mean number checked by the 365 respondents is 47.35, with a standard deviation of 41.15 and a range of 1-192.

Table 20 deals with the applicability of the questionnaire when the respondents are divided into administrators and nonadministrators. The mean number of specialized library functions checked by the administrators is 22.72, which is much higher than the 9.99 mean for the nonadministrators. For the specialized functions the standard deviation also is much higher for the administrators than for the nonadministrators — 19.41 as compared to 9.65. The range was also greater for the administrators. The largest number of items checked by any administrator is 105, while the largest number checked by nonadministrators is 77. By examining the administrative functions in table 20, it is found that the mean for the administrators is 42.77 which is almost seven times as high as the 6.59 for nonadministrators. The standard deviation for the administrators is 26.78 as compared to 9.56 for the nonadministrators. The range was also higher for the administrators. The largest number of items checked by any administrator was 109, while the largest number checked by nonadministrators was 77.

These statistics show that the administrators checked not only many more administrative functions, but also many more specialized library functions than did the nonadministrators. In each instance the standard deviation for administrators is larger than the standard deviation for nonadministrators, which means that there is a greater variation in job items performed among administrators than among nonadministrators. Further, the range is always larger for administrators than for nonadministrators. These statistics might be an indication that because of a shortage of staff, small size of the library, or other reasons, the administrators are spending a considerable amount of time operating at a nonadministrative level. An examination of table 21, which compares the responses in the job inventory by grade level, indicates a tendency for the variance to decrease as the grades increase. The median shows a pattern, namely, that the median goes down as the grade increases for the specialized function, but goes up for administrative functions as the grades increase. This is also true if all the functions are considered together.

Summing up this section on applicability, it can be stated that the respondents presumably found the job items surveyed in the questionnaire adequate, and, furthermore, the large means indicate that the answers are also very dependable. Not only is the information from this

JOB DIMENSIONS

job inventory a valuable source for the selection of courses, but it is also essential for determining job-related statements for training programs and for determining course content that is needed by librarians in their jobs. In the development of individual courses, data are provided which can be used as indicators of the weight to give to various elements of a course, of the level at which to provide training, and of course objectives.

Dimension of Time

The significance of time spent in the performance of job activities can best be judged in combination with other factors, but time is one important measure to use in building well-defined, job-relevant objectives and in deciding on the level of training that will enable the librarian to perform his job at his highest potential. Table 22 is a summary presentation which indicates the highest response rates on the time factor for all respondents. This table does not distinguish between the three time scales; however, it is supplemented in appendix E by table 8, which indicates the number of respondents for each scale. From this latter table, it is possible to arrive at the percentage of respondents answering each question according to a given time dimension. Figure 2 presents graphically the percentages of the "most" and "substantial" responses for the eight top-ranking job activities (according to percentage of respondents checking the item). The source for these percentages is appendix table 8. It also indicates the number and percentage of respondents who checked each job activity and ranks the fifty leading activities according to percentage of respondents checking the items. Such percentages can be used profitably in making decisions concerning course objectives and course content.

To combine different time dimensions and get one score, weights were assigned to three possible degrees of applicability from which the respondent could choose. Thus, a check for "most time consuming" was given a score of 5, a check for a "substantial" amount of time was given a score of 3, and a check for one of the "least time consuming" was given a score of 1. The rated scores for all items were then computed, and table 23 presents the top-ranking 25. These weights were not arbitrarily decided, but were arrived at after careful statistical considerations. In comparing tables 22 and 23, it is to be noted that only 16 items are common to both of them, and of these, 14 are administrative functions, 10 of which fall under the category "Directing" on the questionnaire. It is also to be noted in table 22 that the top 7 items have been checked by 50 percent or more of the 365 respondents; 5 of these items fall in the general category of directing.

TABLE 22

JOB ACTIVITY ITEMS SHOWING HIGHEST RESPONSE RATES ON TIME FACTOR FOR ALL 365 RESPONDENTS: 1968

Job Item Number	Job Item	No. Checking Time Factor For Item	Rank
187.	Directly supervise and guide subordinates	227	1
188.	Assign jobs to subordinates	208	2
191.	Check the accuracy of work of subordinates	202	3
237.	Attend professional meetings and/or conferences	197	4
190.	Train new employees in the performance of their work	190	5
98.	Actively answer reference questions	185	6
193.	Make decisions without consulting others	181	7
194.	Make decisions based on consultation with subordinates	178	8
195.	Give orders to initiate, modify, or stop activities	175	9
206.	Give prompt and full attention to all communications received	175	9
197.	Give subordinates authority to command or to act in certain areas	174	11
217.	Assign priorities for the completion of work	170	12
216.	Schedule activities to insure that deadlines are met	168	13
199.	Stimulate subordinates toward superior performance and creativity	167	14
228.	Interpret library programs to key officials, users, special groups	164	15
198.	Review decisions and/or proposals that are made by subordinates	162	16
201.	Identify and develop potential in subordinates	149	17
192.	Brief subordinates on immediate and continuing library programs	148	18
142.	Help develop new programs and/or activities	144	19
169.	Prepare position descriptions or analyses	143	20
140.	Recommend policy changes	140	21
96.	Have over-all responsibility for the reference services provided	138	22
131.	:ermine needed programs for the library	136	23
64.	Provide research assistance	135	24
166.	Select personnel	135	24

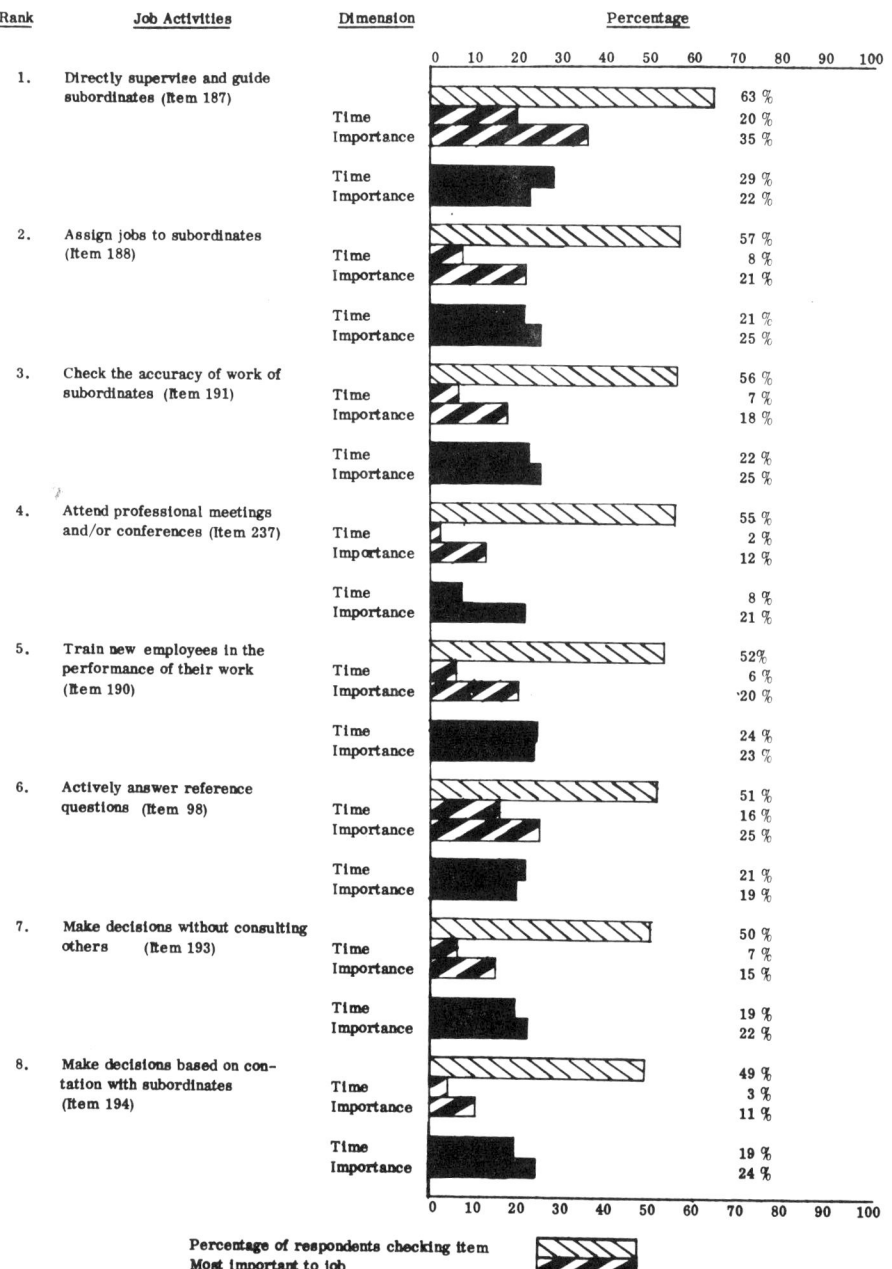

FIGURE 2
JOB ACTIVITIES OF FEDERAL LIBRARIANS SHOWING HIGHEST PERCENTAGE OF RESPONSE
(N=365)

TABLE 23

JOB ACTIVITY ITEMS RANKED ACCORDING TO WEIGHTED TIME SCORE FOR ALL 365 RESPONDENTS: 1968

Job Item Number	Job Item	Weighted Time Score	Rank
187.	Directly supervise and guide subordinates	727	1
98.	Actively answer reference questions	583	2
188.	Assign jobs to subordinates	478	3
191.	Check the accuracy of work of subordinates	464	4
190.	Train new employees in the performance of their work	458	5
206.	Give prompt and full attention to all communications received	443	6
96.	Have over-all responsibility for the reference services provided	436	7
193.	Make decisions without consulting others	415	8
60.	Have over-all responsibility for clientele services	413	9
8.	Am responsible for the over-all acquisitions program	411	10
228.	Interpret library programs to key officials, users, special groups	408	11
216.	Schedule activities to insure that deadlines are met	392	12
64.	Provide research assistance	383	13
29.	Have over-all responsibility for the cataloging program	366	14
62.	Refer clients to sources of information	364	15
194.	Make decisions based on consultation with subordinates	364	15
217.	Assign priorities for the completion of work	360	17
199.	Stimulate subordinates toward superior performance and creativity	357	18
128.	Integrate library programs with missions of parent organization	354	19
108.	Have over-all responsibility for operation of selection system	338	20
131.	Determine needed programs for the library	330	21
114.	Make tentative selection of material from reviews, catalogs, lists	329	22
195.	Give orders to initiate, modify, or stop activities	325	23
142.	Help develop new programs and/or activities	324	24
198.	Review decisions and/or proposals that are made by subordinates	3.6	25

Another item, number 201, "Identify and develop potential in subordinates," was checked for the time dimension by 149 respondents and received a ranking of 17 in table 22, but does not appear at all in table 23, since 91 out of the 149 respondents checked the item under the least time-consuming category, as can be seen in appendix table 8. The reason that this particular item is singled out for comment is because it plays a pivotal role in administration — a fact which is being more and more emphasized throughout management literature.

For an indication of how administrators compare with nonadministrators concerning the time dimension, see appendix table 9. For the administrators, there appear 8 job items of specialized library functions in the 25 top-ranking items, of which 2 — items 50 ("Have over-all responsibility for circulation system") and 86 ("Give over-all supervision to the maintenance of holdings") — did not appear in table 23. This finding indicates that even though these items were enumerated under specialized library functions, the administrators were probably doing these jobs more than the nonadministrators. However, for the nonadministrators, the 25 top-ranking items include 6 items of administrative functions. Further, 5 job items are common to administrators and nonadministrators, of which 4 are administrative in nature. In fact, all of these 4 are under the major job function, namely, directing. This comparison indicates that directing is a very important function both for administrators and nonadministrators. This conclusion is further strengthened when the material is analyzed later from a new perspective, namely, joint time/importance scores.

Another important feature of appendix table 9 is that of the 8 job items of specialized library functions included by administrators in the 25 top-ranking job items, 7 can be broadly called supervisory in nature. A typical example is "Have over-all responsibility for reference services." Henceforth, this type of job item will be referred to as a supervisory type of specialized library function. An examination of this table shows that these supervisory types of job items are not at all represented in the 25 top-ranking job items for the nonadministrators.

For a comparison of grade level to time factor, see data presented in appendix table 10. The important feature of this table is that as the respondents move up in grade, the time devoted to specialized library functions keep decreasing. For grade 9 there are 17 specialized library functions of the 25 top-ranking job items; for grades 10–11 this figure reduces to 13; and for grades 12–14 it drops to zero.

Here again, in grades 12–14, directing plays a major role. Thirteen of 21 job items constituting that major function rank among the 25 top items. However, it is interesting to note that job item 201, "Identify and develop potential in subordinates," is not one of the 13. These tables point out that directing holds a predominant position among major functions for librarians — a fact to be remembered in curriculum building, especially at the post-MLS level.

Dimension of Importance

A different perspective that is indispenable for building courses and determining course content in keeping with training objectives is knowledge of how important a job item is in accomplishing the library's objectives. It may be argued that this dimension is more important than the time dimension since, after all, in the ideal situation time should be completely dependent on the importance which is independent, mathematically speaking, and immutable. However, the limitation associated with this dimension must be borne in mind, namely, that it is not only subjective but also attitudinal. And further, whereas time can be measured, there is no yardstick to measure importance.

Parallel tables to those presented for the dimension of time, and computed in the same manner, are given for the importance factor. It was found that the number checking the importance factor for each item is generally the same as the number checking the time factor for each item (see appendix table 8). Table 24 presents job-activity items ranked according to weighted importance score for all respondents. Here it is found that item 187, "Directly supervise and guide subordinates," is still ranked first. Its weighted importance score of 897 is 196 points more than that of the second ranked item 188, "Assign jobs to subordinates." It is interesting to note that item 201, "Identify and develop potential in subordinates," is rank 18 with a score of 511, whereas it did not appear at all in the top 25 job-activity items ranked according to a weighted time score. Further, only 6 specialized library functions are included in this table, although table 23 (weighted time scores) included 9 such functions. This difference indicates a slight preference toward administrative functions in the importance dimension as compared to the time dimension.

This indication is further strengthened in appendix table 11 where job-activity items are ranked according to weighted importance scores for administrators and nonadministrators. For the administrators there appear 4 job items of specialized library functions in the top 25 items, 3 of these are of the supervisory type; the corresponding figure in the time-dimension table is 8 of the supervisory type. Nonadministrators also show a tendency in the same direction: 8 administrative items find

TABLE 24

JOB ACTIVITY ITEMS RANKED ACCORDING TO WEIGHTED IMPORTANCE SCORE FOR ALL 365 RESPONDENTS: 1968

Job Item Number	Job Item	Weighted Importance Score	Rank
187.	Directly supervise and guide subordinates	897	1
188.	Assign jobs to subordinates	701	2
98.	Actively answer reference questions	698	3
190.	Train new employees in the performance of their work	649	4
191.	Check the accuracy of work of subordinates	645	5
228.	Interpret library programs to key officials, users, special groups	610	6
206.	Give prompt and full attention to all communications received	596	7
216.	Schedule activities to insure that deadlines are met	589	8
217.	Assign priorities for the completion of work	586	9
193.	Make decisions without consulting others	567	10
199.	Stimulate subordinates toward superior performance and creativity	567	10
96.	Have over-all responsibility for the reference services provided	547	12
197.	Give subordinates authority to command or to act in certain areas	542	13
237.	Attend professional meetings and/or conferences	534	14
194.	Make decisions based on consultations with subordinates	521	15
128.	Integrate library programs with missions of parent organization	512	16
195.	Give orders to initiate, modify or stop activities	512	16
201.	Identify and develop potential in subordinates	511	18
60.	Have over-all responsibility for clientele services	508	19
198.	Review decisions and/or proposals that are made by subordinates	506	20
129.	Establish goals and objectives for the library	494	21
64.	Provide research assistance	491	22
8.	Am responsible for the over-all acquisitions program	480	23
62.	Refer clients to sources of information	476	24
131.	Determine needed programs for the library	475	25

a place in the list for nonadministrators; in the corresponding table for the time dimension, the number was only 6. Further, supervisory types of specialized library functions are absent as in the corresponding table for the time dimension. The major job function — directing — continues to hold its predominant position in this dimension, too. Thirteen items under this job function are included in the list for administrators.

Attention is now directed to a comparison of grade levels relative to the weighted importance factor (appendix table 12 is parallel to the weighted time factor presented in appendix table 10). For grade 9, 16 specialized library functions of the 25 top-ranking job items are listed; for grades 10—11 this figure is reduced to 10; and for grades 12—14, the figure drops to zero, repeating the pattern found for the time dimension. Further, the predominant role of the major function — directing — is evident in this importance dimension also. It is noted again that job item 201 ("Identify and develop potential in subordinates") is not anywhere in the section of the table reporting on the GS 9 category; it is rank 22 for the GS 10—11 group; and for the GS 12—14 category, it has moved up to a ranking of 8.

Joint Time/Importance Dimension

The job items in both the dimensions (time and importance) were analyzed separately, and it was found that the conclusions were similar. The last logical step is to analyze the job inventory from a perspective that uses both these dimensions. It has already been remarked that in an ideal situation the element of time should be dependent on importance. Further, the nature of the dependence should be such that similar scores should go together; that is, a job item deemed to be very important should generally take the most time, and, conversely, a job item deemed least important should generally consume very little time in an ideal situation — which, however, rarely seems to be realized.

However, these ideas have been used to construct a joint time/importance score for a job item. For each of the 223 job items the time score for each individual was multiplied by his importance score, and then these scores for each item were added for overall respondents to arrive at a final joint time/importance score for that job item. This joint time/importance score would measure the overall contribution of a job item toward the fulfillment of the objectives of the library. Under this scheme, if an individual checked an item, the joint time/importance for that item for that individual could vary from a maximum of 25 to a minimum of 1. (A score of zero is also possible, since a respondent could check the item for one dimension and leave the other dimension blank, meaning either "no time consumed" or "of no importance."

Table 25 gives the joint time/importance score for the 25 top-ranking job items. The trend noticed in the time dimension and in the importance dimension is accentuated in this new joint dimension. The number of specialized library functions has dwindled to 4 in this table, and 2 of them hold ranks 22 and 25. The administrative functions outscore the specialized library functions. This finding undoubtedly points toward the conclusion that in the minds of these respondents, administration contributes enormously toward the efficient realization of the library's mission and programs. Within the administrative function, the area of directing holds the most predominant position. To substantiate this conclusion, it is necessary to look at the joint time/importance score for an item for administrators and nonadministrators separately, and for the three different grade levels, as has been done in the case of the two dimensions of time and importance separately. These tables are presented in appendix tables 13 and 14.

Administrators show the same characteristics in their joint time/importance dimension as in the time and importance dimensions separately. The few specialized library functions included by them in the top-ranking job items are almost all of the supervisory type. This points toward the conclusion that administrators, when they are engaged in specialized library functions, mostly confine themselves to overall supervision and responsibility rather than actual performance of the job activities that constitute the specialized library functions.

On the other hand, the nonadministrators confine themselves to a great extent to proper specialized library functions. It would not be out of place to mention here how valuable this dichotomy of librarians into administrators and nonadministrators has been for the study of the job inventory. Otherwise, simply because administrators outnumber the nonadministrators by nearly 100 in this study, it would have been difficult to appreciate from the statistical presentation alone the importance of the specialized library function toward the fulfillment of the objectives of federal libraries.

It has already been noticed while studying the job inventory in the time dimension, as well as in the importance dimension, how administrative functions displace the specialized library functions as the grades move up. The same feature is repeated here in the dimension of joint time/importance, and this inescapably points toward the association that exists between high grades and administrative job items in this profession. It is interesting to note that supervisory types of specialized library functions, that are important parts of the job at grade 9, become less important as the grade level increases until at the

TABLE 25

JOB ACTIVITY ITEMS RANKED ACCORDING TO JOINT TIME/
IMPORTANCE WEIGHTED SCORE FOR ALL 365 RESPONDENTS: 1968

Job Item Number	Job Item	Weighted Time/Importance Score	Rank
187.	Directly supervise and guide subordinates	3635	1
188.	Assign jobs to subordinates	2937	2
98.	Actively answer reference questions	2909	3
191.	Check the accuracy of work of subordinates	2612	4
228.	Interpret library programs to key officials, users, special groups	2584	5
190.	Train new employees in the performance of their work	2570	6
216.	Schedule activities to insure that deadlines are met	2528	7
237.	Attend professional meetings and/or conferences	2431	8
217.	Assign priorities for the completion of work	2414	9
199.	Stimulate subordinates toward superior performance and creativity	2373	10
206.	Give prompt and full attention to all communications received	2328	11
193.	Make decisions without consulting others	2311	12
197.	Give subordinates authority to command or to act in certain areas	2290	13
96.	Have over-all responsibility for the reference services provided	2276	14
195.	Give orders to initiate, modify, or stop activities	2209	15
60.	Have over-all responsibility for clientele services	2183	16
201.	Identify and develop potential in subordinates	2171	17
194.	Make decisions based on consultation with subordinates	2146	18
128.	Integrate library programs with missions of parent organization	2102	19
198.	Review decisions and/or proposals that are made by subordinates	2082	20
129.	Establish goals and objectives for the library	2067	21
64.	Provide research assistance	2045	22
166.	Select personnel	2035	23
192.	Brief subordinates on immediate and continuing library programs	1994	24
62.	Refer clients to sources of information	1954	25
	Mean	926.72*	
	Standard Deviation	723.19	

*This statistic was calculated for all the 223 job items.

highest grade level they are completely eliminated from the 25 top-ranking job items.

So far, the study of the job inventory has been made with the job item as the unit. However, since the ultimate objective of this study is curriculum and course building, and since courses are not just a conglomeration of heterogeneous job items, it is necessary that this job inventory be further studied with homogeneous units larger than single job items.

To make the study, the job items in Part I of the questionnaire were grouped under 21 major job functions: 13 listed specialized library functions and 8 listed administrative functions. It is apparent that if the joint time/importance scores of all of the job items constituting a major job function are added up, the sum would be a valid joint time/importance score for the major job functions as a whole.

Table 26 lists the major functions, with the number of job items constituting them, and the joint time/importance score and ranks for administrators, nonadministrators, and both together. Standing alone, this table would seem to indicate that if this data were the sole criteria for deciding the area in which courses are needed, directing and planning in group B and classification in group A would certainly merit priority consideration.

Joint Time (Reversed)/Importance Dimension

If the purpose of this study were simply to analyze the job activities of federal librarians, it would be proper to conclude this section now. However, the main objective of this survey is to build courses and curriculum for librarians at the post-MLS level using information obtained from on-the-job needs of the librarians and certain other factors. With this objective in mind, the dimension of joint time/importance is once more examined.

This score has rated an item or a major job function high if the scores are high in both the time and importance dimension separately. Should this be the only criterion for studying the job inventory to reach a decision on courses and course content? Does this really reflect the true existing situation from a pedagogic point of view? The librarians are working in a library, and they have different types of activities to perform — some important, some not so important — and they devote various amounts of time to the performance of these jobs. As time goes on, the demands for service change, as do the natures of the jobs themselves, and a gap develops between knowledge learned in academic institutions last attended and skill necessary to perform new job activities efficiently. It would seem essential at this stage that the

TABLE 26

MAJOR JOB FUNCTIONS RANKED ACCORDING TO RELATIVE TIME/IMPORTANCE WEIGHTED SCORE BY TYPE OF POSITION: 1968

Major Job Functions	Number of Job Items	Administrative		Non-Administrative		All Together	
		Joint Time/ Importance Score	Rank	Joint Time/ Importance Score	Rank	Joint Time/ Importance Score	Rank
GROUP A							
Abstracting	07	187	21	171	18	358	20
Acquisitions	15	7,577	7	430	11	8,007	7
Bibliography	06	2,576	16	1,093	6	3,669	14
Cataloging and Classification	21	8,063	6	4,003	1	12,066	3
Circulation	10	2,743	15	306	14	3,049	16
Clientele Services	08	5,628	8	2,120	3	7,748	8
Indexing	09	735	19	490	10	1,225	19
Literature Searching	09	1,334	17	947	8	2,281	17
Maintenance of Holdings	10	3,116	14	268	15	3,384	15
Reference	07	4,950	11	1,853	4	6,803	9
Research	05	888	18	368	13	1,256	18
Selection	14	8,558	4	1,495	5	10,053	5
Translation	06	192	20	100	20	292	21
GROUP B							
Planning	23	15,117	2	1,002	7	16,119	2
Organizing	12	5,103	10	104	19	5,207	11
Staffing	24	9,840	3	246	17	10,086	4
Directing	22	23,789	1	2,144	2	25,933	1
Coordinating	06	3,586	13	425	12	4,011	13
Controlling	13	8,257	5	264	16	8,521	6
Representing	11	5,299	9	582	9	5,881	10
Housing	06	4,293	12	30	21	4,323	12

TABLE 27

JOB ACTIVITY ITEMS RANKED ACCORDING TO JOINT TIME (REVERSED)/
IMPORTANCE WEIGHTED SCORE FOR ALL 365 RESPONDENTS: 1968

Job Item Number	Job Item	Weighted Time (Reversed)* Importance Score	Rank
187.	Directly supervise and guide subordinates	1711	1
190.	Train new employees in the performance of their work	1306	2
98.	Actively answer reference questions	1261	3
191.	Check the accuracy of work of subordinates	1240	4
188.	Assign jobs to subordinates	1233	5
206.	Give prompt and full attention to all communications received	1212	6
217.	Assign priorities for the completion of work	1066	7
228.	Interpret library programs to key officials, users, special groups	1064	8
8.	Am responsible for the over-all acquistions program	1045	9
193.	Make decisions without consulting others	1031	10
199.	Stimulate subordinates toward superior performance and creativity	1005	11
96.	Have over-all responsibility for the reference services provided	1000	12
216.	Schedule activities to insure that deadlines are met	1000	12
194.	Make decisions based on consultation with subordinates	974	14
128.	Integrate library programs with missions of parent organization	958	15
197.	Give subordinates authority to command or to act in certain areas	926	16
198.	Review decisions and/or proposals that are made by subordinates	918	17
131.	Determine needed programs for the library	911	18
142.	Help develop new programs and/or activities	880	19
62.	Refer clients to sources of information	878	20
64.	Provide research assistance	865	21
60.	Have over-all responsibility for clientele services	859	22
201.	Identify and develop potential in subordinates	859	22

Table 27 (Continued)

Job Item Number	Job Item	Weighted Time (Reversed)*/ Importance Score	Rank
213.	Anticipate problems and prevent their occurrence through continuous interchange of information and early and direct contact of all involved	859	22
195.	Give orders to initiate, modify, or stop activities	857	24
	Mean	384.08**	
	Standard Deviation	315.56	

*The rationale for reversing the time score is for purposes of training: a highly important task which is seldom performed usually requires more emphasis in training than a highly important task which is performed constantly, as in the latter situation there is much more chance for learning on the job.

**This statistic was calculated for all the 223 job items.

librarian go back to the academic world to acquire training that will give him a solid grasp not only of new societal, technological, and environmental factors, but of administrative skills and processes as well.

However, the importance of on-the-job training, which also helps to bridge this gap, must be remembered, although some kinds of skills and concepts are very difficult to teach on the job. It would seem that curriculum builders at the postgraduate level should pay special attention to the job items which are deemed important but consume very little time, since the gap is expected to be widest for performing these job items efficiently. This observation gives the clue toward the formulation of a new dimension that will open up a new perspective aiding the curriculum builders. Accordingly, it was decided to calculate a new score for these job items by first reversing the time scale and then multiplying the importance score by the new time-reversed score. This score will then possess the necessary property, namely, that an item deemed important but consuming very little time would get the maximum score of 25 while an item deemed least important and consuming the most time would get the minimum score of 1. It was decided to call this score the joint time (reversed)/importance score.

Table 27 gives the 25 top-ranking job items based on this scale. By comparing this table with table 25 it is seen that 21 of the 25 job items are common to both these tables. The close agreement between these two dimensions further strengthens the validity of the method of this study. The reduction of the joint time (reversed)/importance score as compared to joint time/importance score indicates a tendency of time and importance to move together. In his study of executive work in the federal service, Curnow (3:80—81) also reported this tendency of time and importance to move together and concluded that there was some positive relationship between time and importance.

Table 28 gives the joint time (reversed)/importance score for the 21 major functions, and is thus the counterpart of table 26 in this joint time (reversed)/importance dimension. The rankings obtained in this dimension corroborate the conclusion drawn from table 26 regarding the comparative importance of the major job functions — namely, directing, planning, and cataloging and classification — from the point of view of curriculum building at the post-MLS stage.

Conclusions

As discussed in the opening remarks of this section, time and importance are hypothetical measures, but they provide needed substantiation to give confidence to decision-making about the determination of courses offered, course objectives, course content, and level of instruction. All of the data presented thus far are based on the opinion of the job incumbent. An additional rationale for deciding the content and level of a post-MLS program is to seek the judgments of supervisors of the types of positions represented in this survey, and this type of collaborative data is presented in chapter 7.

From this analysis the question arises, How much of the *knowledge* required to perform the chief librarian's job, or the assistant chief librarian's job, is "specialized"? As the study indicates, the duties performed by the administrators are largely managerial rather than of a specialized library nature, but how much of the knowledge required to perform these managerial functions effectively is "specialized" in its very nature? This question would seem especially important at a time when some observers outside libraries are saying that administrative jobs in the library could be performed much better by those trained in business or public administration, rather than librarianship (Carson, 1). One current view of library administration values training in management over that in librarianship. One can draw this conclusion from the dependence in universities upon the college of business for management courses.

TABLE 28

MAJOR JOB FUNCTIONS RANKED ACCORDING TO RELATIVE TIME (REVERSED) /IMPORTANCE WEIGHTED SCORE BY TYPE OF POSITION: 1968

Major Job Functions	Number of Job Items	Administrative		Non-Administrative		All Together	
		Joint Time (Reversed)/ Importance Score	Rank	Joint Time (Reversed)/ Importance Score	Rank	Joint Time (Reversed)/ Importance Score	Rank
GROUP A							
Abstracting	07	167	20	111	18	278	20
Acquisitions	15	4,793	6	318	11	5,111	7
Bibliography	06	1,312	16	561	8	1,873	16
Cataloging and Classification	21	4,739	7	1,935	1	6,674	4
Circulation	10	1,787	15	222	15	2,009	15
Clientele Services	08	3,164	10	1,260	3	4,424	8
Indexing	09	395	19	270	12	665	19
Literature Searching	09	814	17	587	7	1,401	17
Maintenance of Holdings	10	2,180	14	204	17	2,384	14
Reference	07	2,810	12	809	5	3,619	11
Research	05	516	18	220	16	736	18
Selection	14	5,458	5	1,135	4	6,593	5
Translation	06	112	21	100	20	212	21
GROUP B							
Planning	23	10,197	2	682	6	10,879	2
Organizing	12	4,019	8	104	19	4,123	9
Staffing	24	7,740	3	226	14	7,966	3
Directing	22	16,657	1	1,900	2	18,557	1
Coordinating	06	2,566	13	345	10	2,911	13
Controlling	13	6,029	4	244	13	6,273	6
Representing	11	3,639	9	442	9	4,081	10
Housing	06	2,917	11	30	21	2,947	12

JOB DIMENSIONS

In a study of hospital administrators, Underwood (5:24) concludes that it is not enough for the hospital director to be skilled in the general aspects of management and communication; he must have a general awareness of motivations, intergroup relations, responsibilities, and techniques of that specific professional group. He found that while less than 20 percent of the duties performed by the hospital administrator represented specialized hospital functions, more than half of the *knowledge* required to perform effectively in an administrative capacity in a hospital is "specialized" in its nature. Does the same hold true for library administrators? If it does, it would be a strong argument for post-MLS courses being based in the graduate library school.

QUALITATIVE ANALYSIS OF JOB ACTIVITIES

Up to this point in the discussion there has been a quantitative analysis of the job activities in relation to time and importance, but there has been no attempt to assess the quality of the work that was associated with the individual job items. Now, however, is the time to take a step in the direction of qualitative analysis. As it is not possible to analyze qualitatively the whole gamut of the job activities, it was decided to analyze only the two ends of the spectrum as the curriculum builder must always have his eye on these ends.

With this objective in mind, respondents were asked to indicate which three of the activities that constitute an integral part of their job they felt they performed with the greatest competence, and why they had achieved the greatest competence in these. Further, they were asked which job activities they performed with the least competence and why they felt they had achieved little competence in these areas (Part III of the questionnaire, questions 72—77).

Frequency of Response

Considering the nature of the question, there was a high rate of response to these six questions. The question asking about greatest competence was answered by 84.3 percent (308) of the 365 respondents in the study; 68.8 percent (251) listed a second greatest competence; and 55.9 percent (204) gave a third greatest competence. As might be expected, there were fewer respondents who filled in the questions pertaining to least competencies; 73.2 percent (267) gave their least competence; 42.2 percent (154) their area of lesser competence; and 32.6 percent (119) listed an area of little competence. Respondents' answers were reviewed, analyzed, and classified into major categories. Because the answers were free response, the categories used for listing their competencies do not always correspond to the categories used in the printed job inventory in the questionnaire. It is interesting to note that in each case the percentage of administrators and nonadministrators who answered the questions about greatest and least competencies was about the same as that of the two groups in the total number of 365 respondents.

Areas of Greatest Competencies

When the single greatest competence (question 72) is tallied alone, the results are cataloging and classification (62 respondents) and reference (70 respondents). This response probably reflects the fact that there are more respondents specializing in cataloging and reference. In the area of administrative functions, administration received the highest number of checks (30), and planning the second highest (16). When the three greatest competencies (questions 72, 73, and 74) are all grouped together, the totals are:

Library Functions
1. Reference   138
2. Cataloging and classification   109
3. Clientele services   53
4. Selection   50

Administrative Functions
1. Personnel   70
2. Administration   69
3. Representing   51
4. Planning   48

Areas of Greatest Weaknesses

When the single greatest weakness (question 75) is tallied alone, the results are: reference (35 respondents), cataloging and classification (32 respondents), and automation (25 respondents); under administrative functions, personnel administration (34 respondents), representing (21 respondents), and planning (17 respondents) received the largest number of listings. However, when the three least competencies (questions 75, 76, and 77) are all grouped together, the totals are:

Library Functions
1. Reference — 72
2. Automation — 61
3. Cataloging and classification — 57

Administrative Functions
1. Personnel — 65
2. Representing — 43
3. Planning — 37
4. Administration — 32

Reasons for Greatest and Least Competencies

The question also asked why the respondent felt he had competence or lack of it in these areas, and these responses revealed a much more interesting pattern than the frequency distribution of the areas themselves. The reasons for competence in both library functions and administrative functions are training and personal like or interest in the area.

However, when one studies the reasons for lack of competency, it is seen that for administrative functions, the factor of personal dislike or personality traits stays high in frequency of times mentioned, while in the specialized library functions, the factor of personal dislike or lack of ability drops to almost zero. This discovery would seem to indicate that the respondents answering this question entered librarianship with little attraction to administrative functions, and that this type of function is particularly difficult for them because they have a personal disinterest in this activity. This conclusion relates to the answers found in the open-end question concerning most important qualities for replacement, in which it was found that present incumbents rated personal traits very highly. It also indicates that for many people the ideal is not to progress along administrative lines, and that provision should be made for advancement in library positions for those who by personal characteristics are not adept in, or who simply do not like, the tasks of administration. This indication of the importance of providing for the development of a rationale leading to different career progressions in librarianship has been strongly emphasized by Warncke (6:806–8). Thus, a librarian who chooses to pursue his career in bibliographic services or guidance should be able to advance in the profession just as far as the librarian who wishes to hold administrative positions. Lack of training remains consistently high in all the ratings for lack of competence, at each degree, for both library functions and administrative functions.

The analysis of the reasons why respondents felt adequate or inadequate in certain areas also provides insight into the degree to which his job provides possibilities of self-expression for the librarian. It has been found in recent research in the behavioral sciences that a person tends to be highly motivated if he has an opportunity in his job to develop to his highest potential. If a librarian is forced into an administrative position (because it is the only one of advancement in many instances) although he has a personal dislike for and lack of ability in this area, he will not be highly motivated, because he realizes within himself that this is not an avenue that will lead to his making the fullest use of his talents, because his abilities lie in other areas.

It should also be noted that those who listed lack of competency in reference included 24 who stated that it was due to lack of training in a given subject area. In the answer to the greatest lack of competence, 14 said this lack was due to lack of training in a subject area, and 7 said it was due to lack of reference training. Under "little competence," this ratio was reversed; 10 said the lack was due to lack of reference training, and 6 said it was due to lack of training in a specific subject area outside library science.

Automation as Greatest Strength and Greatest Weakness

As it will be evident in later chapters that automation turned out to be of special concern in this study, data from those questions dealing with greatest and least competence in automation are singled out for special analysis. First, to review the frequency responses as they relate to automation:

72. I feel greatest competence	2	
73. My next greatest competence	4	Total
74. My third greatest competence	3	9 people

Thus, of the 365 respondents only 9 felt their greatest competence was in the area of automation. (There were actually 11 checks for these 9 people, as 2 listed automation twice in checking this section.) However,

JOB DIMENSIONS

59 listed it as one of their 3 least competencies (actually there were 61 listings, as 2 people listed it twice):

75. I feel least competent in	25		
76. I am not very competent either in	21	Total	
77. Also, I am not as competent in	13	59 people	

The comments of those listing automation as their greatest competence are quoted here. For more precise analysis training and experience are listed separately. Seven reasons listed are in the area of experience, one in training, and one in training and experience combined.

Experience Cited as Main Reason

> In my last several years, most of my experience has been in information retrieval, also most of my reading. [question 72]

> Information retrieval — through trial and error experience. [73]

> Information retrieval, which I have learned through experience with an automated system. [73]

> Using automation in thesaurus building, because of constructing the first Medical Subject Heading List. [72]

> Information retrieval through trial and error experience. [73]

> Because I have had experience in applying data processing in three different libraries. [74]

> Experience on the job. [73]

Training Cited as Main Reason

> Developing systems for storage and retrieval, because I had good courses in advanced classification and cataloging. [74]

Training and Experience Cited

> Because of my training in symbolic logic and excellent electronic data processing course plus excellent on-the-job training. [74]

Seven of the nine checked the question that they were involved at an administrative or supervisory level in applying automation. All were in libraries where at least some function was automated.

Statements made explaining least competence are listed here to give a more thorough comprehension of why this condition existed. Training and experience are again listed separately. Some responses which seemed to express especially the feeling of the whole group when read together are marked with a dagger. The number of reasons is indicated under each major category (lack of training and/or lack of knowledge; lack of experience and training; lack of experience; and lack of interest and/or ability), but duplicate responses have to a large extent been eliminated.

Lack of Sufficient Training and/or
Lack of Knowledge (26)

†I took a course in computer programming for information storage and retrieval, but it was not applicable to library operations. [question 75]

I have had no training in information theory based on linguistics and math. [75]

I have no courses; I need them. [75]

I have had no training; what I have learned has been on the job. [75]

Have had no training, but now learning and am in training phase concerning computer applications of my job. [75]

I have had no training, but my work does not involve association with computer. [75]

†Planning for the future; I am unfamiliar with automation terminology, capabilities. [75]

†Lack knowledge, and it is not clear just how much of our information can be automated, and which would be the most efficient method. [77]

I have no academic study; only surface acquaintance with principles involved; no knowledge of computer theory. [77]

†The sophistication of the systems with which I deal surpasses the one course I have been able to take. [76]

†No opportunity for training, but I need and want training to use innovations. [76]

†Not touched on when I was in school. [76]

JOB DIMENSIONS

†I feel *I can't plan for the future* as I have no knowledge in information science and automation. [76]

†I don't understand, and everyone seems to be going off in different directions. [75]

Lack of Experience and Training (13)

†Have not taken courses. Our library is not automated, so no experience, but I feel I must learn as much as I can in preparation for automation. [75]

I have had no experience and little training. [75]

I have a weak background, and it is not used in my library. [75]

I have no chance to use in my library, and no opportunity to learn possibilities. [75]

†I lack knowledge. Automation has not reached our library yet; however, new complex is planned and "tempus fugit." [77]

It is not used in my library, and I lack understanding of how and why used. [77]

Lack of Experience (11)

†My library is so small, don't know about from experience — only hear about. [76]

†Have no experience, but it seems to be the coming thing. [76]

†Lack of practice — so much is new; one needs to participate to understand. [77]

Lack of Interest and/or Ability (9)

My interest has not been great in this area, and I am not involved in it in my work. [76]

It is foreign to my thinking — maybe I have a mental block. [75]

I don't understand machines. [75]

I am unmechanical and shy away from all types of machines. [77]

I lack motivation to pursue this whole area; also lack of time. [75]

I lack ability in this area. [75]

I do not grasp the concept easily; I tend to be more of a "traditional" librarian. [77]

I do not care to be involved; only want enough basic knowledge to use as a tool, rather than an end. [76]

I lack interest, as well as knowledge. [76]

These conclusions seem to stand out from this analysis:

1. Very few of the respondents (2.5 percent) feel that their greatest competence is in automation.
2. The chief reason given for competency is experience on the job. Of those who feel their greatest competence is in automation, 89 percent express a desire to take courses.
3. Of the respondents, 16.2 percent list automation as one of their greatest weaknesses.
4. The chief reason given for little competency is lack of training or knowledge.

On the basis of this analysis, several generalizations can be made from this cross section of the respondents' reactions to automation:

Unlike the other activities listed in this section, automation is the only function which ranked in the list of greatest weaknesses which did not also rank in the list of greatest competencies (see pages 117-18). However, from these comments that are presented, it is apparent that the respondents look at automation differently as compared to the other functions on the list of greatest competencies and greatest weaknesses. They listed entirely different causes for weakness in this area than for any of the others. When the respondents discuss automation, there seems to be a psychological element involved. These individuals did not need automation immediately, many of them, but as one respondent put it, "Automation is coming, and 'tempus fugit.'"

The situation seems to be that although they are not engaged in automation at the moment in their jobs, there is a feeling of incompetency. This reaction is obviously partly due to the fear that automation will soon be reaching their sphere of work, and partly to societal changes at the present time, which almost seem to induce a sense of guilt if one is not in the mainstream of technological progress.

These findings would seem to have important implications not only for the post-MLS program, but for the MLS basic required program as well. And, consequently, in the long-range view, changes at the MLS level will have direct implications on the scope and depth of material offered in the post-MLS program.

SUMMARY AND CONCLUSIONS

Quantitative Analysis of the Job Inventory

Not only did the administrators check more than six times as many administrative functions as did the nonadministrators, but they also checked twice as many nonadministrative specialized job items. Also, in each instance the standard deviation for administrators is larger than the standard deviation for nonadministrators, which means that there is a greater variation in job items performed among administrators than nonadministrators. Further, the range of tasks performed was always larger for the administrators. In addition, it was found that the median shows a pattern: namely, that the median goes down as the grade increases for the specialized library functions, but the median goes up for administrative functions as the grades increase. These statistics might be an indication that because of shortage of staff, small size of the library, or other reasons, the administrators are spending a considerable amount of time operating at a nonadministrative level. Awareness of this condition should have implications for course content as well as overall curriculum construction.

From the analysis of the time dimension in relation to the job activities, it was found that as the respondents move up in grade, the time devoted to administrative functions increases and that devoted to specialized library functions decreases. This condition is in accord with the hypothesis of Corson (2) that as one rises in the federal service, one assumes many administrative and management tasks for which he has not been prepared in his basic professional training. For this reason it seems essential to obtain training in administrative skills. Administrators spend more time in directing than in any other job function, an important fact for curriculum builders.

It was found that the number of respondents checking the importance factor for each item was generally the same as the number checking the time factor. Item 187, "Directly supervise and guide subordinates," ranked first according to the weighted importance score, as it had for the weighted time score. There was even a slightly higher

SUMMARY AND CONCLUSIONS

tendency toward administrative functions in the importance dimension than in the time dimension. The process of directing held a predominant position within the dimension of importance, which further emphasized the necessity for special attention to management skills in any post-master's program planned for practicing administrators of libraries.

When a joint time/importance score was constructed for job items in order to measure the total contribution of job activities toward the fulfillment of the objectives of the library, there was shown an even greater displacement of the specialized library functions by the administrators as the grades moved upward.

When the job items were grouped according to the 21 major job functions under which the individual job activities were listed in the questionnaire, directing ranked first by a total joint time/importance weighted score of 25,933 as compared to a score of 16,119 for planning, which received the second highest rating. The fact that planning did rank second in this type of analysis, however, does indicate that it is an area that should receive the attention of curriculum builders at the post-master's level. With the current emphasis inside the federal government on the new techniques of program planning and budgeting, this subject would seem worthy of integration into post-MLS courses now.

Through the construction of a joint time (reversed)/importance score, the conclusion was reached that the dimensions of time and importance have a tendency to move together, and that there is some evidence of a positive relationship between time and importance.

The quantitative data in this section indicate that the duties performed by the administrators are largely managerial rather than of a specialized library nature. The knowledge required to perform these managerial functions effectively in an administrative capacity in a library is technically "specialized" in its nature. If the library administrator must have an awareness of the motivations, responsibilities, and intergroup relations specific to the library profession, a strong argument can be presented for the post-master's program to be based in the graduate library school rather than in other departments of the university. This important question is discussed further in chapter 7, which reports on the interviews with supervisory personnel.

Qualitative Analysis of Job Activities

As it was not possible to analyze qualitatively the whole range of job activities, only two ends of the spectrum were examined. In answering the question about their greatest competencies, the respondents gave top place to reference services and cataloging and classification among the specialized library functions. In the administrative category, personnel work was first, and administration second. The areas listed as those of greatest weakness were very similar. For the library functions they were reference, automation, and cataloging and classification; for the administrative functions, personnel administration, representing, and planning.

The reasons given for the greatest competencies and the greatest weaknesses presented evidence that the respondents felt the need for different career progressions in librarianship, that the only line of advancement should not be that of administration. Thus, a librarian who wishes to pursue a career in a technical speciality should not have to give it up for an administrative position in order to advance his career.

To the curriculum builder, the data in this section provide a reasoned explanation for different areas of specialization at the post-master's level and tend to support the premise that there should be a differentiated program to serve the needs of the individual librarian. The data would also provide evidence that one school's program could not hope to meet the demands of all those wishing a post-master's education, and that different schools might better specialize their programs.

A more detailed analysis was done of those who listed automation as the area of their greatest strength or greatest weakness. It was found that the respondents (only 2.5 percent) who felt that their greatest competence was in automation listed experience on the job as the reason for their competence. On the other hand, 16.2 percent of the respondents listed automation as one of their greatest weaknesses and gave the reason for little competency as lack of training or knowledge.

Comments on Open-End Questions

Two important conclusions can be drawn from the open-end comments that pertained to the job inventory. First, the respondents generally thought the coverage of items in the job inventory was quite adequate. In similar studies in other disciplines, usually some response is obtained criticizing the job-inventory approach itself, but none of the respondents commented negatively on this as a method of approach to curriculum building, and many commented favorably. Second, the respondents were very discouraged by the large amount of clerical and subprofessional duties they were performing; and this reaction, as will be seen as the study progresses, has been reflected in nearly every section of the questionnaire. The respondents pleaded for an answer from the library schools.

REFERENCES IN CHAPTER 4

1. Carson, Lettie Gay. "Remarks at ALTA Meeting, Region VIII." Paper read at the American Library Trustee Association Annual Conference, San Francisco, June 25, 1967. Mimeographed.
2. Corson, John J., and R. Shale Paul. *Men Near the Top: Filling Key Posts in the Federal Service.* Baltimore: Johns Hopkins Pr., 1966.
3. Curnow, Geoffrey Ross. "The Dimensions of Executive Work in the U.S. Federal Career Civil Service: A Factor Analytic Study." Doctor's dissertation, Cornell Univ. Ithaca, 1967.
4. Smith, Robert G., Jr. *The Development of Training Objectives.* Alexandria, Va.: Human Resources Research Office, George Washington Univ., 1964.
5. Underwood, Willis O. "A Hospital Director's Administrative Profile," *Hospital Administration* 8:6—24 (Fall 1963).
6. Warncke, Ruth. "Careers in Librarianship," *ALA Bulletin* 60:805—9 (Sept. 1966).

5
Course Demand and Employee Characteristics

Established course and curricular guidelines for library education at the post-master's level are lacking, yet, as Fryden (2:1) points out, the demands for librarians with some training beyond that obtained in the fifth-year master's program is greater now than ever before. In Fryden's report on the eleven American library schools accredited by the American Library Association that offer a sixth-year post-MLS program, there is abundant evidence that differing philosophies, objectives, standards, program content, and requirements of these programs have produced as many variations of the programs as there are schools offering them. This problem was also recognized by Danton (1:81), who recommended in his study that "the schools spell out clearly and in detail, and put into print, the nature of their programs and what they entail." It should be clear to the student what he "may expect to secure by enrolling, and what will be expected of him." The question arises, and indeed is asked by Fryden (2:26), "On what base do these programs build?"

For a data base beyond that provided by the job inventory, a section of the questionnaire (Part II, items 1—95) was designed to obtain information from practicing librarians about their course needs and interests as an indication of what courses the respondents would be motivated to take if they were offered to them. Practically, it must be remembered that at the post-master's level whether students enroll or not is strictly a matter of personal choice. For, at this point in time, the profession has set the MLS degree as the requirement for entry into librarianship at the professional level, but beyond that there are no criteria established; the choice of courses at this level is strictly determined by the interest and demand of the practicing librarians themselves. Therefore, to build courses in a vacuum without relationship to the actual expressed demands of practicing librarians would seem to be more of an intellectual exercise rather than a realistic approach to meet the on-the-job needs in the profession.

DEMAND FOR COURSES AND WORKSHOPS

The purposes of the course listings in Part II of the questionnaire, entitled Your Educational Needs, were fourfold:

1. To identify those courses which practicing federal librarians are most interested in studying at the post-master's level

2. To identify four degrees of interest in courses: namely, whether the respondent is chiefly interested in a workshop, a "course now," or a "course later" (identified in the questionnaire as three to five years from now) — or has no interest in taking a given course at all

3. To isolate and analyze selected relevant variables and measure their relationship to variables analyzed in other parts of the study

4. To yield data which would permit comparative assessments of course needs from interviews with supervisors of the chief types of librarians represented among the respondents.

Data Analysis

The analyses were made according to the demand for courses under the headings "workshop," "course now," "course later," and "course now or later." The fourth was added because the research staff felt that the designation "now or later," meaning a combination of now and/or later, probably presented a more reliable picture of demand than "course now" or "course later" separately. For the final analysis, to see which courses the respondent ranked the highest overall, another ranking was made which grouped together all the positive approaches to course work — "workshop, course now, or course later."

Appendix tables 15 through 18 show the frequency distribution of the number of people checking "workshops," "course now," "course

TABLE 29

APPLICABILITY OF COURSES BY TYPE OF POSITION AND GRADE LEVEL (Per Cent Distribution of Respondents Checking One or More by Type of Program):1968

Type of Program	Type of Position		Grade Level			Total
	Administrative	Non-Administrative	9	10, 11	12-14	
	(N=230) %	(N=135) %	(N=115) %	(N=140) %	(N=110) %	(N=365) %
Workshop	74.35	62.96	62.61	74.29	70.91	70.14
Course Now	43.47	46.67	40.87	49.29	42.73	44.66
Course Later	49.57	52.59	59.13	48.57	44.55	50.68
Course Now or Later	60.43	67.41	70.43	60.00	59.09	63.01

later," and "course now or later" categories according to type of position and grade level. Analysis of these tables along with table 29 shows that 70.1 percent of the respondents checked one or more courses in the "workshop" category; 63.0 percent of the respondents checked one or more courses in the category "course now or later"; 50.7 percent checked one or more courses in the category "course later"; while only 44.7 percent checked "course now" for one or more items. These responses indicate that the most popular type of continuing education in a formal setting for this group of respondents as a whole was the workshop format. This is further indicated by the fact that the mean number of courses checked for "workshops" was 7.8, as compared to means of 3.7 for "course now," 4.1 for "course later," and 7.5 for "course now or later."

However, when the respondents are broken down by grade and type of job, the "course now or later" category outranks workshops, both for grade 9 and for nonadministrators. This indicates that as the librarians move up in grade or go into administrative jobs, they tend to prefer workshops as a means for continuing education.

The second category that proved to be the most applicable is "course

FIGURE 3
APPLICABILITY OF COURSES ACCORDING TO ALL RESPONDENTS: 1968

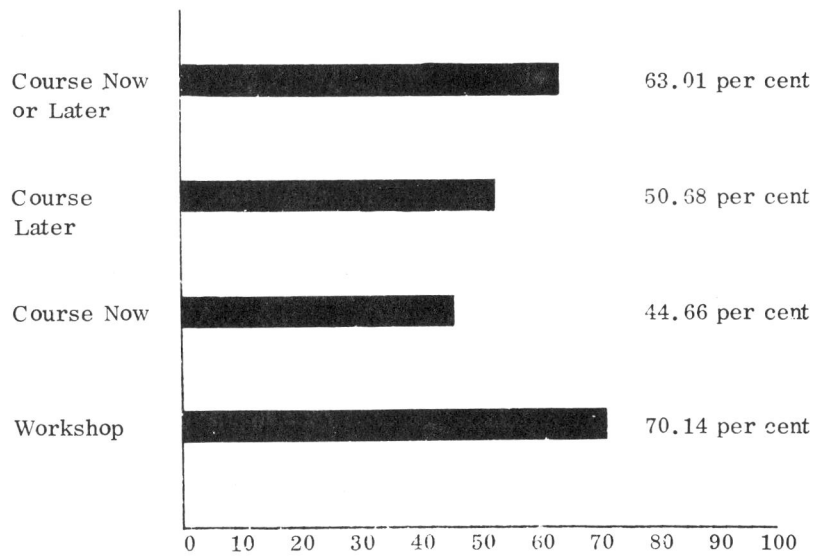

This figure shows the percentage of the 365 respondents who checked one or more course listings under "workshops" or "course now and/or later".

now or later." To show the variations of applicability regarding all types of programs as well as the two most popular categories, figures 3 and 4 are presented showing the percentage of respondents who checked courses under "workshops" and in "course now" or "course later" categories. Every one of the 78 courses was checked by some respondent. The course that received the lowest number of responses was item 80, "Agricultural Literature and Research," and even this course had 3 checks in "course now," 5 in "course later," and 7 in "workshop."

In conclusion, the respondents seemed to find the listing of courses adequate judged by the fact that there were only 6 write-ins which were not listed and the fact that all the courses were checked by some of the respondents. It must be remembered when noting the percentage of the various categories of respondents replying to the questions out of the total of 365, that only 142 of the respondents said they were interested

COURSE DEMAND

FIGURE 4
APPLICABILITY OF COURSES BY FREQUENCY OF "WORKSHOP"
AND "COURSE NOW OR LATER" CHECKED BY
TYPE OF POSITION AND GRADE LEVEL:1968

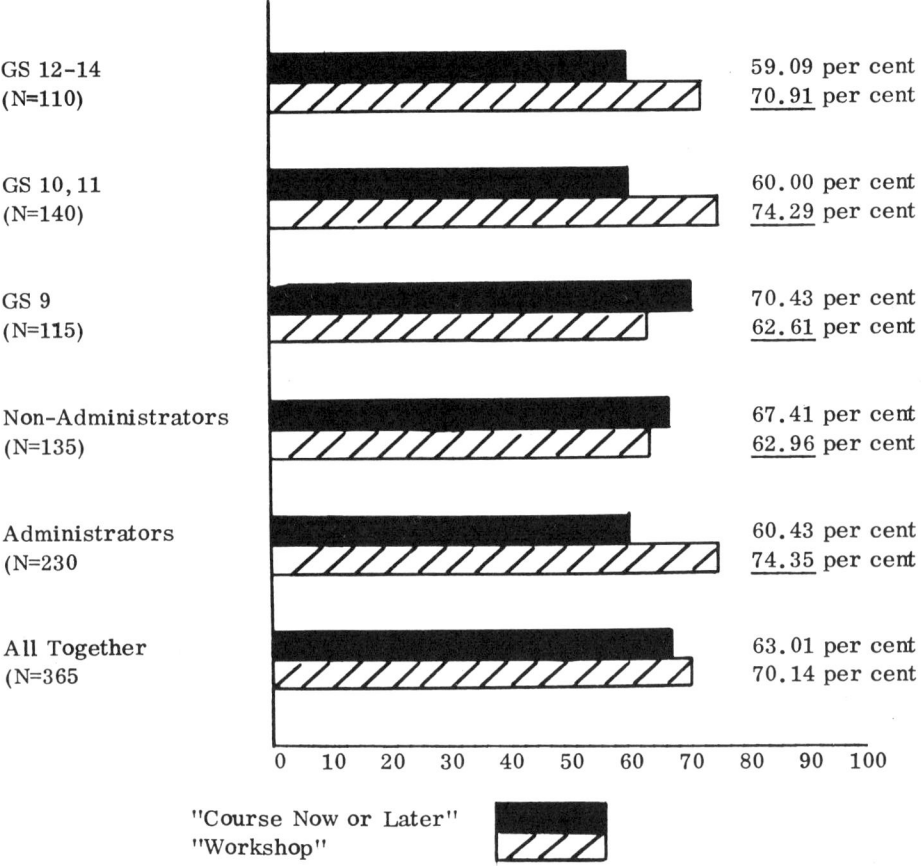

This figure shows the percentage distribution of respondents in various categories who checked one or more course listings under "workshop" or "course now and/or later".

in pursuing a post-MLS program; consequently, many of these respondents checked no courses at all.

To give a clear picture of demand both for all categories of respondents and for types of program ("workshop," "course now," "course later," and "course now or later" combined), rankings were made of the 78 courses according to these categories. The basic table for this section is table 30, which lists the courses showing the highest response rankings according to interest of all the 365 respondents in:

Course Now or Course Later	column 3
Course Now	column 4
Course Later	column 5
Workshop	column 6
Workshop, Course Now or Course Later	column 7

The last column reflects the interests of only those 142 respondents who expressed a willingness to participate in a one-year or more program of post-MLS study in library science.

It was deemed important to ascertain the course demand for all 365 respondents characterized in various ways, but there is the consideration that perhaps those 142 (38.9 percent) who stated they would take a post-MLS program, as distinguished from individual courses, might opt for different courses. Therefore, the premise had to be tested that the course rankings of the 142 respondents who actually indicated an interest in taking a post-MLS program would correlate positively with the course demand of all the 365 respondents.

It was found that there was an almost perfect rank correlation between the 142 stating they would take a post-MLS program and all the 365 respondents in the study at a 1 percent level ($r=0.94$). On the basis of this analysis, it was decided that it was not necessary to repeat all the rankings for these 142 respondents as was performed for all the 365 respondents. The rankings of these 142 respondents for the 78 courses for the category "course now or course later" are presented in the last column of table 30. Examination of this table reveals that the ranking that deviates most from the others is that for workshops. As this is the type of program for which the greatest demand was expressed by the respondents, appendix table 19 is presented, which shows the interest of administrators and nonadministrators in workshops. The overall characteristic that is most noticeable is that many courses in nonadministrative areas have received high rankings. For example, first on the list for administrators is the course entitled Current Practices in Acquisition and Selection of Non-Book Materials.

TABLE 30
COURSES SHOWING HIGHEST RESPONSE RANKINGS INDICATING INTEREST IN
(1) COURSE NOW OR COURSE LATER; (2) COURSE NOW; (3) COURSE LATER; (4) WORKSHOP; (5) WORKSHOP, COURSE NOW OR COURSE LATER FOR ALL 365 RESPONDENTS; (6) COURSE NOW OR COURSE LATER AS CHECKED BY RESPONDENTS STATING INTEREST IN POST-MLS PROGRAM: 1968

Course Number	Course Title	Course Now or Course Later No.	Rank	Course Now No.	Rank	Course Later No.	Rank	Workshop No.	Rank	Course Now or Workshop, Course Later No.	Rank	Course Now or Course Later as checked by respondents stating interest in post-MLS program No.	Rank
26.	Automation of Library Processes	119	1	65	1	57	2	83	8	188	1	79	1
28.	Information Retrieval Systems	116	2	55	2	63	1	58	12	164	2	74	2
27.	Information Processing on Computers	101	3	52	3	51	3	44	30	138	3	66	3
19.	Administration of the Special Federal Library	65	4	38	4	29	8	59	8	117	4	38	9
5.	Administrative Policies and Practices	62	5	30	6	33	4	56	13	114	5	46	5
9.	Human Relations in Library Administration	58	6	29	7	30	5	62	7	112	6	47	4
43.	Information Retrieval for Clientele	55	7	25	11	30	5	59	8	109	8	46	5
8.	General Management	52	8	32	5	20	28	59	8	103	11	42	7
15.	Program Planning and Budgeting	52	8	24	13	28	10	54	14	101	12	37	10
73.	Organization and Administration of Reference Systems	51	10	28	8	25	11	38	36	85	21	34	14
7.	Design of Library Organizations	50	11	22	16	29	8	45	26	93	14	34	14
93.	Systems Analysis and Design for Library and Information Center Operations	49	12	26	10	24	14	26	52	71	30	35	13
12.	Personnel Administration in Libraries	48	13	25	11	24	14	52	15	93	14	39	8
13.	Personnel Problems under the Impact of Technological Change: Library Applications	45	14	21	19	25	11	51	16	90	16	37	10

COURSES AND WORKSHOPS

3.	Current Practices in Acquisition and Selection of Non-Book Materials	43	17	15	37	30	5	76	4	112	6	25	32
6.	Communication Theory and Processes	43	17	27	9	16	40	49	23	89	17	29	19
57.	The Scope of Information Science	43	17	22	16	22	24	51	16	89	17	29	19
68.	Publication in the Library and Information Science Fields	43	17	19	27	24	14	18	61	59	45	36	12
38.	Subject Representation	42	21	20	23	23	18	30	46	68	36	32	17
22.	Information Center Administration	41	22	23	14	19	29	30	46	63	41	29	19
36.	New Advances in Classification Schemes and Cataloging Systems: A Survey	41	22	18	28	23	18	48	25	84	22	26	90
94.	Systems Analysis in Information Science	41	22	20	23	22	24	21	57	58	48	29	19
44.	Literature Searching	40	25	22	13	19	29	49	23	84	22	32	17
50.	Abstracting and Indexing Services	39	26	17	32	23	18	31	42	68	36	29	19
72.	Non-Conventional Library Reference Tools	39	26	18	28	21	27	65	5	97	13	25	32
69.	Publishing in the Twentieth Century: Book and Non-Book Materials	36	28	23	44	23	18	41	34	71	30	29	19
87.	Scientific and Technical Literature and Research	36	28	20	23	19	29	42	33	75	27	27	27
2.	Centralized Processing	35	30	11	52	24	14	50	21	82	24	25	22
30.	Analytical Bibliography	35	30	21	19	16	40	20	58	52	53	29	19
66.	Resources and Services of the Federal Library Complex	35	30	21	19	16	40	77	3	108	9	22	43
92.	Library Management Information Systems	35	30	20	23	15	47	31	42	65	40	27	27
71.	Development and Maintenance of a Reference Referral Center	34	34	16	35	18	33	51	16	82	24	24	39
47.	Library Design and Architecture	33	35	18	28	15	47	35	38	67	38	25	32
34.	Centralized Cataloging at the National Level	32	36	11	52	23	18	51	16	78	26	21	47
77.	Research Development in Libraries	32	36	18	28	15	47	30	46	58	48	26	29

Continued

Table 30 (Continued)

COURSE DEMAND

Course Number	Course Title	Course Now or Course Later No.	Rank	Course Now No.	Rank	Course Later No.	Rank	Workshop No.	Rank	Course Now or Course Workshop, No.	Rank	Course Now or Course Later as checked by respondents stating interest in post-MLS program No.	Rank
1.	Building and Evaluating Library Collection	31	38	11	52	22	24	80	2	104	10	22	43
11.	Management of Records Systems in the Library	31	38	13	44	18	33	37	37	67	38	22	43
89.	Technical Report Literature	31	38	17	32	16	40	34	39	60	42	19	52
84.	Documents or International Organizations and Foreign Governments	30	41	14	42	17	38	18	61	46	58	18	54
33.	Cataloging and Classification of Non-Book Materials	29	42	15	37	15	47	44	30	69	34	18	54
40.	Circulation Systems	29	42	11	52	19	29	63	6	88	19	17	56
52.	Theories of Indexing and Information Retrieval	29	42	14	42	15	47	32	40	60	42	24	39
55.	Linguistics and Information Science	29	42	16	35	14	54	14	69	40	63	26	29
56.	Mathematical Techniques for Information Science	29	42	12	49	18	33	11	72	36	65	25	32
76.	Operations Research in Library Management	29	42	13	44	16	40	24	54	51	54	25	32
10.	Innovation and Planned Change in Library Organizations	28	48	10	58	18	33	32	40	59	45	23	42
17.	Theories of Organization and Management	28	48	15	37	14	54	30	46	57	50	24	39
51.	Content Analysis	27	50	10	58	17	38	16	65	42	61	25	32
64.	Library Networks	27	50	12	49	16	40	51	16	73	29	21	47
78.	Statistical Theory and the Interpretation of Statistical Data for Researching in Libraries and Information Centers	27	50	15	37	13	58	16	65	42	61	22	43
14.	Policy Formation and Decision-Making in Library Organizations	26	53	11	52	16	40	45	26	69	34	19	52
54.	Equipment and Instrumentation	26	53	13	44	14	54	24	54	48	57	21	47
82.	Biomedical Literature and Research	26	53	17	32	11	61	23	56	44	59	14	63

COURSES AND WORKSHOPS

#	Title												
46.	Equipment Evaluation, Selection and Procurement	23	58	13	44	10	67	50	21	70	33	16	61
61.	International Library Services and Resources	21	59	6	71	15	47	17	64	37	64	17	56
63.	The Library Administrator and Government Policy, Organization and Operation	21	59	12	49	9	70	31	42	51	54	17	56
81.	Behavioral Science Literature and Research	21	59	10	58	11	61	18	61	36	65	14	63
16.	Public Administration	20	62	9	62	11	61	16	65	35	67	16	61
31.	Enumerative Bibliographic Systems	20	62	7	67	13	58	13	70	32	70	17	56
37.	Recataloging and Reclassification: Problems and Procedures	20	62	7	67	14	54	41	34	57	50	14	63
59.	Current Issues in Librarianship and Information Science	19	65	8	66	12	60	59	8	75	27	17	56
88.	Social Science Literature and Research	19	65	10	58	9	70	15	68	34	69	14	63
35.	Centralized Cataloging at the International Level	18	67	4	75	15	47	29	51	44	59	13	61
21.	Hospital Library Administration and Service	16	68	9	62	7	74	20	58	35	67	5	77
24.	Rare Book Librarianship	16	68	5	73	11	61	7	76	22	75	12	69
41.	Reprography	16	68	6	71	11	61	45	26	59	45	7	75
48.	Planning and Justifying Library Quarters	16	68	11	52	5	76	45	26	60	42	12	69
83.	Business and Economics Literature and Research	16	68	7	67	9	70	10	74	26	73	13	67
86.	Legal Literature and Research	16	68	9	62	7	74	13	70	29	72	7	75
85.	Fine Arts Literature and Research	15	74	5	73	11	61	11	72	25	74	9	72
20.	Archival Administration	14	75	4	75	10	67	9	75	22	75	8	74
23.	Law Library Administration and Service	13	76	9	62	5	76	7	76	19	77	11	71
62.	Labor Relations and Library Employment	11	77	1	78	10	67	20	58	30	71	9	72
80.	Agricultural Literature and Research	7	78	3	77	5	76	7	76	13	78	5	77

These statistics indicate course interest of the 142 respondents who expressed desire to participate in a year or more post-MLS program in library science. Of the 142, 122 said they would enroll for a one-year post-MLS program in library science, and of these 122, 83 were only interested in this type of program. Fifty-nine stated they would enroll for a doctoral program in library science, of which 20 stated they were only interested in a doctoral program and nothing else. Thirty-nine of the respondents checked both types of program.

Second is Building and Evaluating Library Collections, and Automation, which ranks first on most of the breakdowns that have been made, ranks third. In fact, none of the top five are strictly administrative. This tendency toward nonadministrative courses is even more pronounced among the nonadministrators.

When those indicating "workshop" are broken down by grade level (appendix table 20), it is seen that at the GS 9 level two courses in acquisitions top the list, which would seem to reflect a current awareness that there are many new approaches to the acquisitions activity that librarians feel in need of learning, and that they feel can be acquired in the time allotment given in the average workshop. It is interesting to note that at the GS 9 level Automation in Library Processes ranks only twenty-fifth, while at the GS 10 through 14 level, it ranks first. At the GS 10–11 level the top courses are still largely in specialized services, but at the GS 12–14 level, interest is chiefly in administrative courses. Since the pattern for workshops does seem to be different from that for demand for courses, it would seem that these lists of workshop priorities as expressed by the respondents might give an insight into the type of knowledge and skill that the respondents think it is possible to strengthen and update on a short-term basis, as opposed to the type of knowledge they feel would require a greater investment in time.

Turning now to an examination of the "Combined Listing of Course Now and Course Later" as it is divided by grades (appendix table 21), it is seen that the top three listings for each grade are in the field of automation. For the course entitled Automation of Library Processes, 35.6 percent of the GS 9s expressed an interest, as did 30.7 percent of those in the GS 10–11 category and 31.8 percent of the GS 12–14 respondents. These percentages show that the demand for training in automation is spread fairly evenly through all grades. Generally, as the grades get higher in this table, there is an increase in the demand for administrative courses.

Thus far in this chapter the study of course demand has been made with the individual course listing as the unit of analysis. However, since the ultimate objective of this study is building curricula, and since curricula are more than a collection of courses, it is necessary that the demand for courses be further studied with subject areas as units. This was the reason behind grouping courses under 17 subject areas in the questionnaire. The objective was to build a score for the subject area as a whole denoting the overall demand for the subject area. This score can be used further for ranking the subject areas in relation to demand.

It was decided to have three scores for each subject area corresponding to the headings, namely, "workshop," "course," and "workshop and/or course." Here, "course" is a combination of the two original headings used in the questionnaire, namely, "course now" and "course later," while the third heading is a combination of three headings used in the questionnaire. For each subject area, if an individual checked one or more courses included in the subject area under the heading "workshop," the subject area got a score of one under the heading "workshop." The total number of such respondents was the score for each subject area in the column labeled "workshop." Similarly for each subject area, if an individual checked one or more courses under either the heading "course now" or "course later" in the questionnaire, the subject got a score of one, under the heading labeled "course." The total number of such respondents was the score for each subject area in the column labeled "course."

The two subject areas which received the highest rankings (table 31) under the headings "courses" and "workshops and/or courses" were automation (rank 1) and administration (rank 2), which would be expected from the results in these two general areas shown elsewhere throughout this study. The ranking of the courses further substantiates the conclusions arrived at in earlier pages that automation and administration should play a very important role in the curriculum content of post-MLS programs. It is interesting to note, however, that in the "workshop" column, administration is first, while automation is only sixth. This contrast would seem to imply that the respondents felt that automation was much too large a topic to be covered helpfully in a workshop format, especially if the respondent had had no training or experience in this area and was not currently employed in a library that utilized automation.

The combined ("workshops and/or courses") ranking brings into focus an area which has not stood out in particular in other analyses, namely, Libraries, Government, and Society (rank 3). This subject is covered in the following courses as listed in the questionnaire (Part II, items 59—66); the numbers in parentheses denote the rank under the heading "workshop, course now or later" when the demand for individual courses was analyzed in table 30 in column 7:

Current Issues in Librarianship and Information Science	(rank 27)
Cybernetics and Society	(rank 56)
International Library Services and Resources	(rank 64)
Labor Relations and Library Employment	(rank 71)

COURSE DEMAND

The Library Administrator and Government Policy,
Organization, and Operation (rank 54)
Library Networks (rank 29)
Mass Media in Communication (rank 52)
Resources and Services of the Federal Library Complex (rank 9)

TABLE 31
SUBJECT AREAS RANKED ACCORDING TO NUMBER OF RESPONDENTS CHECKING ANY INDIVIDUAL COURSE WITHIN THE AREA:1968

Item Numbers	Subject Areas	Workshops	Rank	Courses	Rank	Workshops and/or Courses [1]	Rank
1- 4	Acquisitions and Selection	113	3	67	8	153	4
5-18	Administration and General Management of Libraries	134	1	120	2	175	2
19-25	Administration of Special Types of Library Services	76	7	94	4	149	6
26-29	Automation	95	6	137	1	197	1
30-32	Bibliography	21	17	36	17	52	17
33-39	Cataloging and Classification	99	5	83	5	137	8
40-42	Circulation	64	10	37	16	92	11
43-45	Clientele Services	74	9	67	8	121	9
46-49	Housing and Equipment	61	11	46	15	91	12
50-53	Indexing and Abstracting	39	14	47	14	77	15
54-58	Information Science	55	12	65	10	100	10
59-67	Libraries, Government and Society	124	2	77	7	157	3
68-70	Publication	44	13	54	12	84	14
71-75	Reference	102	4	78	6	145	7
76-79	Research	36	15	49	13	73	16
80-91	Specialized Information Sources	75	8	97	3	151	5
92-94	Systems Analysis	32	16	61	11	86	13

[1]Individuals indicating a preference for "Workshop" may have also indicated a willingness to take "Course" work in a particular area. Because of this overlap, the columns will not add horizontally.

The individual rankings of the courses indicate that except for one (Resources and Services of the Federal Library Complex) they were not popular. The high ranking for this group was probably caused by the heterogeneous nature of the individual subjects included in the subject area, and, hence, it seemed to possess some interest for a large number of respondents.

To analyze the volume of demand for courses, the variable that was chosen was the number of courses demanded by an individual in the category "course now or course later." For our purpose it seemed that this variable was the most appropriate one. The objective was to compare the males with the females, reference librarians with cataloging and classification librarians, heads of libraries with those who are not heads, administrators with nonadministrators and people who want to take the post-MLS degree with those who do not want to take the program. Table 32 gives the means and variances for this variable for these subgroups of respondents. An examination of the means and variances shows that there is no difference between the average number of courses demanded by the males and females or between those demanded by reference librarians and classification and cataloging librarians.

To see if the difference between heads of libraries and those who are not heads of libraries is significant, F (1.88) was calculated and found to be significant at the 1 percent level. Thus the conclusion was reached that the heads of libraries and all others formed two different populations for this variable. In other words, the structures of the

TABLE 32
ANALYSIS OF THE STRUCTURE OF THE VOLUME OF DEMAND FOR COURSES AS EXPRESSED BY THE RESPONDENTS: 1968

Variable	Mean	Variance
Male	7.53	99.49
Female	7.52	108.22
Heads of Libraries	9.34	161.81
Non-Heads of Libraries	6.92	85.87
Administrators	7.89	112.43
Non-Administrators	6.89	94.14
Reference	6.95	87.42
Cataloging and Classification	7.00	135.18
Respondents Who Would Enroll In a Post-MLS Program	13.85	151.36
Respondents Who Would Not Enroll in a Post MLS Program	3.44	34.15

volume of demand for these two groups were entirely different, and in order to study the volume of their demands it was necessary to examine them separately. For administrators and nonadministrators the F statistic was insignificant at the 5 percent level ($F=1.19$), and t was also insignificant ($t=0.95$) at the 5 percent level. Therefore, in the demand for "course now and course later," administrators and nonadministrators show no difference in the average number of courses demanded.

Last, the most important comparison was between respondents who wished to pursue post-MLS study and those who did not want to do so. F (4.43) was calculated and was found to be significant at the 1 percent level. Hence we concluded that these two subgroups formed statistically different populations and would have to be studied separately.

Correlation between Demand for Courses and Several Variables

Age. A significant negative relationship ($r=-0.18$) between the age of the respondents and their demand for courses at the 1 percent level was found (table 33). This is to say that as the librarians get older, there is less probability of their actually enrolling for a post-MLS course. The value of the correlation coefficient is quite small, however, which indicates that even though age definitely influences the decision of an individual to enroll for a post-MLS program, the magnitude of the influence is quite small. In other words, the popular notion that the older people become, the less likely they are to go back to school may be true, but the evidence to support it is not conclusive.

Grade. There was found to be a significant negative relationship ($r=-0.13$) between the grade level of the respondents and their demand for courses (table 33). Thus, as the librarian rises in his grade level, he may be less apt to enroll for a post-MLS program; but here again, the correlation coefficient is not as high as might have been expected.

Professional Experience. There was found to be a significant correlation ($r=-0.11$) between the years of professional service and the respondent's demand for courses (table 33). The more years of professional experience the respondent has, the less likely he is to enroll in post-MLS courses. It is encouraging to note that it is just barely significant and need not be a totally discouraging factor in planning for courses.

Years in Present Position. There is also a significant negative correlation ($r= -0.15$) between the years in the present position and the demand for courses (table 33). This means that the longer a person has been in his present position, the less likely he is to engage in post-MLS study.

Years Elapsed since MLS. There is also found to be a statistically significant negative correlation ($r= -0.13$) between the number of years elapsed since the MLS and the respondent's demand for courses (table 33). The more time that has elapsed since his MLS, the less likely the respondent is to enroll for the post-MLS program.

TABLE 33
CORRELATIONS BETWEEN SELECTED VARIABLES
AND THE DEMAND FOR COURSES
AS EXPRESSED BY THE RESPONDENTS: 1968

Variable	Number	Mean	Standard Deviation	Correlation Coefficient
Age	335	44.39	10.53	-0.18**
Grade	365	10.79	1.45	-0.13*
Years of Professional Experience	365	13.99	10.03	-0.11*
Years in Present Position	365	4.92	5.75	-0.15**
Years Elapsed since MLS	348	13.91	10.67	-0.13*
Years between Bachelors Degree and MLS	330	7.13	7.32	-0.06
Hours per Week of Avoidable Detail	321	9.05	7.05	0.12*
Number of People Supervised	344	6.36	11.25	-0.04
Years Worked with Federal Government	353	11.00	9.25	-0.10

**significant at 1 per cent level
* significant at 5 per cent level

Years between Bachelor's Degree and MLS. There is a negative correlation ($r= -0.06$) between the number of years between the bachelor's degree and the MLS degree, but the relationship is not statistically significant (table 33).

Amount of Avoidable Detail. Of all the correlation coefficients obtained relative to demand for courses, that calculated on the amount of avoidable detail is the only one which showed a positive relationship ($r= +0.12$), and it is statistically significant (table 33). Therefore, this positive relationship does indicate a desire on the part of those involved in a great deal of avoidable routines in their jobs to seek a post-MLS program, possibly to escape from such situations.

Number of People Supervised. There was found to be a negative correlation ($r= -0.04$) between number of people supervised and the desire to take post-MLS courses (table 33). However, this relationship is not statistically significant and is so small that there seems to be no relation between number of people supervised and an expressed wish to engage in post-MLS courses.

Years with Federal Government. There was found to be a negative relationship ($r= -0.10$) between number of years worked for the federal government and willingness to engage in a post-MLS program, but it is statistically not significant (table 33). It is large enough, however, to indicate a tendency toward the condition that as the number of years a person has worked for the federal government increases, he is less apt to engage in a post-MLS program.

RELATIONSHIP BETWEEN DEMAND FOR COURSES AND TWO JOB-RELATED VARIABLES

In the previous chapters we have presented information concerning: (1) the needs of the federal library respondents in relation to their jobs; (2) their demand for courses; and (3) selected variables concerning the individual librarian including age, grade, years of professional experience, present position, education, number of people supervised, years between the bachelor's and master's degrees, and time elapsed since the MLS. In this section selections from these three types of data are isolated for purposes of analysis to determine if any significant correlations or associations exist which might determine recommendations for curriculum development.

Type of Position

Demand for a course was expressed in three ways by the respondent: demand for a course now, demand for a course later, or demand for a workshop. These were also formed into various combinations for the purposes of analysis. Hence, in order to choose the courses with highest demand, it is necessary to take into account all of these factors. On this basis, among those courses in administration, the five following were judged to be in greatest demand:

Course 5.	Administrative Policies and Practices
Course 8.	General Management
Course 9.	Human Relations in Library Administration
Course 15.	Program Planning and Budgeting
Course 19.	Administration of the Special Federal Library

The following courses dealing with specialized aspects of library service were judged to be greatest in demand:

Course 3.	Current Practices in Acquisitions and Selection of Non-Book Materials
Course 43.	Information Retrieval for Clientele
Course 73.	Organization and Administration of Reference Systems
Course 93.	Systems Analysis and Design for Library and Information Center Operations

The three courses in automation (courses 26, 27, and 28) were by far in greatest demand; however, it was decided to treat these as one course. Since automation covers both administrative and nonadministrative areas, it was omitted from this analysis.

The objective of this analysis was to find out if there was a difference between the proportion of administrators demanding the course and that of nonadministrators. In other words, whether the administrators differed from the nonadministrators in their attitudes toward taking the post-MLS courses (table 34). However, it was revealed that for each of these courses there was no demand differential. That is to say, that the demand for any of these courses has nothing to do with whether the respondent is an administrator or not. The only possible exception is for course 43, where it seems there is some association between type of position and demand; but even there it is not statistically significant at the 5 percent level. This conclusion has important implications for curriculum building and course content. If this demand schedule portrays reality, then we can expect that in any program that is developed, proportions for administrators and nonadministrators would be maintained. Hence, in planning the courses, it is wise to remember that whether the course is administrative or nonadministrative in its emphasis, there would tend to be students of both of these types of position proportionately represented.

TABLE 34
RELATIONSHIP BETWEEN DEMAND FOR COURSES AND
TYPE OF POSITION: 1968

Course Number	Course Title	Demand for Course: Yes, want course. No, do not want course.	Administrative	Non-Administrative	Chi-Square
3.	Current Practices in Acquisitions of Non-Book Materials	Yes No	31 199	12 123	$x^2=1.72$
5.	Administrative Policies and Practices	Yes No	38 192	24 111	$x^2=0.14$
8.	General Management	Yes No	36 194	16 119	$x^2=1.01$
9.	Human Relations in Library Administration	Yes No	41 189	17 118	$x^2=1.74$
15.	Program Planning and Budgeting	Yes No	38 192	14 121	$x^2=2.63$
19.	Administration of the Special Federal Library	Yes No	139 91	91 44	$x^2=1.79$
43.	Information Retrieval for Clientele	Yes No	29 201	26 109	$x^2=2.94$
73.	Organization and Administration of Reference Systems	Yes No	33 197	18 117	$x^2=0.07$
93.	Systems Analysis and Design for Library and Information Center Operations	Yes No	35 195	14 121	$x^2=1.66$

Type of Work Performed

One objective in collecting data was on the job inventory and on the demand schedule for courses was to relate them and study the influence of the first on the second. To pursue this objective, each course was matched with corresponding job items. This matching meant that a particular job item was assigned to the course where it would be most likely to be discussed. In reverse, therefore, it yields a list of job items for every course. This matching was done by a number of experts in library education independently of each other. It was found that there was a close similarity between these lists; hence, it was possible to produce a final compendium of courses and their corresponding job items. However, it was decided at this stage of the study not to study these relationships for all courses, but only for a few courses deemed to be most popular on the basis of several factors.

The chosen objective, as listed in table 35, was to find out whether people engaged in any one of the selected job items associated with a course tend to demand that course more than those people who are not engaged in any one of these job items. The necessary statistical procedure was to calculate the chi-square statistic for each of these two-by-two resultant tables. These tables, along with the chi-square values, are presented in table 35. For each of these courses, it is important to notice that respondents who are engaged in any of the selected job items tend to demand the courses more often than respondents who are not engaged in any one of the job items. The difference is statistically significant for three courses: namely, course 3, Current Practices in Acquisitions; course 73, Organization and Administration of Reference Systems; and the automation course as combined. Further, courses 43, Information Retrieval for Clientele, and 15, Program Planning and Budgeting, had a difference, which, though not statistically significant at the 5 percent level, was close to it.

Hence it would seem that if a course dealt with nonadministrative matters in general, then it would be more likely that people who actually perform jobs that constitute part of the course would tend to demand it more often than people who were not associated with such job items. However, whether this is true for all the courses listed in our questionnaire can only be ascertained if the other courses are subjected to such analysis. It must be remembered, however, that no such association was seen when the same course was analyzed with respect to administrators and nonadministrators. Therefore, the conclusion seems to be that it is not the type of position that motivates an individual to take a course, but rather, whether the job activities performed by the individual are dealt with in the content of the course.

COURSE DEMAND

TABLE 35

RELATIONSHIP BETWEEN DEMAND FOR COURSES AND
TYPE OF WORK PERFORMED: 1968

Course Number	Course Title	Demand for Course. Yes, want course. No, do not want course	Respondents engage in work with which course deals	Respondents do not engage in work with which course deals	Chi-Square
3.	Current Practices in Acquisitions of Non-Book Materials	Yes No	19 78	24 244	$x^2=7.75*$
5.	Administrative Policies and Practices	Yes No	40 182	22 121	$x^2=0.43$
8.	General Management	Yes No	47 266	5 47	$x^2=1.06$
9.	Human Relations in Library Administration	Yes No	41 183	17 124	$x^2=2.81$
15.	Program Planning and Budgeting	Yes No	27 122	25 191	$x^2=3.09$
26. 27. 28.	Automation of Library Processes Information Processing on Computers Information Retrieval Systems	Yes No	58 98	52 157	$x^2=6.42*$
43.	Information Retrieval for Clientele	Yes No	42 199	13 111	$x^2=3.08$
73.	Organization and Administration of Reference Systems	Yes No	31 140	20 174	$x^2=4.62**$

* Significant at 1 per cent level
**Significant at 5 per cent level

Automation and the Demand for Courses

To get some idea of the number of librarians who engage in automation activities and the number of librarians who work in libraries where some activities are automated, the automated activities list as used in the Schick report (4:17) was given in Part III of the questionnaire. An analysis of the answers to these items for Stratum II (agencies other than the Library of Congress) is presented in table 36. Examination of this table shows that 24 nonadministrators are engaged in departments in their libraries which are using automated procedures. Of 292 respondents in this stratum, 58.3 percent report no automated activities in their libraries.

In the libraries represented by the respondents, the activities which are most frequently reported as being automated are listed in rank order. There is considerable lack of agreement between this rank order and that Schick (4:17) found in his survey, made about one year earlier than this study:

Ranking in This Study		Ranking in Schick Study
1.	Documents information retrieval	10
2	Serial record processing	6
3	Card catalog production	1
4	Bibliography production	2
5	Circulation control	5
6	Thesauri preparation	10
7	Acquisitions	4
8	Book catalog production	9

It is interesting to note that two of the activities for which Schick had only one listing were first and fifth in the present survey, document information retrieval and thesauri construction. The question arises, Are those respondents who indicate on the questionnaire that one or more of the activities in their libraries are automated more likely to check courses in automation than those who said there were no automated activities in their libraries?

Statistical analysis was made of two-by-two table 37. The resulting chi-square indicates that having automated activities in the respondent's library and his wanting to take a course in automation are unrelated ($x^2 = +.0017$). In other words, the analysis showed that a prediction cannot be made concerning whether or not a person tends to want to study automation simply because some of the functions in his own library may be automated.

TABLE 36
FREQUENCY OF AUTOMATED LIBRARY ACTIVITIES
IN RESPONDENTS' LIBRARIES IN STRATUM II
(Libraries other than Library of Congress): 1968

Library Activities	Non-Administrative Respondents whose Primary Activity is Automated	Respondents Indicating Automated Activities in Their Libraries		Total
		Administrative	Non-Administrative	
Accounting	--	8	5	13
Acquisitions	--	14	8	22
Bibliography Production	5	21	8	34
Book Catalog Production	1	13	6	20
Book Indexing	--	9	2	11
Catalog Card Production	2	28	8	38
Circulation Control	--	21	4	25
Document Information Retrieval	7	23	10	40
Graphic Storage of Materials	--	5	2	7
Legislative Indexing	--	3	1	4
Patron Control	--	7	2	9
Personnel Records	1	12	5	18
Reference Queries	2	6	3	11
Report Inventory	--	6	1	7
Selective Dissemination	1	12	3	16
Serial Record	3	24	13	40
Tele-Communication Devices	--	8	3	11
Thesauri Preparation	1	15	9	25
Union Lists	1	14	--	15
Other	--	3	--	3
No Activities Automated	--	135	35	170
Total	24	*	*	*

*Addition of these columns would not be significant because of duplication in answers.

TABLE 37

RELATIONSHIP BETWEEN DEMAND FOR COURSES IN AUTOMATION
AND HAVING AUTOMATED ACTIVITIES IN LIBRARY: 1968

	Respondent wants to take a course in automation	Respondent doesn't want to take a course in automation	Total
Respondent has some automated activities in his library	83	112	195
Respondent has no automated activities in his library	72	98	170
Total	155	210	365

$x^2 = +.0017$ Highly insignificant

Another question was asked concerning automation: Are you involved at an administrative or supervisory level in applying electronic data processing procedures? (Part III of the questionnaire, question 11, p.10.) Of the 365 respondents, 12.3 percent answered yes to this question. A similar question was, Will those who indicate that they are involved at an administrative or supervisory level in applying electronic data processing procedures be more apt to take courses in automation than those who are not so involved?

Statistical analysis based on two-by-two table 38 shows the association between those involved at a supervisory level in applying automation and those indicating an interest in taking a course in automation was not statistically significant ($x^2 = +2.35$). However, in this instance there is some association to suggest a tendency of those involved at a supervisory level toward an interest in taking courses in automation. In other words, it suggests that the librarian who is directly involved at a supervisory level in automation is more likely to want such courses than those who have automation someplace in the library but are not directly involved in the process in their own job.

Data processing was among 38 library activities which the respondents used to indicate their primary engagement. Of the 365 respondents only 2 checked this item as that single professional speciality in which he was primarily engaged. Both were nonadministrators.

COURSE DEMAND

TABLE 38
RELATIONSHIP BETWEEN DEMAND FOR COURSES IN AUTOMATION
AND SUPERVISION OF AUTOMATED ACTIVITIES:1968

	Respondent wants to take a course in automation	Respondent doesn't want to take a course in automation	Total
Respondent involved at supervisory level in applying data processing	24	21	45
Respondent not involved at supervisory level in applying data processing	132	188	320
Total	156	209	365

$x^2 = +2.35$ Not significant

ATTAINMENT OF OBJECTIVES

Courses Federal Librarians Are Most Interested in Studying

The devotion of a major portion of this section to those courses with the highest rankings makes further detailed presentation here redundant. However, there were two types of courses that received the highest overall rankings in several dimensions: courses in automation (items 26, 28, and 27) and courses in administration and management of libraries, especially Administrative Policies and Practices, Human Relations in Library Administration, General Management, Program Planning and Budgeting, and Administration of the Special Federal Library.

The courses dealing with specialized aspects of library service which were judged to be the greatest in demand are: Current Practices in Acquisition and Selection of Non-Book Materials (course 3),

Information Retrieval for Clientele (course 43), Organization and Administration of Reference Systems (course 73), and Systems Analysis and Design for Library and Information Center Operations (course 93).

The hypothesis was tested whether the course rankings of the 142 respondents who actually indicated on the questionnaire an interest in taking a post-MLS program would correlate highly with the course demand of all the 365 respondents. There was found to be an almost perfect correlation between the two rankings. The courses were ranked according to the main categories being studied in each section of this questionnaire, namely, type of position, grade level, and stratum, as well as all of the 365 respondents together. Further, as an aid to curriculum building the seventeen main subject areas were ranked in relation to demand. The subject areas which received the highest rankings as a result of this analysis were, first, automation and, second, administration.

Types or Degrees of Interest

The analyses were made according to types or degrees of interest in courses; namely, whether the respondent was chiefly interested in a "workshop," a "course now," a "course later" (identified in the questionnaire as three to five years from now), or a "course now or later" (meaning a combination of now and/or later). Analyses were also made to see which courses overall ranked the highest in a category entitled "workshop, course now or later" and which aroused no interest at all. An indication of the respondent's preference for course format is seen by listing the percentage of respondents who chose courses within each format:

> 70.14 percent checked 1 or more courses under "workshop"
> 50.68 percent checked 1 or more courses under "course later"
> 44.66 percent checked 1 or more courses under "course now."

When "course later" was combined with "course now," it was found that 63.0 percent of the respondents had checked one or more courses. Further, it was found that "course now" and "course later" as checked by the respondents had a very similar pattern of response, but there were obvious differences in the rankings of courses listed under "workshop " The courses receiving the highest rankings under the workshop format tended to deal more with the specialized aspects of library service. For example, the top five rankings are: Automation (course 26), Building and Evaluating Library Collections (course 1), Resources and Services of the Federal Library Complex (course 66), Current Practices in Acquisition and Selection of Non-Book Materials (course 3), and Non-Conventional Library Reference Tools (course 72).

Free-Response Comments

From a cross section of the respondents' comments, it seems that five generalizations can be drawn:

1. Generally, respondents thought the suggestions for courses were quite comprehensive as only six courses were mentioned that were not included in the scope of the questionnaire.

2. The practical aspects of administration were stressed not only in the comments relating directly to administration courses, but also in relation to other courses such as those on federal libraries and in the behavioral sciences.

3. The importance of understanding and using the new technology was mentioned in relation to several courses, such as audiovisual materials, automation, and federal libraries. Of particular interest was the suggestion that a course on federal libraries should be made available to librarians everywhere through the use of closed-circuit television.

4. Concern for the user was mentioned by reference to courses in such terms as: training in the methodology of user surveys, development of sensitivity in understanding the user's needs, ways of reaching the nonuser, and training to enable the librarian to "climb over the mound of details to reach people."

5. The value of the workshop as a means of continuing post-MLS education was mentioned by seventeen of the respondents. It is interesting to note that although the open-end question to which the librarians were responding said nothing about suggestions for workshops, this method of professional growth was stressed often and in such terms as being available to all librarians, in all areas, and at all times.

Selected Course-Related Variables
and Their Relationship to Other Variables

To determine if there is any relationship between the *number* of courses chosen in the combined category "course now/course later" and various groups of the respondents, a statistical analysis was made to determine the structure of the volume of demand for courses. It was found that there is no difference between the average number of courses demanded by males and females, reference librarians and classification and cataloging librarians, and administrators and non-administrators.

There is a distinct difference between the average number of courses demanded by the following groups, and to study the volume of their demands, each category of respondent must be studied separately (each group forms a statistically different population in relation to *number* of courses checked): those who are heads of libraries and those who are not heads of libraries, and those who indicate that they would participate in a post-MLS program in library science and those who indicate that they would not participate.

The relationship between demand for courses in relation to several variables was analyzed. The possibility of the respondents' enrolling for a post-MLS course decreases in association with factors concerned with the amount of time elapsed since receipt of the MLS. It increases as the amount of avoidable detail work on the job increases but seems to show no relation to the number of people supervised.

Demand for Courses and Type of Position. The findings seem to indicate that the course needs of federal librarians stem from the job activities that are performed. If the course content deals with the work in which the individual is currently engaged, the individual is more likely to take the course than if its content does not pertain to the job activities in which he is currently engaged.

This finding is in agreement with that of a recent study (Stone, 5:234) which found that the content of formal course work which can be related to the librarian's actual job was the most influential factor in motivating the librarian to enroll in formal courses. Further, this conclusion would seem to bear a relationship to the studies by Herzberg (3:59) which maintain that motivation in the work situation is closely related to the opportunity to grow in job competence.

Demand for Courses and Type of Work Performed. The findings seem to indicate that the expressed willingness to take these courses was not dependent upon the type of position, namely, administrative or non-administrative. Further, the total volume of demand for courses does not differ appreciably between the administrators and the non-administrators. The problem then arises, Should they be taught together or should they be taught separately? In other words, when he is building the course and writing the behavioral objectives for it, the curriculum builder has to keep constantly in mind the group for whom the course is being offered.

These findings were also reinforced in the free-response section of the questionnaire. The respondents pointed out rather forcefully that they did not wish to return to school to take courses which were not oriented to their present job needs. Courses which were on the same level as those they had taken at the MLS level or courses in which there were enrollees who did not have similar backgrounds, training, and experience to their own were singled out as of no interest.

Automation and Its Relationship to Demand for Courses. Through analysis it was shown that having automated activities in the respondent's library and wanting to take a course in automation are unrelated statistically. That is to say, a prediction cannot be made concerning whether or not a person tends to want to study automation simply because some of the functions in his own library may be automated. However, it was also shown statistically that the librarian who was directly involved at a supervisory level in automation was more likely to want to take courses in automation than one who has automation someplace else in the library but is not directly involved with automation.

A related condition was observed in the data presented in chapter 4. Of nine respondents who said automation was their greatest competence, eight checked that they wanted to take course work in this area, and only one of the nine checked no automation courses. These conditions provide supportive evidence for the principle, mentioned in the previous sections of this chapter, that a person who is engaged in a particular type of work tends to want to take courses in that area.

On the other hand, 16.2 percent of the respondents listed automation one of their greatest weaknesses and gave the reason for little competency as lack of training or knowledge. Of those listing automation as the area of their least competency, 71.2 percent indicated a desire to take some type of formal course work. Reading the responses of these individuals, one finds the reason for their stated willingness to take courses seems to be that they feel automation will be needed in their present jobs in the near future. It would seem, therefore, that in this special situation both responses supply supportive evidence for the premise that content directly related to the job situation provides the greatest motivation for enrolling in post-MLS courses.

REFERENCES IN CHAPTER 5

1. Danton, J. Periam. *Between M.L.S. and Ph.D: A Study of Sixth-Year Specialist Programs in Accredited Library Schools.* Chicago: American Library Assn., 1970.
2. Fryden, Floyd N. "Post-Master's Degree Programs in Some American Library Schools." Research paper, Graduate Library School, University of Chicago, Chicago, 1968.
3. Herzberg, Frederick. "One More Time: How Do You Motivate Employees?" *Harvard Business Review* 46:53—62 (Jan.-Feb. 1968).
4. Schick, Frank. *Survey of Special Libraries Serving the Federal Government.* Washington, D.C.: National Center for Educational Statistics, U.S. Dept. of Health, Education and Welfare, 1968.
5. Stone, Elizabeth W. *Factors Related to the Professional Development of Librarians.* Metuchen, N.J.: Scarecrow, 1969.

6
Additional Data about Building a Post-Master's Program in Library Science

In chapter 5 the needs for individual courses and workshops, as perceived by the federal librarian respondents, were studied in depth. This analysis provided the background data needed to achieve the ultimate objective of the project, namely, the development of a post-master's curricular program in library science. The base for a curricular structure is further enlarged in this chapter through a thorough study of data collected in the questionnaire pertaining to post-master's programs as a whole.

INTEREST IN FORMAL POST-MASTER'S PROGRAMS

In the data-gathering instrument, eleven questions were asked concerning the respondent's future interest in formal post-master's programs of a year's duration or more (Part II of the questionnaire, questions 96—105, p.9). It is to be noted that the replies to these questions in each instance implied a commitment to a "program" of a certain time duration as distinguished from the responses discussed in the last chapter, which sought the interest of the respondents about specific courses, not necessarily a part of a total program package.

TABLE 39
FREQUENCY DISTRIBUTION OF RESPONDENTS WILLING TO ENROLL FOR ONE-YEAR POST-MLS AND/OR PH.D. PROGRAM IN LIBRARY SCIENCE BY TYPE OF POSITION, GRADE LEVEL, AND SEX: 1968

Category	Yes Post-MLS		Yes Ph.D.		Yes to Either Post-MLS or Ph.D.	
	No.	%	No.	%	No.	%
Type of Position						
Administrators (N=230)	73	31.73	36	15.65	85	36.96
Non-Administrators (N=135)	49	36.29	23	17.04	57	42.22
Sex						
Male (N=96)						
GS 9 (N=17)	8	8.33	6	6.25	9	9.38
GS 10,11 (N=30)	9	9.37	8	8.33	14	14.58
GS 12-14 (N=49)	16	16.66	13	13.54	21	21.88
Subtotal (N=96)	33	34.38	27	28.13	44	45.83
Female (N=269)						
GS 9 (N=98)	35	13.01	10	3.72	38	14.13
GS 10,11 (N=110)	42	15.61	17	6.32	47	17.47
GS 12-14 (N=61)	12	4.46	5	1.86	13	4.83
Subtotal (N=269)	89	33.09	32	11.89	98	36.43
Grade Level						
GS 9 (N=115)	43	37.39	16	13.91	47	40.87
GS 10,11 (N=140)	51	36.43	25	17.86	61	43.57
GS 12-14 (N=110)	28	25.45	18	16.36	34	30.91
TOTAL	122	33.42	59	16.16	142	38.90

One-Year Post-Master's Program in Library Science

Of the 365 respondents 122, or 33.4 percent, answered in the affirmative the question "Would you enroll for a one-year post-MLS program in library science?" (Part II of the questionnaire, no.96.) The breakdown of these answers by sex, type of question, and grade level (table 39) would seem to warrant the following conclusions:

Interest in taking a post-MLS one-year program was generally the same for men as for women, as 34.4 percent of the men in the study and 33.1 percent of the women checked yes to this question.

In general, the interest in taking a post-MLS program was the same for administrators as for nonadministrators, as 31.7 percent of the administrators and 36.3 percent of the nonadministrators checked that they would enroll for a post-MLS program.

Interest in taking a post-MLS one-year program was generally lower for grades 12—14 than for grades 9—11. This is reflected in the following statistics:

37.4 percent of those in GS 9 stated they would enroll.
36.4 percent of those in GS 10—11 stated they would enroll.
25.5 percent of those in GS 12—14 stated they would enroll.

Thus, it would seem that as the grade level increases, desire to take a post-MLS program has a tendency to decrease.

Of the 122 respondents (33.4 percent) indicating an interest in a post-MLS one-year program, 111 respondents, or 90.9 percent, listed certain conditions under which they would enroll in such a program (question 97). Question 98 asked for a listing of these conditions. As shown in figure 5, the most frequently mentioned condition involved making satisfactory financial arrangements. Partial financial help was stated as a condition by 45 (36.9 percent) of the 122 respondents answering this question, and total financial help was listed as a condition by 16 respondents (13.1 percent). From reading the conditions stated by the 122 persons answering this question, the general impression was that a large proportion of those respondents who said they would return to school would require major financial assistance to enroll, even those who did not indicate the need for total financial support.

The second-largest group of responses stated leave of absence as a condition for enrollment. These 25 respondents (20.5 percent) wanted assurance that their jobs would be waiting for them on the completion of the post-MLS program.

The third-largest cluster of responses was related to the curricular program of the one-year post-MLS program. Twenty-one respondents, or 17.2 percent, listed conditions relating to the library schools' obligation for building a program. The largest subgroup in this category related to the quality of the program. Because stipulations about curriculum are particularly important in regard to this study, some examples of the type of answers given follow:

INTEREST

Courses must have "real" content, as opposed to the dull, tedious and empty content of courses I had in the MLS program.

I will only return if I have an indication of tangible evidence that the courses are more sophisticated and advanced than MLS programs. ... Practicing librarians lose enthusiasm for scholarship and intellectual endeavor. Their work becomes simply a job. Perhaps enforced continuing education, similar to the requirement that teachers have, might be helpful.

FIGURE 5
CONDITIONS LISTED BY RESPONDENTS AS NECESSARY FOR THEIR ENROLLING IN A ONE-YEAR POST-MLS LIBRARY SCIENCE PROGRAM: 1968

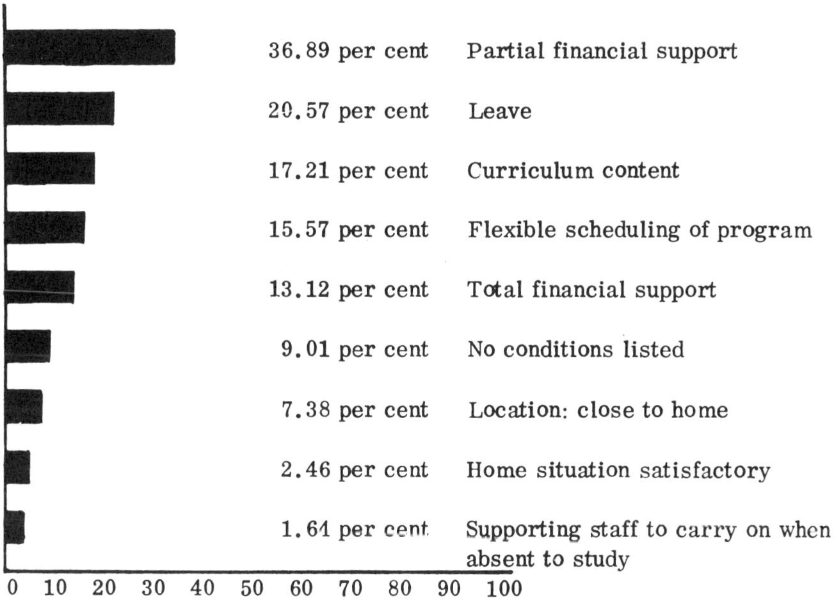

Percentage	Condition
36.89 per cent	Partial financial support
20.57 per cent	Leave
17.21 per cent	Curriculum content
15.57 per cent	Flexible scheduling of program
13.12 per cent	Total financial support
9.01 per cent	No conditions listed
7.38 per cent	Location: close to home
2.46 per cent	Home situation satisfactory
1.64 per cent	Supporting staff to carry on when absent to study

The conditions that the respondents listed as necessary for their enrolling in a one-year post-MLS library science program are charted here. Of the 365 Federal librarians in the study 33.4 per cent indicated an interest in a one-year post-MLS program. Of the 122 respondents who said they would enroll for such a program, 111 respondents listed necessary conditions. This chart shows the percentage of respondents listing factors in the clusters given above. The total percentages of the columns do not add up to 100.0 per cent as some respondents listed more than one condition.

ADDITIONAL DATA

> The program must be "proven." I do not want to repeat material I have already covered at the undergraduate and graduate levels.
>
> I want to be sure the program has adequate research in progress.
>
> If I return, I want an indication that there will be tangible results in terms of increased job opportunities.
>
> I want to be able to use any post-master's credits toward a Ph.D., if I should decide to go on for that.

Nineteen of the respondents (15.6 percent) were concerned with scheduling of courses. The emphasis was on flexible scheduling which would permit the respondents to keep their jobs and attend at night, on Saturdays, and on a part-time basis. The remainder of the conditions cited related to location (close to home), which was mentioned by nine respondents; satisfactory home situation, which was listed by three respondents; and a support staff in the respondent's library to carry on efficiently in his absence (two respondents).

Before leaving this section, it should be noted that the large majority of those saying they would enroll for the post-MLS program appeared to desire to retain contact with their present employer. This response suggested a point to raise in interviewing top-level administrators of libraries. If they realize that the general feeling of librarians in the federal service is that they intend to come back to the same library with improved skills and knowledge, rather than use this training as a stepping stone to another library situation, these managers might be inclined to encourage participation and not see it as a threat to their own programs.

Doctoral Programs in Library Science

Of the 365 individuals in the study, 59 (16.2 percent) indicated an interest in enrolling for a doctoral program in library science. The breakdown of the answers by sex, type of position, and grade level (table 39) shows several factors that are itemized below. However, it must be borne in mind that the total number of people willing to study in a doctoral program in library science is small, compared to the number interested in a post-MLS one-year program; and, therefore, the conclusions here have much less reliability. With this limitation in mind, some general statements would seem warranted:

> A smaller proportion of women than of men is interested in a doctoral program. Only 11.9 percent of the women, as compared to 28.1 percent of the men, stated that they would enroll for a

doctoral program in library science. For the one-year post-MLS program, interest of men and women was about the same.

The interest in taking a doctoral program was nearly the same for administrators (15.7 percent) as for nonadministrators (17.0 percent). This parallels the finding that was made in regard to type of position related to taking a one-year post-MLS program.

At the GS 9 level, interest in enrolling for a doctoral program, based on the limited number of people involved, was generally lower than for higher grades. This is opposite to the pattern that pertained for the post-MLS program relative to grade level. On the basis of the limited statistics available, it would seem that those who would be most interested in a doctoral program would be men at a grade level above GS 9.

Of the 59 respondents (16.2 percent) who stated they would enroll for a doctoral program in library science, 56 stated that certain conditions would have to be met in order for them to enroll (Part II of the questionnaire, question 102). In answering these questions, the respondents indicated certain clusters of conditions as being predominant (see figure 6):

1. Partial financial help
2. Curriculum content
3. Satisfactory leave arrangements
4. Total financial support
5. Flexible scheduling on the part of the library school.

Because conditions necessary for enrollment are particularly important in this study, some direct quotations from the respondents regarding curriculum content are included here:

I would have to be convinced that the program was worthwhile and intellectually challenging.

I would want a program that was tailored to my individual needs.

There must be proven merit and need for such a program, before I would go.

Because I want to study, but not just for the sake of another degree, I would need a school that offered iconoclasts in library science and no more unpurposeful busy work.

I would want reasonable freedom in selection of courses; I would like to pursue independent study.

ADDITIONAL DATA

FIGURE 6
CONDITIONS LISTED BY RESPONDENTS AS NECESSARY FOR THEIR ENROLLING IN A DOCTORAL PROGRAM IN LIBRARY SCIENCE: 1968

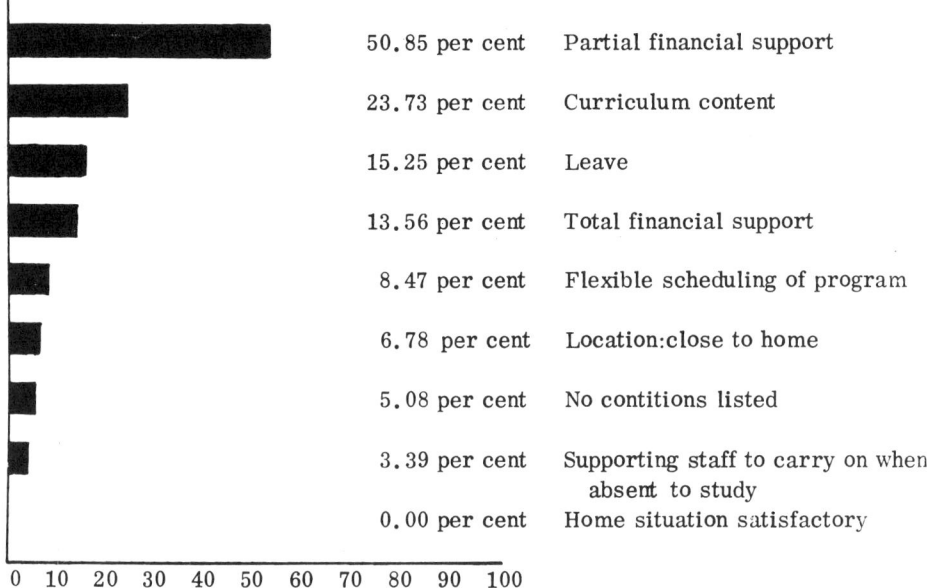

50.85 per cent	Partial financial support
23.73 per cent	Curriculum content
15.25 per cent	Leave
13.56 per cent	Total financial support
8.47 per cent	Flexible scheduling of program
6.78 per cent	Location: close to home
5.08 per cent	No contitions listed
3.39 per cent	Supporting staff to carry on when absent to study
0.00 per cent	Home situation satisfactory

0 10 20 30 40 50 60 70 80 90 100

The conditions that the respondents listed as necessary for their enrolling in a doctoral program are charted here. Of the 365 Federal librarians in the study, 16.2 per cent indicated an interest in a doctoral program in library science. Of the 59 respondents who said they would enroll for such a program, 56 respondents listed necessary conditions. This chart shows the percentage of times of respondents listing factors in the clusters given above. The total percentages of the columns do not add up to 100.0 per cent as some respondents listed more than one condition.

Graduate Programs Other than Library Science

When queried about their interest in postgraduate work in fields other than library science, 40 (11.0 percent) said they would enroll in a doctoral program, and 106 (29.0 percent) would enroll in programs below the doctoral level. The disciplines in which they showed interest are presented in table 40.

TABLE 40
A LIST OF THE FIELDS OF STUDY AND SUBJECT AREAS (OTHER THAN LIBRARY SCIENCE) IN WHICH RESPONDENTS INDICATED INTEREST IN STUDYING AT THE GRADUATE LEVEL, WITH THE CORRESPONDING NUMBER OF PEOPLE INTERESTED: 1968 [1]

Fields of Study	Subject Areas	Number of Respondents Interested in graduate programs below doctoral level	Number of Respondents Interest in program at doctoral level
Behavioral and Social Sciences	Administration, Business	7	1
	Administration, General	12	2
	Administration, Public	5	2
	Behavioral Sciences (general)	4	0
	Communications	0	2
	History	14	9
	International Relations	0	2
	Law	5	0
	Political Science (general)	5	2
	Psychology	3	0
	Social Science (general)	5	0
	Sociology	3	0
	Urban Planning	1	0
	Miscellaneous	0	5
	Subtotal	64	25
Education		4	3
Engineering		1	0
Humanities and Arts	Fine Arts	4	3
	Foreign Languages	5	7
	Literature	12	3
	Music	0	2
	Writing	1	0
	Miscellaneous	0	7
	Subtotal	22	22
Information Science		8	2
Sciences, Basic and Applied	Biological and Medical Sciences	6	0
	Earth Sciences	0	1
	Mathematical Sciences	1	1
	Oceanography	1	0
	Subtotal	8	2
	TOTAL	107	54

[1] The table shows the number of different subject areas listed by the respondents. The total number of subject areas is greater than the total number of respondents, as some people listed more than one subject area.

ADDITIONAL DATA

For programs below the doctoral level, administration and management were in the majority (24); history was second (14), with literature a close third (12). At the doctoral level, history was the most popular subject area (9); the second most popular was foreign languages (7), with the third choice being administration and management (5). Thus the courses most frequently checked by the respondents were concentrated in the behavioral and social sciences and the humanities with only 8 respondents (2 at the doctoral level) listing courses in the sciences. This distribution of courses has significance because it generally indicates that the overall knowledge that would be added to the profession would be, except for the administration and management, in areas already heavily represented (humanities and the social sciences) within the profession, rather than in additional areas which would add breadth to the coverage of various related disciplines within librarianship.

Interest in graduate study below the doctoral level reflected the same general pattern as that in a one-year post-MLS program in library science; namely, as the grade increased, the number who said they would enroll decreased. This is evident in the following listing:

Grade Level	Percentage of Those Interested in Graduate Study (below Doctoral Level in a Subject Field)
GS 9	40.5 percent
GS 10—11	35.8 percent
GS 12—14	23.5 percent

Library School and the Professional Development of Its Graduates

The last question (no. 106) in Part II of the questionnaire, entitled Your Educational Needs, asked, "In what other ways do you see that the library school could help you in your professional development?" Only two respondents replied that the library school is probably doing enough. The general attitude of the respondents seemed to be that the library schools should be giving much more serious thought to their role in continuing education — especially in ways that they are not presently functioning. They offered suggestions which challenged the library school not only to improve in quality and quantity its services to its alumni, but also to the community at large. Some of the specific suggestions made have been grouped to suggest the wide scope of additional activities the respondents thought within the realm of the school's responsibility.

Clearinghouse for Information

Keep in continual touch by mail through publication of information bulletins with content and substance which will keep former students in touch with the latest developments in the profession, at the school, and in the area.

Specific publications mentioned to mail to alumni were acquisitions lists (in library literature) and pertinent "occasional papers."

A newsletter of a scholarly nature should be sent to all librarians which should include: review of significant publications; state-of-the-art papers; composite picture of library development as a whole—all latest trends. It would serve as a quick and valuable "current awareness tool" for everyone in the field. This, too, would be continuing education.

Continuing statistical surveys of the career development of the members of each class with results sent periodically to former students.

Counseling Center. According to the respondents, the counseling service would include: initial placement, career development, continuing placement, counseling help for older graduates in adequate placement.

Discussion and Idea Center

Inviting library directors to school to participate in pertinent colloquia.

Forums to provide for the presentation and discussion of professional papers so they can be reviewed *before* publication. These could be organized by subject interest in various geographical locations.

Educator. Even though the direction on the questionnaire was for suggestions other than courses and workshops, many respondents did include comments on types of courses and their content.

ADDITIONAL DATA

Offer correspondence courses.

Conduct more surveys and find out exactly how meaningful the courses are that are being offered now.

Prepare outlines of selected readings on subjects so that the alumni may keep up on the job. Hard for the non-expert to sift the important from the unimportant.

Use modern technology to take library school courses to people who need them and cannot travel.

Survey various subject areas of value to those in the field and then offer courses that incorporate all updating that has been done.

Provide opportunities for the alumnus to come back to library school to observe new techniques in action and audit class lectures.

In all forms of continuing education, library schools should put a stronger emphasis on administration, personnel management, budget planning, and automation.

Provide refresher courses for those who have been out of the field and now want to re-enter.

One year is too long. Post-master's should be concentrated into a six-month period — or into one-quarter or one-semester programs.

Agent for Improving Librarianship

Use the library school's influence to encourage attendance of librarians at association meetings.

Take the lead in writing a pamphlet clearly defining various working groups in the library — professionals, supporting staff, etc.

Actively work for librarians to receive academic status in university situations.

More careful screening of applications for admission to school. By getting activists, not cast-offs from other professions, the whole profession could be upgraded. The library school must bear a large share of the responsibility for the image that librarians have today because of admission policies.

Impress on administrative personnel that professional librarians should not be given clerical duties.

The Library School in the Community

Offer consultants for local associations and other groups planning workshops and training sessions, and consultative service for practicing librarians.

Give lectures on new trends in librarianship to staffs of libraries in the area.

Think through and devise new library concepts of service to reach the functionally illiterate in our society. More stress on readers services at all levels and to all groups.

Implementer of Effective Legislation

Actively work for the continuation of grants for study.

Bring influence to bear on Congress and the Civil Service Commission to improve remuneration for continuing education engaged in; to eliminate anti-intellectualism; and to upgrade library technicians.

Variables Affecting Interest

The question arises, What variables are related to interest in taking a one-year or more post-master's program? Two variables were selected to test if any prediction might be made from them concerning participation. One of them did prove a basis for prediction and the other did not.

One variable was distance from an accredited library school, and the premise tested was whether or not this had any association with willingness to participate in a post-master's program. The research staff determined the distance from an accredited library school for every individual respondent in the sample since this information was not available from the questionnaire. Statistical analysis was made, using these figures, to see if distance from an accredited school had any relationship to expressed willingness to take a post-MLS program. The particular test used was chi-square. It was found that these two variables were statistically independent of each other, indicating that distance from a library school does not influence one's decision to enroll in post-MLS programs (table 41).

ADDITIONAL DATA

TABLE 41

DISTRIBUTION OF RESPONDENTS ACCORDING TO WILLINGNESS TO TAKE A POST-MLS PROGRAM IN LIBRARY SCIENCE AND DISTANCE FROM THEIR NEAREST ACCREDITED LIBRARY SCHOOL: 1968

Distance of Place of Work from Accredited Library School	Respondents Interested in Post-MLS Study (including Ph.D. Study) in Library Science		Respondents Not Answering Question or Stating Not Interested in Post-MLS Study in Library Science	
	No. (N=142)	%	No. (N=223)	%
0- 30 Miles	84	59.16	139	62.33
31-100 Miles	23	16.20	42	18.83
Over 100 Miles	18	12.68	31	13.91
APO	17	11.97	11	4.93
TOTAL	142	100.00	223	100.00

$x^2 = 0.12$ (Excluding APO)   Insignificant

The other variable was the extent of formal course work undertaken after the MLS. To determine whether there was any relationship between having taken formal course work since the completion of the MLS degree and an expression of willingness to take a post-MLS program, the respondents were asked in the questionnaire to note participation in all formal study (in any subject area) following their MLS. Such study included formal courses for credit and noncredit and participation in institutes, workshops, and seminars. As shown in table 42, 57.3 percent of the respondents indicated that they had not taken any formal course work either in library science or in other subject areas since the completion of their MLS degree.

Of those participating in the study, 15.1 percent indicated that they had taken six or more hours of formal course work for credit (indicated in table 42 as "some formal course work"); and 27.2 percent had either taken six hours of formal course work and/or had participated in one or more institutes, workshops, or noncredit courses (indicated in table 42 as "very little formal course work"). A summarization of these findings is given in figure 7. A statistical analysis was made of the relationship between those in this survey (39 percent of 365) who expressed the intention of taking post-MLS work, including willingness to participate in a doctoral program, and those respondents who had engaged in some type of formal study following their MLS degree. It was found that there is a statistically significant relationship between the amount of

TABLE 42

AMOUNT OF FORMAL STUDY ENGAGED IN BY RESPONDENTS FOLLOWING MLS DEGREE BY TYPE OF POSITION AND GRADE LEVEL: 1968

Amount of Course Work Following MLS	Type of Position				Grade Level								Total Respondents	
	Administrative		Non-Administrative		9		10, 11		12-14					
	No.	%	No.	%	No.	%	No.	%	No.	%			No.	%
Some Formal Course Work[1]	36	9.86	19	5.21	9	2.47	23	6.30	23	6.30			55	15.07
Very Little Formal Course Work[2]	72	19.73	29	7.94	22	6.03	51	13.97	28	7.67			101	27.67
No Formal Course Work	122	33.42	87	23.84	84	23.01	66	18.09	59	16.16			209	57.26
TOTAL	230	63.01	135	36.99	115	31.51	140	38.36	110	30.13			365	100.00

[1]Six or more hours of formal course work for credit.

[2]Under six hours of formal course work and/or participation in one or more institutes or workshops or non-credit courses.

FIGURE 7
AMOUNT OF FORMAL STUDY ENGAGED IN BY RESPONDENTS
FOLLOWING MLS DEGREE: 1968

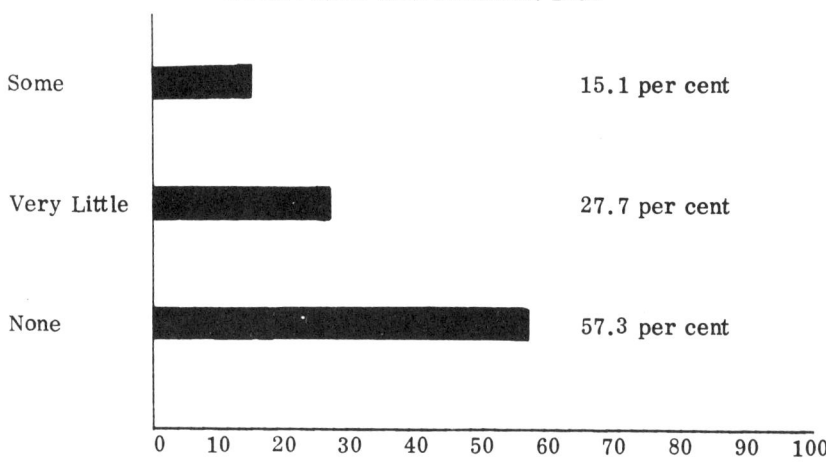

The formal study attainments of the Federal librarians responding to the study as of the year 1968 are charted here. The category "Some" represents six or more hours of formal course work for credit. The category "Very Little" represents under six hours of formal study and/or participation in one or more institutes, workshops, or non-credit courses.

TABLE 43
DISTRIBUTION OF AMOUNT OF FORMAL STUDY ENGAGED IN
BY RESPONDENTS FOLLOWING MLS DEGREE
VS. EXPRESSED INTENT TO ENGAGE IN POST-MLS FORMAL STUDY: 1968

Amount of Formal Course Work Following MLS Degree	Expression of Intent to Take Post-MLS Work				Total	
	Yes		No			
	No.	%	No.	%	No.	%
Some formal course work[1]	28	7.67	27	7.39	55	15.07
Very little formal course work[2]	51	13.97	50	13.69	101	27.67
No Formal course work	63	17.26	146	40.00	209	57.26
Total	142	38.90	223	61.09	365	100.00

Chi-square is 15.78, which is significant at the .01 level.

[1]Six or more hours of formal course work for credit.
[2]Under six hours of formal course work and/or participation in one or more institutes or workshops or non-credit courses.

formal course work taken since the MLS degree and the expression of intent to take a post-master's program. That is to say, if the respondent has taken no formal course work since his MLS degree, he is less apt to engage in any kind of a post-master's study than the respondent who has taken some kind of formal course work since the completion of his MLS degree (table 43).

SELF-PERCEIVED DEFICIENCIES IN PROFESSIONAL TRAINING

In the questionnaire two questions were designed to give those who plan post-MLS programs an idea of gaps in the librarian's training which are especially notable in his present position.

Scientific, Technical, or Professional Courses

The respondents were asked: "Are there any formal scientific, technical, or professional courses which you lack which you feel would have been especially helpful in your position? . . . If yes, please specify courses or course areas" (questionnaire, Part III, question 49, p.1).

Of the 365 respondents in the study, 177 (48.5 percent) listed courses which they lack and which they feel would have been especially helpful to prepare them for their present positions. Of this 177, 93 respondents (52.5 percent) listed one course, and 52 (29.4 percent) listed two courses. Five was the greatest number of courses specified on any one questionnaire. It is interesting to note that of the 177 responding to this question, 119 (67.2 percent) are administrators, and 58 (32.8 percent) are nonadministrators. This ratio of administrators to nonadministrators is nearly the same as the ratio in the overall sample.

The library science courses the respondents felt to be most needed and usually unavailable were:

1. Scientific and technical literature and research (31 respondents)
2. Automation of library processes (26 respondents)
3. General management (22 respondents)
4. Biomedical literature and research (17 respondents)
5. Personnel administration in libraries (16 respondents)

TABLE 44
DEFICIENCIES IN FORMAL SCIENTIFIC, TECHNICAL OR PROFESSIONAL EDUCATION AS EVALUATED ACCORDING TO COURSE AREAS BY TYPE OF POSITION: 1968

Course Areas	Number of Times Course or Course Area Listed by Respondents[1]		Total
	Administrative	Non-Administrative	
Library Science Areas:			
Specialized Information Sources	46	31	77
Administration & General Management of Libraries	46	8	54
Automation	32	18	50
Cataloging & Classification	5	6	11
Indexing & Abstracting	3	7	10
Administration of Special Types of Library Services	8	1	9
Housing & Equipment	7	0	7
Systems Analysis	6	1	7
Acquisitions & Selection	5	1	6
Research	4	1	5
Information Science	3	1	4
Publication	2	1	3
Clientele Services	2	0	2
Bibliography	0	1	1
Reference	1	0	1
SUBTOTAL	170	77	247
Non-Library Fields:			
Humanities & Arts			
Foreign Languages	12	11	23
Miscellaneous	3	0	3
Sciences, Basic & Applied	4	5	9
Behavioral & Social Sciences	2	3	5
Miscellaneous	3	2	5
Engineering	1	0	1
SUBTOTAL	25	21	46
TOTALS	195	98	293

[1] The total number of respondents answering was 177. Of these 119 were administrative respondents, and 58 were non-administrative.

SELF-PERCEIVED DEFICIENCIES

When the answers in this section are categorized by major subject areas, the greatest gaps are in these areas:

1. Specialized information sources (77 respondents)
2. Administration and general management of libraries (54 respondents)
3. Automation (50 respondents)
4. Cataloging and classification (11 respondents)
5. Indexing and abstracting (10 respondents)

Forty-six respondents, or 26.0 percent of those listing deficiencies, mentioned specific subject areas outside the field of library science. More than half of these respondents (24) listed courses in the area of foreign languages, with German and Russian noted the most often. Table 44 shows the breakdown, first by library science areas and second by non-library science fields of study.

Unperformed Job Activities

A question about educational background was: "In relation to your present position, are there any activities you should be engaged in for which your previous training has not prepared you? ... If yes, please specify these activities" (questionnaire, Part III, question 50 p.11).

Of the 365 respondents in the study, 81, or 22.2 percent, specified activities they should be engaged in but are not because their previous training had not prepared them. Of these 81, 58 respondents (71.6 percent) listed only one activity, while only 16 respondents (19.8 percent) listed two activities. Five was the greatest number of activities specified on any one questionnaire. It is interesting to note that of those 81 listing unperformed job activities, 62, or 76.5 percent, were administrators and 19, or 25.5 percent, were nonadministrators. This is a higher ratio of administrators to nonadministrators than is the ratio for the entire sample. Thus, there is some evidence that an administrator was more likely to feel that he should be engaged in activities in his present position for which his previous training had not prepared him.

The answers given by the respondents were coded by the job activities as listed in Part I of the questionnaire. Table 45 shows these job activities listed by the respondents grouped under the twenty-one types of job activities listed in the questionnaire. The three needed areas of competence receiving the most mention were as follows:

Automation	23 respondents listed 23 job activities
Representing	20 respondents listed 23 job activities
Planning	10 respondents listed 11 job activities

ADDITIONAL DATA

TABLE 45
NUMBER OF RESPONDENTS LISTING ACTIVITIES THEY SHOULD BE ENGAGED IN FOR WHICH THEIR PREVIOUS TRAINING HAS NOT PREPARED THEM BY TYPE OF POSITION: 1968

	Type of Position		All Together
Job Area Heading	Administrative (N=62)	Non-Administrative (N=19)	(N=81)
Specialized Library Functions:			
Abstracting	2	0	2
Acquisitions	4	0	4
Bibliography	1	0	1
Cataloging and Classification	3	2	5
Circulation	0	0	0
Clientele Services	3	1	4
Indexing	2	0	2
Literature Searching	3	0	3
Maintenance of Holdings	3	0	3
Reference	2	1	3
Research	1	1	2
Selection	2	0	2
Translation	0	1	1
General Administrative and Management Functions:			
Planning	9	1	10
Organizing	4	3	7
Staffing	6	1	7
Directing	4	0	4
Coordinating	0	0	0
Controlling	2	1	3
Representing	17	3	20
Housing	2	0	2
Automation:	21	2	23

The proportionately large number of people indicating automation was not surprising in view of the answers to question 49, where automation courses were felt to be lacking by 28.2 percent of those indicating a gap in their education. It is interesting to note that of the 23 respondents stating inability in automation, 20 were administrators. This would seem to illustrate further the importance of automation in the curriculum at both the MLS and the post-MLS levels.

As 76.5 percent of those listing activities unable to be performed were administrators, it is not surprising that there was a heavier concentration of these problems in the administrative and management category than in the specialized library category of job activities. Because automation cuts across both administrative and management functions as well as specialized library functions, it is listed separately in table 45.

KNOWLEDGE, ABILITIES, AND/OR SKILLS FOR REPLACEMENT

In Part III of the questionnaire, item 78, the respondent was asked:

> Suppose you were leaving your library for another position, and the administration asked you to <u>recommend someone as your replacement</u>. You know that your views would weigh heavily in the final decision. Let us assume that you are leaving your present position with great reluctance and that you have great affection for your library. Hence, you want to see yourself replaced with the type of person most likely to do a top-notch job after you have gone. Keep in mind also, the changes that you foresee coming and the necessity of your replacement anticipating and adapting to these changes.
>
> Based on these considerations, what knowledge and which abilities or skills would you consider most important for your replacement to have?
>
> A. <u>Most Important Knowledge</u>   B. <u>Most Important Abilities and/or Skills</u>

This question was answered by 313 or 85.8 percent of the respondents. Of these, 306 offered comments under section A, "Most Important Knowledge," and 298 respondents entered remarks under

ADDITIONAL DATA

"Most Important Abilities and/or Skills." From the 313 librarians answering this question, a total of 1,615 comments were written, 809 under "Most Important Knowledge" and 806 under "Most Important Abilities and/or Skills." It should be stated at this point that in the respondent's mind there did not always seem to be a clear distinction between "knowledge" and "skills and abilities." In discussing the comments, these two categories, A (knowledge) and B (skills and abilities), will be grouped together.

From an examination of figure 8 it is possible to see why it was important to include this question in the instrument. Some additional facts are brought out here which are not found anyplace else in the respondents' data. Probably the most striking result from the replies to this question is the emphasis that the respondents placed on personal characteristics required on the job. Of the 313 answering the question, 229 (73.2 percent) listed items in this area. It is interesting to note that whether the respondents are analyzed by grade, by agency, or by stratum, there is a representative response in this area. The number is particularly noticeable when compared with the importance the respondents placed on experience, which was mentioned the least number of times by the respondents.

In the current literature on curriculum building, little emphasis has been found relating to personal characteristics, but Peterson (8:8) does state that in building curriculum, in addition to other factors "personal characteristics required by the job, such as a high degree of accuracy, above-average mental application, creative ability, and use of independent judgment" should be used as criteria. Hall (5:42), in studying the educational objectives for the public service librarian, set up five major classes against which education for public librarianship might be measured and analyzed, one of which was personal traits. But she immediately commented, "no consideration of them in relation to education objectives will be included in the analysis." This statement is explained: "Personal traits are not considered the 'learned' knowledges which fall within the cognitive domain and were not originally intended for inclusion in this study. However, as is often the case in service-oriented institutions, they were reflected, at least indirectly, in so many descriptions of incidents that acknowledgement of their existence is hereby noted."

Specifically, the personality traits ranked the highest by the respondents were: getting along with people, which was mentioned by 114 of the 229 who answered this section of the questionnaire; adaptability or flexibility, mentioned by 38; patience, by 22; dedication and loyalty, by 18; and fortitude, which was listed by 10.

FIGURE 8

SUMMARY OF RESPONDENTS' EVALUATION OF KNOWLEDGE, ABILITIES, AND SKILLS MOST IMPORTANT FOR THEIR REPLACEMENTS TO HAVE: 1968

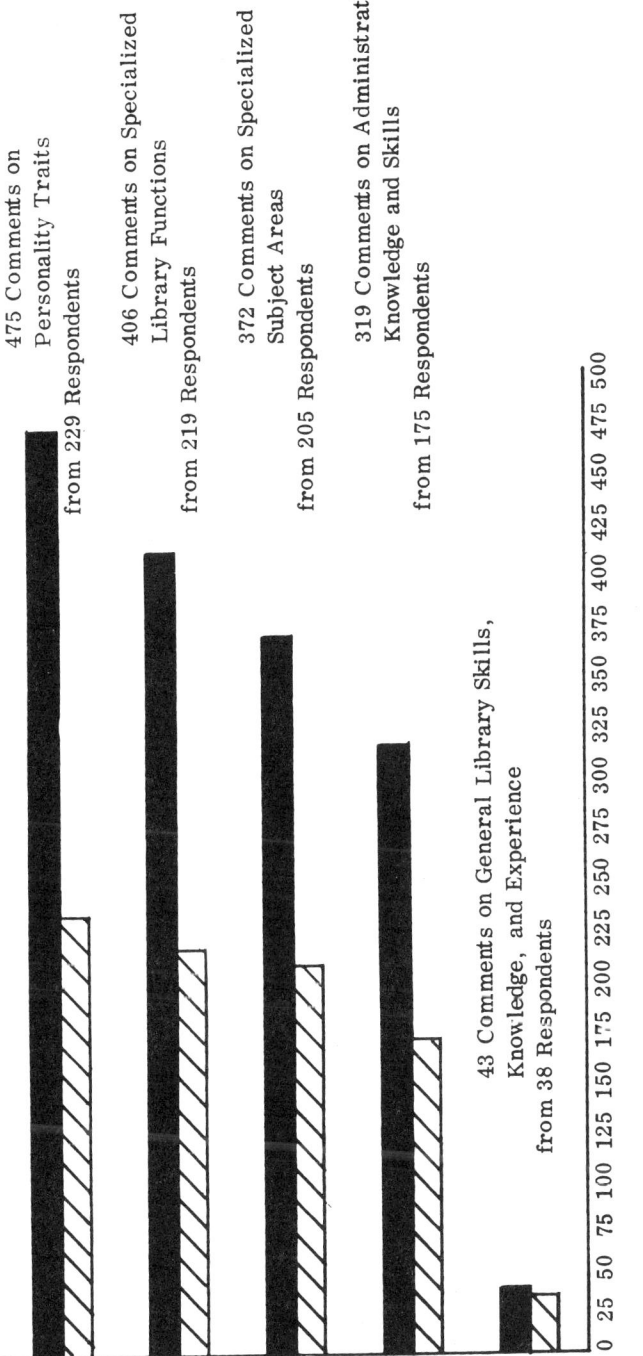

In answer to Question 78, Part III of the questionnaire, 313 (85.8 per cent) of the 365 respondents made 1615 recommendations of which 29.4 per cent were related to personality traits, 25.1 per cent were related to specialized library functions, 23.0 per cent related to specialized subject knowledge; 19.8 per cent related to administrative knowledge and skills; and 2.7 per cent concerned general library skills, knowledge and experience. Of the 313 respondents answering this question, 229 respondents (73.2 per cent) listed personal characteristics.

ADDITIONAL DATA

One of the surprising features of this particular analysis was the small number of times knowledge or skill in automation was mentioned, whereas the demand for courses in this area is so marked. Automation was listed 39 times, but cataloging, for example, was listed 134 times by the respondents, and reference 87 times. In the section where the question appears there are 409 responses, and automation accounted for only 9.5 percent of them. A possible explanation of this might be that the respondents did not actually need automation in their present work, but indicated great interest in taking formal study in the area because they feel that in the future, possibly in their present jobs, they may need such comprehension. They perhaps feel insecure without it, but do not see it as a present necessity.

It was also rather surprising to find the humanities receiving such a high score at a time when there is so much emphasis on the sciences in federal libraries. When the responses are analyzed by agency, an explanation for this can be found. Thirty-one of these comments were in the area of foreign languages and were made by those working at the Library of Congress where there is a constant demand for expertise in translation.

A final area that deserves comment is the recommendations for successors in the areas of administrative knowledge and skills, where there was a heavy concentration (85 items) in personnel supervision and human relations. Also, the problems of dealing with the government itself were mentioned 53 times. In the area of administration a total of 319 suggestions was made. These findings, however, coincide with the emphasis placed in all other parts of the study on the need for ability, skill, and knowledge in this area.

SUGGESTIONS ABOUT A POST-MLS PROGRAM

The last page of the questionnaire asks for the respondent's ideas and comments on the study as a whole. Volunteered were 352 suggestions that definitely aid in attaining the objectives of the study. Slightly more than 50 percent of them (181 comments) related to curricular development. These comments have been edited and summarized to express those ideas which appeared to be fairly universal, or those that were original and unique. The degree of attention given to various areas, as indicated in appendix table 22, is in itself interesting and affords one type of evidence of the importance attached to the various items mentioned by the respondents. Some of the areas commented upon are: (1) suggestions regarding non-library science study; (2) work-study programs; (3) doctoral programs; (4) general comments about continuing education in a university setting; (5) comments about time, location, and format of courses; (6) attitude toward post-MLS study; (7) undergraduate admission requirements for the MLS program as they affect post-MLS study; (8) suggestions regarding library technicians; (9) reactions to the study as a whole; and (10) surveys of other similar groups.

Non-Library Science Study

Twenty-eight of the respondents spoke of the importance of studying in subject fields other than librarianship. Sixteen made statements similar to the following, listing preferences such as language, business, mathematics, finance, banking, and chemistry:

> Some research libraries will not employ librarians for their libraries because of lack of appropriate subject background among professional librarians.

> At present almost any offering in philosophy, humanities, history of ideas, aesthetics in art or music, to name a few, seems more intellectually interesting (than a program just in library science). (Administrative librarian)

> Although when I started out, I found library work interesting, satisfying and sufficient; with increasing administrative duties, which for me are low in intellectual appeal, I now find library work insufficient. Rather than pursuing further study in the library field, I am now more likely to continue in philosophy and humanities. (Administrative librarian)

> I don't feel that library education beyond the master's degree can compare in value with an advanced degree in a subject area — subject specialization is of highest importance. (Reference librarian)

The chief ideas presented in the other twelve comments concerning non-library science courses are expressed in the following:

> What is needed is a sabbatical year, or a half-year, in order to get *outside the library itself*. This time could be used to study in other subject areas or to travel or to do research. Such a program is

rarely possible without resigning one's job. We need *outside* contacts. (Administrative librarian)

I have earned fifty graduate credit hours in non-library subject fields. It seems much easier for other types of professionals to continue their education than librarians. I investigated postgraduate programs in library science, but few were even relevant, so took work in other subject areas. (Administrative librarian)

Patrons want to talk to someone in a library who understands their subject field. This probably would mean advanced degrees in subject fields (not library science). This should mean such specialized subject courses *every six or seven years.* (Reference librarian)

There should be some control over electives. Courses should be selected from areas that are based on needed knowledge and skills in libraries, such as personnel management, report writing, technical reports, languages. (Head librarian)

There should be available an optional "survey course" which could be comprised of "guest" lecturers from the various university subject areas. Each "guest" lecturer would give lectures for one week (two or three sessions) covering the basic subject matter, terminology, etc., of his particular speciality (e.g., nuclear physics, biology, botany, geography, anthropology, etc.). This would provide outstanding benefits to those in specialized libraries and also for reference librarians in non-specialized libraries. (Cataloger)

Work-Study Programs

Three respondents pointed out the value of imaginative work-study programs in such terms as the following:

The library school should offer a work-study program rather than just theoretical study. Recent graduates under my supervision have no concept of the service part of the librarian's job in order to satisfy patrons' needs. Too much emphasis is on "professional" duties vs. "non-professional" duties. They should be willing to learn and know so-called non-professional duties in order to perform better as "professionals" and supervise personnel. (Head librarian)

Doctoral Programs

As there were only four specific suggestions relating to the doctoral program, each of these has been summarized below. Two of these emphasize the research orientation of such programs and the other two benefit administrators in the field who wish to gain proficiency for their positions.

> Existing doctoral programs are exclusively research oriented. There is a *parallel need* to impart a higher level of training to those who will actually be operating at a *high level in the field*, which will give them increased ability and skill in the real-life library situation. This type of program should be conceived and planned in a manner similar to the *Doctor of Business Administration programs.* (Library administrator)

> Doctoral education, or a post-MLS program, should be built around symposia: colloquia involving both faculty, practicing library administrators, and graduate students. *Interaction* of these personnel in problem-solving, decision-making processes (using case studies), preparing staff studies, rounded off with visits to appropriate institutions and *rotating internships* would add to the viability of such a program. (Head librarian)

> Both the doctoral program and the sixth-year program could conceivably be largely research oriented, with part-time residence at one of the "think-tanks" such as Hudson Institute, Rand, or Arthur D. Little, where candidates are engaged in *interdisciplinary research in relation to information science.* (Head librarian)

> The doctoral program in library science should be scholarly and research based, requiring a knowledge in depth of previous work. Such a program should make a *new contribution* to the profession. It should not be merely an inflated MLS. It should also possibly include broad cultural and scientific knowledge not directly in the field of library science; for example, a survey of the advancement of knowledge thoughout history. (Bibliographer)

Formal Education in a University Setting

Thirty-three suggestions were made to library educators covering a wide range of subjects. In the area of *curriculum development* there were four general suggestions, five comments on the relation of theory to practice (three emphasizing the practical, and two a balanced relationship between theory and practice), and five statements stressing the importance of specialization. Sample statements of the main ideas expressed in these areas follow:

> Library school deans should meet together and evolve a standard curriculum — a truly *professional* curriculum so that graduates of master's and post-master's programs will no longer have to compete with business and education majors for library jobs. (Cataloger)

> In my opinion, continuing education for practicing librarians might be divided into two fields: (1) For newer graduates, programs to keep them abreast of new policies and practices in literature, subject areas, technical processing, automation. (2) Comprehensive courses in automation, government documents and other fields which *older professionals* did not have the opportunity to take and which the *younger professionals* may not have been able to work into their MLS schedules. (Library administrator)

> Library schools should *always* be broad-based in their curricula, because one never knows in what type of specialization he may work. (Library administrator)

> Continuing formal education is not only an excellent idea — *it is essential to professional awareness and advancement.* But it should be geared to practical applications. (Library administrator)

> Courses must cover both theory and practical application. (Library administrator)

Five respondents stressed the importance of specialization in today's library in such terms as:

> The library school must take cognizance of areas of specialization — perhaps this would require lengthening the period of education, but it seems to me that librarianship is now much too diverse to avoid specialization. The content of courses for different types of libraries should be different. (Head librarian)

> It seems to me that specialization should be handled by certain library schools specializing in training people for college, for public, for school, or for special librarianship. (Head librarian)

> In the post-master's degree, specialization should be in a subject

field, whether it be chemistry, literature, or languages. This might be worked out through part-time programs developed across the country, so that this would be possible, and one could keep one's job. (Cataloger)

Since libraries are becoming technological and scientific information centers, science subject matter should be incorporated in all degree programs. (Bibliographer)

Nine respondents mentioned ideas related to methodology recommendations:

Please try to eliminate "busy" work for more practical course assignments which are geared to a particular size and kind of library in which the individual proposes to work. If he masters one kind of library situation successfully, I believe he can successfully change to another kind of library. (Cataloger)

Stress reading, reading, reading. There should be mostly discussion courses with very few students enrolled so that individual attention can be given to them, and their reading can be individually directed. There should be few written papers. (Cataloger)

Do not "over-teach" rules created by other librarians. A rule should be only a means to an end — not an end in itself. (Library administrator)

Similar to student teaching programs, practical training or internship programs should be provided for the librarian. (Library administrator)

The school should provide more opportunities for the individual to actually see other librarians at work in the field. (Cataloger)

Courses must be taught in reference to all types of materials and media, not just conventional printed materials. (Head librarian)

Attention should be focused on problems and projects such as how to deal with adverse situations, such as low budgets. The library school tends to present everything from the ideal standpoint which is *very* unrealistic. (Head librarian)

The post-MLS program should be conducted through *seminars* in the theory of library work, new developments in the field, place of automation, and personnel administration. (Head librarian)

ADDITIONAL DATA

> The course work should not be concerned with things that can be more easily and better learned on the job. (Librarian)

Two respondents urged innovative approaches:

> There are too few new ideas advanced in libraries as too much time is wasted on detail, and there is little rapport among professional librarians. This shows lack of administrative ability to create an environment that fosters creativity. Courses should be revamped to teach professionals in this area. Conventions offer little help here. (Library administrator)

> Any courses offered at a university in continuing education for the librarian should take into consideration past experiences and offer something really new and challenging — *not just a rehash* of the same old ideas taught the same old way. (Head librarian)

The responsibility of the library school to be concerned about the development of personal traits and attitudes was stressed by three respondents:

> Librarians must be taught to be more flexible. If they were more responsive to user needs, perhaps it would not have been necessary to have created information centers. (Library administrator)

> I would suggest that in all library school curricula great emphasis be placed on personal integrity, dedication to service, and above all, respect for human dignity and proper expression of appreciation for work well done. (Library administrator)

> Librarians must be concerned with the philosophy of librarianship. More concern must be given to service to patrons and less to performing other "professional duties." (Head librarian)

The remaining five suggestions covered additional points as summarized below:

> Professional certification should be formalized by a certificate from ALA/SLA with a five-year renewal dependent upon continued study and publication. The range of competence among "professional" librarians is appalling. (Library administrator)

> The library school needs to build bridges between traditional methods of library management, today's chaos, and the automated potential of tomorrow. (Head librarian)

> Whatever you do, publicize to the working librarians *widely and often* the opportunities (and necessity) of continuing education and the benefits that would derive. (Head librarian)

> The library school needs to explain to administrators that the BLS before the early 1950's was a *graduate* degree. What consideration will be given to us regarding admission to post-MLS programs? (Head librarian)

Time, Location, and Format of Courses

Twenty respondents were concerned about time and location factors which they saw as a major deterrent to continuing education of professional librarians. They made suggestions about course format, scheduling, and location of courses that would overcome these two major obstacles:

Course Format (6 suggestions)

> To realistically reach all librarians, the university library schools must realize that non-resident courses will have to be developed of a quality nature, such as programmed instruction, talk-back TV, and correspondence courses. (Library administrator)

> I am not near a library school, and although I very much want to take post-master's courses, the only way I could do it would be if I could remain in this location. I suggest TV instruction for credit as is now being done by many universities for engineers, educators, nurses and others. (Reference librarian)

> Please! Correspondence courses for federal librarians who wish to continue their education with or without credit, but are presently located where it is impossible to attend classes. (Head librarian)

> I would like some reading courses — or something based on the English system. Where I can study on my own — then take the post-master's exam. I'm not keen on being too directed as in a master's program. (Reference librarian)

Scheduling (8 suggestions)

> Not too many people can leave their present position for various reasons. As an alternate solution a series of summer sessions could be offered (cf. Russian Studies Program at Middlebury College,

Vermont, leading to an M.S. degree). Thus employees who could secure a two-months' leave of absence during the summer could still achieve the same goal at a slower pace. (Indexer)

I am very interested in obtaining a post-master's through six-week sessions — intensive — on a particular subject — broken up perhaps into three-week sessions — easy to get that amount of time on administrative leave. (Reference librarian)

Location (5 suggestions)

Have you considered *bringing the course to the librarian* rather than the librarian to the course? TIME is major deterrent for librarians in continuing education. If the school could provide the instructor to go to groups of students, then travel time for working librarians would be negated. (Administrative librarian)

Why not some extension off-the-campus courses where no library schools exist? (Head librarian)

Extended Leave (1 suggestion)

If librarians could become eligible for a type of sabbatical leave as frequently is offered educators and for the same type of time span, librarians could then attend post-MLS program without resigning. (Head librarian)

Post-MLS Study

Seventeen respondents voluntarily offered their reaction toward post-MLS education. Of these, 15 were strongly negative; only 2 were positive — to the extent of recommending that such study be required.

Negative

For a person engaged in cataloging, particularly in a large library, very little can be gained from a formal course of instruction that would directly apply to his work. The vast majority of his day-to-day activities are concerned with the details involved in applying cataloging rules and procedures required by his particular library. Apart from some general theoretical principles, which he supposedly learned in the MLS program, and an acquaintance with current developments in the field — which can be acquired from selective perusal of library literature — he must depend almost entirely on actual experience to develop his working skills. (Cataloger)

Library experience is far more important than continuing formal education. (Acquisitions librarian)

Cataloging, reference, circulation, filing, etc., can be learned in any library on the job in a short time. No need for further education. (Head librarian)

When studying for my MLS, I was so bored I rarely attended lectures. Why go back? (Library administrator)

I submit that library science is only a technique that is learned quickly, then refined and sharpened by practice and common sense; if one returns to school, the important knowledge is subject knowledge in all fields. (Library administrator)

I have a very poor attitude toward my library degree — most of my courses were simplified to the extreme, the faculty was inexperienced and/or poor teachers, and I felt after completing the five quarters that I had done nothing to earn or deserve my diploma. I have at this time no intention of ever returning to school to study library science more fully. For forty hours each week I live in a library, and I feel my time to be better spent in studying other fields. I have spoken to other degree holders who feel the same way I do about my degree. (Cataloger)

Positive

Post-MLS training should be required after one or two years experience. Then we have a better understanding of what is needed for the job. (Reference librarian)

Continuing education is essential for librarians. It should be mandatory; or encouraged by the Civil Service Commission by offering step increases or grade promotions. Courses related to an agency's mission as well as library courses are needed. Short courses or workshops should also be frequent and made available to federal librarians in all areas. (Administrative librarian)

Although not suggested in any way by the question asked, two other areas were mentioned in the suggestions to library schools: one in the area of requirements for admission to the MLS program and the other regarding the use of library technicians.

ADDITIONAL DATA

Undergraduate Requirements (7 suggestions)

To raise professional standards *do not make the entrance requirements so easy!* We are surrounded by librarians who do not think that there are countries outside of the USA, but are supposed to be making a contribution to science and advanced research in medicine. There must be more emphasis on academic preparation for librarianship if standards are ever to be raised. (Coordinator)

The greatest single deficiency is that it is possible to get, for example, a BS in physical education from some obscure but accredited school, and then with supposedly a B average, apply to library school, be accepted, and emerge with an MLS in library science — which hardly makes one a librarian. We are fighting for consideration as so-called professional librarians, but we aren't educated enough to begin with to qualify. With such a background how can anyone be anything but a highly paid clerk? And to my mind this is what the vast majority of librarians are. (Administrative librarian)

One of the main problems in library education is the lack of quality of education on the part of librarians generally. A strong and broad liberal education in one of the historic disciplines should be a basic requirement. Undergraduate degrees in education, nursing, home economics, etc., leave much to be desired in furnishing a broad liberal education that is necessary for developing good librarians. (Head librarian)

Admissions policy is one of the basic weaknesses in the profession. Much more emphasis needs to be placed on applicant's subject backgrounds. We do need people with majors in things other than history and English. Such a background does not prepare one to answer reference questions in the physical sciences or the biological sciences. Some research firms will not employ librarians for their libraries because of their lack of appropriate subject background. (Cataloger)

Before admission to library school every candidate should be required to have had some practical experience in a library. Then he will have something on which to build. (Administrative librarian)

SUGGESTIONS

Library Technicians (4 suggestions)

> Much of descriptive cataloging is really non-professional. An MLS degree is *not required* to do most of this work. Large libraries can train their own, but smaller installations need training courses. Have you given any consideration to training courses for the technicians? (Administrative librarian)

> Library schools or vocational schools should include courses for technicians. (Administrative librarian)

> Any chance of developing meaningful workshops for library technicians? There is a real need for stimulation, encouragement and training of such staff — a task which only the largest libraries can do. (Administrative librarian)

The Study as a Whole

The third section of the open-end comments page, entitled "Your ideas for the study as a whole," directed the respondents as follows:

> We would also appreciate your general or specific recommendations as we proceed with the ultimate objective of curriculum building. After going through this material, is there anything that we have omitted to ask that you feel we should know in order to do a better job for you? This questionnaire represents input from the librarians practicing in the field. Do you have suggestions or advice on other groups we should question or interview such as supervisors, users, or officials in an agency who are served by the library? If some of your ideas seem "way-out" don't hesitate to list them, as we want to consider innovative and creative approaches as well as those that are more generally accepted.

Questionnaire

Altogether there were 96 comments distributed over all grades, of which the greatest number of comments (49) related to the questionnaire itself, a favorable or neutral attitude toward the survey was manifest in 35 of these comments. Some 14 comments were unfavorable regarding some phase of the study. Some typical positive and neutral comments were:

> I am pleased to find someone asking the working librarians what they would like to, or need to, study. (Reference librarian)

191

ADDITIONAL DATA

> This is a wonderful study, long overdue, and I look for significant results. (Head librarian)
>
> There is a definite requirement for the type of program you have under consideration. (Head librarian)
>
> I would like to compliment the compilers of this study. It seems to present the most exhaustive overview of all aspects of the library and information sciences. (Indexer)
>
> I must say that this questionnaire is impressively comprehensive and very, very thorough. I do thank you very much, for asking me to take part in this study. (Reference librarian)
>
> Thank you for the opportunity of filling out this questionnaire, even though it is the most difficult one I have ever seen. I will be very interested in the results. Perhaps the most difficult part was the comparison of job importance. To me, every item is important. Some things that take only a microscopic part of my time are very important. (Head librarian)
>
> If this study could reflect the need to allow a person to move into the area of *his* greatest ability, hence being of greater service, it would be worthwhile — people get pigeon-holed in this field, and this is not good. (Administrative librarian)
>
> I'll tell you, supervisors aren't so much — they stand in need of many old maid librarians to get the work done. (Bibliographer)
>
> There's not much emphasis on medical or hospital field. (Head librarian)

The areas covered by the unfavorable comments are reflected in the following responses:

> I doubt if this study will do any more good than any of the previous studies, which have apparently done no good. These questionnaires are a terrible waste of time, and there are too many of them. (Head librarian)
>
> The definition of "professional" is unrealistic. There are many highly educated professionals in the government without a library science degree. (Cataloger)
>
> You seem not to recognize that a majority, or at least a large percentage of persons with professional training find themselves in

subordinate positions for some time after library school, and that the needs and problems of such positions also need to be defined. (Cataloger)

Although the survey is relevant to special librarianship, it is irrelevant to public librarianship. The whole structure of the survey and actual practice of public librarianship is different. (Library administrator)

It is difficult to answer many of these questions since military libraries depend so much on the present commanding officer's feeling and attitude toward them. (Head librarian)

Survey of Other Groups. The second highest category of responses in this section related to other groups that should be questioned. These fell into three main groups: officials of agencies, supervisors, and users. In addition, there were several miscellaneous suggestions outside these three categories. In all there were thirty comments relating to obtaining information from other groups.

Of the suggestions made, the largest number, thirteen, suggested user surveys. The following comments are typical of these suggestions:

Check on users. They are a very good measure of library service. (Library administrator)

Would be significant to find out what role the users assign to the library. (Personnel librarian)

Please question some honest users who won't be afraid to point out our shortcomings, and let's see what can be done about them. (Head librarian)

Users should have an opportunity to participate in these interviews. Otherwise, the information obtained tends to be one-sided and biased by the librarian's point of view. Libraries should meet needs rather than just offer services. Librarians must know what these needs are, in order to meet them with maximum effectiveness. (Library administrator)

Eleven comments suggested going to agency officials and supervisors above or outside the library. Typical of these suggestions are:

Find out what agency officials think of their libraries. Are they getting what they need? (Defense librarian)

> What role do agency officials think the library should be playing? (Public Relations)
>
> Essential to find out if agency officials think the library services are adequate. No one ever asks them. (Reference librarian)
>
> Question supervisors who are not librarians to find out what they think adequate library service should be. (Library administrator)
>
> Interview those responsible for the budget to see if it might be possible for the librarians far from a library school to take time away from work to attend programs. (Head librarian)
>
> Interviewing agency officials and non-library supervisors will point up library weaknesses which need attention. (Library administrator)

In addition there were others suggested as sources of information for the study: library school students, new graduates (who may be highly dissatisfied and disillusioned), contractor personnel. Three specific suggestions were:

> Check on the opinion of the subordinates. I think we supervisors are pretty sure we're the greatest — and we aren't. (Library administrator)
>
> A study of the relationships between various types of librarians and libraries might tend to change the study and course requirements for certain groups in library schools. (Head librarian)
>
> Believe more daring and original criticism coupled with new ideas will come from new graduate who is leaving his first job because he is dissatisfied, bored, or disillusioned. There needs to be a place for the heretic who's impatient. (Library administrator)

Deterrents to Formal Study. Five respondents stressed deterrents to formal study: nearness to retirement age, need for grants approaching salaries received, and lack of available time.

Miscellaneous Suggestions. Finally, there were twelve general suggestions, including:

> Library schools should become interdisciplinary and utilize faculty in other departments. (Library administrator)
>
> Professional associations should insist that librarians do only

professional work. This would greatly decrease the shortage of manpower in the field. (Library administrator)

Perhaps, *enforced continuing education* similar to the requirement that teachers periodically return to school would be helpful. If this is not possible, then the library school needs to initiate continual communication with practicing librarians in order to achieve a measure of continuing education. (Bibliographer)

I would like to see a survey of automated libraries. Do practicing librarians find them satisfactory? What problems turned up in automating; what solutions were found? Does automation really make for faster, more effective reference? What does automation do to staff needs? Do librarians who work in automated libraries find less or more job satisfaction than in non-automated libraries? (Library administrator)

Library schools need to "loosen up," *concentrating on needs* rather than concentrating on formal academic programs leading to a degree. (Head librarian)

Library school teachers should visit libraries and observe anonymously daily routines and problems. (Head librarian)

Our jobs would be easier if those in other professions realize the tremendous value and contribution that libraries make to the successful completion of any mission. Can you help? (Library administrator)

SUMMARY AND CONCLUSIONS

The most pertinent findings concerning the respondents' interest in post-master's study, both in library science and in other disciplines, provide insights for the curriculum builder concerning potential demand for post-MLS programs and some indications of the conditions that do presently affect demand.

Interest in Post-Master's Programs

It was found that 38.9 percent of the respondents stated that they would enroll in either (both in some cases) a post-MLS year-long program or a doctoral program in library science. The interest was far greater, however, in the one-year program (33.4 percent) than in the doctoral program (16.2 percent). The degree of interest in both of these programs was generally the same for men as for women, and the same for administrators as for nonadministrators.

It was found that as the grade level increased, the interest in the one-year post-MLS program tended to decrease. In spite of this, however, 30 percent of the respondents in the study at grades 12—14 indicated a willingness to take a post-MLS program (as compared to 38.9 percent overall demand); thus there is evidence that, even in the higher grades, there would be a considerable demand for such courses if they were provided. The findings do indicate, however, that special motivational factors would have to be taken into account if a substantial percentage of those in the upper grades are to be reached by post-MLS training. These personalized criteria are the same for the one-year program as for the doctoral program. Some practical considerations of the prospective scholars are: the need for partial or total financial support, stipulations about curricular content, leave of absence concerns, accessibility, and the desirability of flexible scheduling (figure 6).

Information which sheds light on the conditions related to curricular content is of particular interest to this study — conditions which can either lead toward participation in formal course work or discourage individuals from further study. As documented by the investigators, the curriculum-centered conditions listed in the order of highest frequency were: quality of program, courses relevant to present position, opportunity to specialize, programs that might lead to better jobs, freedom of selection from a wide variety of courses, credits that would apply to a doctorate, new content that had not been covered at the MLS level, balance between library science and subject specialization, no comprehensives or thesis, and admission requirements.

It was found that of the respondents interested in formal course programs, 29.0 percent would choose fields other than library science at the predoctoral graduate level, and 11.0 percent at the doctoral level. The most popular areas of study were: administration and management, history, and literature at the predoctoral level. At the doctoral level, history, languages, administration and management, and information science were the favorites.

Many of those who opted for courses outside library science spoke out strongly and itemized their reasons for choosing to pursue their studies in other disciplines. For example, a number of respondents said they were interested and were willing to go back for postgraduate work. But based on their past MLS experience, they would not consider

SUMMARY AND CONCLUSIONS

returning to library school. In view of the amount of interest in administration and management, it is conceivable that if a library school-based program, which was relevant and of high quality, were to be offered in this area, some of these individuals might consider continuing their education under the banner of library science.

The respondents in this study had many suggestions of ways in which the library schools could be of additional help to them in their continuing education other than through formal programs. These are grouped under the following headings:

1. The Library School as a Clearinghouse of Information
2. The Library School as a Counseling Center
3. The Library School as Educator
4. The Library School as Agent to Help Improve the Profession
5. The Library School in the Community
6. The Library School as an Implementer of Effective Legislation for Librarians and Libraries

At first consideration, it might be asked exactly what all these "extra" services on the part of the library school have to do with developing a curriculum for post-master's programs in library science. Perhaps this relationship is best summed up by quoting McGlothlin (7:29): "The [professional] school must judge itself and be judged on its influence over the full careers of its graduates. Nothing less than endless growth can be considered success." Surely today, society would gain with these respondents in validating the need for any such services to prepare practicing librarians to adjust with all considered speed to the contemporary library realities.

It is quite evident from the large number of replies to the open-end questions that many librarians feel that the library schools have not nicked the surface so far as the endless growth of their alumni is concerned. Based on their past experience, some of the respondents doubted that any post-master's programs sponsored by library schools could ever really meet their needs. Many tended to look to other disciplines and areas of study to seek the reinforcement needed in their career development. On this basis, even as McGlothlin states, they are judging the library schools and finding them woefully lacking.

Deficiencies in Professional Training

The purpose of another section of the questionnaire was to ascertain: (1) whether or not there are any formal scientific, technical, or professional courses the respondents lack which they feel would have been especially helpful in their positions; and (2) whether or not, in relation to their present position, there are any activities they should be engaged in for which their previous training has not prepared them. The following statements summarize the findings which seem especially interesting and which may provide a basis for further research and for the initiation of specific programs in continuing education at the post-master's level.

Before discussing specific course deficiencies, it should be noted that nearly one-half (48.5 percent) of the respondents (67.2 percent of the administrators and 32.8 percent of the nonadministrators) listed courses they lacked that would have been especially helpful to them in their present positions. These deficiencies, as listed by the respondents, suggest the necessity for corrective measures both at the master's and the post-master's level:

1. The fact that the highest-ranking single course deficiency was scientific and technical literature reinforces the frequent observation that the library profession as a whole is heavily specialized in humanities and the social sciences. In this connection it is significant to note that Lilley (6:122—25) found that knowledge of basic sciences (chemistry, first priority; biology, second priority) and mathematics is a most especially necessary prerequisite for the graduate education of information specialists, with the social sciences and humanities much lower on the priority scale. This finding suggests that to meet actual job requirements at the present time, the library school at the master's level might well consider requiring courses in history and methods of science, and technology and its literature.

    In addition, it should be noted that when courses were categorized by major subject areas, specialized information sources ranked first. Many respondents seemed to want not just an overall course in scientific and technical literature, but a particular speciality within science, such as the literature of chemistry, physics, or engineering. This would seem to imply that at the post-master's level there should be the opportunity for the individual to take at least a seminar in such a specialized area.

2. The second highest-ranking subject area deficiency was the administration and general management of libraries. Designers

SUMMARY AND CONCLUSIONS

of library school curricula should carefully consider the evidence here, as well as in all sections of this study, of the pressing need for more training within the library school at the master's level in the area of administration and management. Obviously, particular attention should be paid to the development of post-master's programs in this area. Based on the expressed needs of the respondents in this section of the report, two courses that would seem to merit serious consideration for inclusion at the post-MLS level would be general management and personnel administration.

3. The third highest-ranking subject area deficiency was automation. Combined with evidence of need in this area found in nearly every section of this report, the findings would seem to reinforce the current opinion prevalent among some library educators that the time has come when a basic course in automation should be a requirement at the MLS level, to be supplemented by a more advanced course at the post-master's level.

4. A final observation is related to the fact that in some schools there is pressure being exerted to drop any foreign-language proficiency requirement for the MLS degree. The data collected in this study provide evidence that foreign-language competency is an important area for many librarians today, and that the foreign-language proficiency requirement should not be dropped without further research. This point of view is reinforced by the findings in the recent research by Lilley (6:123–25), who found that knowledge of foreign languages was the second most important prerequisite (basic science, first; mathematics, third) for the graduate education of the information specialist.

Deficiencies in training led more than one-fifth (22.2 percent) of the respondents to report that they were not performing duties in their jobs which they felt they should have been. This fact is in itself a matter for serious consideration by library educators. The following specific points seem worthy of emphasis:

1. There was evidence that an administrator, rather than a non-administrator, is more likely to feel that he should be performing activities which he is not, and for which his previous training has not prepared him. Generally, this

conclusion would be in keeping with the theories of Fayol (4:7—13) and Corson (2:131—40, 155—57) that for effective performance in any position above the beginning level in the hierarchy of organization, managerial concepts and competencies must be acquired.

2. The activities most frequently listed as not engaged in because of lack of previous training were in automation. It is interesting to note that of the 23 respondents listing automation as an unable-to-be-performed activity, 20 were administrators.

3. These data brought into focus one type of job function more clearly than in any other place in the findings. Designated in the questionnaire as "Representing," this area constituted the second largest area of unable-to-be-performed activities. It covers such individual activities as public relations, publicity, report writing, editing, and the layout of publications. The findings in this section would seem to support Hall's statement (5) that good public relations techniques are not taught by library schools, and graduates are left to their own devices in the crucial facet of communication. Adequate training in this area might help to intensify efforts and improve abilities throughout the profession for reaching the nonuser of library services and for conveying to current users the full extent and potential value of library services.

4. The administrative function of planning constituted the third largest area of unable-to-be-performed activities. With the current emphasis on program planning and budgeting, as prescribed by the Bureau of the Budget for all federal facilities — and with the concept spreading rapidly to the private and public sectors generally — this would seem to be an area which should receive special attention in the development of post-master's programs. Commenting on the fact that the infusion of federal money into libraries is now forcing the library to justify how its services warrant public support, de Prospo (3:30—32) points out that it has become more readily recognized that better and more sophisticated administrative skills must be utilized by the heads of libraries, especially in the area of better planning for improving library services.

SUMMARY AND CONCLUSIONS

Knowledge, Abilities, and/or Skills for Replacement

The most striking result from the replies received from the question asking what knowledge, abilities, and skills the respondents would consider most important for a replacement was the emphasis placed on job-connected personal characteristics. The heavy response to the question (85.5 percent of the 365 respondents), which came at the end of page 12 of a long questionnaire, is in itself indicative of the importance attached to this question by the respondents. Specifically, the personality traits ranking the highest were getting along with people and adaptability or flexibility.

This emphasis on personality traits suggests two avenues of approach for this present project: (1) in addition to academic prerequisites, careful consideration of personal characteristics that seem to be necessary to the efficient functioning of the librarian in screening applicants for admission to the program as suggested by Clayton (1:84—99) and Lilley (6:3); and (2) the use of teaching methods to emphasize the importance of these characteristics, even though one might accept the premise of Hall (5:42) that they cannot be educationally "learned." However, deep implications are involved in both the above approaches and considerable research has to be done before any final conclusion is reached. The objective of post-MLS programs is to train librarians for better performance on the job. There is no way for this study to determine the measure of these characteristics in the totality of librarianship.

Suggestions from Open-End Questions

From examining in detail the wide range of comments given in response to the final open-end questions, it would seem that the following have the greatest relevance to curriculum planning at the post-MLS level:

1. New programs should be just that — "new" — based on innovative methods which make full use of the modern technology available today.

2. Relevant research findings from other disciplines, particularly the behavioral sciences, should be integrated into the content of the post-master's library science program.

3. Certain personalized criteria must be met in the post-master's

201

programs if they are to attract a large number of enrollees and so meet the profession's continuing education needs. These would include: personal satisfaction, freedom of choice, accessibility, convenience, and continuity of programs. In essence, this concept envisions the library school's accepting the technological advances now available to bring the courses and programs to the librarian wherever he may be.

Specific suggestions for meeting these personalized criteria included:

Taking the campus to the library by the development of courses utilizing the newest technology such as video tape, closed-circuit educational television, talk-back television, and radio communications networks.

Taking the campus to the library through the development of *individualized* learning centers including an inventory of equipment such as: study console; 8mm-cartridge motion picture projector; stereo tape recorder and placer; cassette player; cartridge audiotape and filmstrip projector; headphones; equipment storage facilities; desktop daylight projection screen; slide handviewer; bulletin board; chalkboard; index file; and question box.

Taking the campus to the *individual* by means of correspondence courses which could include the use of programmed instruction, cassettes, filmstrips, slides, tape recordings, telephone access to recordings, and electronic video recorder (EVR).

That admissions standards be high at the entering MLS level so that the type of persons receiving the MLS degree would be those who would later be drawn to the concept of continuing education.

That library schools take cognizance of the fact that many respondents have a strongly negative feeling toward taking further formal study in library science based on their own past experience, and that there was considerable feeling among some of the respondents that post-MLS work might be better taken in a subject field other than in library science itself. Further research on the reasons for this negative reaction might result in corrected concepts which would in turn attract librarians at the post-MLS level.

That valuable additional information relative to building post-master's programs might be sought from officials in agencies outside the library and from users of library services.

That there is a need in the profession for two types of doctoral programs, each different in its objectives, content, and approach: (1) one based on the needs of the practicing administrator which should be aimed at imparting a higher level of training to those who will actually be operating at a top management level in the field, and which will give them increased ability and skill in the real-life library situation — a program conceived and planned in a manner similar to the doctor of business administration programs; and (2) one based on the needs of those who are preparing to make a career in teaching library science or in doing research in librarianship.

That the library school must be concerned about the development of personal traits and attitudes of librarians as well as their technical knowledge and skills.

That continuing formal education is not only an excellent idea — it is essential to professional awareness and advancement.

The question arises, Are the free-response reactions of federal librarians, as summarized in this section, typical of those of other types of librarians in regard to continuing education programs sponsored by library schools? A partial answer in the affirmative to this question is found in the recent study by Stone (9:208—13) in which the respondents (MLS graduates now employed in all types of libraries) made free-response suggestions very similar to those presented in this study by the federal librarians. The participants in that study were in general agreement that the library schools should focus on formal continuing-education programs in areas in which there were definite and expressed needs by librarians in the field; that those programs should be presented in varying and flexible formats which would meet the personalized criteria of practicing librarians; that the library school had a definite responsibility to improve and increase its contacts with its graduates; and that the central focus of all programs and activities developed should be on content that could be of actual help to them in their present job situations.

ADDITIONAL DATA

REFERENCES IN CHAPTER 6

1. Clayton, Howard. *An Investigation of Personality Characteristics among Library Students at One Midwestern University.* Final Report. Brockport: State Univ. of New York, 1968 (ED 024 422).
2. Corson, John J., and R. Shale Paul. *Men Near the Top: Filling Key Posts in the Federal Service.* Baltimore: Johns Hopkins Pr., 1966.
3. De Prospo, Ernest R., Jr. "Contributions of the Political Scientist and Public Administrator to Library Administration," in: Neal Harlow and others, eds., *Administration and Change: Continuing Education in Library Administration,* pp.29—38. New Brunswick, N.J.: Rutgers Univ. Pr., 1959.
4. Fayol, Henri. *General and Industrial Management.* London: Pitman & Sons, 1949.
5. Hall, Anna C. *Selected Educational Objectives for Public Librarians: A Taxonomic Approach.* Pittsburgh: Univ. of Pittsburgh, 1968.
6. Lilley, Dorothy Brace. "Graduate Education Needed by Information Specialists and the Extent to Which It Is Offered in Accredited Library Schools." Doctor's dissertation, Columbia Univ., New York, 1969.
7. McGlothlin, William J. *The Professional Schools.* New York: Center for Applied Research in Education, 1964.
8. Peterson, Clarence E. *Electronic Data Processing in Engineering, Science and Business: Suggested Techniques for Determining Courses of Study in Vocational and Technical Education Programs.* Washington, D.C.: U.S. Office of Education, 1964 (ED 013 325).
9. Stone, Elizabeth W. *Factors Related to the Professional Development of Librarians.* Metuchen, N.J.: Scarecrow, 1969.

7
Interviews with Top-Level Library Administrators

In the preceding chapters the findings obtained through the first data-gathering instrument, the questionnaire, have been studied and analyzed. This chapter is devoted to the findings obtained from the second data-gathering instrument used in this study, namely, the interviews with top-level library administrators. It should be understood at the outset that since only 20 (14 men, 6 women) were interviewed, the data collected through the interview cannot be analyzed statistically in the same manner as the findings collected from the questionnaire. The number of interviewees was small because the total number of people in top-level library administrative positions (grade 15 and above) was only 46, as reported by the Civil Service Commission in the fall of 1969. A reflection of the attitudes and opinions of the administrators has been supported by actual quotations from the interviewees to illuminate further each concept under consideration.

The characteristics common to the twenty interviewees were: (1) they were top-level administrative personnel in federal libraries; (2) they held a grade level of GS 15 or above; and (3) they were all from one to three steps of authority above the level of professional librarian respondents who answered the questionnaire. For reasons of convenience and economy, all of the interviewees, with the exception of one, were located in the greater Washington area. As far as possible, all the agencies represented by the questionnaire respondents were proportionately represented in the interviews. The quota sampling method, based on a proportionate number of administrators for each category of positions represented in the responses received from the practicing librarians who answered the questionnaire, made it possible to compare the results obtained from the interviews with the results obtained from the questionnaire.

It was decided at the outset that each interviewee would be asked questions pertaining to a particular type of position so that the answers could be specific rather than too general in nature. Hence, each interview centered around a particular type of position. At the time of selection of an interviewee, the type of position about which he would be queried was also determined. (For a list of the positions about which interviewees were queried, see table 6, chapter 2.) The main difficulty encountered while the interview structure was being planned was how to eliminate consideration of the individual incumbent in the position about which the interview was to be conducted. It was solved by asking the interviewee at the start of the interview to think in terms of a replacement for the particular position about which he was being queried. All of the interview was then conducted with this hypothetical replacement in mind. This approach removed individual personalities from the discussion and set it in the future tense.

It should be mentioned that no attempt was made to collect additional data on the job inventory. Instead, the questions in the interview included desirable courses and competencies needed by the replacement for a particular position being discussed. In addition, several other questions of particular interest to the curriculum builder pertaining to post-MLS study were included. In conjunction with the data obtained from the questionnaire, these interviews provide some feasible guidelines for the curriculum builder by throwing light on the possible content and structure of a post-MLS program.

COURSE NEEDS AT THE POST-MLS LEVEL

The interviewees were asked about the courses most needed at the post-master's level, and at the end of the interview they completed the card sort of the 78 courses listed in the questionnaire as described in chapter 2. The objectives of the card sort were: (1) to identify and rank the courses that the library administrators agree are the most desirable for post-MLS study; and (2) to compare and correlate the assessments made by them with the assessments made by the middle- and upper-level respondents in the questionnaire. These objectives were accomplished through different methods of analysis, but it should be pointed out that the discussion in this section is limited to courses (as distinguished from workshops), and is only comparable to the category labeled "course now and/or course later" used in the analysis of the questionnaire as described in chapter 5.

Courses Selected by the Interviewees

The curriculum deck used in the card sort contained the same 78 course titles with descriptive notes as were listed for the respondents in Part II of the questionnaire. The top-level administrators (also referred to as the interviewees) were asked to examine each of these courses from the point of view of its helpfulness to the replacement in question in the successful performance of his professional responsibilities. The interviewee indicated the degree of helpfulness by putting each course card in a stack under one of the mutually exclusive categories: (1) "should have," (2) "could use," or (3) "don't really need."

Fifty percent or more of the interviewees indicated the hypothetical replacement should have the nine courses graphically shown in figure 9. Eight of the courses selected by 50 percent or more of the interviewees as being needed at the post-master's level were in the area of administration and general management of libraries. Only one, Automation of Library Processes, did not fall in that category as listed in the questionnaire.

To achieve a ranking that would include some recognition of the "could use" category into which curriculum cards had been placed, a score was established for each course according to the group into which the course card was placed by the interviewees:

Each card item rated as "should have this course"	2 points
Each card item rated as "could use this course, but not essential"	1 point
Each card item rated as "don't really need this course"	0 points

The foregoing procedure for arriving at a weighted score to use for the interviewee rankings was considered appropriate to the statistical goals of the study because the values assigned to each response represented an ordinal relationship among the three possible responses which is consistent with the card-sort operation as it was performed by the respondents.

On the basis of the weighted scores thus achieved for the course needs of respondents as perceived by the interviewees, the ten top-ranking

FIGURE 9
PERCENTAGE DISTRIBUTION OF EDUCATIONAL NEEDS OF FEDERAL
LIBRARIANS AS PERCEIVED BY INTERVIEWEES:1969

Course Number	Course Title	Per Cent
9.	Human Relations in Library Administration	75% / 25 / 0
5.	Administrative Policies and Practices	70 / 20 / 10
14.	Policy Formation and Decision Making in Library Organizations	70 / 15 / 15
26.	Automation of Library Processes	65 / 25 / 10
8.	General Management	60 / 35 / 5
6.	Communication Theory and Processes	55 / 40 / 5
10.	Innovation and Planned Change in Library Organizations	50 / 45 / 5
15.	Program Planning and Budgeting	50 / 30 / 20
13.	Personnel Problems and the Impact of Technology	50 / 30 / 20

Should Have
Could Use
Not Needed

courses (listed by number and title as found in the questionnaire) were:

	Course	Rank
9.	Human Relations in Library Administration	1
5.	Administrative Policies and Practices	2
8.	General Management	3
14.	Policy Formation and Decision-Making in Library Organizations	3
26.	Automation of Library Processes	3
6.	Communication Theory and Processes	6
10.	Innovation and Planned Change in Library Organizations	7
1.	Building and Evaluating Library Collections	8
13.	Personnel Problems under the Impact of Technological Change	8
15.	Program Planning and Budgeting.	8

Examination of figure 9 quickly reveals that the weighted scores of the course rankings by the interviewees are very similar in content to the listing of the courses chosen in the "should have" category by 50 percent or more of the interviewees. In fact, all of the same courses appear, but they are ranked in a slightly different order. Also, one additional course appears, Building and Evaluating Library Collections, which was placed in the "should have" category by 45 percent of the interviewees.

Comparison of the Course Rankings

To determine the degree of relationship between the ranking of the courses by the interviewees and by the questionnaire respondents, the rankings obtained from the weighted scores of the interviewees were correlated with the "course now and/or course later" rankings of all the 365 questionnaire respondents and with the administrative and non-administrative respondents with the following results:

Rankings of Courses by Interviewees with:	Correlation Coefficient
The "course now and/or course later" rankings of all the 365 questionnaire respondents	0.64
The "course now and/or course later" rankings of the administrative respondents to the questionnaire	0.66

> The "course now and/or course later" rankings
> of the nonadministrative respondents to the
> questionnaire   0.48

The correlation coefficients calculated above reflect the degree of concurrence between the different rankings. The correlation between the rankings by the interviewees and the respondents is not as high as might be expected. It only shows the importance of a separate survey of top-level administrators. The correlation between the ranking of the interviewees and the respondents who were administrators is of the same magnitude as the above correlation, although it could have been expected to be larger because of similarity in types of jobs, even though at different levels. However, the correlation between the rankings by the interviewees and the respondents who are nonadministrators is smaller in magnitude compared to the other two correlations. This, too, was expected because of the differences in their types of jobs.

In many instances the opinions of the interviewees have closely coincided with the view of the questionnaire respondents. However, in other instances, it is quite obvious that the interviewees have placed a different value judgment on some of the courses in the post-master's program than did the respondents to the questionnaire.

Administration and Management Courses. As one basis for comparing rankings, all the 13 courses listed in the course area entitled Administration and General Management of Libraries (questionnaire, Part II, questions 5—17, p.7) were listed side by side in table 46 and the rankings compared. It is interesting to note that of the 13 courses, the ranking by the interviewees for 9 courses was higher than that by the respondents, and for 4 of them it was appreciably higher. For 2 courses, the ranking remained the same. For 3 courses the ranking by the interviewees was lower, but for only 2 of them was it appreciably so. To what do these findings add up? The following conclusions can be drawn from this comparison of rankings within the administration and management course areas:

1. From the analysis of the data obtained from the questionnaire, the importance of the courses in administration was clear, but from the viewpoint of the interviewees it is now found that the administration courses are considered even more important for inclusion in a post-MLS program. The higher rank given some courses is so pronounced and sufficiently backed up by data obtained from the interview proper that it would seem such course or course content should be seriously

TABLE 46

RANKING OF ADMINISTRATION AND MANAGEMENT COURSES TO INDICATE EDUCATIONAL NEEDS OF FEDERAL LIBRARIANS (GRADES 9-14) AS PERCEIVED BY INTERVIEWEES COMPARED TO RANKING ACCORDING TO CATEGORY "COURSE NOW AND/OR COURSE LATER" BY ALL RESPONDENTS: 1969

Course Number	Course Title	Ranking by Interviewees (N=20)	Course Now and/ or Course Later Rankings by Respondents (N=365)	Difference
9.	Human Relations in Library Administration	1	6	+ 5
5.	Administrative Policies and Practices	2	5	+ 3
8.	General Management	3	8	+ 5
14.	Policy Formation and Decision Making	3	53	+50
6.	Communication Theory and Processes	6	17	+11
10.	Innovation and Planned Change in Library Organizations	7	48	+41
13.	Personnel Problems under the Impact of Technological Change	8	14	+ 6
15.	Program Planning and Budgeting	8	8	0
7.	Design of Library Organizations	11	11	0
12.	Personnel Administration in Libraries	15	13	- 2
17.	Theories of Organization and Management	15	48	+33
16.	Public Administration	28	62	+34
11.	Management of Records Systems in the Library	56	38	-18

considered for inclusion in a post-MLS program even though the rankings of the questionnaire respondents standing alone might not seem to warrant such inclusion.

2. The perspective of the top-level administrators in relation to a specific job is different from that of the librarians at the middle and upper level. The administrator seemed to look at a job as a part of the whole mission of the library system and tended to attach more importance to the administrative and management portion of the position than did the individual librarian, who, perhaps, did not see exactly where his individual job fit administratively into the total mission and goals of the library.

3. The top-level administrators ranked the course Innovation and Planned Change in Library Organizations much higher than did the

questionnaire respondents. The interviewee from his broader experience and perspective tended to see that a substantial part of management involves the responsibility for continual innovation and for taking the lead in bringing about changes, and therefore rated the course much higher (7 as compared to 48) than did the questionnaire respondents. This response would seem to imply that the librarian returning for a post-MLS program basically needs to be shown or taught to recognize the necessity for continual adaptation to change as well as recognition of the ways consensus for change can be achieved and implemented within the library system.

In their response, the top-level administrators seemed to be aware of and anxious to do something to correct the lethargy toward change that has characterized the profession, and seemed to be in agreement with the statement of Bundy and Wasserman (5:25—26) that

> Progress in librarianship is made by only a relatively small number. Innovation remains on trial when it should be encouraged. The field stands conservative and deeply rooted in the past at a time when such a stance exposes it to danger.

4. The greatest difference in ranking in the administrative course area was in the difference in rankings by the interviewees as compared to the questionnaire respondents). The top-level administrator frequently referred to the importance of decision-making and to that part the person in the job about which he was interviewed had in decision-making, and to the fact that so often knowledge in this area was lacking. He saw decision-making in terms of informed and debated views that needed to be presented as logical and feasible alternatives before any decision could be made; of matching resources with priorities; of being able to make compromises; and of recognizing that it is primarily a group process, and seldom the task of an all-powerful individual working alone. The respondents, on the other hand, appear not to have seen decision-making in its multifaceted aspects.

5. The importance that the top-level administrators placed on theory seemed to be grounded in their observation that managerial actions of librarians were very often based only on past experience, which might be very inadequate, or on hunches rather than on theories which have been developed, researched, and tested. The questionnaire respondents did not attach the same importance to this broader outlook, nor seem

to realize the real problems that they would need to face in this area as they move up in the organizational hierarchy of the library. The interviewees saw that theory and practice were inseparable and lamented the fact that so many librarians had never had any background or training in the theory of organization and management on which to base their practices.

6. The importance of public administration seemed to be related in the minds of the top-level administrators to gaining an understanding of the external environment — especially the governmental framework within which the librarian has to work as a part of the subsystem of his agency. They saw the library not as an isolated unit, but as an important segment in the total governmental framework. One administrator expressed it this way:

> I very strongly believe that a good course in public administration would be desirable at the post-MLS level. One thing you're not prepared for from your library training is the real problem of working in a framework of Congressional delays in appropriation, the need to respond rapidly with long-range programs; the necessity of meeting the requirements of higher administration, but the inability to do really any concrete, meaningful short-range planning because of a lack of authorization for appropriation.

7. Communication Theory and Processes was also ranked considerably higher by the interviewee than by the questionnaire respondent (rank 6 compared to 17). The importance of communication skills in the mind of the administrator was reflected not only in his ranking of this course, but also in repeated comments by a majority of the interviewees that librarianship demands skill in communications. Unfortunately, the administrators found these skills weak or lacking among librarians.

According to many of the top-level administrators, the librarian's accomplishment may depend largely on his ability to communicate with others — in writing and orally — to gather needed facts and views; to put these in terms that the user, or an agency official, or a congressman, can understand; to persuade subordinates of the wisdom of following certain courses of action; to be able to sell the library's program to users, agency officials, bosses; to put needed data in a form that his superior can use effectively for decision-making purposes; to win the confidence and support of the library's program throughout the

INTERVIEWS

agency; and to gain support for raising the library's budget. The importance of communication skills in relation to serving the user was stated forcefully by one of the interviewees:

> It is essential to understand that the core of success in a library, if you had to take one element, is the degree of communication between the user and the librarian — this is the core. Unless you have that, the house collapses on you. This is the most sensitive of all elements; I would make this a critical point above everything else.

Commenting on the common lack of communication skills among librarians, one interviewee stated:

> All these people [librarians] suffer from almost the same weakness. They've never really learned how to communicate. It's an odd thing that people in the business of transferring information are the poorest communicators that I've ever run into. They are neither able to communicate upward, nor are they able to communicate downward. The chief complaint that I get from the lower level of employees is: "We really don't know what the boss wants. We want to do what he wants; we want to do the best possible job, but nobody tells us what to do." This is the principal problem everywhere I have been. They just are unable to communicate — they can't do it verbally, and they can't do it in writing.

In summary, the top-level administrators saw skill in communication as a competency which could and should be improved and strengthened through post-MLS courses.

8. Finally, it should be noted that the course Human Relations in Library Administration ranked first with the interviewees, and sixth with the questionnaire respondents. The importance that the administrators attached to this course is further indicated by the fact that in both ways of ranking the results of the card sort performed by the interviewees, Human Relations ranked first. They also put this course into the "should have" group by a higher percentage than any of the other 78 courses; it was the only course not put into the "do not need" column by any of the interviewees. Further, it is interesting to point out that after the courses on automation, it was the first choice of the 142 questionnaire respondents who stated that they would return for a post-MLS program. It would seem that regardless of how

the data were analyzed, this course should be a prime candidate for inclusion in a post-MLS program.

Automation Courses. Perhaps the most significant difference in rankings was between the interviewees and the questionnaire respondents in the area of automation, as shown in table 47. Further, it should be pointed out that Automation of Library Processes was ranked first (listed first in the "should have" stack of cards) by only two of the interviewees, and 30 percent of the interviewees did not even include it in their "should have" group. The percentage distribution of the three automation courses in the three categories of the card sort is shown in table 48.

These statistics seem to reflect a different outlook toward training in automation on the part of the interviewees than was found among the respondents to the questionnaire. All three courses in automation, as indicated in table 30, were ranked high by the respondents (ranks 1, 2, and 3); however, only Automation of Library Processes (rank 4) is

TABLE 47
RANKING OF AUTOMATION COURSES TO INDICATE EDUCATIONAL NEEDS OF FEDERAL LIBRARIANS (GRADES 9-14) AS PERCEIVED BY INTERVIEWEES COMPARED TO RANKING BY ALL RESPONDENTS: 1969

Course Number	Course Name[1]	Ranking by Interviewees	Ranking by Questionnaire Respondents	Difference
26.	Automation of Library Processes	3	1	- 2
27.	Information Processing on Computers	12	3	- 9
28.	Information Retrieval Systems	19	2	-17

[1]The courses were described in the questionnaire as follows:
AUTOMATION
26. Automation of Library Processes: Application of computer technology to library processes.
27. Information Processing on Computers: The functions performed, and organization of computers; principles of programming and symbol manipulation.
28. Information Retrieval Systems: Structure and operation of information systems, including question analysis, search strategy, thesaurus construction.

INTERVIEWS

TABLE 48

PERCENTAGE DISTRIBUTION OF AUTOMATION COURSES TO INDICATE EDUCATIONAL NEEDS OF FEDERAL LIBRARIANS (GRADES 9-14) AS PERCEIVED BY INTERVIEWEES:1969 (N=20)

Ranking	Course Number	Course Title[1]	Should Have %	Could Use %	Don't Really Need %
4	26.	Automation of Library Processes	65.00	25.00	10.00
21	27.	Information Processing on Computers	30.00	60.00	10.00
21	28.	Information Retrieval Systems	30.00	50.00	20.00

[1] The courses were described in the questionnaire as follows:
AUTOMATION
26. Automation of Library Processes: Application of computer technology to library processes.
27. Information Processing on Computers: The functions performed, and organization of computers; principles of programming and symbol manipulation.
28. Information Retrieval Systems: Structure and operation of information systems, including question analysis, search strategy, thesaurus construction.

given a top ranking by the interviewees, while Information Processing on Computers and Information Retrieval Systems have a considerably lower priority (rank 21).

Careful observation reveals that these two lower-ranking courses are more closely allied with information science than with library science, and it may be that the interviewees made this distinction between the two areas. The interviewees did not completely eliminate Information Processing on Computers and Information Retrieval Systems as possible courses at the post-MLS level, but they did not give them a high priority, whereas the respondents seemed to attach much importance to them. From this, it is not certain that the interviewees really distinguish between information science and library science, but they certainly give lower priority to the two courses in automation which are more closely oriented to information science.

Essentially, the opinion of the interviewees toward training in automation was summed up by one of them:

> I think many schools have been a little misled about what the librarian should know about automation. Librarians need to have

an understanding of what the total library system is and how automation can help information flow through that system and increase the service output, but they shouldn't have to worry or become expert in how to use computers themselves. They don't need to be able to write a program — that is a very specialized skill and properly should be left to those trained to write programs — they need to know what kind of information to communicate to a programmer, a systems designer, and a systems analyst in order to develop an improved flow of information or improve library processes.

The fact that this attitude predominated among the interviewees is borne out in the statistics. It should be noted that two of the interviewees thought it was not necessary to offer any courses in automation at the post-MLS level at all. Their opinion was based on the fact that they thought a good basic course should be offered at the MLS level and that thereafter the librarian would be able to get the additional knowledge he needed in this area through on-the-job training and/or through attendance at an occasional workshop or seminar which would keep him abreast of the latest developments in the field.

As the more experienced top-level administrators felt that the need for courses in automation was considerably less than that indicated by the questionnaire respondents, the interviewees were queried about their reaction to the heavy demand of the questionnaire respondents for all the automation courses listed. They doubted whether close familiarity with automation processes is useful and gave such answers as:

> They are afraid that they will need all the knowledge and skills they think may be in these courses.

> They are afraid that the day may come when they will need the content of these courses, although they don't really need them in their jobs today.

Other interviewees offered the theory that perhaps the reason automation was so heavily checked was that since it now seems the popular thing to do, they wanted to get on the bandwagon of automation skills; none wanted to be left behind.

Specialized Library Courses. As the basis for comparing the rankings of selected specialized library courses, table 49 was compiled. Looking

TABLE 49
RANKING OF SELECTED SPECIALIZED LIBRARY COURSES TO
INDICATE EDUCATIONAL NEEDS OF FEDERAL LIBRARIANS
(GRADES 9-14) AS PERCEIVED BY INTERVIEWEES COMPARED
TO RANKING ACCORDING TO CATEGORY "COURSE NOW
AND/OR COURSE LATER" BY ALL RESPONDENTS: 1969

Course Number	Course Title	Ranking by Interviewees (N=20)	Course Now and/or Course Later Rankings by Respondents (N=365)	Difference
1.	Building and Evaluating Library Collections	8	38	+30
3.	Current Practices in Acquisition and Selection of Non-Book Materials	12	17	+ 5
19.	Administration of the Special Federal Library	38	4	-34
73.	Organization and Administration of Reference Systems	32	10	-22
77.	Research Development in Libraries	32	36	+ 4
78.	Statistical Theory and the Interpretation of Statistical Data for Researching	45	50	+ 5
76.	Operations Research in Library Management	24	42	+18

at these statistics, we are again faced with the question, What do they mean in the light of course offerings at the post-master's level? The following paragraphs suggest some possible implications for the curriculum builder especially when these rankings are further interpreted by comments of the interviewees:

1. In examining this comparative list of rankings for a group of specialized library courses, the most noticeable difference in rankings is between the interviewees and the respondents in relation to the course Administration of the Special Federal Library, which in the questionnaire was listed under the area cluster entitled Administration of Special Types of Library Services. After the three courses in automation, this course was most frequently checked by the respondents (rank 4), perhaps because it seemed to embody the opportunity to improve their administrative and management skills

within the bounds of a course. On the other hand, the interviewees rated this course much lower, perhaps because they felt that the knowledge and skills of library management are the same for any type of library. If the interviewees considered management the central process which is the same in any type of organization, they probably saw no practical reason for such specificity.

In fact, some interviewees stated that the things that make the federal library distinctly different in some of its specialized features, such as procurement, should be properly learned on the job. It was felt by the interviewees that the administrative courses offered at the post-MLS level should be of a depth, content, and caliber that would be basically applicable to any type of library. A further point made was that every type of library is represented within the federal library complex. One said, for example:

> I don't really see the need to concentrate just on the "Federal" library in a course in the post-MLS curriculum. Federal libraries as a group are not that different from special libraries as a whole — they are just one type of special library. They all operate within the framework of a larger organization. There are just as many differences among Federal libraries as [there are among] any other group of special libraries.

It is interesting to note in this connection that the educators (8 to 2) in the Lilley study (18:208) recommended that a related course — The Administration of the Scientific Information Center — be offered as a separate entity at the master's level. The respondents in that study felt that an organization that is different from that of business is needed where research scientists are working. Lilley stated it this way, "The difference in organization, however, is not only to accommodate the scientist, but because the organization needs his increased productivity."

The same rationale that led those interviewed to affix a much lower priority to the Administration of the Special Federal Library seemed to apply to the course entitled Organization and Administration of Reference Systems, which was ranked 32 by the interviewees as compared to a rank of 10 by the questionnaire respondents. In the reasoning of the interviewees, basic courses in organization and administration would apply to a reference system as well as to any other system, and there was no reason to separate this particular type of service for a special course.

219

2. The interviewees evaluated the course Building and Evaluating Library Collections much higher than did the questionnaire respondents (rank of 8 compared to a rank of 38). As one interviewee phrased it, "I like to think in terms of collection development in which the person responsible translates successful book selection into a development program that will benefit the whole library."

The Acquisition and Selection of Non-Book Materials rated considerably higher in the minds of the questionnaire respondents, but it still lagged a bit behind the value assessment placed on it as a course at the post-MLS level by the interviewees (rank of 15 compared to a rank of 17 for the questionnaire respondents). Several of the administrators spoke of the importance of the library's increasing its acquisition of nonbook materials, especially audiovisual. One commented:

> We have got to bring to the library an awareness that books and periodicals are basic, but not all inclusive in the library's collection. Audio-visuals are here to stay and must be used in the library, not in a vacuum, but in conjunction with our other collections.

It should be pointed out that the questionnaire respondents recognized the need for additional training in acquisition of nonbook materials as well as in building and evaluating library collections generally. They felt, however, that these added concepts were best offered through the workshop format, ranking the course Building and Evaluating Library Collections second, and Current Practices in Acquisition and Selection of Non-Book Materials fourth in the workshop format.

3. In spite of the fact that some library leaders like Joeckel (13) as far back as 1939 emphasized the value of using applied research as an active management tool in libraries, and in spite of an increase in recent literature and conference programs emphasizing this concept, it was apparent both from the replies of the interviewees and from the respondents that the value of applied research within the library had not been widely accepted by them. In fact, one of the interviewees, seeing this deficiency, stated:

> I don't think we do nearly as much research in our libraries as we should. That's one of the reasons we're vulnerable when they say, "Well, really, is librarianship a profession? Are you really professional people?"

Inasmuch as it was apparent that neither the interviewees nor the questionnaire respondents give a high priority to research as a part of the curriculum at the post-master's level, it can be surmised that both the groups believe in a separate or differentiated type of training for the practical administrator and/or practicing librarian from that for the librarian who is returning to take further postgraduate work in order to do research or to teach.

As research was not rated highly among the interviewees and the respondents, it is not surprising that the course entitled Statistical Theory and Interpretation of Statistical Data for Researching did not rate high with either group, although it received a higher ranking from the interviewees than from the questionnaire respondents. Several interviewees spoke, however, of the value that statistics could be to the profession. One implied that the reason research was not accorded a high priority was that librarians did not have an adequate concept of the use of statistics and, believing that it was necessary for competent research in applied situations in the library, assiduously shied away from such research efforts. He stated it this way:

> There should be no question; there should be at least an elective course in statistics available at the MLS level. I don't think that every person who works in a library should know statistics, but I do think that a lot of people need to know a lot more of statistical research methods — not at a high level, but at least at a level which gives them confidence to experiment. From teaching in a library school, I know that lots of our library students know nothing in this area (probably as high as 90 percent). It was difficult for them to even read library literature that included any statistical concepts, let alone literature from other disciplines. If we hope to make applied research a common experience in libraries, students must have at least an elementary introduction to statistical methods.

Several of the interviewees stated that they thought statistics should be interwoven into nearly all the administration courses, that problems or simulated exercises should be provided that would necessarily involve the use of statistics, and that this would be a better form of training than having statistics offered as a separate course at the post-MLS level. However, when the course Operations Research in Library Management was examined, it was found that the interviewees gave an appreciably higher ranking to it than to Statistical Theory and Interpretation of Statistical Data for Researching. This preference would

INTERVIEWS

seem to support the view, already mentioned, that in the minds of practicing library administrators, most post-master's courses should be professionally oriented to on-the-job rather than to research situations. In this particular case, it would seem that the interviewees felt that Operations Research in Library Management would have more job applications for practicing librarians than would Statistical Theory, which presumably (at least to the interviewees) is oriented more toward research use.

Information Science Courses. Just as the administration and the automation courses were singled out and analyzed by comparing rankings, so courses from the questionnaire related to the area of information science are presented with comparative rankings. An examination of them, as presented in table 50, reveals that for all the courses the rankings by the interviewees were less than the corresponding rankings given by the respondents. This situation is almost the reverse of the case with the administrative courses, where the rankings for the interviewees were, in almost all cases, higher than those of the

TABLE 50
RANKING OF COURSES RELATED TO THE SUBJECT AREA OF INFORMATION SCIENCE TO INDICATE EDUCATIONAL NEEDS OF FEDERAL LIBRARIANS (GRADES 9-14) AS PERCEIVED BY INTERVIEWEES COMPARED TO RANKING ACCORDING TO CATEGORY "COURSE NOW AND/OR COURSE LATER" BY ALL RESPONDENTS: 1969

Course Number	Course Title	Ranking by Interviewees (N=20)	Course Now and/ or Course Later Rankings by Respondents (N=365)	Difference
57.	The Scope of Information Science	51	17	-34
94.	Systems Analysis in Information Science	51	22	-29
54.	Equipment and Instrumentation	61	53	- 8
55.	Linguistics and Information Science	61	42	-19
60.	Cybernetics and Society	67	56	-11
56.	Mathematical Techniques for Information Science	69	42	-27
22.	Information Center Administration	71	22	-49

222

respondents. This would seem to indicate that as far as these courses related to information science are concerned, the interviewees as a group gave them a lower priority than the respondents did.

One explanation for this could be that the interviewees were answering in regard to one particular type of position, and for the position discussed they saw little need for courses in information science at the post-master's level. Another explanation might be, as was suggested in the section comparing the automation rankings, that the interviewees felt that skills involving specialization in information science techniques such as systems design and programming were better performed by specialists brought into the library for that purpose, and that such functions did not constitute the role of the librarian. Further, in some of the libraries represented, much of this type of responsibility is concentrated in a centralized office, and the librarian in the field has little direct involvement.

MOST-NEEDED SKILLS AND COMPETENCIES AT THE POST-MASTER'S LEVEL

The data presented thus far in this chapter give a summary of the types of courses that the top-level administrators considered most important for inclusion at the post-MLS level, and compare them with the highest-priority courses as suggested by the questionnaire respondents. Another purpose, however, for interviewing these administrators was to obtain suggestions about the content and structure of courses which are to be taught at the post-master's level. The data thus supplied provide additional information for determining behavioral objectives and in developing specifications for model courses for a post-master's program. The opinions of the interviewees, therefore, stressing skills and practices they recommended for inclusion in post-MLS education, add an extra dimension to the whole study and complement the job-inventory section of the questionnaire.

This extra dimension was accomplished by asking the interviewees to list the skills and competencies over and above those achieved at the master's level which they felt were necessary to perform more efficiently the job about which they were being queried. As the object of the project is building courses, and since these skills and competencies are to be translated or incorporated into terminal behavioral course objectives, the data were analyzed from the point of view of three broad area clusters of courses: (1) administration, (2) automation, and (3) specialized library courses. Most of the skills and competencies suggested by the interviewees fell in the first two areas. This division in itself is an indication of the degree of importance they attached to the administration and automation activities of the librarian.

In the following sections the interviewees' suggestions regarding skills and competencies are presented largely in their own words under the broad areas of administration and management, automation, and courses in specialized subject areas. A note of caution needs to be inserted here, however, against putting too much weight on the findings from the interviews, as they stand alone and are the central focus of this chapter. It must be kept in mind constantly in reading the data in this chapter that the interviews constituted only a small part of the study and were designed chiefly as an extra dimension, or a supplement, to the data that were obtained from the basic study, namely, the questionnaire responses from 365 practicing librarians (grades 9 through 14) as presented in chapters 3 through 5.

Further, it must be remembered that the findings are based on the reaction of the interviewee to needs concerning the replacement for just one job about which he was being queried. Finally, it should be emphasized that the findings in this chapter represent spontaneous free-response answers to general questions posed to only twenty interviewees, so no precise statistical findings can be presented as a result.

Administration and General Management of Libraries

As reported in the previous section, the interviewees gave the highest priority for training at the post-master's level to courses in the area of administration. In this section it is found that answers of the interviewees to a general question asking what competencies they felt were most needed for the hypothetical replacement for the particular job about which they were being queried covered a wide range of administrative concepts, skills, and practices beyond those possessed by the average MLS graduate. The knowledge and skills were thought to be necessary because the MLS graduate's first position usually involves him in some specialized library activity, such as cataloging, acquisitions, reference, or circulation. He soon finds himself, however, in a position of supervising others.* This situation was recognized by Kortendick (16:92) in an article on the curriculum of administration in library education:

> If capable, periodically they [library school graduates] will move up to new tasks for which they are not yet adequately prepared, and by the time they master one work level they will be moved on to another. If the rise is too spectacular, the young top administrator may begin to stagnate, lacking the stimulation of a supervisor or of competition.

The dilemma of this situation within the sphere of ongoing library activity was described by one of the interviewees:

> An individual comes to us with a master's degree and takes a position cataloging, and gains a facility for cataloging our materials according to our set of procedures. That is all we require, and probably all that can be required. However, when we go looking for people to promote we look for people who have certain abilities as supervisors, but they are very hard to find. If there could be training for the individual which would include administration courses which emphasize the things that a supervisor should know and how he should act under certain circumstances, it would be the most valuable post-master's training you could give.

Increased skill in supervision, however, was but one area in the broader area of administration in which the interviewees saw a need for further training. As one interviewee stated:

> Regardless of the type of library, there is a vast array of administrative problems that always exists. For example, the information systems that we are trying to build in libraries today cut across organizational lines, and this makes the necessity for expertise in administration greater than ever before. The librarian often has to direct the work of others from some distance. In

---

*Regarding the rapidity of advancement, it was found in Stone's recent study (27:256) that 67.4 percent of the graduates who have been in library work for 5 years had achieved administrative responsibility either as library director, associate or assistant librarian, department or division head or branch head; of those who had been out of library school 10 years, 78.8 percent were in administrative posts. The graduate out 10 years was supervising an average of 15 employees; the 5-year graduate, an average of 11 employees.

addition, they may have skills in which he is not an expert. Increasingly, he has to achieve the goals of the library through those who are not his subordinates, but whose support he hopes to win. He has to develop skills as a communicator, as a long-range planner, as a decision maker, [and] as a negotiator for the library.

The opinions of the interviewees regarding the precise competencies in the field of administration and management revealed what they felt are most necessary for efficient performance. To the curriculum builder, the data about desired knowledge and competencies beyond the MLS degree can be useful in determining the courses to be offered and in focusing on skills and practices that deserve special emphasis within courses to be developed at the post-master's level.

In what competencies and skills do the interviewees feel librarians most urgently need to have additional training in a post-master's program? Those mentioned most often in the free-response conversations with the interviewees were: capacity for directing others — including interpersonal skills and employee motivation (18)*; communication skills (16); understanding the management process (15); skill in decision-making (13); skill in program planning and budgeting (12); developing and merchandising user services, including public relations and publicity (11); innovation — taking the lead in bringing about changes (10); and gaining an understanding of systems design and analysis, including understanding of networks (10). After these activities, there was a drop in frequency: understanding the external environment outside the agency (6); understanding the other units in the agency (5); cultivating a sense of social responsibility, which in turn is revealed in user services (3); managing by objectives (2); and mention of other single skills or practices (5).

The added competencies (beyond those received at the MLS level) which were given the highest priority in the free-response statements of the interviewees are indicated by the following eight generalizations about the role and expertise desired of the professional librarian in the area of administration and management. In addition, appendix table 23 relates these added elements as suggested by 50 percent or more of the interviewees to the major job functions and courses as listed in Parts I and II of the questionnaire.

"Skill in the capacity for directing others is probably the most universally needed added competency," one interviewee stated. His

---

*The numbers in parentheses indicate the number of responses.

opinion in this regard was borne out in conversation with a majority of the interviewees. However, within the term "work direction" a number of supervisory competencies were singled out for special comments: ability to perceive the attitudes, expectations, and values of subordinates; skill in interpersonal relationships; ability to delegate; ability to discern what motivates employees to develop to their full potential.*

In general, the importance they gave to skills in this area are borne out in the words of the interviewees:

> The main thing I would look for in relation to the replacement for this position [branch head] would be the administrative ability to direct the work of others, to develop staff to their full potential, and the ability to supervise the total operation without having to do all of the work himself.
>
> The librarian has to deal with a whole array of unstructured problems involving interpersonal skill in dealing with subordinates. Often motivation of those he is working with may be the supervisor's chief concern. Training in human relations is needed at the post-master's level, I think, if any real gain is to be made in understanding these areas, however, cooperative arrangements will have to be made with faculty from other disciplines (especially psychology) to become directly involved in the development and presentation of the program.
>
> Supervision involves directing small groups and large groups, as well as individuals. Training in group dynamics is needed in order to do an effective job in this area.
>
> The capacity to direct others is the ability to motivate, and personality makes the difference. Therefore, those selected for further training in this area should have the capability to grow in the understanding and practice of human relations concepts.
>
> One of the most important aspects of work direction is realizing the potential represented by the people currently working in the library. This implies laying out duties within the library; the fitting, adjusting, and adapting job assignments to an individual's

---

*The interviewees also included a number of communication skills while talking about the capacity for directing others, but because communication skills were spoken of so forcefully and by such a large number of the interviewees they are separated for special consideration in the following section.

particular abilities so that each individual can develop the talent necessary to meet the library's objectives. This means knowing how to assign work to all who work in the library — the college graduate without library training, the clerk, the high school page, the volunteers.

Rather than stating one particular competency, I would like to group the three which I think are the most important together: good human relations, good staff relations, good public relations. In other words, the image of the person should be a very positive one, as one who can get along very easily both with the agency and without. In terms of administration and supervision, but also just keeping everything on a positive keel, the person should have positive attitudes rather than negative, toward both the library and its future and librarianship. Also, it should be a person who not only is good in what he is doing now, but seems to show potential for future growth. He should be interested in the new developments, he should not be dragging his feet.

There is an urgent need at the post-master's level to improve communication skills. The ability to communicate (and be communicated with), as well as the importance of understanding the significance of the many facets of communication, was mentioned more often in the free-response conversation than any other single competency discussed — 16 out of 20 interviewees stressed the ability to communicate as being extremely important, mentioning it almost immediately when asked the general question about added skills needed. Several interviewees stated that it was *the* most important and critical area in which they thought learning was possible through training and, therefore, a prime candidate for coverage in the post-MLS program. The urgency of providing added training in the area of communication is portrayed vividly in the words of the interviewees themselves:

> Many librarians have trouble in expressing what they know. I have often had people come to me with problems of classification in their grades, and in almost every case the job descriptions had not been stated in such a way that they would be intelligible to a classifier who did not know the library. The same problem occurs when they present programs to management: they rarely explain their program fully enough or graphically enough.

Basically, I think librarians need a tremendous amount of training in how to present programs. It seems to me that most of the difficulties that the federal libraries are having are concerned with their relations to management. They aren't able to sell a program, and it seems to me they need to be trained in just presenting information about their programs. They need to learn how to think about a program; you can't present a program unless you've done some systems analysis.

I think there should be a course in how communication occurs — what's supposed to happen. Communication doesn't occur unless there's a reaction — the concept that a noise is not a noise without an ear to hear, that communication doesn't occur unless someone hears and reacts. There is no communication unless something happens — unless there is feedback.

I think one of the things you could successfully teach at the post-master's level, especially in higher echelons, is how to present data — communication in the sense of how to give background information in an organized fashion so that the data can be used for decision-making. Many librarians can't do this either verbally or in a written form. For example, they should be able to develop a position paper, a summary of what are the issues, what is the background information, how did this originate, what are some possible solutions, what do they recommend be done. For important things, it should be written; for other things, it can be informal.

We need improved communication skills in so many areas of library work. For example, in order to interview a systems analyst with ease and to discuss the problem at hand — to be able to sit down in a quiet place and discuss the information needs of the library in relation to his problem of finding a solution.

I find that on every professional level, it is very difficult to find librarians able to write and prepare position papers, to prepare a paper on a special service or idea that they have, even an announcement explaining the background and purpose of a service. It's not only report writing they can't do, but just preparing a simple position paper. Unless librarians can succeed in voicing their ideas (which are often excellent) in terms that management and the clientele understand, they have failed in the communication process.

229

INTERVIEWS

Librarians need post-MLS continuing-education opportunities to develop a fuller understanding of the management process. Emphasis in the program offered at the post-master's level should be, the interviewees recommended, on skills of management and the attitudes appropriate to their effective use. Emphasis on skill in application, rather than on knowledge itself, suggested to the interviewees that the program should provide opportunities for practical problem solving with less emphasis on lecturing, listening, and note-taking. The value of using simulations which would approximate real-life library situations and give students valuable training in both problem solving and achieving effective interpersonal relations was stressed by some of the interviewees. The necessity of the interdisciplinary approach to deepening the librarian's understanding of management was also emphasized. Several interviewees suggested that the development of such a program should have close working relationships with practicing library managers.

> The chief added element I would look for in a replacement in this position [head of a department] would be a greater understanding of management — the whole idea. When I look at a library, I don't think of it as any different from a business. The bigger it is the more it is like any other business enterprise. You need the same management skills for both.

> One urgent need is providing training in skills to improve their ability as managers. They are not good managers; they are not good organizers; they don't have a systems approach to management. Rather, they sort of crawl into their library and let the rest of the world go by.

> A person in this position should primarily realize that libraries operate as part of a larger system — no library is an island. The important thing is to see how to relate to the system as a whole. I think the bigger management picture is more important for them to get at the post-MLS level than any specialized type of library subject. Management knowledge from other disciplines should be part of the tools of contemporary librarianship; such concepts should become the common knowledge of our profession.

> When I look for someone to fill this position [head cataloger] I don't look for someone with great competency in cataloging — we have that in journeyman catalogers. I look for someone who can analyze what's going on in our system; who can analyze the staffing requirements; who can organize the cataloging department

so it relates to other functions of the library; who can relate it to other libraries, who can motivate the staff to production. In addition, this person should have ability to direct others, to coordinate, to use analytical techniques. In short, I am chiefly looking for a good manager.

Considerable attention needs to be given at the post-master's level to developing skill in the decision-making process. The interviewees pointed out many facets of the decision-making process and believed that at the post-master's level, training should be given which would unify all these elements:

Competence in decision-making is the chief added competency needed by the replacement for this type of position [head of a library]. This involves the ability to establish priorities in the use of resources: people, money, and collections. Since we cannot do everything that is considered ideal in operating libraries, we have to make many compromises: people have to have an ability to match the needs of their bureaus — needs that are not always specified very clearly by their heads — to be able to match these needs with existing resources and then be able to negotiate, to convince the users to hold the line in their demands.

How do they work under extreme stress? They need an ability to operate independently, using the most general guidelines. They need to understand all that goes into decision-making.

The ability to adapt and to set priorities comes into play; knowing when to step back and when to step forward. Alternative features can be built into the program, knowing what they do about librarianship. I think what I have been describing is a *decision-making ability*. If I had my way, librarians would be trained in only two things: the general characteristics of librarianship — what can be done in libraries (what are the technologies with which we deal in librarianship) — and decision-making training.

Decision-making should be emphasized — the willingness to do it rather than knowing how. I have to force some of my people into making decisions.

It is necessary to educate your clientele. Tell them what service you can give them. In a way it is all a matter of advertising. Your service has to be promoted. For example, we give an hour slide presentation of the type of information service we give plus a walk through our operation to demonstrate just how we operate and conclude the session by giving them samples of our products (reports, etc., we have produced). This pays off in building confidence levels and making people aware.

No matter how good your service is, it won't reach the maximum number of users unless you publicize it.

Communicating with users, finding out what they need and telling them what the library can do for them: I think this is one of the greatest weaknesses. We do not communicate what the library is and can do for us.

One of the major problems within the profession is that we've been prone to communicate just within our own little world. This is perhaps because we have been shy and haven't been responsive to the newer needs of the science and research people and, now, the disadvantaged. Perhaps we need to bring the behavioral scientist or the sociologist to the library school.

I consider the most important added element is the degree of communication between the user and the librarian. This, to me, is the most critical emphasis that should be made at the post-master's level.

The necessity of the library's manager recognizing and accepting responsibility for continual innovation, that is, for taking the lead in bringing about changes which will make the library more consistent with contemporary organizational requirements. Much of the library manager's time, the interviewees believed, should go into activities (resulting from long-range planning) that are undertaken to make changes in pervading policies, to improve the processes and procedures, and to adapt organizational arrangements to the new technology. The interviewees felt that one reason the librarians were hesitant to innovate was their lack of familiarity with new research-based developments in related fields which would give them a broader perspective and would tend to make their approach to library problems more change oriented.*

*Wasserman (30), in his paper on library and information center management, makes an important distinction between innovation and imitation. Genuine innovation, he states, requires the kind of research and development activity which is far more costly than adapting procedures and arrangements which have already been plotted, developed, and implemented elsewhere. To the interviewees in this study, innovation was chiefly related to the imitative process based on results already successfully obtained elsewhere, rather than on research and development activity within the library itself.

232

SKILLS AND COMPETENCIES

One of the things a library staff is paid for is to suggest and implement innovations, to create new programs, and to improve them. That is one of the most important things a staff can do. But it just doesn't happen. They are all bright people, but they haven't been trained (or motivated) to come forth with things they feel. Perhaps if they were more familiar with management literature in other areas they might understand that a part of management involves the responsibility for continuous innovation.

The library manager must be willing to assume active leadership in the effort of making changes within the library. The profession has been quite slow in keeping current; I find it extremely hard to convince people that librarianship is any different today than it was 20 years ago.

To be able to develop a skill to negotiate changes, to make them move faster (or to make them slow down) is an exceedingly important area and one in which I am most troubled at the present time. But the question in my mind is: Can formal education do very much in this area? It takes a very thoughtful leader with constant attention on what he is doing with people over a period of time. If it can be shown that training at the post-master's level can help the individual develop this type of skill, then certainly it should be offered.

The practicing librarian should have sufficient familiarity with the concepts and phases of systems study — analysis, evaluation, and design — to be able to work cooperatively toward increasing the efficiency and productivity of the library, whether or not there is an automated system within the library. The key word here is *cooperatively* for the interviewees seemed in agreement with those who have written in the field (Chapman, Minder, Asheim, Wasserman) that librarians have different roles to play in a library systems study which represents a demanding total library effort involving the entire library staff. For example, in addition to creating an atmosphere conducive to systems study throughout the library, the head librarian should play a leadership role by being fully involved in planning the study and by being responsible for appointing a library systems analyst (preferably trained in librarianship, as well as systems analysis and design as taught in modern management courses) to conduct the study. Only with the support and involvement of the total library staff, however, will the resulting system design and its implementation achieve the desired objectives.

INTERVIEWS

As an introduction to the comments by the interviewees, it should be noted that there are generally two types of major systems in a library: (1) the data-processing system which is involved with methods to improve the efficient management operations within a library, and (2) the informational system which has as its objective the library's service requirements and goals (Chapman, 6). Some interviewees addressed their remarks to both, some to only one. Some expanded the systems concept farther to include the point of view of "being a part of a network or networks of librarians throughout the United States and what the librarian's part should be in that total system."

> The element I think that needs most to be added by the library school is to make the librarian realize that the library is a total system whose object is to provide information. Every librarian should think of his job as being part of a whole, rather than as a separate segment; actually the whole function — the end product — of what all are doing is providing information. Each step ties into the next one; it's necessary to break down completely any barriers or any idea that what you do in reference is different from what you do in cataloging. This concept — held by all the staff — is basic to any successful systems study or implementation in a library.

> All librarians do not need to be skilled in systems designing, but they should be skilled enough in analyzing the functions within their library in order to specify what they want from their system and be able to communicate these objectives to the professional designer who can then analyze inputs and outputs with great detail and be able to discover what problems exist and how to design a new system that will correct these conditions.

> I think that courses in systems study should pay less attention to analysis — collection of information, flow-charts and their symbols — and give more attention to the fundamentals of systems design, of information systems design. Even if the librarian does not design the system by himself, he will better be able to relate to the professional systems designer if he has had such training.

> Every librarian should have sufficient know-how to be able to interact with a systems designer and know what his objectives in life are — the way he looks at life. The basic objective should be to further the objectives of the library by improving the flow of information through the library. The basic interest should be in moving toward building an information system which, although it

interacts with the actual physical movement of materials through the library and may result in improving the flow of these materials, has as its chief objective not to improve the flow of material, but to build an information data base. The real world of information is not the world of physical things. It implies a different way of looking at things than the way an industrial engineer would look at them, and that is why it is advantageous to have a system designer who is also trained in library science.

The importance of this area of administration was further stressed in a different context in the interview. In the questionnaire it was found that the respondents spent an average of 9.1 hours a week doing avoidable detail work. When the interviewees were asked if they saw any solution to this situation, they confessed that there was no magic solution they could offer. Fifty percent of the interviewees, however, saw it as primarily an administrative problem revolving chiefly around the fact that the respondents did not understand the system and consequently could not make the system work for them. It was possible, the interviewees observed from their experience, to get sufficient clerical help and library assistants so that time could be spent by the professional staff on professional work.

Several interviewees believed the difficulty was that administrators were not able to plan for a staff sufficient and competent to fulfill the system's requirements under the currently applied methods and procedures. Such ability requires knowledge of the capacities and skills or special training of all individual workers and the ways of reassigning jobs to workers to fit their levels of competency and their potential.

> Unfortunately, most of our people do not have this kind of awareness. They see themselves as library operators. They lack the systems approach to the whole information system we are trying to develop. They see their function as only seeing that the circulation desk is manned, and that the procedures are set up. They don't see themselves as promoters or advancers of the total library system.

> It's primarily an administrative problem. There are ways of getting around the red tape and getting the support needed, but so many librarians, especially those in the field, don't seem to have the kind of skill necessary to bring about the needed change. If the librarian isn't completely aware of the potential that is available to him and the channels that he must use in order to

> accomplish certain things and procedures, he's in pretty poor shape.

One of the interviewees succinctly expressed the attitude of an administrator with sufficient familiarity with the concept of system study — an attitude which is conducive to curtailing such waste of manpower and which enables librarians to realize their full potential:

> I ask frequently, "Do you do anything you shouldn't be doing — anything unprofessional?"

Automation

Although the administrators' expression of need for post-master's training in automation was, on the whole, less extensive than that of the questionnaire respondents, some of the interviewees took the occasion to speak of the concerted effort necessary at the post-master's level in this subject. The profession, they felt, needs to understand the full capabilities of the modern technology. They stated that to use it to benefit library service, it was necessary for the leaders in the profession to understand the potential offered by automation. If major improvements in library service were not made by librarians, then society would turn to other agencies to supply its information needs, as predicted in the report of the National Advisory Commission on Libraries (14:321).

Speaking of the universality of the need for correctly relating librarianship to automation, one interviewee stated:

> Every library is probably going to be involved directly or indirectly with automation in the next decade. Every librarian, therefore, needs to have an understanding of how the computer can help, both in improving library procedures and in increasing the speed and accuracy with which data can be supplied to the user. Training in automation is a necessity.

The general feeling of the interviewees seemed to be that today it should be expected that every working librarian should have had some introduction to the use of automated procedures in the library, but that for those that had had no such exposure a library school course should be available. They seemed also to be of the opinion that those who had been exposed to an introductory course during their MLS training should have the opportunity of taking a more advanced automation course.

To keep abreast of rapidly changing developments in technology that make automation a viable tool in the library, the interviewees pointed out, takes more than exposure in one course: it takes continuing education. Two interviewees stated:

> Every librarian needs a basic course in automation, and the library school should be able to come up with one that would meet the need. But I don't think it's something you can expose a person to for a semester and forget it. Once they have one course, they are then involved and motivated to go onwards. Once their attitude toward the computer and computer-related things has been favorably altered, if they are not offered other courses, they should at least be offered periodic seminars or workshops to keep them up-to-date with changes in technology.

> The librarian needs to express a confident willingness to work with superiors in adopting as many automated routines and practices as we can build into the normal library set-up. It takes more than just an open mind; it takes a willingness to do some continuous learning on one's own.

The interviewees were almost unanimous in their feeling that courses in automation at the post-master's level should be based in the library school, and that it was up to the school to structure courses so that they would be able to meet the librarians' varying degrees of familiarity with the subject matter. One approach to this problem was seen in the modular design of courses, in which the student might not be required to take those modules which were already familiar to him.

In discussing the free-response answers of the interviewees regarding what they considered were the chief skills and practices the librarian should have presented to him in a course at the post-master's level, it must be remembered that the interviewees — 65 percent of them — thought the replacement for the job about which they were being queried "should have" the course in automation of library processes, and that only 30 percent thought the replacement "should have" the courses in information processing on computers or information retrieval systems as indicated in table 48. Therefore, the preponderance of the skills and competencies detailed by the interviewees are related to this opinion of what the course should be. And as cautioned in the preceding administration section, it must be remembered that the interviewees were giving free responses in relation to just one position about which they were being questioned.

INTERVIEWS

The interviewees were generally in agreement on the type of skills and competencies that were most needed at the post-master's level in automation. A large proportion of their comments, directly or indirectly, related to the role they felt the librarian should play in relation to automation. From these statements drawn from a cross section of federal library experience at the top administrative level, five generalizations can be drawn about automation at the post-master's level:

There are certain basic concepts which should be included in the automation course at the post-master's level. The student should see that automation is really a branch of modern logic, and the presentation of the course should be more philosophical than that typically made by either the Civil Service Commission or the hardware producer. Broader philosophical concepts should be stressed. Technicalities can be learned on the job, but the broader concepts will usually not be presented there, or if they are presented, are not apt to be given completely and correctly. When a librarian is trained to appreciate these principles, he will learn to look at the computer not only as a means to encompass a given function but also — taking the total systems approach — as a utility in terms of all other related functions. A total systems approach demands great detail in system study. On the basis of such study, long-range planning can be considered, and the problems defined by later research and development. Indeed the experimental character of systems installation permits only incremental change to automation.

The librarian needs to know enough about automation to see how it can be applied to different systems. In other words, he needs to think of automation in terms of: (1) the data-processing system which supports internal operations of the individual library; (2) the information system which is concerned with storing and retrieving information to meet the needs of his library's clientele; and (3) the network of libraries throughout the United States and the individual library's part in that total system. Installation of systems is seldom considered as complete and fixed. No major automated information system which is presently operating, including systems in the military, is designed completely from the ground up and turned on for a whole library.

All of the interviewees stressed the importance of mastery of terminology in the field of automation. In the world of automation and information systems, labels are often attached to the basic concepts which are very misleading. The most usual connotations of many words do not apply: for example, *information, channel,* and *capacity.* These semantic difficulties warn that "things are not as they seem" and that the precise meaning for the terms used must be arrived at by the student. He must handle the jargon well enough to understand a textbook on computer operation — and what is meant by "library automation," what stage it has reached, and what directions it may go in the future. The science is further complicated by the use at this time of several different computer languages. It was agreed that the student must have some general knowledge of the more widely used languages since it is important that he understand language level and control.

The librarian must be aware of potential applications of automation in his library. This awareness would include knowing basic existing applications, advanced applications now technically possible, and future possible applications. The time is rapidly approaching when every competent library administrator, like every other professional practitioner, will find it necessary to be well enough versed in automation to read the literature, listen to salesmen, observe applications in other libraries, and judge the adequacy of their findings and claims for his own library *for himself.* This skill is no more than is expected of other professional practitioners in disciplines relevant to their work. In other words, the librarian needs to be immersed in, but not completely merged with, or submerged by, the computer-automation tide. He must learn the exact nature of the computer applications that have been made in his library and those that can be made. Thus he would need to determine those outputs that can be automated in his library. The course should not only teach what the computer can do, but it should show the various uses to which products of the computer can be put. Applicable uses are phototypesetting and card preparation. The limitations of library automation in relation to his library should be understood. For long-range success in automation it is just as important that the librarian be as discriminating in his automation efforts as he is enthusiastic. It is undeniable, too, that he will be subject to pressures from those who will presume upon his ignorance. Computer salesmen are not alone in educational establishments in seeking to foster their own goals upon unarmed librarians.

One interviewee also pointed out:

> The course should not only teach what the computer can do, but it should show the various uses to which the products of the computer can be put, including at least some techniques such as phototypesetting, preparation of catalog cards — the type of

activities that librarians become involved with which are peripheral to the computer itself.

The areas of possible library use of automation mentioned by the interviewees included computer-based acquisitions systems, serials systems, circulation systems, as well as applications in reference and indexing. Many interviewees thought the librarian should understand MARC (Machine-Readable Cataloging) and its possible applications to his library.

The librarian needs to put automatic data-processing operations in perspective with regard to the "Economics of Information." Information economics makes one aware of the cost of automation — utility trade-off, feasibility, and maintenance — that must be thoroughly investigated before automation is installed in the library if disappointment (sometimes disaster) over increased costs is to be avoided. Speed does cost:

> The librarian should be given some kind of presentation on cost analysis techniques, because these things can get very fuzzy. The feeling often is, machines are fast — therefore cheap, but that is not necessarily so. The librarian needs to have brought home to him that the computer rarely saves money.

> First there is the cost to install and operate the automated system that is being proposed.

> Subsequently there are the cost implications of automation; for example, the manual catalog versus on-line machine cataloging.

It is necessary to take the mystery out of computers and bring an understanding of how they operate. This would include the ability to relate hardware to software but, more importantly, to understand the capability of the hardware and the satellite machines. This familiarity will permit the librarian to relate inputs and outputs to the computer process.

> The customer must have parity with the salesman. The computer manufacturer's representative often feels no continuing responsibility toward his customers — he is there to sell hardware.

> Librarians should learn that they must insist on actual information on how the computer can serve the library.

They should be able to specify the product and services wanted for the library that should be automated and be able to describe those data needed for input.

One of the best ways to take away the fear of the computer is to build into the course some "hands-on" experience. This would not be for the purpose of training one to program, but to give one enough actual experience to realize the problems involved and to get a feel for what is totally involved in any computerization of processes. It would seem that learning to use a few machines would be helpful in this regard, such as the key-puncher and the card sorter.

I think that it is not only computerization, but the new technology in its entirety that should be presented in the course at the post-MLS level. I think many people use the term *automation* but really mean this whole complex of the new technology in the field of communication, reprography, microforms, TWX — all are very significant as well as computers.

Specialized Library Functions

The fact that in their free responses the interviewees mentioned relatively fewer specialized library functions than administrative and automative functions would seem to indicate that they felt management skills to be more important than technical skills at the middle and upper job levels. Library personnel, as they move upward organizationally, usually require a different combination of skills and competencies than were needed in their first library assignments. The findings by Fayol (9:7—13) and Corson (7:131—36), noted earlier in this report, that management assumes its own unique functions apply to librarianship.

Actually, for a large percentage of the positions about which the interviewees responded, there seemed to be little need for depth of understanding of specialized library functions. However, the interviewees felt that the supervising librarians should have at least a working knowledge of the specialties their staffs were engaged in. Most of them did not think it necessary to take a full course in order to attain the knowledge requisite to an effective supervisory performance. The interviewees believed that the needed degree of familiarity beyond the MLS could be attained by participating in seminars or workshops or, in many cases, by watching and talking and by keeping up with the literature.

INTERVIEWS

A convincing case is made for this kind of reasoning by Jacques Barzun (3:11—12), who refuted the formula that one has to practice any kind of science, art, or trade or process in order to understand it and to supervise it as carried out by others:

> We forget that every age has carried with it great loads of information, most of it false or tautological, yet deemed indispensable at the time. Of true knowledge at any time, a good part is merely convenient, necessary indeed to the worker, but not to an understanding of his subject: one can judge a building without knowing where to buy the bricks; one can understand a violin sonata without knowing how to score for that instrument. The work may in fact be better understood *without* a knowledge of the details of its manufacture, for attention to these tends to distract from meaning and effect. Even if one sets apart those arts and sciences that require special preparation, there remains a large field to which Intellect has access in its own right. With a cautious confidence and sufficient intellectual training, it is possible to master the literature of a subject and gain a proper understanding of it.

To sum up: the interviewees thought it necessary that the incumbents be conversant with the positions about which they were being queried and generally knowledgeable about the work that came under their direction in order to make wise decisions and to maintain the respect of those whom they supervised. The administrators did not think that the librarians needed to gain expertise in these areas themselves — essentially the same attitude the interviewees had toward the amount of knowledge and skill needed in the area of automation.

Specifically, the interviewees mentioned some special knowledge and skills enough to warrant a generalized statement about them. In no case, however, did as many as 50 percent of the interviewees list these as "must" competencies for inclusion in a post-master's program. Those mentioned by three or more interviewees are summarized in the following paragraphs:

Greater expertise is needed in providing reference service to the library clientele. Four interviewees placed stress on the need for improvement in the librarian-client relationship in terms of the reference function if full professional service is to be provided to the library user. Greater expertise was seen to be needed in two areas:

1. Greater skill in understanding the psychology of the user is needed for meeting client needs. A number of the interviewees implied in varying ways that greater skill was needed in decoding the users' reference questions. For example, one interviewee explained it this way:

> An essential competency is for the librarian to know how to negotiate the reference question. That should be the prime object of a separate course — the approach to the user. It involves psychology, but much more than that. There have to be methods of assessment in a hurry; there has to be an understanding of interpersonal relationships; there has to be an understanding of the psychology of reading — the behavior and flow of information, including an understanding of the invisible college. It's not essential that they be expert catalogers, or expert bibliographers, but it is essential for them to get into the minds of the user.

2. Added competence is needed in an innovative approach to little-used and nonconventional library reference tools. A number of interviewees felt that the MLS graduate left school with a fair competency in the conventional reference courses, but appeared to have no vision of how to approach creatively clients' problems for which no standard tools were available. Some of the approaches suggested for study to meet this need were: the vital nature of the telephone; private collectors; other libraries; associations; consulates; congressmen; archives; patents; technical reports; commercial catalogs; newspaper morgues; minutes of meetings; etc.

The librarian needs to cultivate a sense of social responsibility which will be reflected in the service patterns of his library. Whether it is interpreted as serving minority groups in the community, or researching data on environmental pollution to be used in a campaign against pollution, the interviewees felt that sensitivity to the needs of the library's community and clientele should dictate the type of library service offered.

> The librarian has to know what the community's needs are so that he can develop his collection and provide the service that best meets those needs.

> It seems to me that a course that might be of great value at the post-master's level would be one in community relations. This would give the librarian going into a new community some background on how the feelings of groups develop; how groups interact

with each other; how groups function; and how the individual can best relate to these groups.

Much thought is needed in order to convert libraries into learning resources centers. Three of the interviewees believed that librarians generally resisted incorporating educational technology into their own libraries because they were not technically competent and were not willing to think through what the library's position should be.

> A facet of education which should be demanded of the replacement for this position [head of library] is the ability to change the library into a learning resources center. This person should know about audio and video tape and slides and all the software associated with a suitable media program for the library.

An experimental approach to traditional practices is needed throughout the area of technical services. The three interviewees who mentioned the possibility of improved skills in technical services thought that there was a place for such study at the post-master's level if it "were lab work and experimental — not book research." Here is an example cited by one interviewee of the type of experimental studies he had in mind:

> There are always lots of questionnaires and surveys of what people *think* would happen if technical services were organized differently or changed, but there have been very few experimental studies. For example: to experiment with giving up the catalog completely and then measuring what effect this has on service; or what would happen to a file if you treated a title as a main entry all the time; or take the subject approach to cataloging. Some preliminary research seems to indicate that the subject approach in a library catalog is of minimal value within a research library and that the lay user doesn't need highly specialized subject headings either. This is another area for experimentation.

To solve practical library problems, efficiency and ease in handling research methods are needed. Seven interviewees stressed the importance of using research methods to solve the large problems that arise in the ongoing operations of a library.

> Most librarians I know use a kind of hit-or-miss method when they try to solve a practical library problem. How do you compile data

ADDITIONAL DATA

and analyze it statistically to get reliable information from it? There is a great lack on the part of my staff in this whole area. If such a course were offered, I'd not only send all of my staff, I'd go myself.

I have found consistently in our analysis of technical services, for example, that there is a tremendous amount of statistical information involved. The skill comes in reducing all this data to a few statements of fact, but these seemingly simple statements are the basis on which we make all of our major decisions — so statistics becomes exceedingly important. I find sampling techniques suitable for use in libraries are simply not known to most librarians. And — sadly enough — not enough are willing to admit their ignorance and go to an expert, or they don't have enough cash. Librarians should know enough statistics to do this kind of work "in the house."

The general consensus among those wanting additional training in research techniques seemed to be:

I don't think every person working in a library has to have expertise in statistics, but I do think at least some elementary statistical methods should be a part of a post-master's program.

I don't think every librarian has to be a statistician, but perhaps there could be a conscientious attempt to work standard statistical practices into every course that involves quantification in problem solving.

These generalizations cover all the skills and competencies in the area of specialized library functions that were mentioned by three or more interviewees. Two specialized nonlibrary information source areas were mentioned as being worthwhile courses at the post-master's level: (1) urban literature and research, which would cover environmental sciences, technology, and sociology; and (2) literature and research for the natural and applied sciences.

ADDITIONAL DATA ABOUT BUILDING A POST-MASTER'S PROGRAM

For the remainder of the chapter the emphasis is shifted from individual courses to possible post-master's programs of one year in duration. The interest of the interviewees in such programs, the role of workshops and institutes, and other related variables of interest are analyzed with quotations from the interviewees. The idea for a year-long post-master's program was presented in the questionnaire, but suggestions for the particular content that should be included in such a program were derived from the responses of the librarians themselves.

Formal Post-Master's Programs

Throughout the interview, the top-level administrators alluded to their general reaction to library school-centered post-master's programs. In order to quantify these reactions to present a clearer picture, nine specific written questions were asked of the interviewees. The answers to these questions are summarized in table 51. Examination of this table reveals that the interviewees as a group were in favor of a post-master's program being offered, in fact, nineteen of them (one did not answer the question) considered the program important enough that they would allow full-time employees to attend on a part-time basis.

Sixteen of the interviewees agreed either strongly or mildly that certain schools should specialize in certain areas. During the interview, possible areas that were mentioned for specialization were administration, information science, automation, and research. If schools did specialize in certain areas, it would not seem feasible that they could meet the varied needs of all who might wish to attend, but 8 of the interviewees did indicate that they thought an effort should be made in this regard (4 strongly agreed; 4 mildly agreed).

In an attempt to discover some criteria that should be set for admission to such a program, the interviewees were asked the amount of time they thought should ideally elapse between the master's degree in library science and post-MLS study. The average number of years suggested was three and one-half. The responses ranged from no years (one respondent thought the student could profit by continuing immediately following the MLS degree) to six years (two respondents).

Although this study has indicated that in administrative positions at the upper and middle levels, a high percentage of the duties performed represented universal management skills and competencies, there is still a solid component of specialized knowledge, abilities, and attitudes which can be acquired only through substantial study and experience in the library field. In other words, while an increasingly small percentage of the duties performed as one rises in the organizational hierarchy represent specialized library functions, a considerable part of the

ADDITIONAL DATA

TABLE 51
ATTITUDES OF THE INTERVIEWEES TOWARD POST-MASTER'S
PROGRAMS IN LIBRARY SCIENCE:1969
(N=20)

Statement Given Interviewee for Reaction	Extent of Agreement			
	Strongly Agree	Mildly Agree	Disagree	No Opinion
I consider a post-master's program important enough that I would let full-time employees attend on a part-time basis.	12	7	0	1
I think certain schools should specialize in certain areas.	7	9	3	1
I think that every school having a post-MLS program should try to meet the varied needs of all who wish to come back.	4	4	11	1
I think the maximum advantages from a post-MLS program will be obtained only if the person involved has had some experience in a job following the MLS.	10	8	0	2
I feel the school should offer courses in the library science department, but that they should be highly interdisciplinary in their approach.	15	5	0	0
I would expect certain terminal behavior patterns from persons who come back after participating in a post-MLS program.	6	7	3	4
I would be interested, myself, in going back for certain types of training.	8	6	2	4
I feel that updating is done best in the job situation rather than by returning to library school.	0	2	10	8
Courses and in-service training programs aren't in my mind the answer to continuing staff development. Understanding and a developmental type of leadership on the job are much more important for the development of the individual in his job.	0	3	16	1

knowledge required to perform these supervisory library jobs is "specialized." For example, it is not enough for a library administrator to be skilled in the general aspects of communication. To communicate successfully with a group of catalogers he must have, among other things, a general awareness of the responsibilities, techniques, motivations, and intergroup relationships of catalogers. It was for reasons such as these that the majority of the interviewees felt it was preferable to have the courses at the post-master's level based in the library school rather than in other departments on the campus, such as psychology, sociology, educational technology, or business or public administration. Here are two such statements from interviewees:

> I think we err to think that because something is a little unusual it is outside the library school framework. To me, management is an integral part of libraries; therefore, management should be taught in that context. There are many things about library management that are different. In most management positions you can immediately come to a reasonable judgment as to the value of your output products, because most managements deal either in profit-making services or turn out a commodity. When you deal with a library, the benefit of what you do is very much like a church — it's not a very tangible thing. And so you take it with a great deal of faith. But when you come to selling people on a budget, you have to have some tangible way of demonstrating your value. Some of the faith has to be translated into body — some substance somewhere. This is one of the big problems that librarians have with the whole budget program. It shows up again when you want to go into a computer operation. If you want to take on any new kind of program that is terribly expensive, your order of magnitude of cost goes up two or three times. To justify this takes a lot of selling.
>
> Handling information is different from handling commodities; so, although the basic management skills you need for a library are pretty much the same as for business or any other organization, the specialized library knowledge you need to perform these basic management functions is different. Therefore the management and administration courses we are talking about should definitely be taught in the library school.
>
> I would be reluctant to turn over those who come back for post-MLS study to graduate schools in business administration. For most of them are fully oriented toward industry, and libraries have specialized characteristics that must be accounted for. There is a large amount of the profit motive in the decision-making process in industry. Therefore, I would like to see any post-master's program based in the library school, but going out to and bringing in professors who will add to the library environment needed concepts from other disciplines such as psychology, sociology, and public administration.

It is interesting to note that though there is an essential interchangeability of administrative skills, there is also a core of specialized knowledge and concepts which is best acquired through study and experience in the library field. This approach is essentially the same as that favored by Underwood (29:24) in his study of the role of the hospital administrator. It should be noted further, however, that this view is different from the current thrust of the schools of business administration which have developed into much broader areas than business administration. Today the emphasis is on management, both as the newest profession and as the central process in the conduct of any organization, according to a recent paper published by the System Development Corporation entitled "Grooming Tomorrow's Managers" (28:4). Thus business schools are dropping the word *business* from their titles to become "schools of management" and, through the use of interdisciplinary faculties, to meet the specialized requirements of management education so their graduates can possess broad management capabilities.

Although most of the twenty interviewees agreed with offering administration courses in library school, five only "mildly" agreed. Their reservations were related to the difficulty of obtaining qualified faculty to teach at the interdisciplinary level desired:

> If you had someone who was skilled enough in teaching these courses, it would make no difference where they were taught. But, if they were being taught by someone who was not really a broad expert with wide experience and knowledge in other disciplines, they would be too confined by the library school. It might be desirable to have the course taught by other graduate school faculties under direction from the library school.

> In relation to this higher administrative position about which we are talking, I am not so sure that the crucial question is so much the administration of the library as the broader concept of administering within a government framework. From my experience I would suspect that the administration requirements of even a deputy chief in a relatively large library are different from a high-ranking librarian in a smaller library — this is the kind of frontier that does not involve traditional library backgrounds. Perhaps, for these higher level administrative positions in government libraries, provision would have to be made either for them to take work in the Department of Public Administration or have professors from that discipline come to the library school.

INTERVIEWS

The many suggestions of the interviewees on how to get adequate interdisciplinary concepts represented in the courses that are to be offered at the post-master's level in the library school bore a general uniformity. The most practical suggestions made in this area may be synthesized:

> That library schools bring in specialists in other disciplines to teach, especially in the area of administration and management, or, better still, that the courses be designed by a team of experts drawn from library school and other faculties such as business psychologists, who know how to negotiate change; social psychologists, who understand human relations; economists, who understand professional manpower problems; educational technologists, who understand educational philosophy as it applies to using different media and different methods of teaching in actual presentation of the course; and public administrators, who understand the unique problems of administration within a governmental framework. This recommendation would be in keeping with that of economist Ginzberg (10), who concluded at the end of his study on manpower for library services that:

> To some extent, the shortages of faculty in library science can be relieved only by drawing into the field more subject-matter specialists: men and women who can make a significant contribution to the training of future librarians even though they themselves are not professional librarians. There is no other possible source. This is a pattern that graduate schools of business, social work, and even law schools have followed and continue to follow. . . . it does not follow that every library school must add specialists to its faculty. One of the strengths of a major university is its large number of specialized departments of instruction. Library schools should do more to tap into the departments which can help train their students [10:57—58].

That the courses offered at the post-master's level concentrate on the skills of management and the attitudes appropriate to their effective use in the job situation in order to achieve a balance of objectives which will more fully accomplish the library's goals and, at the same time, yield greater satisfaction to the individual employed. It is interesting to note that a practical emphasis at this level of training, as opposed to a theoretical approach (presumably presented at MLS level), is in keeping with current trends in schools of management as reported by the System Development Corporation in its paper on "Grooming Tomorrow's Managers" (28).

Beyond the confines of a specific course in human relations, the human factor is an important variable to be considered. The interviewees thought that the emphasis should be on achieving a curriculum that would effect a balance between the behavioral and technical aspects of the work situation. Here again, they were in line with the thinking of the deans of leading schools of management, who predict to a man that "behavioral studies" will "bulk larger and larger in importance in coming years." Said one dean, "Managers must deal with a whole range of unstructured problems that don't lend themselves to solution by quantitative methods. The human factor is the dominant variable, and while we don't yet have the goals to deal effectively with this range of problems, I believe the schools will be attaching much more emphasis to behavioral science methodologies. Perhaps the key will be the interdisciplinary faculty" (28:14).

> That although the courses should be presented in an interdisciplinary framework, in actual teaching "applications should be made," as stated by one interviewee, "whether it's a problem to be solved, an involvement in a team action situation, a simulated situation, a case study, a research paper, or a role-playing activity."

> That teaching methods should be broadened to include the type of activities mentioned above, and that there be less lecturing, listening, and note-taking and more thinking and problem solving related to their real jobs.

> That as full use as possible be made of the new technology and the new media in making course presentations.

When asked what terminal behavior patterns the interviewees would expect the librarian to have gained by participation in a post-master's program, the answers were almost uniform. The desired objectives were affective toward their jobs in general, rather than cognitive, specifying skills or competencies. The comments can be put into two categories: attitude toward change, and improved work performance:

> Unwillingness to accept status quo; strong desire to innovate and experiment with new systems and services.

INTERVIEWS

Motivation toward new development.

Open-mindedness and flexibility; initiative to try new ideas.

Broader involvement and willingness to make policy recommendations.

Improved performance generally, but wouldn't expect miracles.

Greater contribution generally, either in ideas or in actual production.

Broader understanding and scope of thinking enlarged.

Greater analytical ability to solve problems.

Better prepared to do the job.

When the interviewees were asked if they themselves would be interested in returning for certain types of training, 70 percent answered in the affirmative, mentioning from one to three courses they would be willing to take. The courses listed were:

Administration
Automation
Communications Technology
Communication with Management (outside the library)
Current Issues and Problems in Librarianship
General Management
Human Relations (outside the library)
Information Networks
Logic
Network Planning and Design
Personnel
Research Methods
Systems Design and Analysis

Finally, two questions dealt with the preferred method for continuing education at the post-master's level. One question asked if updating was better done on the job than in the university. Fifty percent of the interviewees disagreed with this statement and thought that going to a university was the better way. Ten percent preferred on-the-job training. Forty percent did not answer the question, explaining that they did not think there was "one best way," but rather a combination of ways. The 50 percent who considered the university campus the best locale for training programs gave reasons very similar to those listed by Kortendick (15:269—70) in regard to short-term training programs based on the university campus; namely, that participants are removed from the supervisors and from the environment of the job, and are thus able to get a new perspective and to look at their work more objectively. The experience is to be intellectually stimulating, in approach and in content. There can be an opportunity for discussing problems with faculty and with people from other libraries. The theory which underlies the practice is often better transmitted in such an environment.

Finally, when asked about the importance of a developmental type of leadership on the part of the top library administrators in relation to either courses in the university setting or in-service training programs, only 15 percent thought that developmental type of leadership was more important. Eighty percent disagreed. The 15 percent reflected the philosophy of McGregor (21):

> The individual will grow into what he is capable of becoming provided we can create the proper conditions for that growth. Such an approach involves less emphasis on manufacturing techniques and more on controlling the climate and fertility of the soil, and on methods of cultivation [21:192].

In other words, these interviewees stress the importance of the librarian working for supervisors who delegate and who are constantly making it possible for their subordinates to further their own self-development. One interviewee underscored this by saying that when he was looking for a replacement for the position about which he was being interviewed (head of a library), he put prime importance on knowing who the candidate's previous supervisors had been. He put it this way:

> In looking for a replacement I would want to see whom he had worked for. I have passed several by because I felt that they would not have had the kind of training that I require in problem solving, decision making, or opportunity to grow on the job working under Librarian X. In other words, I am judging their capability for the job by their boss.

Perhaps the most important observation to make relative to this discussion is that courses taken in the library school at the post-master's level will have the maximum effectiveness only if the employee who enrolls comes out of an environment that is conducive to growth and that will permit him to use any gains he makes or concepts he learns in the classroom.

Summing up this section, it can be said that the top-level library administrators were sympathetic toward a post-master's program. They felt (to the extent that 70 percent of them were willing to come themselves and take courses offered in the program) that the chief gains from such a program would be to: (1) create a desire on the part of the participants to be an agent for change in their libraries, and (2) improve work performance generally. The majority of the interviewees saw advantages in developing a one-year program, as opposed to merely a selection of courses at will, and in offering a degree (preferred) or certificate at the end of the program, as opposed to no formalized recognition of completion. Two quotations from the interviewees illustrate their feelings in this regard:

> I think the post-master's program would be a very good thing, because it doesn't seem to me that a person need necessarily commit himself to earning the doctorate. If he wants to take work beyond his master's degree, he should get some credit for it. If you offer a person some goal, it is much better than his simply taking this course and that course.

> Yes, I certainly think the person should have a degree at the end of the program. That is recognition of the person's having completed an organized course of study. Because, after all, when you start to select and take what you need here and there you often end up with a sort of mishmash. If you were to offer this type of degree, you might induce some people to go back for additional training who are unable financially to go back for a doctorate.

The interviewees were in agreement that the content of the curriculum for upper- and middle-level library personnel should be heavily oriented toward achievement of management skills and attitudes, and that, whatever the problems involved, the curriculum should be strongly interdisciplinary. The program, they thought, should be based in the library school because, although a relatively small percentage of the managerial and administrative duties performed represent specialized library functions, a large proportion of the knowledge required to perform successfully at middle and upper levels is of a "specialized" nature. Therefore, the interviewees recommended that the applications used in course presentation should be library oriented. The interviewees believed that librarians with some experience (3-1/2 years was the suggested average) would benefit most from such a program.

Workshops and Institutes

When asked their opinion about the value of institutes, short-term courses and workshops, 85 percent of the interviewees felt that the library school should be involved in these forms of continuing education in addition to whatever full-length courses the school might offer as part of a formal post-master's program. Three of the interviewees, however, felt that rather than dissipating their efforts too widely, the library schools would be well advised to concentrate on full-length courses at the post-master's level, but suggested experimentation in the timing, scheduling, and format of such course offerings so that a wider audience might be reached. Their reasons for questioning heavy involvement in short-term continuing-education programs centered on their belief that the content of such short-term programs was so intensive that there were apt to be no lasting changes realized from such participation, either in the participant's attitude or knowledge. Too often, they felt, a person returning highly motivated from such a program found, when back in the same old job environment, that in the eyes of his supervisor his brief exposure did not give him the right to try out new concepts in the job; his enthusiasm soon changed to discouragement.

However, one of these interviewees, out of personal experience, suggested a way in which these short-term programs might be made more meaningful in meeting the needs of the job situation. It seems worthwhile to mention this individual recommendation because of possible application to library school short-term programs in general. For reasons mentioned in the preceding paragraph, this interviewee felt short-term programs had little merit. However, in one specific case from this person's experience, it was possible for a group from one library to go together to a short-term workshop which concentrated on problem solving in a specific type of library situation. The interviewee found this particular type of group experience to be of great value because it touched on practical problems their library was facing at the moment, and, more important, because a group from the library went together, it was actually possible to bring about changes in their library when they returned. Several people with improved knowledge or attitudes can make a potent catalyst of their common experience in a given library situation. The interviewee in question endorsed this approach as a valuable suggestion to make to library schools. By getting together a group of people coming from one library at the same time, rather than trying to fill the workshop with individuals coming from separate libraries, a greater impact would result. It is interesting to note that Vroom (28:11) of the Carnegie-Mellon School of Administration states a similar solution to lengthening the life of lessons learned in short-term programs: "I expect that in the next few years we'll be focusing away from individual managers and concentrating on management systems. That is, bringing in teams of working managers in an effort to foster real environmental change."

Returning to the 85 percent who endorsed the library school's involvement in workshops and institutes, it was discovered that about half were in favor of shorter workshops (one day to one week) and the others in favor of longer workshops (preferably three weeks or more). Those preferring the shorter term said they were just being realistic in terms of the number of people that could attend on that basis. The shorter term would permit anyone to attend without his job suffering. Another advantage is lower costs which make possible wider participation. Another reason given for the preference for the short-term format was that "there is an inclination to pack into them what is really needed — the nub of the problem." On the whole, those for short-term programs admitted, however, that they were beneficial chiefly from the point of view of exposure to new concepts and cited the MARC institutes as being a good example of this. They stated that they realized the institutes were too short to provide any lasting attitudinal change for the individuals participating.

Speaking in defense of the long-term workshop, these interviewees still thought that it is probably not long enough to serve as an effective attitudinal-change device (a long-term course was necessary for that), but if the workshop is primarily information-oriented, then a great deal could be accomplished. A three-week period is still short enough to permit participation by many librarians without having their jobs suffer, and may be more easily financed than longer-term kinds of educational programs.

Generally, the type of subject coverage considered by the interviewees most suitable for institutes and workshops paralleled that favored by the respondents. In some subject areas the interviewees thought that the time factor prevented maximum gains. Courses in personnel management and human relations were generally put in this category. In addition to the time being too short for any type of attitudinal change, one interviewee expressed the idea that seemed to speak for many:

In order for a workshop or institute to be effective, the participants have to know enough so that they can update themselves in a few days, at the most three weeks of concentrated effort. On the other hand, management is a foreign discipline, and I wouldn't expect much in the way of results.

Subjects mentioned by the interviewees as a suitable base for a workshop or institute presentation included: new reference books for professional librarians; reference and resource material in a given area such as science or behavioral studies; acquisitions (especially nonbook); federal library resources; and, as mentioned earlier, the MARC program.

Finally, the interviewees stated certain criteria for workshops that they believed would be beneficial to those of any length:

1. The groups should be homogeneous, such as military librarians who all work under the same regulations, federal librarians all under the same civil service system, or any group subject to the same regulations.

2. The level of experience and background of all participants should be similar — otherwise a lot of needless time is spent in explanations.

3. Coverage should tend toward the narrow rather than the broad. "I generally find workshops are aimed at too broad a group of people, and therefore are not satisfying, because they are not specific enough to help me in my job. They have a little for everybody, and not enough for any one individual to make it worthwhile." Several of the interviewees spoke with enthusiasm of special courses for top-level executives or for middle managers in which all had a similar background of experiences to share and a similar amount of knowledge to use in problem-solving situations presented in the programs.

4. The content should be related to needs of the participants in their job situations.

Admission Criteria

The designer of any educational program must give adequate thought to its admission requirements. As the analysis of the data from the respondents progressed, a tentative curriculum for a post-master's program slowly emerged. To build upon this, the interviewees were asked for their suggestions for admission criteria to a post-master's program. Their recommendations were multidimensional, and they will be discussed one by one:

The program would be more meaningful if the participant in the program had had some experience between his MLS degree program and enrollment in a post-master's program. This was the most definite recommendation made. The average time suggested by the interviewees, as reported earlier in this chapter, was three-and-one-half years, but the range was from zero number of years to six years. No clear-cut answer emerged:

> There's no clear-cut answer on how many years should elapse. It depends on the person. If he's a real go-getter and really keeps up with the field, I don't think it matters when he goes back. I think that he should take something he needs to know more about for his present job, or he should be considering new developments or what was lacking in his MLS preparation. In other words, I don't believe in going back to school to take a course just because it is beyond the master's degree; he should only be admitted to the program if it is based on a real need.

> Many of the things you would offer in a post-master's course would not be understandable until they had been out on the job for a while and had seen how they fit into their daily work. For example, it's pretty hard to teach someone about personnel management unless they've run across some personnel problems, and that's the best time in the world for them to learn — when faced with actual problems related to the work situation. It's the old principle: when an individual sees the need for certain courses, then he is motivated to learn.

> It seems to me you should not only be looking for technical competencies, but for the person with a broad background in librarianship; a person who seems to have, or has demonstrated, an ability to administer, to think and plan, and to work with people. So experience is important and also the type of experience. I think the breadth of experience is particularly important, for such a person can relate the library's mission and library services and materials to those in the agency outside the library.

A master's degree in library science would assure that all in the program started with a common background in specialized library functions. This requirement was considered necessary because a large proportion of the knowledge required to perform successfully at the middle and upper levels in a library is of a "specialized" nature even though a relatively small percentage of the managerial and administrative duties performed represent specialized library functions.

Certain prerequisites should be required for enrollment in certain courses. For example, as a prerequisite to a course in human relations, the applicant should have had a course at the MLS level in the principles of administration. Or, as a prerequisite to a course at the post-master's level in automation, the applicant should have had an introductory course at the MLS level in automated procedures in the library to ensure that all in the post-master's program would have the same background on which to build. It was suggested that in the case of mature students with extensive experience in automation, work experience might be considered in order to reach an acceptable standard for admission to the course in automation.

The admissions program should be flexible enough to provide for a mixture of people with different value orientations. Corson and Paul (7:138—39) pointed out that there is evidence that a group excelling in academic work may not include proportions of individuals with the proper "mix" of talents necessary to handle the full variety of management and administrative responsibilities. The value orientations which Ginzberg and Herma (11:117—22) found to affect profoundly organizational performance, and which ideally should be represented in an organization, are: (1) those wanting to achieve leadership roles with groups of individuals; (2) those content to gain and hold acceptance by other members of their work group as a prerequisite to achieving organizational advances; (3) those dedicated to ideals who are likely to provide the zeal and enthusiasm, if not the intellectual leadership, that inspire organizational advances; and (4) those insistent upon their right to structure their own activities and to be able to work as independently as possible.

The implication is that admission requirements should be liberal enough about previous academic record to provide for differing value orientations which determine the role the individual wishes to fill in the library's program. It is thought that through this procedure, an adequate supply of talent will be developed for the middle-, upper-, and top-level management and administrative positions.

The final admission criterion considered was personality characteristics. The suggestion is being made in the literature today that applicants to graduate library programs be screened in order to obtain individuals with certain personality characteristics (Lilley, 18:171—72).

Therefore, questions were asked both of the respondents and of the interviewees which yielded information on the great importance each of these groups placed on personality characteristics in relation to job performance. Twenty percent of the interviewees felt that personality characteristics were so important (and so little subject to change) that they recommended that all applicants to a post-master's program should be carefully screened in order to obtain certain personality traits for the program and keep those with less-desired traits (according to the value judgments of the interviewees) out of the program. As there was so much interest expressed in personality characteristics on the part of both the interviewees and the respondents, the possibility of screening for personality traits at the time of admission to the post-master's program is discussed at some length.

Just as information-center experts have insisted (Lilley cites many examples: 18:171—73) that certain personality traits are needed to serve the scientific community effectively,* the interviewees believed that certain traits were needed for the positions about which they were being interviewed. Twenty percent suggested that the library school should look for these qualities of personality in those seeking admission to the program:

> A good outgoing, forceful personality, but a pleasant one that doesn't get rattled easily, is patient, can meet deadlines, and, most important, is receptive to change.

> Decisiveness is a key factor. We're going to have to look at their skills at doing professional management tasks. We need decision makers who can quickly fight their way through to what is the real issue, what is the problem that we are faced with, and develop some mechanisms to solve the problem.

> The most important thing needed is someone who can organize and motivate people and look at the whole operation very critically and very analytically. This can be the key difference in the management of an operation.

> We've got to have people who have not just gotten along for years, but people who can make imaginative, innovative suggestions for program improvement.

---

*Longnecker (19:12) states that "They must have personality traits that are opposite from those of the librarian or information specialist who works alone, independent of others."

Those who advocated an admissions policy that would screen out certain kinds of personality traits mentioned more or less the same ones that have come in for heavy criticism by many observers (Bergen, 4:478; Harvey, 12:1; Lothrop, 20:132—33; Muller, 24:1128; Schultz, 26:513) and appear in the research findings of Morrison (23:365—68) and Douglass (8):

> Librarians tend to be highly introverted types; basically they lack an aggressive character. These people now are being asked to supervise other people, and they are not equipped to do this. They don't have the insight. This is an overwhelming problem to the profession.
>
> The personality traits of librarians are one of our great problems. They simply don't have the personality to reach out to the user, and by the time such a person is ready to go for postgraduate work, his personality traits are so ingrained that he is not going to change.
>
> A librarian tends to be a gentle, easy, nondecisive person who wants no problems with the world. He just wants his books, his periods, his commas, and his cards to be in order. He is retiring and not aggressive enough; he favors the status quo to change. Unfortunately this is the type, because they often made straight "A's" in their MLS program, that is appointed to the top positions.
>
> In general, the type of persons that are attracted to librarianship are not what you would call aggressive, outgoing types.

The characteristics the respondents described as the most important for their replacement (chapter 6) are very different from those found in the responses by the interviewees or in the literature. For the respondents, the three most important personal traits for a replacement were (1) getting along with other people, (2) adaptability or flexibility, and (3) patience. They refer to getting things done routinely, rather than to characteristics that a leader should have.

The comparison between the type of characteristics suggested by the interviewees and the respondents is significant, especially when examined in the light of a research paper by Porter and Henry (25) on perceptions of the importance of certain personality traits as a function of job level. This study investigated managers' perceptions of the relative importance of 10 personality traits for success in their managerial roles as a function of level of position within management. The 10 traits consisted of 5 other-directed, or organization-man, traits and 5 inner-directed traits. The inner-directed traits (forceful, imaginative, independent, decisive) were perceived as more important at successive higher levels of management, while the other-directed traits (cooperative, adaptable, agreeable, tactful) were seen to decrease at each higher level of management. It would appear that the inner-directed traits, showing a strong emphasis on individual capabilities, are very similar to the most desirable characteristics as perceived by the interviewees, namely, being decisive, innovative, forceful, outgoing, and an agent for change.

On the other hand, it would seem that the other-directed traits, showing a concern for adapting to the feelings and behavior of others (Porter, 25:31), are very similar to the characteristics cited by the respondents, namely, getting along with other people, adaptability, flexibility, and patience. The results of the Porter and Henry study point clearly to the fact that the psychological demands of the job, in terms of relative emphases on different types of personality qualities, change from one part of the management hierarchy to another, and the data from this study (from the respondents and from the interviewees) substantiate these findings.

Speaking of criteria of admission to library schools, Lilley (18:171) states, "At this juncture, it would seem appropriate to recommend that library schools look not only to academic preparation . . . but to the personality of the students who are to be admitted to a graduate program." After citing many examples showing how seriously librarians lack initiative and leadership and showing that certain personality traits are needed in order to serve clients more effectively, she reaches the following conclusions:

> Under the circumstances, it would seem that library schools ought either to screen their applicants for personality characteristics in terms of what is needed or to provide the kind of education that will develop in them the necessary qualities of initiative, creativity, and competence [18:176].

The data from the present study would seem to indicate a conclusion different from that stated by Lilley about the inclusion of personal characteristics in admission criteria, at least those for a post-master's program. The present findings would seem to indicate that individuals at different levels of the library organizational hierarchy perceive different personality characteristics as important for job success. From the whole spectrum of personality traits, some seem more useful in attaining success at one level of the library structure and some at another level; at different levels of management they are, to a certain degree, at variance with one another. Therefore, it would not seem very judicious to accept a single set of personality characteristics. Library schools need to ensure the proper balance of people to handle the variety of responsibilities which must be borne by the library in order to give quality service.

Returning to the second suggestion in Lilley's recommendation to library schools, it will be remembered that she stated that if applicants were not screened for personality characteristics, then the school should "provide the kind of education that will develop in them the necessary qualities of initiative, creativity, and competence." Many of the interviewees asked whether a course in human relations could have any effect in changing attitudes. The interviewees seemed to feel that only through attitudinal change would it be possible for there to be any great improvement in the ability of the individual librarian to interact with others with whom he worked. The interviewees agreed that, to a large extent, the success of a library's operation depends on how effectively the manager or administrator uses this personal interaction, but some wondered if much could be done in equipping those who came back from the program to learn how better to handle these personal problems.

In answer to the question whether or not a course in human relations could be helpful to the librarian in coming to grips with the problems growing out of personal characteristics, 30 percent of the interviewees expressed doubt that a lot could be accomplished, but saw it as probably the best way of trying to help librarians with this problem. Two of the five who expressed doubt about the final outcome expressed it this way:

> I think courses in human relations could do a lot, but am afraid that when the librarians are back in their same old job environment, not many changes will be possible. However, I think that it would make them aware of the challenge they have as supervisors and that they may become more competent in some ways. Certainly they should become more professional from having had such a course. In the free atmosphere of the university there is a greater chance that improvements could be made than back in the job situation.

> Courses won't necessarily help in the development of personality traits or in the ability of the supervisor to understand the

personality traits of others. I'm afraid that so much is dependent upon native ability, energy, self-assurance. I don't know how to develop skill in human relations, or if it can be taught, but it would be at least worth a try to see what could be accomplished in a course.

The general opinion seemed to be, in spite of questions raised about outcomes, that libraries have become increasingly more complex and businesslike organizations that impose tremendous communication and personal interaction requirements on their managers, and that somehow the library school should be able to help the library managers deal with such unstructured problems as arise each day and claim a large proportion of their time. Such a course should also help the participant develop a greater awareness and understanding of his own values and attitudes as they affect his relationships with others in the job situation. It becomes apparent that in the development of such a course the whole spectrum of personality characteristics in relationship to job levels would need to be included if the participant is to gain increased insight into the motivation and behavior of library staff members as they interact with peers, supervisors, and subordinates. The interviewees were in complete agreement that this was one of the areas which called for interdisciplinary cooperation, especially in the area of behavioral science methodologies.

To sum up, it is unrealistic to expect that one course or program can develop the range of personality characteristics that are necessary to operate effectively at each of the levels of the library hierarchy. However, a course in human relations can be used as a powerful aid in understanding human relations theory and research and their applications in library administration, providing there is a positive environment in the job situation that supports the educational gains made in the classroom. It was noted in this connection that during the interviews one phrase repeatedly occurred in regard to courses, programs, and institutes, "but I'm afraid they [course enrollees] won't really be changed much back on the job." This emphasizes what has been shown over and over again in recent research — that a negative environment will wipe out all the gains that may have been achieved in the classroom. In fact, Likert (17:127) goes so far as to say:

> To expose managers to new and challenging data and ideas and then make it impossible for them to make use of their new insights and even penalize them for doing so, is highly frustrating. One can safely predict that managers so treated will have their performance

adversely affected, and many, especially the more able, will seek a different company with a management system more compatible with their new insights.

If it is not feasible to rely simply on screening out applicants based on personal characteristics at the time of entry into the post-master's program in order to improve personal interaction in the library organization, and if it is not realistic to think that the whole range of unstructured human problems can be solved through a single course in human relations, the question arises, Is there another method available to deal with this range of problems?

In view of the fact that personality characteristics play such an important role in library administration, it might be worthwhile to try the educational method for improving the skills of social interaction that has been widely advocated by some leaders (Argyris, 1; and McGregor, 21), namely, the sensitivity group, or T (for training) group. The common pattern, which involves a two-week program during which the T-group meets daily for two hours, might be provided on an optional basis, as a supplementary program for those who complete a course in human relations. In other words, it would be a module of the program that the individual could participate in or not as he chose.

There is nothing mysterious about this form of training. Conditions are created by which individuals can increase their understanding (1) of the impact of their own behavior on others, (2) of their reactions to the behavior of others, and (3) of the phenomena of group activity and their significance. It is not expected that such training would bring about dramatic changes. A librarian who has been to a sensitivity training group does not become a new person, but he gets acquainted with the process of self-discovery and the opportunity is present for him, because participation in the group involves practice and feedback of a unique nature, to improve his skills of social interaction.

All of this discussion adds up to the conclusion that including personal characteristics among admission criteria for any post-master's program is a complex and many-faceted problem, one for which imaginative research is needed. It must be emphasized that the characteristics reported on in this section from the interviewees and that respondents are both based on perceptions by librarians themselves. However, before any firm conclusions or recommendations can be reached, it will be necessary to survey the users concerning desirable personal characteristics found in an efficient librarian, for, in the final analysis, it is they who are the consumers of the product.

INTERVIEWS

It can be surmised that the personal traits listed by both the interviewees and the respondents are oriented largely toward successful human relationships within the library organizational framework, but this, after all, is not the sole criterion for judging the efficiency of the library's service. It is quite conceivable that a librarian might be extremely poor in his interactions with other personnel within the library organization, but might do excellent work in isolation in producing the information demanded by the clientele. The personal traits perceived by the librarians concerned interpersonal relations with others in the library hierarchy of employees. Research needs to be undertaken, as was pointed out by a number of the respondents, which will come to grips with the quality of service given to the clientele, both actual and potential.

Career Development

It was the general feeling of the interviewees that, as expressed by one of them, "Right now, the only way our people can progress is the administrative way." However, 35 percent of the interviewees hoped that a rationale might be developed providing for different career progressions in librarianship as brought out in Asheim's (2) recent paper "Education and Manpower for Librarianship." In stating his reasons for thinking that administration should not be the only career ladder, one interviewee said:

> I don't like to think of administration as the only way to the top, because I have seen some very good people who are natural catalogers, or geniuses at matching people with books or people with the information they need, or at being able to communicate with just a few questions, finding out what the individual is really after and getting it to him. To me, we would be losing one of the purposes, if not the main purpose, of librarianship to push them into administration and not to provide an alternative ladder to higher salaried positions for them. This is one thing I liked particularly about Dr. Asheim's position paper. He brings this out — career ladders for the nonadministrator as well as for the administrator; and I would certainly hope to see this.

However, today there is only one career ladder. The jobs at the top are mostly administrative positions. Hence, the individual librarian should be aware of the requirements for this advancement in the profession, whether he chooses to pursue his career in bibliographic services or clientele guidance, or whether he wishes to advance in administrative positions. If the librarian chooses to advance as an administrator, he will need, for example, certain competencies, such as the ability to direct others; an understanding of the processes of management; a respect for the importance of motivation; and a thorough understanding of the library as a total system, as well as an understanding of the environment in which the library is situated.

To provide for these administrative competencies, the interviewees saw the post-master's program as possibly being developed with a specialization in administration. However, for those pursuing career advancement in paths other than administration, the librarians felt a differentiated program at the post-master's level might be developed by different schools. Eighty percent of the interviewees thought schools at this level should specialize in certain areas to meet specific career needs. Only 20 percent felt strongly that every school offering a post-master's program should try to meet the varied career needs of all who might wish to come back.

The interviewees generally give preference to promoting from within the library if they have a qualified person responsible for the job, although the Civil Service Commission's policy on promotion is open. If this is the general policy, as one interviewee pointed out, then it is necessary that provision be made for training those already in the library. One interviewee stated:

> Because I felt the internal training program was unusually poor, I had to fill all my jobs when I first came from without. This creates quite a morale problem, and I wouldn't have done it by choice if I thought I had any alternative. Unless management makes training a very significant part of its management process, there is no other way of doing it. Therefore, one of the first things I did was appoint a training officer. They didn't have such an animal. I took a trained librarian on the staff and said, "From now on your job is to see to it that there are adequate training and development opportunities for the rest of the staff — to see that all of the staff is trained." By now, over one-third of the staff has participated in some sort of a training program. Morale has gone up, and turnover has gone down. I realize that it cannot all be attributed just to training, but it is certainly a major factor.

To develop a staff over the years, one needs to plan for their career development as well as to do some forecasting to estimate just what kinds of positions and competencies will be needed ten or more years hence. Once such a rationale has been developed, there is a need for regularly examining and improving the process of assignment, training, and promotion. It was apparent that the large majority of the interviewees did not think that they had an integrated program to develop the individual librarians to their greatest capacity. Nor did they believe that keeping up to date is done better on the job than in library school (table 51). This feeling was well expressed by one of the interviewees:

> I think formal course work is very necessary, as the on-the-job training is not sufficiently well organized to give them what they would get in a formal course. However, each library has its own peculiar procedures; these must be taught through on-the-job training.

Hence, the need is for each library administrator to establish career-long processes that develop the talent required to operate the library at the highest level possible. This would mean development by all means of training — one important means of such training is post-master's education at a university.

When asked if the librarian returning to work with an additional degree or certificate from a sixth-year program would have an advantage for consideration for higher grade and/or salary, the interviewees generally stated that they "would consider it a plus." But specifically just what this "plus" would be seemed to be unclear and to vary greatly in the minds of the interviewees. On the whole, the attitude seemed to be one of waiting to see what the program contained before any type of statement could be made.

> I suspect a good test of a training program would be a person coming back and beginning to perform as a manager just as he began to perform as a librarian when he came out of library school. I would hope so. This would have implications for me. I would suspect and hope he could do many things in the management line that at present I find necessary to do myself, for example, in the area of budget preparation.

> I think the person with the additional sixth-year program might have a chance of making a higher grade than the one with only a master's. I'm not sure this could be borne out by any actual experience. Generally, we would tend to equate an additional master's with one year of experience, I believe.

The research team was also interested in discovering the attitude of the interviewees about whether the librarian returning after participating in a post-master's program would have an opportunity to use the acquired skills in the job environment. The general response was that they would try, but in no formal way. What the team was looking for here was whether or not the interviewees would be receptive to the librarian's experimenting with new ideas and concepts in the old environment when he returned to it. However, in the spontaneous responses, not too much of a definite commitment came through. The general response seemed to be that they would provide no formal way for the librarian returning to his job to apply acquired skills and knowledge, but that inasmuch as he could use new concepts and skills in the performance of his job, he would be free to do so.

Almost all of those interviewed expressed their willingness to support their employees' efforts toward further formal professional schooling, and there was a wide range of opinion on the actual on-the-job feasibility of such action. Although the same training act is in force for all federal employees, the interpretations of how its provisions might be applied toward librarians participating in a post-master's program ranged from authorized payment for one or two night classes only (no leave involved) to leave and financial support for a whole year's program. These variations are in part accounted for by the differences within the individual federal libraries represented, such as size of library staff, promotion policies, status and character of the career development programs in various agencies, and individual interpretations of how much help would be available from the training act.

The size of the library staff seemed one crucial barrier to the actual ability to release an employee for a semester or a year's study, and to have a post vacant for him on his return:

> If our library were very large, I would look for several to send all the time — three, four, or six-month classes — hoping they would return and be able to fill vacancies as they arose. But we are small, and I can't do that. If they were gone and an opportunity to promote came up, I couldn't wait for them to return. I would have to look outside for a replacement.

The larger the staff, the greater the chance to handle this efficiently. For this reason there was considerably more expression of possible support for leave and funds to study on a part-time basis than on a full-time.

> I would have no objections to employees taking courses which

might lead them to something better, except that I would probably not pay their tuition. When a person wants to broaden his knowledge in a subject field or librarianship, I think I would say, "Do it on your own time and financing."

I don't see how I could let them off for a semester to study. I don't see how we'd get the work done. Once our people are in line to advance and have a great deal of loyalty to the institution, we would rather not send them off.

If I gave an employee time for study, the course would have to relate very closely to either what he was doing today or what we were hoping to do as the next step in the area the person was working in. The course description would have to convince me that the level is beyond that of the person now in it, or we couldn't afford to send him. For example, we are facing automation work in the library, and everyone in the library is slowly picking up some knowledge. However, I need but one automation project manager for the major task. I would be willing to send the one person I thought best for that post and tell him that he could take all the time he wanted to take one or two courses in data processing and systems analysis. I think the payoff to me in that one person in three or four years would be great enough to provide justification.

I would certainly encourage anyone who wanted to take a post-master's program. But whether we could send them, I very much doubt. I don't think the library could pay for their cost under the training act, for instance. Because we want to encourage them we would consider giving them time off.

I can't spare incumbents too much. I want them to develop; I want them to move along on the job, but I would prefer to have short courses, because we just don't have much time.

If a program is needed by an individual, I would send them with salary plus per diem allowance and travel expenses.

If I felt the program was to be worthwhile and needed, I'd be willing to give them as much as a year to study.

We give as high as a third of our staff time off with pay to go to school now. We even pick up the cost of the courses. We have a great deal of flexibility in letting people have time off.

On special occasions I could send people for a whole degree as part of a career progression program we have in our agency. They will give people as much as a whole year off from their jobs and pay them for it.

We could send people within the regulations on which our career development system is structured. It works like this: we nominate people for courses and we justify this — the funding of it. The training officer concurs or does not concur. He screens out all requests that are not job related. A person might wish to take two courses, and one would be approved on this basis — the other might not be. We generally have pretty good luck and normally have several people in continuing education each semester.

I think we are heading in the direction of letting people take time off from their jobs to participate in the type of post-master's program we are discussing. I believe I could get money for courses, textual materials, as well as leave, because we have a rather extensive career development program. The Committee on Librarians has met regularly for about a year to discuss what could be done to promote career development of librarians and information specialists. Our emphasis in these meetings is on the individual, not the institution — to help the individual grow. It goes without saying that sometimes this will mean the individual's moving outside the department. Now they haven't moved around; they haven't been promoted; they haven't progressed. They've just been confined to one little spot in one department.

Realistically, in view of these statements, it seems that the majority of government employees have to study in these programs on a part-time basis. This conclusion is arrived at from a joint consideration of what the respondents said in answering the questionnaire and what the interviewees said about the financial aspect for participating in a post-master's program. This, of course, is very discouraging, because of the large number of federal librarians living far from an ALA-accredited library school (table 41), even though willingness to take a post-master's program was found to be independent of the distance from an accredited library school. However, if the librarians have to attend on a part-time basis, actual participation would depend on their distance from the library school. Hence, for this program, distance from a library school would turn out to be an important barrier.

SUMMARY AND CONCLUSIONS

In this chapter, the data presented were obtained from the interviews with top-level library administrators (grades 15 and up). The findings reflect the educational needs and desired competencies and skills of middle- and upper-level librarians (grades 9 through 14). The twenty interviewees were selected on the basis of quota sampling, and the findings are thus comparable. Some salient features of this chapter seem worthy of reiteration:

1. The interviewees put into three mutually exclusive categories all of the 78 courses listed in the questionnaire, and from that a ranking was developed. The correlation coefficient between the two sets of rankings of the courses — the one by the interviewees, and the one by the respondents — was found to be moderately high (0.64).

2. In particular, the courses in administration were ranked higher by the interviewees, and courses related to information science ranked lower, as compared to the rankings of the respondents. In the area of automation, only one course — namely, the one entitled Automation of Library Processes — maintained the same high ranking with the interviewees, while the other two courses in automation slipped in ranking.

3. In the area of administration, the course that topped the list was Human Relations in Library Administration, which was one of the top courses selected by the respondents also.

4. Specific skills and competencies needed by middle- and upper-level library personnel, as perceived by the interviewees, were analyzed by major course areas. The fact that most of them fell within the areas of administration and automation further stressed the importance of these two areas.

Summarizing the attitude of the interviewees toward the concept of offering post-master's programs, the following predominated:

1. There was in general a favorable reaction from the interviewees toward offering post-master's programs.

2. The interviewees recommended that in the development of such programs certain conditions should prevail: (a) that the programs be based in the library school itself; (b) that there be

a heavy emphasis on an interdisciplinary approach to all content presented; (c) that content be closely related to on-the-job needs; and (d) that a given school concentrate its offerings in one area and not try to meet the needs of all librarians who might wish to enroll.

3. The interviewees believed that on-the-job training had value, especially in orienting the individual to the particular routines and practices of a given library, but that such training cannot replace a further need for formal courses.

4. Generally, the interviewees indicated that individuals who had completed a post-master's program would receive preference in regard to promotion. The possibility of utilizing the advanced skills of sixth-year program graduates within their old positions was not apparent to the interviewees.

5. After a thorough analysis of the favorable personality characteristics, as listed by the interviewees and compared with those listed by the respondents, the conclusion was reached that it would be inadvisable to adopt a policy of screening out certain personality traits at the time of admission to post-master's programs, even though such a procedure was suggested by some interviewees. Instead, the problem of personality characteristics should be dealt with in the program itself and not be left to admission policies.

6. Finally, regarding the financing of post-master's continuing education, the statements made by the interviewees represented the whole range of possibilities from no support to total support. On the basis of the necessity for financial support as made evident by the respondents and the majority of the opinions of the interviewees, the conclusion was reached that, realistically, unless the trend now present against federal financing of post-master's programs below the PhD level is reversed, the majority of those wishing to participate in programs would have to be accommodated on a part-time basis.

INTERVIEWS

REFERENCES IN CHAPTER 7

1. Argyris, Chris. "T-Groups for Organizational Effectiveness," *Harvard Business Review* 42:60—74 (Mar. — Apr. 1964).
2. Asheim, Lester E. "Education and Manpower for Librarianship: First Steps toward a Statement of Policy," *ALA Bulletin* 62:1096—1106 (Oct. 1968).
3. Barzun, Jacques. *The House of Intellect.* New York: Harper, 1959.
4. Bergen, Daniel P. "Librarians and the Bipolarization of the Academic Enterprise," *College and Research Libraries* 24:467—80 (Nov. 1963).
5. Bundy, Mary Lee, and Paul Wasserman. "Professionalism Reconsidered," *College and Research Libraries* 29:5—26 (Jan. 1968).
6. Chapman, Edward A., John Lubans, Jr., and Paul L. St. Pierre. *Library Systems Analysis Guidelines.* New York: Wiley, 1970.
7. Corson, John J., and R. Shale Paul. *Men Near the Top: Filling Key Posts in the Federal Service.* Baltimore: Johns Hopkins Pr., 1966.
8. Douglass, Robert R. "The Personality of the Librarian." Doctor's dissertation, Univ. of Chicago, Graduate Library School, Chicago, 1957.
9. Fayol, Henri. *General and Industrial Management.* London: Pitman & Sons, 1949.
10. Ginzberg, Eli, and Carol A. Brown. *Manpower for Library Services.* New York: Conservation of Human Resources Project, Columbia Univ., 1967 (ED 023 408).
11. Ginzberg, Eli, and John L. Herma. *Talent and Performance.* New York: Columbia Univ. Pr., 1964.
12. Harvey, John. "The Educational Needs of Special Librarians." Paper delivered at the 5th annual IBM Librarians' Conference, White Plains, New York, Dec. 13, 1963.
13. Joeckel, Carleton B., ed. *Current Issues in Library Administration.* Papers Presented before the Library Institute at the University of Chicago, August 1—12, 1938. Chicago: Univ. of Chicago Pr., 1939.
14. Knight, Douglas M., and E. Shepley Nourse, eds. *Libraries at Large: Tradition, Innovation and the National Interest.* New York: Bowker, 1969.
15. Kortendick, James J. "Continuing Education and Library Administration," *ALA Bulletin,* 61:268—72 (Mar. 1967).
16. ———"Curriculum: Administration," *Drexel Library Quarterly* 3:92—103 (Jan. 1967).
17. Likert, Rensis. *The Human Organization: Its Management and Value.* New York: McGraw-Hill, 1967.
18. Lilley, Dorothy. "Graduate Education Needed by Information Specialists and the Extent to Which It Is Offered in Accredited Library Schools." Doctor's dissertation, Columbia University, New York, 1969.
19. Longnecker, Henry C. "Staffing an Information Group." Internal report. Philadelphia: Smith Kline & French Laboratories, 1958.
20. Lothrop, Warren C. *Management Uses of Research and Development.* New York: Harper, 1964.
21. McGregor, Douglas. *The Human Side of Enterprise.* New York: McGraw-Hill, 1960.
22. Minder, Thomas. "Library Systems Analyst — A Job Description," *College and Research Libraries* 27:271—76 (July 1966).

REFERENCES

23. Morrison, Perry D. "The Personality of the Academic Librarians," *College and Research Libraries* 24:365—68 (Sept. 1963).
24. Muller, Robert H. "The Research Mind in Library Education and Practice," *Library Journal* 92:1126—29 (Mar. 1967).
25. Porter, Lyman W., and Mildred M. Henry. "Job Attitudes in Management: V. Perceptions of the Importance of Certain Personality Traits as a Function of Job Level," *Journal of Applied Psychology* 48:31—36 (Feb. 1964).
26. Schultz, Claire. "Things They Don't Teach in Library School," *Special Libraries* 54:513 (Oct. 1963).
27. Stone, Elizabeth W. *Factors Related to the Professional Development of Librarians.* Metuchen, N.J.: Scarecrow, 1969.
28. System Development Corporation. "Grooming Tomorrow's Managers," *SDC Magazine* 13:3—15 (Jan. 1970).
29. Underwood, Willis O. "A Hospital Director's Administrative Profile," *Hospital Administration* 8:6—24 (Fall 1963).
30. Wasserman, Paul, and E. Daniel. "Library and Information Center Management" in Carlos A. Cuadra, ed. *Annual Review of Information Science and Technology,* v.4, p.405—32. Chicago: Encyclopaedia Britannica, 1969.

8
Conclusions and Recommendations

By way of introduction, a few statements regarding the methodology of the study seem worthy of reiteration. The random sampling of the librarians lends validity to the questionnaire results reported in the earlier chapters. The study demonstrates how a job inventory, competently analyzed, can provide valuable information toward curriculum building. The project also uses information from two different hierarchical levels of professionals effectively fused to provide guidelines for continuing education within the profession. The overall design of the study and the combination of methods used to complement it support the contention that professional curriculum building need not be an unscientific trial-and-error method unrelated to actual, data-verified needs.

The study concentrated on the continuing-education needs of librarians at the middle and upper level (grades 9 through 14) in the federal complex. However, as has been pointed out, conclusions reached in this study for these levels may be applicable in large part to the whole profession. It would seem apparent that federal librarians form a representative sample of practicing librarians from each comparable level. The precise degree to which the segment of the profession under study here is representative of the whole profession at these levels can be verified only when comparable investigations are made for other segments. These are suggested in Recommendations for Further Study and Research, page 308.

PROFESSIONAL PROBLEMS REFLECTED IN STUDY

Although the central thrust of this analysis has been in the area of curriculum building at the post-master's level, the study is broad in its dimensions and indicates the multiplicity of problems that the library and the library profession face today. In his penetrating and thorough study entitled *Professional Education and the Public Services*, Mosher (18:66—67) outlines four major underlying problems facing professional education today. The present study produces evidence that all of these problems are present within the profession of librarianship. It is not within the scope of this study to answer all of these questions, and it must be borne in mind that the information about the problems that is presented by these research findings reflects the opinions of but two groups within the profession — the federal librarians at the middle and upper levels of management, and the top-level administrators of federal libraries — although their reactions are probably typical of the profession as a whole.

Answered or not, the problems themselves are important, and they certainly merit the close consideration of educators who are concerned with restructuring the basic professional MLS program as well as educators who are planning post-master's programs. They also indicate lines of research which would be beneficial at this particular time. The problems that have particular relevance to professional education are:

1. *Professional Boundaries.* To what extent should professional education for librarianship go beyond the traditional boundaries of the profession? More broadly, how should educators define the content of the profession? For example, should it include automation and computer science? information science? systems design and analysis? When a profession uses the strategy of widening the boundaries of its own activities by taking in a broader foundation of knowledge and enlarges its operation to include a broader range of activity and responsibility, Mosher (18:25) warns, "The process of assimilation in competition with other professions may be difficult and highly competitive.... The ensuing digestion can be most disruptive, even destructive of the unity and integrity of the profession itself."

2. *Intraprofessional Fission.* To what extent and at what stage should subspecialization be recognized or encouraged in the

educational process? The broadening of knowledge at the base of the profession, coupled with the widening boundaries of its legitimate operations, tends to have a divisive effect upon the profession as a whole. Individual groups whose work is focused on common problems, distinct from the profession as a whole, develop a subcommunity of interest. As these subgroups grow strong, the ties to the broader parent profession become weaker. Thus the process of specialization forces subdivision into professional segments and subsegments which weakens their identity with the parent profession. The question arises, How much of this type of subdivision based on specialization should the professional school encourage? It is important to realize, as Mosher points out, that professionals can only continue to exercise social and political influence as long as they can maintain to the public the appearance, or the illusion, of internal unity. As a consequence:

... there is a continuing striving for a basis of unity which will tie the many strands together, yet maintain a clear distinctiveness from other professional groups. There is a search for a common basis in doctrine, acceptable to all, but not so generalized as to be meaningless. And there is a search for a common, central core of knowledge and technique [18:27].

3. *Obsolescence.* How should professional educators cope with the accelerating growth of knowledge relevant to an individual profession? How much emphasis should the profession as a whole give to continuing education? In a rapidly developing profession, a practitioner may be at his peak between the ages of 25 and 35; by the time he reaches 50 he may be totally obsolete unless he has taken positive steps which are within his range to cope with obsolescence. Fortunately, the educational process by which the professional is kept up-to-date can be studied and made to cope with this problem. The pertinent questions would seem to be: (1) How can older professionals gain the skills and competencies that are essential for the continuing successful fulfillment of their jobs? and (2) How can they be motivated to take advantage of the opportunities that are offered?

4. *Organization and Management.* To what extent and at what stage should professional education recognize and prepare

students for managerial responsibilities which a large percentage of them will subsequently assume? This is one of the main problems dealt with in this study, but it is not unique in librarianship. It is a problem for all of the professions, for it has been found that a growing proportion of positions in business, as well as in public administration, are filled by those who have been given little, if any, training for their role as administrators and managers. It is the same problem that Corson and Paul (3) devoted major attention to in their writing which has been cited earlier in this study.

The data from the study mirror existing problems in these four areas. Of critical importance, however, is the impression gained from the totality of the findings that there is an urgent need for a general upgrading of the profession. The latter term carries with it many meanings,* but as used here it refers chiefly to raising the standards of professional education, especially at the postentry level. Emphasis on education is important for the advancement of a profession, for a scientific society emphasizes rational analysis for the solution of problems. Knowledge of subject areas furnishes insight into library needs, and methods of inquiry used to develop areas of knowledge provide the tools for problem solving in librarianship. Sound education will raise standards and even create new definitions of performance.

It should be pointed out, however, that as the profession is successful in this upgrading process, a bilevel differentiation will undoubtedly emerge as it has in other "upgraded" professions. On one level, supporting the occupation of librarianship, will be the further development

---

*Mosher (18:30—31) has defined *upgrading* in the following terms: "Within most of the professions, there seems to be a continuing, restless pressure for what is often somewhat ambiguously referred to as 'upgrading.' And within many of those occupational fields, there is similarly a pressure for upgrading in the direction of being recognized as a profession. The word is itself a catch-all, carrying a variety of different connotations, but these are seen as related and mutually self-supporting. Most generally, upgrading refers to the standing and esteem in which the occupation is held in society — or at least among persons closely associated with it, and this of course applies to the individual practitioners of the occupation. It applies also, in some but not all cases, to the income-commanding power of the profession, its strength in the labor marketplace. Indeed, its most literal meaning, in civil service terminology, is reclassification upward to higher-salaried grades. It means the raising of standards of professional education, of entrance, and of performance, and enforcing such standards with increasing strictness. It means, in a scientized society, becoming more and more scientific, rational, and objective. It means attracting better and better recruits into the profession; developing and enforcing codes of ethics; eliminating amateurs; and divorce from politics."

CONCLUSIONS AND RECOMMENDATIONS

of subprofessionals to perform essential clerical work that does not require professional training. This study provides ample evidence that professionals feel quite strongly about this differentiation and the need to train clerks where the decisive skills and knowledge of the true professional are not required.

The respondents were very discouraged by the large amount of clerical and subprofessional duties they were performing. Their attitude was reflected in nearly every section of the questionnaire. To give an indication of how fully the respondents' talents were being used, the questionnaire asked how many hours a week were spent on avoidable detail work that the respondents felt should not be a part of their jobs. Ninety percent reported spending from 1 to 38 hours a week. Only 10 percent of those answering this question reported "no time" spent in this manner. This is in marked contrast to the 17 percent who spent more than 16 hours a week on avoidable details. The mean number of hours spent by the 321 respondents answering this question was 9.1. A hope was expressed that the library school might be concerned with this problem. Several respondents thought that in its training of managers a method of work organization more satisfying at least to professional employees might be found. It is interesting to note that the possibility of respondents enrolling for a post-MLS program (based on their statements of interest) tended to increase as the amount of avoidable detail work on the job increased.

At the second level will be the growth of professionalism in librarianship. With the standards and qualifications constantly rising for new recruits to the profession, an increasing obligation is put on older practitioners to keep up through some form of continuing education in order to qualify for positions of leadership. Unless the older professional engages in continual professional development, experience alone can become actually disqualifying.

This study, as well as other recent ones cited in it, has shown that a very large number (46.6 percent in the study) have come to librarianship from other professions. These individuals from other professions have two characteristic variables: (1) they are older (average age of the respondents in the study was 44.4 years); and (2) they have a greater number of years between the bachelor's and the MLS degrees — which this research shows tends to decrease the likelihood that they will engage in continuing-education programs. As upgrading of the profession increases, it will be increasingly difficult for those from other professions to enter because of the number of years of education and the number of skills that will be necessary for them to qualify as professionals. Those who have already entered by this gate will often find themselves at a disadvantage.

LIBRARY EDUCATION NEEDS AT THE POST-MASTER'S LEVEL

The primary means of meeting the need for upgrading the profession recommended in this study is a library school-based post-master's program, interdisciplinary in nature and one year in duration. The section of the report dealing with this major recommendation is divided into three main parts. The first part attempts to identify the "why" and deals with the character of educational needs at the post-MLS level as revealed from the data collected in this study. Specifically, it presents answers that emerge from the survey to two questions: (1) Is there a need for formal course work at the post-master's level in librarianship? and (2) Are librarians with several years of experience (average of 14 years in this study) interested in taking courses at this level? In other words, if a program is offered, what will be the probable demand for it? The second part discusses the "how," or the form and attributes that those in the survey recommended for such a program. The third part considers the "what," that is, what should be the content or course design of the program as indicated from the findings in the study.

Character of the Educational Needs

In the study, the post-master's educational needs of middle- and upper-level librarians were elicited in several ways. The self-perceived needs of the respondents to the questionnaire and the views of the top-level library administrators concerning the needs of this same group of middle- and upper-level librarians are summarized. Taken together, they yield an overall view of the needs for post-master's education of middle- and upper-level (grades 9 through 14) librarians today. It was found that the character of the educational needs is closely related to, and results from, their present (as opposed to possible future) job activities.

In Part II of the questionnaire, entitled Your Educational Needs, the librarians indicated their interest in post-MLS library education in relation to three categories "course now," "course later," and "workshop." Seventy percent of the respondents checked courses they would take in a workshop format; 51 percent checked "course later"; and 45 percent checked "course now." There were, however, 135 respondents, some of whom checked "workshop," who did not check either the "course now" or "course later" categories. Of the 78 courses listed there was no course that was not checked by some of the respondents.

CONCLUSIONS AND RECOMMENDATIONS

Of the 10 courses which the librarians ranked the highest in the categories "course now" and "course later," 7 were in the area of administration and management, and 3 dealt with the automation of library processes and information retrieval. It is significant to note that this high interest in administration was also brought out in the job inventory where the highest-ranking categories were directing, planning, and staffing; and by far the highest single job activity, in the dimensions of both time and importance, was "Directly supervise and guide subordinates."

More evidence of interest in post-MLS education was provided by asking the respondents if they would enroll for a one-year post-MLS program (as distinguished from single courses) in library science. It was found that 38.9 percent of the respondents stated that they would enroll in either (both in some cases) the post-MLS year-long program or a doctoral program in library science. The interest was far greater, however, in the one-year program (33.4 percent) than in the doctoral program (16.2 percent). The degree of interest in both of these programs was generally the same for men as for women, and the same for administrators as for nonadministrators. As the grade level increased, the interest in the one-year post-MLS program tended to decrease. In spite of this, however, 30 percent of the respondents in the study at grades 12—14 indicated a willingness to take a post-MLS program (as compared with 38.9 percent overall demand); thus there is evidence that, even in the higher grades, there would be a considerable demand for such courses if they were provided.

The findings do indicate, however, that special motivational factors would have to be taken into account if a substantial percentage of those in the upper grades are to be reached by post-MLS training. These personalized criteria are the same for the one-year program as for the doctoral program. Some practical considerations of the prospective scholars are: partial or total financial support, curricular content, leaves of absence, accessibility, and flexible scheduling.

In addition to post-MLS programs in library science, 29 percent of the respondents stated that they would enroll for a graduate program in other subject areas at a predoctoral level. Administration and management (24 respondents), history (14), literature (12), information science (8), and biological and medical science (6) were the most frequent fields listed. In answer to the question, "Would you enroll for a Ph.D. program in another subject area?" 15 percent of the respondents answered yes. History (9 respondents), foreign languages (7), and administration and management (5) were the most frequent fields listed. Only 2 listed any of the natural sciences (earth science and mathematics); 2 listed information science.

When related to the professional problem of obsolescence, the following findings seem significant:

1. Respondents were asked to indicate what formal study they had engaged in since receiving their library science degree. Only 15.1 percent reported they had taken six credit hours or more; 27.7 percent had taken a workshop and/or less than six hours; and 57.3 percent had taken no formal course or workshop in any field. A further analysis showed that those who have already engaged in some more or less formal continuing education were predominantly those who are interested in post-MLS degree programs.

2. Nearly one-half (48.5 percent) of the respondents (67.2 percent of the administrators and 32.8 percent of the non-administrators) listed courses they lacked that would have been especially helpful to them in their present positions.

3. It was found that because of deficiencies in training, more than one-fifth (22.2 percent) of the respondents reported that they were not performing duties in their jobs which they felt were required.

The top-level library administrators revealed through the interviews that they were in favor of a post-master's program being offered. Generally, they considered such a program important enough that they would allow full-time employees to attend on a part-time basis. Relating possible post-MLS programs to on-the-job training, the interviewees felt there would always be a need to provide on-the-job and in-service training opportunities, but that such training programs did not take the place of, nor did they serve the same function as, education by means of library school-based formal courses at the post-MLS level.

Although the interviewees agreed on the importance of the availability of post-master's educational opportunity, they differed somewhat with the respondents in their priority rankings of the courses to be offered (correlation cocfficient of .64 between the ranking of interviewees as compared with respondents). The specific skills and competencies needed by middle- and upper-level library personnel, as perceived by the interviewees, were mostly in the areas of administration and automation. In particular, the courses in these two areas were

CONCLUSIONS AND RECOMMENDATIONS

ranked higher by the interviewees, and courses related to information science lower, than by the respondents. In the area of automation, only one course, the one entitled Automation of Library Processes, maintained the same high ranking with the interviewees, while the other two courses in automation slipped in rank as compared to those given by the respondents.

The study revealed that 63 percent of the respondents were administrators, that 44.8 percent of the administrators were heads of libraries or library systems, and that the average number of people supervised by this group was ten library employees. The question arises whether, on the basis of their professional degrees and experience gained on the job, these library administrators had acquired a solid grasp of the management skills necessary to fill these positions. Specific training for administrative positions was not apparent from the findings of the study.

What the responses revealed concerning the administrators was: (1) the graduate degree in library science was the last degree received for 94.3 percent of the administrators; (2) English (24.4 percent) and history (10.9 percent) majors predominate; and (3) the total humanities (43.5 percent), the social sciences (25.2 percent), and the sciences (10.9 percent) provided the subject backgrounds for the library administrators. Only 3 (1.3 percent) of the administrators had an undergraduate major in administration or management, and only 1 had obtained a master's degree in administration or management. Of the 81 respondents listing activities that they should have been performing but were not because of deficiencies in their educational background, 76.5 percent were administrators. Courses for credit following the library degree generally concentrated again in the humanities and social sciences, which would not directly contribute to managerial skills. Although the administrator averaged 17 years since completion of his library degree, 53 percent had taken no formal course work (including workshops) since receiving it, and only 15.7 percent had taken 6 or more hours of formal course work. It is true that these administrators had the advantage of experience, but as Harlow (9:6) pointed out:

> Experience is a famous but unorganized teacher, and most people learn to "role" with it rather than let it strike off fresh ideas and solutions. Its lessons are often poorly structured, are inferred rather than obvious, and are overlooked or forgotten because they happen in such an ordinary way. Only the discipline of formal education — systematic, questioning, interpretative, open-ended,

284

and demanding — can hope to keep up to date with today's growth and change.

Perhaps the most hopeful sign from this study is that overall, 39 percent of the respondents (average age 44) and 37 percent of the administrators (average age 47), all of whom will continue to exercise leadership for the next 10 to 20 years, themselves acknowledged the need for increased training in the areas of administration and management, and automation. Through retraining they can overcome limitations growing out of their past education and build upon their past. Such programs, however, are costly for the library school that provides the opportunity for formal study and also for the individual in time and resources.

It would be highly unrealistic to reach any conclusions concerning the real demand for a program at the post-master's level without taking into account conditions which the respondents indicated would be necessary for their enrollment — and more than 90 percent listed such conditions. Such personalized criteria as recommendations for curriculum format and content are discussed elsewhere in this chapter, but here special attention is focused on the primary hurdle — financial aid. Of those interested in a post-master's program of one-year duration, 36.9 percent stated that partial, and 13.1 percent that total, financial support would be a necessary prerequisite. In addition, 20.6 percent said leave from their present position would also be a requirement. As might be expected the percentages were even higher for those expressing an interest in doctoral programs: 50.9 percent indicated the necessity for partial financial support; 13.6 percent said that total financial support would be required; and 15.3 percent would expect leave of absence from their present jobs.

At the time of the interview the interviewees saw little possibility of giving full support to those employees interested in post-master's education on a full-time basis. They did indicate that they would support employees attending on a part-time basis by granting leave, and in some cases the interviewees indicated that they thought they could get funds to cover the cost of tuition if the course were closely related to present job needs. In view of the comments made, however, it was apparent that the majority of federal librarians would have to participate in continuing education at the post-master's level on a part-time basis. It was found that 40.8 percent of those librarians indicating they were interested in studying in a post-master's program were living more than thirty miles from an accredited library school. Though it was found that the respondents' willingness to take post-master's work was not affected by their distance from an accredited library school, if attendance was possible only on a part-time basis, actual participation would become dependent on distance. Therefore, taking all these factors into consideration, unless the trend now present against federal financing of post-master's programs below the PhD level is reversed, our sample indicates that the majority of those wishing to participate in programs would have to be accommodated on a part-time basis, and approximately 40.8 percent would not be able to attend at all on this basis.

Imparting knowledge is by no means an exclusive prerogative of the university. Practicing librarians can learn from many sources and many experiences, but educational institutions have traditionally been looked on as a source of additional knowledge. The education of the librarian should be a continuing process, and it can be aided periodically by his participation in formal academic programs, which can use the newest educational methods as well as recognize and enforce high standards needed to ensure that time spent in study is worthwhile. Financial means must be found to prepare and offer up-to-date instruction in the selected fields where the demand is widespread if we are to make the best use of our professional personnel in the administrative and technological areas of librarianship.

Form of the Education

Findings from the questionnaire and the interviews shed considerable light on attributes of post-master's education which could lead either toward or away from participation in formal course work. High-quality programs and practical courses relevant to their present positions were the two curriculum-centered conditions that were mentioned most often by the respondents. From the free-response answers of the respondents and the interviewees, "quality" seemed to be equated with interdisciplinary and systems-oriented course content, which provided for a variety of teaching methods. Or, as one respondent expressed it, "New programs should be just that — 'new' — based on innovative methods which make full use of the modern technology available today."

The recommendation that all work at the post-master's level be highly interdisciplinary in its approach was brought out strongly both by the respondents and the interviewees. It was felt that this approach is necessary to tie together the general and specialized understandings of librarianship today and express them in some coherent framework that has practical application in a real library situation. This suggestion is in line with a pattern that is generally being followed in management schools today. In librarianship it is particularly important for two reasons. First, the recent introduction of the computer into the library has brought with it a variety of related techniques. Second, it has been found in recent studies, including this one, that librarianship has few within its ranks who have had academic training in the necessary quantitative and behavioral concepts, or the administrative skills, that are important for the library's fulfillment of its present objectives or the probable requirements of tomorrow's libraries.

The emphasis by the respondents and the interviewees on the necessity of an interdisciplinary approach is very significant, because it indicates that the solution they see as the best way to bridge the gap between the traditional and the new spheres of library science is to enter into some kind of a cooperative team arrangement with those who have highly specialized knowledge in the fields of mathematics, social science, and information science. This attitude is reflected not only in the choice of courses considered most important for inclusion in the post-master's program, but also in the heavy demand for automation. In each instance, the findings indicate that the solution will not be to have the librarian become an expert in such divergent new fields as computer programming, game theory, cybernetics, and the requisite mathematical frameworks, but rather to have him develop an ability to cooperate and communicate with experts in these fields so that problems could be worked out cooperatively.

The research team is using the cooperative approach in the courses it is planning. One of the courses will be developed by a social psychologist, with the assistance of the research team and the cooperation of an educational technologist, a public administrator, and a library administrator. It should be noted, also, that this drawing into library education of those from other disciplines represents a practical way of handling existing, and likely to be continuing, library science faculty shortages.

The foregoing remarks underscore the need expressed by the interviewees for a systems perspective as a way of applying an interdisciplinary approach in the development of courses and curricula. A systems approach is concerned with providing a coherent framework for describing general relationships as a unitary whole. "The term 'systems' is generally used by social scientists to refer to an assemblage of components (characteristics of individuals or of groups of individuals) that have an ordered pattern of interrelationships. A systems

CONCLUSIONS AND RECOMMENDATIONS

perspective has five characteristics: there is a set of identifiable elements or components; these system components have interrelationships; the relationships have consequences; these consequences have further consequences (including the future set of relationships); both sets of consequences have effects on the objectives or outputs of the system" (Katz, 13:17—18). In addition there are analytic techniques associated with, and helpful in, the use of systems.

The systems approach to education, as summarized by Ofeish (19:763), "involves the specifications of behavioral objectives, the assessment of student repertoires, the development of instructional strategies, testing and revision of instructional units (validation), and finally packaging and *administering a validated learning system.*" Such an approach results in the development of learning experiences which are adjusted to students' needs and learning modes. The learning experiences are designed to produce the behaviors specified for each course. In other words, the specified behavioral objectives would be the constants of the system. With a systems approach, behavioral objectives become allocated during the construction of the whole program. The integration of knowledge from many sources is brought to bear on each particular course in line with course objectives. It is recommended that the systems perspective, therefore, should suffuse all of the courses planned at the post-master's level.

It is further recommended that while using a systems approach in the development of courses and curriculum, the program should assure that the student's central focus will be on practical library problems. Therefore, the program should be located in the library school rather than in other departments or schools of the university. The study indicated that while only a small percentage of the administrator's time might be spent in performing specialized library functions, the respondents and the interviewees felt that a large proportion of the knowledge required to perform library administrative and management functions is of a specialized library nature. Therefore, examples and practices used in administration courses at the post-master's level should be drawn from librarianship. The vocational interchangeability of the administrative function will need to be modified by the administrator's specialization in a given area. Specially oriented management competence must be the instructional objective. Bridging gaps between theory and practice was a need expressed in other ways, too. It was pointed out by some of the respondents that education at the master's level seemed to be devoting more and more attention to theory and less attention to application. Instructional reference to wide-ranging theory is possibly a reaction against the lingering effect of the origin of library education as apprenticeship training. It is important to view post-master's education as structuring of theory to bear upon problems faced by librarians on the job.

The interviewees stated quite positively that they would not let an employee take time to attend classes that did not relate specifically to his present job situation. The respondents likewise stated they would not be motivated to take courses unless these related to their work. Several of the respondents made the further suggestion that the professors seek out administrators to enable them to develop simulation exercises or case studies that were grounded in real library situations. The urgent necessity of formal course work related to the practical is emphasized by Mosher (18:108—9). He sees as a serious threat the fact that there seems to be an ever-widening gap in professional education between the professors — "the men who search for truth" — and the administrators, who decide and do. Further, he postulates that as scholars proceed more deeply into their subject matter, the problem of converting their findings and their wisdom into social policy becomes even greater and more important. If the present gap continues and increases in this area, he foresees that specialism may lead to "trained incapacity" for social decision.

Since the research team believes that there would indeed be many gains if professors in graduate schools had closer working relationships with the practicing administrators of libraries, one of the courses to be developed will be taught entirely by simulation techniques and will be based on actual practical data and problems obtained from a number of federal libraries. Never has a closer relationship been more needed than at the present, yet some library school faculty members seem to stand somewhat apart and aloof from their natural allies — the library administrators. It is recommended that this trend be reversed and that research be undertaken to determine ways and means by which closer working relationships may be established.

The respondents were quite emphatic in their insistence that instruction should not be limited to the lecture method. They urged a multimedia approach including the use of new technology in the teaching of all courses offered at the post-master's level. In the development of these courses it is recommended that a range of instructional methods be used, including newer media when they best fit given strategies and objectives. Faegre (6) has developed a helpful instrument for the evaluation of proposed media systems in higher education. This process consists of five steps: (1) preparing behavioral objectives (as indicated above); (2) describing the types of learning which can be inferred from the specified behaviors and then selecting one or more types from the learning categories; (3) with these behaviors and learning types in mind, describing one or more instructional strategies which could be used to accomplish the objectives; (4) identifying various media alternatives which best fit the objectives and instructional strategy description; and (5) selecting the one medium which best fits the characteristics in steps 1, 2, and 3; and the alternative in step 4. This procedure would result in the preparation of a media specification for a particular unit of instruction involving one medium, or in some cases a combination of media. A very similar process is described by Briggs (2:28—73), and illustrations of the analysis procedure for a group of behavioral objectives from a course are described in some detail.

It was apparent from the open-end responses of the respondents, as well as from the fact that only 15 percent of the respondents had taken as much as six credit hours since receiving their MLS degree (average of 14 years since the graduate degree in library science has been received), that motivational factors will have to be taken into account if a substantial number of librarians are to be reached by post-MLS training. The Graduate School of the Department of Agriculture (7), Hilgard (11), Crawford (4), and Jerkedal (12), are but four of those writing in the area of continuing education who stress the importance of motivational factors in relation to professional development. These authors feel that it is of prime importance that the student be adequately motivated for changes (in knowledge, comprehension, skill, attitude, values) to occur. Since enrollment at the post-MLS level is voluntary and not prescribed by the profession as mandatory for practice or promotion, the student must be motivated to attend. Concerning the participation of librarians in continuing education, a recent study of librarians (Stone, 22) discovered that librarians were most likely to be motivated to engage in formal continuing education when the content of the experience offered was directly related to the job situation and to on-the-job activities being performed by them. This finding is in keeping with the research of Herzberg and his associates (10, 20) who have found that factors that motivate the individual in the work situation are related to the work itself, achievement, and opportunity for personal growth. Jerkedal (12:229—30) in his study of top-management education concluded that the two most important factors which tended to cause changed behavioral patterns on the part of participants in advanced management educational programs are: (1) the degree of motivation that impelled participants to take the training, and (2) the determination on the part of the organization which sends the individual to take courses to impress upon every participant why the course content would meet his training needs — "in other words, motivate him before the training starts."

Once the individual has enrolled in the course, motivation must be kept sufficiently high for learning to take place. Whether original motives can last or can be transposed into ones strong enough to bring about the learning set for the students is in large part dependent upon the instructional skills and the conscious effort of the teacher. The *Faculty Handbook* of the Graduate School of the Department of Agriculture (7:40) states:

> The problem of motivation becomes one of organizing... activities in such a way that the student will begin to derive satisfaction from new ways of behaving before old patterns are relinquished.... Intellectual mastery is rewarding when the student recognizes that learning one thing allows him to go to something which before was out of reach. Thus the cumulative power of learning is eventful to the student himself.

These conditions make it imperative that the student perceive the proposed learning task as personally important or significant to his job or career. It puts on the teacher the responsibility for helping the student find materials that are relevant to his concerns in relation to his job. A student unwilling to attempt certain kinds of changes may fear failure or see changes as an attack on his attitudinal patterns which he values. Group forces, if skillfully used, can provide a supportive atmosphere and can exert great influence on attitudes and values. It has been found that involvement in class activities related to the work situation is an important way of sustaining student motivation. McKeachie (16) suggests that the use of roles drawn from work situations is one of the most effective ways of bringing down barriers to involvement in class activities. Involvement is, of course, evidence of the formation of more favorable attitudes toward learning experience. It is recommended, therefore, that library schools give special attention to those factors which up to the present time have been found important in motivating participation in formal course work at the post-MLS level, especially high-quality course work relevant to the librarian's job situation, as well as certain personalized criteria — the need for financial support, leave of absence, accessibility, timing, and the desirability of flexible scheduling. It is also recommended that the library administrator be helped to see that he plays an important part by his encouragement or discouragement in whether or not the

CONCLUSIONS AND RECOMMENDATIONS

individual is motivated to engage in further formal education following the MLS degree.

The most popular format chosen for course content was the workshop (70.1 percent of the respondents chose this category as compared to 63.0 percent for the categories "course now" and "course later" combined). The respondents and the interviewees recommended that library schools offer workshops regardless of what type of full-length courses at the post-master's level might be developed. One major advantage of the workshop, seen by both respondents and interviewees, is the ease of financing it. The interviewees stated that if the content covered related to the job situation, both financing and leave would be possible. Of special interest is that the courses receiving the highest rankings under the workshop format showed a different pattern from those in the "course now" or "course later" categories.

Content of the Education

A coherent picture of a post-master's program for middle- and upper-level library personnel has begun to emerge from this study. Based on the research findings, continuing education at the post-master's level is visualized as consisting of three main elements that interweave to form the whole fabric of content. These elements respond directly to the greatest needs of middle- and upper-level library personnel as revealed by the respondents and interviewees, namely, courses in the areas of (1) administration and management, (2) automation, and (3) specialized library subjects. Depending on such variables as the background and needs of librarians in a given geographical area, on present content of a school's MLS program, on available qualified faculty, on resources to develop programs, and on results from other surveys, a varying combination of courses might be undertaken. An overview of suggested program content is displayed in table 52.

Administration and Management. The overwhelming opinion of the respondents in answering the questionnaire seemed to be "Courses in administration should be a *must for all* in any post-master's program." After the courses in automation, they far outranked any course area in the questionnaire chosen by the respondents. The interviewees ranked the administration courses first in importance and considered them even more important for inclusion in a post-MLS program than did the respondents. The higher ranking given some of these courses by the interviewees is so pronounced and backed up by such convincing data obtained from the interview proper that it would seem such courses should be seriously considered by educators for inclusion in a post-MLS program, at least as electives, even though the rankings of the questionnaire respondents standing alone might not seem to warrant such inclusion. These differences in rankings between the respondents and the interviewees were due chiefly to the fact that the perspective of the top-level administrators in relation to a specific job is different from that of the librarians at the middle and upper level. The administrator

TABLE 52
LIST OF HIGHEST PRIORITY COURSES[1] FOR POST-MASTER'S EDUCATION OF MIDDLE AND UPPER-LEVEL LIBRARY PERSONNEL BASED ON RANKINGS BY RESPONDENTS AND INTERVIEWEES: 1969

Major Elements	Number of Course in Questionnaire	Educational Content (Courses)
Library Administration	9.	Human Relations in Library Administration
	5.	Administrative Policies and Practices
	8.	General Management
	6.	Communication Theory and Processes
	15.	Program Planning and Budgeting
	*10.	Innovation and Planned Change in Library Organizations
Automation	26.	Automation of Library Processes
	28.	Information Retrieval Systems
Specialized Library Courses	* 1.	Building and Evaluating Library Collections
	* 3.	Current Practices in Acquisition and Selection of Non-Book Materials
	*19.	Administration of the Special Federal Library
	*43.	Information Retrieval for Clientele
	*74.	Search Logic and Tactics
	*93.	Systems Analysis for Library and Information Center Operations

[1] For the purposes of this paper, a course is assumed to consist of three class hours and six to nine hours of non-class preparation per week for about fifteen or sixteen working weeks. Four or five of these courses would constitute a full term.

* Suggested as electives.

293

tends to look at a job as part of the whole mission of the library system and sees more clearly how the job relates to the overall goals of the library. These distinctions were particularly noticeable in the case of six courses: Communication Theory and Processes, Policy Formation and Decision-Making, Innovation and Planned Change in Library Organizations, Personnel Problems under the Impact of Technological Change, Theories of Organization and Management, and Public Administration.

Before going into detail about the courses which were rated highest by the respondents and the interviewees, it is interesting to note that in chapter 3 it was postulated that the continuing-education needs of federal librarians would be similar to those of other types of librarians. Indeed, three recent studies offer support for this assumption. The three studies cited below quite uniformly show that a strong need is felt by all types of librarians for knowledge in the area of administration, often coupled with needs in the area of library automation. These results are very similar to those reported in chapter 5 of this study which reveal automation and administration to be the top priority needs of federal librarians also.

In 1967, DeProspo and Huang (5:25) of Rutgers sent a questionnaire to a stratified sample of 184 academic, public, and school libraries. They found the most urgently needed areas in which the administrators of these libraries wanted continuing education were: (1) application of machines, (2) personnel administration, and (3) evaluation of library problems. After these there was a drop in frequency and the next three were: communications, systems analysis, and budgeting. From the data collected, the authors concluded that "librarians seem not to be familiar with the more recent developments in the field of administration and management."

In New York, in 1969, Meyer (17) conducted a statewide survey of continuing professional education needs of public librarians (small, medium, and large libraries). Top needs indicated were for training in: (1) group dynamics, (2) personnel development, and (3) management skills.

Also, in 1969, the American Association of School Librarians sent out a questionnaire to members which asked for the self-perceived needs of school librarians in the area of continuing education. Whether the results were analyzed by weighted choices (1, 2, 3) or all lumped together, they were the same: coming out on top each time as "management philosophy and techniques" (1).

Hence, the conclusions arrived at in this study are supported by two approaches: one is direct, and one is indirect. The latter has been provided by evidence that federal libraries resemble other libraries in their major budget allocations and size. As for the former, there is evidence from independent sources that the areas in which the respondents in this study most urgently need to have continuing education are the same as, or closely related to, the areas most urgently needed by other types of librarians.

The courses in the area of administration and management that would seem to have the highest priority for inclusion are: Human Relations in Library Administration, Administrative Policies and Practices, General Management, Program Planning and Budgeting, Communication Theory and Processes, and Innovation and Planned Change in Library Organizations.*

1. Human Relations in Library Administration: Exploration of the interpersonal and inter-group relationships in a library organizational setting: employee motivation; the managerial environment (course no.9, Part II of the questionnaire).

With the interviewees this course ranked first of all the 78 courses in the questionnaire, and was, as a matter of fact, the only course that none of the top-level library administrators considered "not really needed" at the post-master's level. Taking the replies of all the 365 respondents together in the category "course now" or "course later," it ranked sixth, and for those respondents stating a definite interest in enrolling in a post-master's program, it ranked fourth. In addition, the open-end free responses of both the respondents and the interviewees showed that current environmental conditions in libraries demonstrate the great need for this course.

The areas most often mentioned in the free-response conversations with interviewees as important for inclusion in this course were: skills in interpersonal and intergroup relationships; motivational factors in organizational behavior; administrative ability to develop staff to their full potential, including accountability for employee development; and recent social and psychological research findings regarding leadership roles. If the course Personnel Problems under the Impact of Technology is not to be offered in the program, it was the recommendation of the interviewees that its main insights be included in the human relations course with special emphasis on the importance of maintaining a balance between the personnel subsystem and the technological subsystem in the library.

*In addition to these six courses, other courses that contain the chief competencies that the interviewees indicated should be covered at the post-master's level are presented in appendix table 23.

CONCLUSIONS AND RECOMMENDATIONS

> 2. Administrative Policies and Practices: Emphasis on library organization and its operational problems relevant to top levels of administration (course no.5 in Part II of the questionnaire).

Competencies mentioned by the interviewees included practical experience in policy formation and the recognition that it is not something that can be delegated to others; skill in executing policies agreed upon; and an understanding of the ethics of policy and the political and social forces which affect it. They also suggested that the course include a study of the nature, reliability, and accessibility of information upon which administrative decisions are based and the impact on decision-making that computer technology may have in the future. Finally, the interviewees emphasized the importance of the top administrators' recognizing the need for a systems approach in administering the library with emphasis on the various subsystems in the library and the interdependent, interacting character of these subsystems. It should also be noted that the second highest-ranking area of deficiencies in previous training which are now important in the respondents' jobs was in the area of administrative skills.

> 3. General Management: Developing the skills of the middle-level library manager by focusing on the basic processes of management (course no.8 in Part II of the questionnaire).

This course, focusing on the functions of the management process, was ranked third in importance by the interviewees and eighth by the respondents. Its importance was further emphasized by the number of competencies the interviewees mentioned that they hoped would constitute the terminal behavior patterns of those who might take the course. Summarized, these are: (1) skill in directing, which the interviewees considered the most universally needed competency among librarians; (2) development of a fuller understanding of the management process; (3) necessity of realizing that the library is part of a larger system and finding ways of relating to that system; (4) ability to understand staffing requirements; (5) ability to organize a department so it relates to all the other functions of the library; and (6) ability to use analytical techniques.

The interviewees emphasized that this course should be taken by returning librarians even though they may have had an introductory course in principles of management or administration at the MLS level. At the MLS level, they said, the course emphasized knowledge and theory, but after a few years' experience the returning librarian needed to take a course in which the emphasis was on skill in application and in solving the type of problems that he was now facing. As a matter of fact, it was suggested that the introductory course now offered in most accredited library schools should be a prerequisite for admission to this course, and if the enrollee had not had it, he should be required at least to audit it before admission to this course at the post-master's level, which they saw as being taught quite differently than the MLS course in management. It should also be noted here that the job inventory, as filled out by the respondents, gave important clues to the weight that various segments of a course on management processes should have. For example, by far the top-ranking job activity in relation to the dimensions of time and importance was directing, and by far the highest-ranking single job activity, both for time and importance, was "Directly supervise and guide subordinates."

4. Communication Theory and Processes: The communication processes: media techniques employed by the library manager; public relations (course no.6 in Part II of the questionnaire).

The course Communication Theory and Processes was ranked considerably higher by top-level administrators than by the respondents (rank 6 compared to 17). However, the importance of communication skills in the minds of the interviewees was reflected not only in their ranking of this course, but also in repeated and forceful comments by a majority of the interviewees that successful librarianship demands skill in communications perhaps to a greater degree than any other single skill — but, unfortunately, the top-level administrators found this skill weak or lacking among librarians.

The importance of the many facets of communication for the librarian was reflected in the many related competencies listed by the interviewees, including: the ability to communicate the objectives of the library to those in other disciplines when required; the ability to present a position paper and/or alternative choices to a superior for him to use in decision-making; the ability to communicate to subordinates what is wanted and expected of them; and the ability to listen and be communicated with. All data stressed the urgent need for improved efficiency in librarian-library user communication.

A further reason for including this course is that the questionnaire course area entitled Representing in the job inventory, covering such individual activities as public relations, publicity, report writing, editing, and the layout of publications, was the second-largest area in which respondents said that they were leaving activities unperformed

CONCLUSIONS AND RECOMMENDATIONS

due to lack of training. Therefore, these findings would seem to support the observations of the interviewees that good communication techniques are not widely taught by library schools, and that graduates are left to their own devices in this crucial facet of communications. This condition was also noted by Hall (8:146) in her survey of public library training.

> 5. Program Planning and Budgeting: Library applications. The processes and instruments of planning, programming, and budgetary functions of the library, with special emphasis on the current approaches of the federal government in this function (course no.15 of Part II of the questionnaire).

Program Planning and Budgeting was one of the few courses which received the same rating from the respondents as from the interviewees (rank 8). Sixty percent of the interviewees specifically mentioned competency in program planning and budgeting (PPB) as one of the skills that should be developed at the post-master's level. They pointed out that because of a complete lack of such training, librarians are not able to prepare budgets in today's style.

Planning is an essential part of PPB, and in the job inventory it was found that planning ranked second among the processes of management desired by the respondents (directing, first) in terms of time and importance. Another indication of the need of such a course is that activities falling under the administrative function category of planning constituted the third-largest area of unable-to-be-performed activities due to lack of training. Also, as explained by Schultz (21:23):

> A crucial aim of the PPB system is the analysis of alternatives to find the most effective means of reaching basic program objectives, and to achieve these objectives for the least cost. The goal is to force Federal agencies to consider particular programs not as ends in themselves — to be perpetuated without challenge or question — but as means to objectives, subject to the competition of alternative and perhaps more effective or efficient programs.

In other words, the techniques of program budgeting also include the techniques of decision-making, and decision-making was one of the chief competencies that the interviewees (65 percent of them) said should result from any post-master's program.

And finally, one does not need to search very far in library literature to find that budgets and financial matters make up one of the chief areas in which libraries are having difficulties today, difficulties which call for all the expertise that a librarian can possibly master. Based on a review of the educational background of the respondents, it is an area in which they have probably had the least training for their administrative tasks.

   6. Innovation and Planned Change in Library Organizations: The social psychology and management implications of change (course no.10 in Part II of the questionnaire).

This course was rated very high by the interviewees (rank 7), but only rated a rank of 48 from the respondents. The difference in rating would in itself seem to imply that the librarian returning for a post-MLS program basically needs to be shown or taught (or persuaded) to recognize the necessity for continual adaptation to change as well as the possibility within any library system of the consensus for change and action. The interviewees were aware of, and anxious to correct, the lethargy toward change that has characterized the profession.

Much of the librarian's time, the interviewees believed, should go into long-range planning, undertaken to bring about a change in prevailing policies and to improve the processes and procedures for adapting an organization to the new technology. The 50 percent of the interviewees who mentioned this competency were quite emphatic in its importance. In their opinion, the library manager must be willing to assume a beneficent control over official politics to make changes within the library. They would cast the librarian in the role of the agent for change.

This role, according to Lippitt (14:119—26) includes: (1) diagnosing the problems of the system to be changed; (2) assessing its motivations and capacities to change; (3) appraising the agents' own motivations and resources; (4) guiding the selection of appropriate change objectives; (5) assuming an appropriate helping role; (6) establishing and maintaining the helping relationship; (7) understanding and guiding the change process; (8) choosing the techniques and modes of behavior appropriate at different stages of the process; and (9) contributing to the development of basic skills and theories. It is evident that to fulfill such a role, the librarian needs to engage in research and development activity, and that he should be familiar with new research-based developments in related disciplines which would provide a broader perspective and would tend to make him more amenable to change.

CONCLUSIONS AND RECOMMENDATIONS

Furthermore, the library manager needs to look to the behavioral sciences to provide information about his problems—not to solve them, which would deprive him of his managerial role. The behavioral scientist can indirectly serve as an agent of change by planning the applications of theories and principles. The librarian, then, can apply them to his own area.

A further rationale for offering this course is that when asked what terminal patterns the interviewees would expect the librarian to have gained by participation in a post-master's program, the answers suggested attitudinal rather than cognitive changes. Rather than listing any specific competencies desired, their comments centered around objectives. The control over customary functions would by a long-range plan achieve the implementation of rational objectives.

Automation. Regardless of how the data from the questionnaire are analyzed, the chief demand for courses by the respondents was in the area of automation. Probably the most significant difference in rankings between the interviewees and the questionnaire respondents was in the area of automation. By the interviewees Automation of Library Processes was ranked third (as compared to first by the respondents), Information Processing on Computers twelfth (as compared to third), and Information Retrieval Systems nineteenth (as compared to second). Two of the interviewees did not think automation should be offered at all at the post-master's level, but that it should be required at the MLS level. The interviewees, on the whole, emphasized the necessity of the librarians' being able to communicate their needs and the library's objectives effectively to the computer and systems men. They seemed to be in agreement with Andrews (23:15) of Harvard who felt the critical task thus becomes "training the managers to ask and insist on answers to those questions that are of importance to them, not to the programmer or systems man."

A few factors showing the relationship of automation to the demand for courses by the respondents bear repetition:

1. The automation of some library functions does not assure that the library's employees want to study automation.

2. Involvement in automation at the supervisory level seems to bear the greatest relation to desire for such study.

3. Of the 9 librarians (2.5 percent) in the study who said that understanding of automation gained through on-the-job

experience was their greatest competence, 8 wanted to take course work in this area.

4. The 16.2 percent of the respondents who listed automation as one of their greatest weaknesses stated their little competence was due to a lack of training or knowledge.
5. The activities most frequently listed as not engaged in because of lack of previous training were in automation. Of the 23 respondents listing automation as an unable-to-be-performed activity, 20 were administrators.

The reason that so many showed a desire to take courses in automation, even though they were not presently engaged in it, seemed to indicate that they felt automation would be needed in their jobs in the near future. Librarians have come to an uneasy, but positive, feeling that automation — chiefly in the form of computer systems — has a part to play in their activities, but they are uncertain about what this part is and exactly how they should be prepared for it, and how it should be introduced to their libraries. It is recommended, therefore, that two courses in this area be offered as core courses in the post-master's program to help the individual bridge this information gap which seems to present a real threat to him in many instances. From the findings in the study the two courses recommended are: (1) Automation of Library Processes, and (2) Information Retrieval Systems.

1. Automation of Library Processes: Application of computer technology to library processes (course no.26 in Part II of the questionnaire).

This course was ranked first by all respondents and third by the interviewees. Twenty-five percent of the interviewees did not include it in their "should have" group of courses at the post-master's level and 10 percent thought it was not needed at all at that level. The interviewees electing the course were agreed on the relevant competencies that should be taught:

Certain basic concepts about the computer in society today and its use in a library system

An understanding by librarians of their role in automation

The mastery of terminology in the field of automation

Awareness of the potential applications of automation in libraries

CONCLUSIONS AND RECOMMENDATIONS

Need to put ADP operations in perspective with regard to the "economics of information."

Finally, this course was not considered a basic offering of the sixth-year program. The interviewees thought that now all students should be exposed to a general introductory course in automation at the master's level. One coming back for work at the post-master's level should be required to have that course or the equivalent at the MLS level as a prerequisite for admission to the program so the class might be able to start with a similar entry level for all the students.

2. Information Retrieval Systems: Structure and operation of information systems, including question analysis, search strategy, and thesaurus construction (course no.28 in Part II of the questionnaire).

The respondents uniformly ranked this course as their second choice, regardless of how the categories were formulated, except in one instance where it was ranked first ("course later"). Although the interviewees gave it a much lower rating (rank 21), their free-response answers during the interview indicate that they did not completely eliminate this as a possible course at the post-MLS level.

On the basis of the free-response statements of the respondents and the interviewees, particular course attention should be given to information flow and modes of retrieval, selective dissemination, current awareness programs, retrospective retrieval, and evaluation of retrieval effectiveness based on knowledge of user requirements. The master's level course, Automation of Library Processes, would be a prerequisite for admission to this course.

Specialized Library Functions. As the objective of this study was to determine post-master's educational needs for middle- and upper-level library personnel, it is not surprising to find that the preponderance of respondent demand falls within the areas of administration and automation or that in their free-response answers the interviewees mentioned fewer specialized functions than administrative or management functions, thus indicating that they thought management competency more important at this level than technical skills. It was found, as would be expected, that as the respondents moved up in grade, the amount of time devoted to administrative functions increased and that devoted to specialized library functions decreased. However, the findings also brought out the important concept that

302

although the administrator's tasks were largely managerial rather than of a specialized library nature, the knowledge required to perform these managerial functions effectively was technically "specialized" in its nature, and that administrators and supervisors needed to have at least a working knowledge of the specialities that constituted the operations they directed. The interviewees did not, however, think it necessary to take a full course in order to attain the requisite knowledge for effective supervisory performance. This same feeling was echoed by the respondents who specified freedom of selection from a variety of courses which balanced specialized subjects with other courses. The respondents also preferred the workshop, rather than the formal course, as a means of presenting specialized library functions.

Competencies mentioned most often by the interviewees that would probably best fall within the scope of Specialized Library Functions were: (1) greater expertise in providing reference service to library clientele; (2) greater understanding of the psychology of the user; (3) an innovative approach to little used, nonconventional library reference tools; (4) development of a sense of social responsibility to be reflected in library service; (5) an experimental approach to traditional practices in the area of technical services; and (6) efficiency and ease in using research methods to study library problems, with special emphasis on the need for the use of statistics.

From these suggestions, a number of courses emerge as possible electives in this area. These suggested electives are not discussed in detail as some version of most of them is already offered in library school programs and their content is familiar to library educators. However, it should be stressed that it is important in offering such electives to weigh certain other curriculum-related conditions that the respondents said were necessary if they were to return to study at the post-master's level. Worth noting among these conditions are: the provision of new content rather than old MLS material; job relevant content that will give them an opportunity for problem solving in a university setting; and an opportunity to acquire skills lacking in their previous training.

The courses in specialized aspects of library service which have the greatest demand and which are recommended electives are:

1. Building and Evaluating Library Collections: Criteria for evaluating and selecting library materials, and for devising and maintaining an acquisition system (course no.1 in Part II of the questionnaire).

CONCLUSIONS AND RECOMMENDATIONS

The interviewees in particular (they gave the course rank 8; the respondents, 38) seemed aware of the many new approaches to acquisitions activity which could be of value in facing up to the problems brought about by the proliferation of publications in all subject areas which has made it virtually impossible for any type of library to select title-by-title from current in-prints. Basically, the problem they voiced was identifying what is needed by their users and finding the most expeditious and economical ways of getting these materials on the shelves.

    2. Current Practices in Acquisition and Selection of Non-Book Materials: Including an understanding of the new technology which governs the selection and use of video tapes, dial access sets, audiovisual materials, etc., in libraries (course no.3 in Part II of the questionnaire).

The field of media is a large one, encompassing audiovisual education, books, special devices such as reading equipment, television, computers, photographic equipment, and a wide array of other materials. Media programs can range from almost no emphasis on the machinery to almost total emphasis, stressing the 8- and 16mm motion picture production, and video- and audio-tape production. As the range of media becomes more and more encompassing, programs are being centered in the library. Thus the librarian may no longer be concerned solely with selection, preparation, organization, and retrieval of printed materials; his position is rapidly becoming that of media specialist, and he must prepare himself to meet that challenge. This change as the interviewees (who ranked the course 12; the respondents ranked it 17) pointed out, is rapidly coming to all types of libraries.

    3. Administration of the Special Federal Library (course no.19 in Part II of the questionnaire).

Although the course entitled Administration of the Special Federal Library received a high priority (rank 4) from only the questionnaire respondents (rank 38 with the interviewees), it would seem that the course offering would merit consideration at the post-MLS level for several reasons. First, the field of administration is such that a concrete type of structure against which to project specific cases would seem to have value. The federal libraries would seem to provide one such example. Also, in a course on administration, the hierarchy of the personnel plays an important role. The federal libraries, with a well-

LIBRARY EDUCATION

defined common hierarchy of library personnel, are particularly well-suited to this purpose. Since the respondents stressed the need of added knowledge in the area of automation, the study of federal libraries, many of which are highly involved with automation, offers the opportunity to consider these aspects as part of the course. Further, since an individual federal library is likely to be part of a larger library network, such a course would offer a unique opportunity to present insights into the relationships of an individual library to its concomitant system.

Because of Washington's favorable library environment and the cooperation offered by several federal libraries, the research team will develop a model course on federal libraries which will be taught through the techniques of simulation. The verbal model (as opposed to a mathematical model) to be developed will consist of a description of a hypothetical library, giving a framework of facts, policies, procedures, and other information needed to make decisions about the library. A series of interrelated problems, each of which requires one or more administrative decisions, will be developed for use in the course. The model will describe a typical federal library, and the problems will be typical of upper management and administrative problems in a federal library.

4. Information Retrieval for Clientele: Forecasting and analyzing clientele needs; the psychology of the user; initiating user services; development of orientation programs for users; instructing users in reference methods and sources (course no.43 in Part II of the questionnaire).

Twenty percent of the interviewees spoke forcefully of the great need for a course covering these areas of clientele service. The chief competence emphasized was greater skill in understanding the psychology of the user, particularly in negotiating the reference question. This course was given rank 7 by the respondents; 15 by the interviewees.

5. Search Logic and Tactics (course no.74 in Part II of the questionnaire).

In general, the interviewees (by whom the course was given rank 12) felt a post-master's program should provide for added expertise in the area of search logic and tactics. One competency they mentioned particularly was the development of an innovative approach to little used and nonconventional library reference tools. Respondents ranked the course 14.

CONCLUSIONS AND RECOMMENDATIONS

>   6. Systems Analysis and Design for Library and Information Center Operations (course no.93 in Part II of the questionnaire).

Whether or not there is an automated system within a library, the interviewees felt the librarian should have sufficient familiarity with the concepts and phases of systems study — analysis, evaluation, and design — to be able to work cooperatively with professional systems designers and analysts toward increasing the efficiency and productivity of the library. The word emphasized was *cooperatively*, for the interviewees seemed in agreement that librarians of a given library have different roles to play in a library systems study which represents a demanding total library effort involving the entire library staff. The interviewees suggested that special emphasis be given in the course to (1) the ability of the librarian to relate the library's objectives to the professional systems designer; (2) the librarian's possessing enough knowledge to make the final decisions about redesign without having to turn them over to an outside analyst; and (3) the librarian's being able to balance the human needs with the technological needs of the library in order to obtain a balance in the whole library system. Some interviewees saw in systems design and analysis the potential for eliminating much of the avoidable detail work that many of the respondents complained so much about in the study. This course was given rank 12 by the respondents; 15 by the interviewees.

To sum up; these elective courses in specialized library subjects should be clearly associated with practical applications. The particular combination of electives offered would depend on the needs of the students enrolling as well as on the available faculty and teaching resources of the library school. It should also be pointed out that in developing a program for a particular school, a library educator might like to select, to meet special needs, electives other than those suggested in this section. A final note: Within each of these elective courses the instruction should be geared as much as possible to the job-related interests and needs of the individual student.

Workshop Courses. The study revealed that the most popular topics chosen for the workshop format showed a considerably different pattern from those in the course categories ("course now and/or course later"). The most obvious difference was that there were more non-administrative areas receiving high rankings. The subjects receiving the highest ranking for workshops were: (1) Automation of Library

Processes, (2) Building and Evaluating Library Collections, (3) Resources and Services of the Federal Library Complex, (4) Current Practices in Acquisition and Selection of Non-Book Materials, (5) Non-Conventional Library Reference Tools, (6) Circulation Systems, (7) Human Relations in Library Administration, (8) Administration of the Special Federal Library, (8) Information Retrieval for Clientele, (8) General Management, and (8) Current Issues in Librarianship and Information Science.

Detailed analysis of the workshop listings by many different types of breakdowns of the respondents (grade, age, type of position, etc.) led to the conclusion that in some subject areas, such as administration and automation, courses were too large in scope to be covered in the short period of time available in a workshop, thus preventing maximum gains from the time invested. Demand for type of course was related to responses to two questions: (1) "Are there any formal scientific, technical, or professional courses you lack which you feel would be especially helpful in your position?" (2) "In relation to your present position, are there any activities you should be engaged in for which your previous training has not prepared you?" It was found that demand for courses rather than workshop was positively related to activities named as responses to these questions. The respondents felt this was particularly true in subject areas in which they had no previous training or experience. On the other hand, the reason so many non-administrative courses were high on the list seemed to be that respondents had had training in these areas at the MLS level and merely wished now to use the workshop as a medium of bringing themselves up to date.

The following statement sums up the probable relationship between a library school's post-master's program and its workshop activity: To keep abreast of rapidly changing developments in technology that make automation a viable tool in the library, as well as to keep up with today's growth and changes in library school and related disciplines, takes more than exposure to courses at one point of time, as in a post-master's program. It takes continuing education of a formal character which is "systematic, questioning, interpretative, open ended and demanding" (Harlow, 9:6). Therefore, it is concluded that the library schools have an obligation, even as pointed out by the respondents and the interviewees, consistently and continually to offer workshops and institutes in the areas of administration, management, and automation, regardless of how effectively and comprehensively the post-master's program of one year's duration may be developed.

CONCLUSIONS AND RECOMMENDATIONS

Conclusion

In the preceding section the research findings from this study have been used to summarize the educational needs of middle- and upper-level library personnel and to make suggestions concerning the form and content of formal education at the post-master's level. Many implications can be drawn from these data to help understand and guide the design of programs at the post-master's level, but in and of themselves the data are not relevant to formulate the details of such programs. They do provide an information base for developing specifications for courses responsive to knowledge and skill requirements, especially through the analysis of the job-inventory findings and the analysis of needed competencies as suggested by the interviewees. Subsequently, three of the high-priority courses will be selected for development and packaging by a systems approach to educational planning: Human Relations in Library Administration, Administration of the Special Federal Library, and Application of Computer Technology to Library Processes.

As the study was not designed to produce data for building a doctoral program for practicing librarians, there can be no positive suggestions for a program at this level. What indications did emerge showed that the demand for such a program is not high (16.2 percent of the respondents), and that 95 percent of those expressing an interest stated that certain conditions (chiefly financial) would have to be met in order for them to enroll. As the real motivation for those who are willing to participate in a doctoral level program is not clearly understood, it may turn out that the proposed post-MLS program may provide the training these librarians are seeking. However, if it develops that the proposed post-MLS program cannot satisfy the training requirements for practicing librarians, a doctoral program created around their needs might well be contemplated.

RECOMMENDATIONS FOR FURTHER STUDY AND RESEARCH

There are many suggestions for further study and research that flow from this study. The ones that seem, in the minds of the authors, to be the most relevant and to have emanated most directly from these findings are:

1. Although it is postulated that the educational needs of middle-

and upper-level federal library personnel are similar to those of other types of librarians, parallel research based on other types of librarians, especially academic, public, and nongovernment special librarians (the current School Library Manpower Project is already providing similar data for school librarians) is needed for conclusive acceptance of this hypothesis.

2. Paralleling advances that are being made in other professions — such as medicine, engineering, and education — is a need for research on the practicality and effectiveness of extending educational opportunities beyond the walls of the professional school. As one respondent phrased it, "Use modern technology to take library school courses to where people are who need them and cannot travel." To meet the personal criteria that respondents said were necessary for them to participate in continuing education programs — namely, excellence of content, accessibility, flexibility, and continuity of offerings — it is recommended that research be undertaken to determine by what means formal library school courses can most effectively be taken to the individual or to groups in other locations. Ways of development suggested by the respondents were: (a) taking the campus to classrooms in libraries by the development of courses using the newest in technology, (b) taking the campus to the library through the development of individualized learning centers which would be available in libraries in every state, (c) taking the campus directly to the individual in his home by the use of the new technology, and (d) correspondence courses. In essence, what is needed is research and cooperative effort which would lead to the development of a conceptual and practical blueprint for the provision of equal, coordinated education opportunities throughout the country for all those librarians who need, want, and will continue their lifetime of post-graduate learning.

3. As it was found that a majority (57 percent) of the respondents had not been motivated to participate in any form of formal course work (including workshops and short-term courses) since receiving their graduate degree, it is recommended that a comprehensive study be undertaken which would seek to establish the most important factors related to the individual librarian's motivation toward participating in continuing-education activities. It would supplement the pilot study already completed in this area (Stone, 22) and should be based

on a much broader population base. Such a study should seek answers to such questions as: (a) What motivates librarians toward or deters them from participating in continuing education programs? (b) What are the necessary personal criteria that must be met in planning for continuing education if there is to be wide participation by all librarians? (c) What is the degree and kind of support that administrators need to give their employees regarding professional development activities? (d) How can the library school instill in the student the need for a lifelong program of professional growth? (e) Is there any relation between the amount of continuing education that librarians participate in and the fact that the profession itself has no standard recognition for advanced training? and (f) To what extent is continuing education the responsibility of the whole profession?

4. Inasmuch as the respondents indicated that workshops were the form of continuing education in which the highest percentage of librarians were likely to participate at the post-master's level, it is recommended that a more comprehensive approach to educational planning for short-term institutes and workshops is necessary, which would result in the raising of standards for such projects. The need for such a comprehensive approach to workshop planning and management becomes increasingly acute as the number of proposals submitted for federal funds for this form of continuing education increases, as greater allocations of money and personnel are being invested in workshops, as the range of subject areas continues to widen, and as the number of different agencies proposing workshops increases. It is further suggested that a comprehensive model be developed for planning, managing, and evaluating short-term institutes and workshops. Such a model should apply to every important phase of a project from its inception to its termination. Such a model should include such elements as: statement of criteria for proposal development of needs, priority considerations, staff and management, program activities and curriculum, facilities and evaluation. The model should be in a form which could be used by (a) those who write proposals, (b) those who operate projects, (c) those who evaluate proposals, and (d) those who evaluate the outcome of the programs. Such a model should result in the improvement of programs by providing specific criteria from

the conception to the culmination of a project and by providing feedback data throughout.

5. This study has shown that, in the eyes of the respondents, a great deal of professional time was spent on jobs that the librarians considered to be of a clerical nature. In fact, the librarians urged help from the library schools to correct this situation. The effects of this constant pressure for upgrading are pervasive, and correction will have to come from several sources. As the libraries make use of more paraprofessionals, as a result of better utilization of manpower and economic pressure, it will become increasingly necessary for the library school to provide not only adequate training for such supportive staff, who will be performing essential work which does not require professional training, but also instruction in efficient personnel management for the professional librarian.

It is recommended that several research studies be undertaken to determine more precisely the specific skills and knowledge needed by technicians in various types of libraries, the areas of training appropriate to the curricula of schools undertaking to prepare library technicians, the problem of absorbing this type of personnel into the library system, the evaluation of their contribution, and the skills and techniques needed by the professional supervisor to utilize supportive staff more effectively.

6. In the free-response answers of both the respondents and the interviewees, there were frequent suggestions that user studies should receive more attention from the profession. These suggestions took two forms: First, the largest single number (13) of suggestions concerned the need for further inquiry related to user studies. The respondents felt that querying actual users would point out shortcomings of practice that had become blind spots to the librarians as they worked. Further, they stated that without the users' points of view the data for developing continuing-education programs tend to be one-sided. "Librarians," they said, "should meet users' needs rather than just offer services. Librarians must know what these needs are in order to meet thm with maximum effectiveness." Second, it is recommended that a study paralleling the one on public library use conducted for the National Advisory Commission on Libraries be made of other types of libraries in order to explore the use and nonuse, and the adequacy of other

CONCLUSIONS AND RECOMMENDATIONS

types of libraries — such as academic, professional, federal and other special libraries — from the point of view of the user.

The transition from research to practice is always a slow and measured one rather than a single leap. It is a slow process from investigation to development, to production, and finally to evaluation. Sometimes it may seem that the evaluation takes so long that it can be bypassed, but as McConnell (15) has warned, "without evaluation, development may easily become quackery." To date, slow or cumbersome as it may seem, the authors still believe firmly that a progression from investigation and research through development and implementation and on to evaluation is the most promising way to assure that improvement and progress will be made in the formal continuing education of professional librarians.

REFERENCES IN CHAPTER 8

1. American Association of School Librarians. Supervisors Section. "Summary Sheet of Responses Received from 'Questionnaire About Continuing Education for School-Library-Media Supervisors'." Mimeographed. Questionnaire published in *School Libraries*, 18:53 (Summer, 1969).
2. Briggs, Leslie J., and others. *Instructional Media: A Procedure for the Design of Multi-Media Instruction, A Critical Review of Research, and Suggestions for Future Research*. Final Report. Pittsburgh: American Institutes for Research, 1967 (ED 024 278).
3. Corson, John J., and R. Shale Paul. *Men Near the Top: Filling Key Posts in the Federal Service*. Baltimore: Johns Hopkins Pr., 1966.
4. Crawford, Meredith P. "Concepts of Training," in Robert M. Gagné, ed., *Psychological Principles in Systems Development*, p.301—41. New York: Holt, 1962.
5. DeProspo, Ernest R., Jr., and Theodore S. Huang. "Continuing Education for the Library Administrator: His Needs," in Neal Harlow and others, eds., *Administration and Change: Continuing Education in Library Administration*, p.21—27. New Brunswick, N.J.: Rutgers Univ. Pr., 1969.
6. Faegre, Christopher L., and others. *Analysis and Evaluation of Present and Future Multi-Media Needs in Higher Education*. Final Report. Pittsburgh: Communication Research Program, American Institutes for Research, 1968 (ED 024 351).
7. Graduate School of the U.S. Department of Agriculture. *Faculty Handbook: Part II. Improving Teaching*. Washington, D.C.: Dept. of Agriculture Graduate Schools, 1967.
8. Hall, Anna C. *Selected Educational Objectives for Public Service Librarians: A Taxonomic Approach*. Pittsburgh: Univ. of Pittsburgh, 1968.

REFERENCES

9. Harlow, Neal, and others, eds. *Administration and Change: Continuing Education in Library Administration.* New Brunswick, N.J.: Rutgers Univ. Pr., 1969.
10. Herzberg, Frederick. "One More Time: How Do You Motivate Employees?" *Harvard Business Review* 46:53—62 (Jan.—Feb., 1968).
11. Hilgard, E. R. *Theories of Learning.* 2d ed. New York: Appleton, 1956.
12. Jerkedal, Ake. *Top Management Education: An Evaluation Study.* Stockholm: Svenska Tryckeri Bolagen STB AB, 1967.
13. Katz, Saul M. *Education for Development Administrators: Character, Form, Content and Curriculum.* Pittsburgh: Univ. of Pittsburgh, 1967.
14. Lippitt, R., J. Watson, and B. Westley. *The Dynamics of Planned Change.* New York: Harcourt, 1958.
15. McConnell, T. R. *Research or Development: A Reconciliation.* Bloomington, Ind.: Phi Delta Kappa International, 1967.
16. McKeachie, Wilbert N. *The Learning Process as Applied to Short-Term Learning Situations.* Conference Proceedings. National University Extension Association, Purdue University, West Lafayette, Ind., Apr. 23—27, 1965 (ED 019 532).
17. Meyer, Ursula. "New York's Statewide Continuing Professional Education Program: The Early Stages of Development." Paper presented at the first annual Staff Development Micro-Workshop, American Library Association Convention, Detroit, June 28, 1970.
18. Mosher, Frederick. *Professional Education and the Public Services: An Exploratory Study.* Final Report. Berkeley: Center for Research and Development in Higher Education, Univ. of California, 1968 (ED 025 220).
19. Ofeish, Gabriel D. "The New Education and the Learning Industry," *Educational Leadership* 26:760—63 (May 1969).
20. Paul, William J., Keith B. Robertson, and Frederick Herzberg. "Job Enrichment Pays Off," *Harvard Business Review* 47:61—78 (Mar.—Apr. 1969).
21. Schultze, Charles L. *The Politics and Economics of Public Spending.* Washington, D.C.: Brookings Institution, 1968.
22. Stone, Elizabeth W. *Factors Related to the Professional Development of Librarians.* Metuchen, N.J.: Scarecrow, 1969.
23. System Development Corporation. "Grooming Tomorrow's Managers," *SDC Magazine,* 13:3—15 (Jan. 1970).

APPENDIX A
QUESTIONNAIRE AND COVER LETTER SENT TO PROFESSIONAL FEDERAL LIBRARIANS

The Catholic University of America
Washington, D. C. 20017

DEPARTMENT OF LIBRARY SCIENCE

Dear

"What can a library school do to help you in your career development?" This was one of the questions we asked a group of librarians in a recent study. The response of many was most tersely expressed by one: "Find out our real needs and concentrate on these. Don't just guess--ask us."

There is widespread interest today in improving and expanding the curricula of library schools. The question is: "Where to begin?" We agree that the first thing to do before offering more courses is to find out what you are actually doing in your job and what opportunities you would like in relation to your career development. This, we feel, is one significant base on which to build.

Therefore, we ask your help in answering the questions which follow. Those in the pre-test groups reported, that although it took from one to one hour and a half of their time, the experience was interesting and profitable to them. You have a unique contribution to make because the details about what you are doing and what continuing education programs you would be interested in can only come from you.

This research project, entitled "Post-M.L.S. Education for Middle and Upper-Level Personnel in Libraries and Information Centers," is being conducted by the Department of Library Science of The Catholic University of America, in cooperation with the Federal Library Committee. The over-all results will be shared with the library education community as a whole.

Individual responses to the questionnaire will be confidential. They will be available neither to your agency nor to the Federal Library Committee. Although no one will see your questionnaire except the few professional members of our research staff here on the campus, we have assigned you a number in order to determine returns and to send you a summary of the results. No individual will be identified in any way in the results reported. Please do not put your name on the questionnaire.

A self-addressed stamped envelope is enclosed for your convenience in returning the questionnaire. While we wish to give you a reasonable amount of time to complete the questionnaire, we have scheduled time to put this data through a computer. Thus, it would be greatly appreciated if you would mail your completed questionnaire to us within two weeks, that is by Monday,

Thank you very much for your assistance in what we feel is an important endeavor.

Cordially yours,

(Rev.) James J. Kortendick, S.S., Ph.D.
Project Director and Head of the Department

(Mrs.) Elizabeth W. Stone, Ph.D., Associate Project Director and Assistant to the Head of the Department

APPENDIX A

DEPARTMENT OF
LIBRARY SCIENCE OF
THE CATHOLIC UNIVERSITY
OF AMERICA

A STUDY OF JOB DIMENSIONS AND EDUCATIONAL NEEDS:
POST-MLS EDUCATION FOR MIDDLE
AND UPPER-LEVEL PERSONNEL IN LIBRARIES AND
INFORMATION CENTERS

PART I. EVALUATING JOB ACTIVITIES YOU PERFORM IN RELATION
TO TIME AND IMPORTANCE

Directions for completion of Part I of the Questionnaire:

On the following pages you will find a number of statements about job elements and activities which might apply to your position. We ask you to rate each in terms of how time-consuming and important it is relative to other activities in your job at this time. To the left of each statement are two sets of symbols under the headings, "TIME" and "IMPORTANCE."

First, decide whether the statement applies to your position. Base this decision on what your position requires that you actually do, and not on your job description or position specification. If the statement does not apply, or is not true, leave the boxes under TIME and IMPORTANCE corresponding to that statement blank.

TIME

● --One of the most time-consuming functions of the position

◐ --Consumes a substantial amount of time

◯ --One of the least time-consuming functions of the position

Then, indicate how important you feel the activity is RELATIVE TO OTHER ACTIVITIES in terms of its contribution to effective performance in your entire job. Do this in the boxes under the IMPORTANCE Column, by checking the symbol which best describes the importance of this activity for your effective performance. The symbols and their meanings follow:

APPENDIX A

If the statement does apply to your position, indicate in "TIME" Column how time-consuming the activity is RELATIVE TO OTHER ACTIVITIES in your entire job, by checking the symbol which best describes the time factor to you. The symbols and their meanings follow:

●—One of the most important parts of the position

◐ —A substantial part of the position

○ —One of the least important parts of the position.

IMPORT-
ANCE

Please Note:

In Part I, please check only those position activities which you engage in directly and actually perform yourself. If the statement describes something that does not apply to, or is not true for your position because it describes something that is:
 (1) delegated by you to a subordinate; or,
 (2) is strictly the concern of a superior,
it is not a part of your position. Please leave the boxes that pertain to it blank.

You will find that the job activities are listed by two major categories:

A. SPECIALIZED LIBRARY FUNCTIONS--
    If you are responsible for, or oversee, all the activities for a specialized library function, evaluate the first sentence(s) of that category relative to Time and Importance, indicating that you have over-all responsibility for that function. If a job element describes something which is strictly the concern of a superior or a subordinate, leave the boxes that pertain to it blank.

B. GENERAL ADMINISTRATIVE AND MANAGEMENT FUNCTIONS--
    This category includes statements which may describe something that you do in your job in the areas of Planning, Organizing, Staffing, Directing, Coordinating, Controlling, Representing, and Housing. These questions apply to the administrative and management functions you now perform in your job as related to your area of responsibility, whether it be for the whole library, a department, a branch, or the specialized library functions which are assigned to you.

A. Performing Specialized Library Functions

In this Section A, you need only refer to and put a check in the boxes of the parts of the questionnaire that apply to your job. For example: if all of your job activities are in the areas of Bibliography and Indexing, you would need only to consider Items 23 through 28 and Items 68 through 76. Then you could skip to Section B, Page 4. To help you find your special areas more easily, the following list is provided:

- --Abstracting, Items 1 through 7
- --Acquisitions, Items 8 through 22
- --Bibliography, Items 23 through 28
- --Cataloging and Classification, Items 29 through 49
- --Circulation, Items 50 through 59
- --Clientele Services, Items 60 through 67
- --Indexing, Items 68 through 76
- --Literature Searching, Items 77 through 85
- --Maintenance of Holdings, Items 86 through 95
- --Reference, Items 96 through 102
- --Research, Items 103 through 107
- --Selection, Items 108 through 121
- --Translation, Items 122 through 127

JOB ACTIVITIES

IN MY POSITION, IN THE AREA OF ABSTRACTING, I:

1. Supervise the preparation of all abstracts and/or abstract services
2. Prepare descriptive abstracts
3. Write abstracts of content of materials
4. Evaluate material and state critique in an annotation
5. Make extracts of materials
6. Provide abstracting services through special announcement devices
7. Other:

IN MY POSITION, IN THE AREA OF ACQUISITIONS, I:

8. Am responsible for the over-all acquisitions program
9. Establish policies for determining acquisitions
10. Establish ordering and checking systems for books
11. Establish ordering and checking systems for reports and/or documents
12. Establish ordering and checking systems for serials
13. Procure books
14. Procure non-book materials
15. Am responsible for acquisitions received by donation or exchange
16. Establish interlibrary loan system

APPENDIX A

19. Procure materials for the library's document depository
20. Appraise highly specialized and/or rare materials
21. Publish new-acquisitions bulletin
22. Other:

IN MY POSITION, IN THE AREA OF BIBLIOGRAPHY, I:
23. Am responsible for the over-all compilation of bibliographies
24. Maintain continuing bibliographies
25. Compile bibliographies in specialized subject areas
26. Produce demand bibliographies upon request
27. Prepare bibliographies using automated methods
28. Other:

IN MY POSITION, IN THE AREA OF CATALOGING AND CLASSIFICATION, I:
29. Have over-all responsibility for the cataloging program
30. Have over-all responsibility for the classification program
31. Establish cataloging policies and procedures
32. Establish classification policies and procedures
33. Expand, develop, and improve classification schemes
34. Develop terminology control schemes
35. Classify and/or reclassify books
36. Classify and/or reclassify non-book materials
37. Expand, develop, and improve lists of subject headings
38. Do descriptive cataloging of books
39. Do descriptive cataloging of non-book materials
40. Do subject cataloging of books
41. Do subject cataloging of non-book materials
42. Work on the production of book catalogs
43. Use reprography for catalog card reproduction
44. Establish and revise filing rules or special codes
45. Maintain cataloging records
46. Revise cataloging and/or classification done by others
47. Catalog and/or classify rare books
48. Catalog and/or classify public documents and technical reports
49. Other:

319

APPENDIX A

A. Performing Specialized Library Functions (continued)

TIME	IMPORTANCE	JOB ACTIVITIES
		IN MY POSITION, IN THE AREA OF CIRCULATION, I:
		50. Have over-all responsibility for circulation system
		51. Develop circulation systems
		52. Circulate holdings on request
		53. Circulate holdings using an EAM-based system
		54. Circulate holdings using an EDP-based system
		55. Circulate interlibrary loan materials
		56. Develop procedures for providing photoduplication of materials
		57. Route periodicals on request
		58. Route pertinent clippings and ephemeral materials
		59. Other:
		IN MY POSITION, IN THE AREA OF CLIENTELE SERVICES, I:
		60. Have over-all responsibility for clientele services
		61. Initiate user services
		62. Refer clients to sources of information
		63. Instruct users in reference methods and information sources
		64. Provide research assistance
		65. Plan and/or conduct orientation programs for clientele
		66. Compile reading lists
		67. Other:
		IN MY POSITION, IN THE AREA OF INDEXING, I:
		68. Supervise the preparation and/or production of all indexes
		69. Provide Key-word-in-context indexing service
		70. Do concept indexing
		71. Do coordinated indexing
		72. Do citation indexing
		73. Do conventional indexing
		74. Index data for storage and retrieval
		75. Prepare thesauri and/or terminology control schemes
		76. Other:

APPENDIX A

IN MY POSITION, IN THE AREA OF LITERATURE SEARCHING, I:
77. Have over-all responsibility for the literature searching program
78. Establish selective dissemination of information program
79. Establish and/or maintain a field-of-interest register for users
80. Match information against field-of-interest profiles
81. Notify users of material that match their profiles
82. Conduct retrospective searches
83. Analyze and evaluate data for users
84. Publish contents of selected periodicals
85. Other:

IN MY POSITION, IN THE AREA OF MAINTENANCE OF HOLDINGS, I:
86. Give over-all supervision to the maintenance of holdings
87. Maintain hardbound holdings
88. Supervise binding of softbound documents
89. Keep serial bindery records
90. Keep non-serial bindery records
91. Store material in microform
92. Provide viewing and printing equipment for microforms
93. Plan a program for updating material
94. Weed out-of-date material by a planned program
95. Other:

IN MY POSITION, IN THE AREA OF REFERENCE, I:
96. Have over-all responsibility for the reference services provided
97. Establish reference service policies
98. Actively answer reference questions
99. Develop and/or maintain a referral reference center
100. Organize systems for quick reference
101. Reference other material pertinent to information under consideration
102. Other:

IN MY POSITION, IN THE AREA OF RESEARCH, I:
103. Am responsible for the adequacy and soundness of research activity
104. Research with information
105. Do information scouting using non-print sources
106. Prepare analytical, evaluative state-of-the-art reports
107. Other:

321

APPENDIX A

A. Performing Specialized Library Functions (continued)

TIME IMPORTANCE JOB ACTIVITIES

IN MY POSITION, IN THE AREA OF SELECTION, I:

108. Have over-all responsibility for operation of selection system
109. Formulate policies for selection
110. Allocate funds between departments, subjects, collections
111. Make final decisions on selection of material for unit or subject area
112. Serve as a selection official for materials purchased centrally for distribution to branch, mobile, extension, or regional collections
113. Identify needs of clientele
114. Make tentative selection of material from reviews, catalogs, lists
115. Prepare lists of materials needed in specific subject areas
116. Decide on number of duplicate copies and on editions
117. Decide on acceptability of gifts
118. Select serials
119. Select non-book materials
120. Make recommendations on selection of materials
121. Other:

IN MY POSITION, IN THE AREA OF TRANSLATION, I:

122. Have over-all responsibility for my library's translation program
123. Translate material into foreign languages
124. Translate material from foreign languages into English
125. Abstract and translate
126. Extract and translate
127. Other:

B. Performing General Administrative and Management Functions

In this Section B, the items apply to the administrative and management functions you perform now in your job as related to your area of responsibility, whether it be for a whole library, a branch, department or division, or the specialized library functions to which you are assigned. To help find the administrative and management functions you perform, the following list is provided:

APPENDIX A

- --Planning, Items 128 through 150
- --Organizing, Items 151 through 162
- --Staffing, Items 163 through 186
- --Directing, Items 187 through 208
- --Coordinating, Items 209 through 214
- --Controlling, Items 215 through 227
- --Representing, Items 228 through 238
- --Housing, Items 239 through 244

TIME	IMPORTANCE	JOB ACTIVITIES
		IN MY POSITION, I:
		128. Integrate library programs with missions of parent organization
		129. Establish goals and objectives for the library
		130. Forecast new and/or changed demands for service
		131. Determine needed programs for the library
		132. Direct over-all preparation of the program budget
		133. Compute costs of the library's programs and/or activities
		134. Compare the cost and effectiveness of feasible alternatives
		135. Make budget request decisions
		136. Provide analytical studies justifying budget request decisions
		137. Prepare a multi-year summary tabulation of library programs in terms of their outputs, costs, and funding for at least 5 years in advance
		138. Negotiate with higher management about allocation of funds
		139. Prepare material for inclusion in policy statements
		140. Recommend policy changes
		141. Devise detailed procedures to implement general policy
		142. Help develop new programs and/or activities
		143. Provide for participation of employees in planning programs
		144. Use PERT as an aid in planning
		145. Use Operations Research methods as an aid in planning
		146. Plan for the installation of mechanized systems
		147. Identify and plan research activities
		148. Advise on application of research findings
		149. Keep informed about the latest relevant research and developments
		150. Other:

PLANNING

323

APPENDIX A

B. Performing General Administrative and Management Functions (continued)

TIME	IMPORTANCE		JOB ACTIVITIES

IN MY POSITION, I:

ORGANIZING

151. Group activities necessary to attain library's objectives
152. Assign each grouping to a supervisor with authority necessary to manage it
153. Allocate personnel to the various activity groupings
154. Distribute material resources among the various parts of the library
155. Determine line and staff authority relationships
156. Prepare and/or update organization charts
157. Create and/or maintain a staff manual
158. Modify organizational structure to meet changes
159. Organize the clerical processing of information
160. Sometimes use committees to undertake line or staff functions
161. Provide each department with a clear definition of results expected
162. Other:

STAFFING

163. Codify personnel philosophy, policies and procedures
164. Forecast future staffing needs
165. Recruit additional staff members
166. Select personnel
167. Use probationary period as a testing program before final appointment
168. Study and implement the Civil Service Classification Standards
169. Prepare position descriptions or analyses
170. Develop employee orientation programs
171. Determine training needs at each organizational level
172. Build training programs
173. Serve as an instructor in training programs
174. Use some psychological approaches to training, such as sensitivity groups and/or role playing
175. Arrange for personnel to go outside agency for training
176. Develop and/or implement a system for career development
177. Make and/or approve recommendations for promotion
178. Nominate employees for awards and/or special recognition
179. Make and/or approve recommendations for separation of employees

324

APPENDIX A

DIRECTING

180. Conduct exit interviews
181. Make performance appraisals using traditional formal systems
182. Make appraisals using "management by objectives" techniques
183. Provide a feed-back or suggestion system for employees
184. Maintain adequate personnel records for all employees
185. Participate in meetings with employee associations
186. Other:

187. Directly supervise and guide subordinates
188. Assign jobs to subordinates
189. Harmonize individual objectives with library's objectives
190. Train new employees in the performance of their work
191. Check the accuracy of work of subordinates
192. Brief subordinates on immediate and continuing library programs
193. Make decisions without consulting others
194. Make decisions based on consultation with subordinates
195. Give orders to initiate, modify, or stop activities
196. Install operating procedures for new activities and/or programs
197. Give subordinates authority to command or to act in certain areas
198. Review decisions and/or proposals that are made by subordinates
199. Stimulate subordinates toward superior performance and creativity
200. Use "job enrichment" as a means of motivating subordinates
201. Identify and develop potential in subordinates
202. Counsel subordinates about their career development
203. Administer discipline
204. Formulate communication and express it understandably
205. Use the informal organization as a means of communication
206. Give prompt and full attention to all communications received
207. Frame and transmit communications to support organizational objectives
208. Other:

COORDINATING

209. Coordinate the activities of separate groups within the library
210. Exchange ideas and reach understandings through direct contact with others in the library who are not my subordinates
211. Hold group meetings with subordinates
212. Participate in developing inter-library cooperative networks
213. Anticipate problems and prevent their occurrence through continuous interchange of information and early and direct contact of all involved
214. Other:

325

APPENDIX A

B. Performing General Administrative and Management Functions (continued)

TIME	IMPORTANCE		JOB ACTIVITIES
			IN MY POSITION, I:
		CONTROLLING	215. Establish standards in terms of specific criteria
			216. Schedule activities to ensure that deadlines are met
			217. Assign priorities for the completion of work
			218. Use the budget to monitor progress of activities
			219. Solicit and evaluate clientele reactions to library's services
			220. Measure performance against standards, schedules, budgets, surveys
			221. Correct the deviations from standards that are discovered
			222. Use statistical analysis and/or special reports as control devices
			223. Use systems analysis as a means of control
			224. Use the techniques of work simplification to correct inefficiencies
			225. Account for the utilization of resources and meeting of goals
			226. Prepare regular progress reports to higher management
			227. Other:
		REPRESENTING	228. Interpret library programs to key officials, users, special groups
			229. Approve material prepared for public use
			230. Am responsible for a publications program
			231. Issue news releases
			232. Edit drafts of reports, statements and/or technical documents
			233. Write articles of a professional nature
			234. Write or dictate at least 25 letters per week
			235. Negotiate with other groups in agency to get goods and/or services
			236. Arrange for the services of contractors and/or consultants
			237. Attend professional meetings and/or conferences
			238. Other:
		HOUSING	239. Plan and justify library quarters
			240. Determine equipment needed and compute costs
			241. Procure equipment needed
			242. Manage the use of library space
			243. Manage library's physical maintenance
			244. Other:

APPENDIX A

PLEASE MAKE ANY ADDITIONAL COMMENTS WHICH YOU FEEL ARE NEEDED TO GIVE AN ADEQUATE PICTURE OF YOUR JOB ACTIVITIES ON THE LAST PAGE OF THE QUESTIONNAIRE WHERE SPACE IS PROVIDED FOR ADDITIONAL REMARKS.

PART II. YOUR EDUCATIONAL NEEDS

Listed below are some courses that could be offered at the post-MLS level to help librarians in mid-career upgrade and update their present knowledge. Please check your interest in studying in these areas according to the following headings, which are also given at the top of the columns to the left of the course listings.

WORKSHOP: If you are interested in spending time in a short-term (few days to four weeks) workshop or institute;

COURSE NOW: If you are interested in taking a post-MLS course for credit at the present time;

COURSE LATER: If you are interested in taking a post-MLS course for credit at a later time (three to five years from now).

[ ] [ ] [ ] If you are not interested in formal study in a given course, please leave the boxes that pertain to it blank.

COURSE AREAS

WORK-SHOP	COURSE NOW	COURSE LATER	
			ACQUISITIONS AND SELECTION
[ ]	[ ]	[ ]	1. **Building and Evaluating Library Collections:** Criteria for evaluating and selecting library materials, devising and maintaining an acquisition system.
[ ]	[ ]	[ ]	2. **Centralized Processing:** Principles and problems of developing centers for acquisition, cataloging, and the physical preparation of materials.
[ ]	[ ]	[ ]	3. **Current Practices in Acquisition and Selection of Non-Book Materials.** Including an understanding of the new technology which governs the selection and use of video tapes, dial access sets, audio-visual materials, etc., in libraries.
[ ]	[ ]	[ ]	4. Other:

APPENDIX A

PART II. YOUR EDUCATIONAL NEEDS (continued)

WORK-SHOP	COURSE NOW	COURSE LATER	COURSE AREAS
			ADMINISTRATION AND GENERAL MANAGEMENT OF LIBRARIES:
[ ]	[ ]	[ ]	5. Administrative Policies and Practices: Emphasis on library organization and its operational problems relevant to top levels of administration.
[ ]	[ ]	[ ]	6. Communication Theory and Processes: The communication processes; media techniques employed by the library manager; public relations.
[ ]	[ ]	[ ]	7. Design of Library Organizations: Developing structures that effectively organize all resources necessary to achieve the library's organizational objectives. Consideration of re-design necessitated by impact of technological changes in the library.
[ ]	[ ]	[ ]	8. General Management: Developing the skills of the middle-level library manager by focusing on the basic processes of management.
[ ]	[ ]	[ ]	9. Human Relations in Library Administration: Exploration of the interpersonal and inter-group relationships in a library organizational setting; employee motivation; the managerial environment.
[ ]	[ ]	[ ]	10. Innovation and Planned Change in Library Organizations: The social psychology and management implications of change.
[ ]	[ ]	[ ]	11. Management of Records Systems in the Library: Emphasis on the development and installation of records management program.
[ ]	[ ]	[ ]	12. Personnel Administration in Libraries: Procedures of the major personnel sub-functions including recruitment, selection, classification, placement, appraisal, and training.
[ ]	[ ]	[ ]	13. Personnel Problems Under the Impact of Technological Change: Library Applications. Emphasis on adjusting the individual to ADP conversions; job redesign; reclassifying jobs; training and retraining.
[ ]	[ ]	[ ]	14. Policy Formation and Decision-Making in Library Organizations.
[ ]	[ ]	[ ]	15. Program Planning and Budgeting: Library applications. The processes and instruments of planning, programming, and budgetary functions of the library, with special emphasis on the current approaches of the Federal Government in this function.
[ ]	[ ]	[ ]	16. Public Administration: Introductory survey with library applications.
[ ]	[ ]	[ ]	17. Theories of Organization and Management: Library applications.
[ ]	[ ]	[ ]	18. Other:

APPENDIX A

ADMINISTRATION OF SPECIAL TYPES OF LIBRARY SERVICES
19. Administration of the Special Federal Library.
20. Archival Administration.
21. Hospital Library Administration and Service.
22. Information Center Administration.
23. Law Library Administration and Service.
24. Rare Book Librarianship.
25. Other:

AUTOMATION
26. Automation of Library Processes: Application of computer technology to library processes.
27. Information Processing on Computers: The functions performed and organization of computers; principles of programming and symbol manipulation.
28. Information Retrieval Systems: Structure and operation of information systems, including question analysis, search strategy, thesaurus construction.
29. Other:

BIBLIOGRAPHY
30. Analytical Bibliography.
31. Enumerative Bibliographical Systems.
32. Other:

CATALOGING AND CLASSIFICATION
33. Cataloging and Classification of Non-Book Materials.
34. Centralized Cataloging at the National Level. Emphasis on the Library of Congress MARC II Project, its uses and implications.
35. Centralized Cataloging at the International Level. The importance, uses and implications of "The National Program for Acquisitions and Cataloging" as provided under Title IIC of the Higher Education Act of 1965.
36. New Advances in Classification Schemes and Cataloging Systems: A Survey.
37. Recataloging and Reclassification: Problems and Procedures.
38. Subject Representation: Theory of knowledge, descriptor systems, nature of classificatory languages.
39. Other:

329

APPENDIX A

PART II. YOUR EDUCATIONAL NEEDS (continued)

WORK-SHOP	COURSE NOW	COURSE LATER	COURSE AREAS
			CIRCULATION
[ ]	[ ]	[ ]	40. <u>Circulation Systems</u>: Overview and evaluation of new circulation systems with special emphasis on EAM and ADP based equipment and procedures for installing a new system in a library.
[ ]	[ ]	[ ]	41. <u>Reprography</u>: Using reprographic processes (printing, duplicating, copying, microreproduction) to maximize library service.
[ ]	[ ]	[ ]	42. Other:
			CLIENTELE SERVICES
[ ]	[ ]	[ ]	43. <u>Information Retrieval for Clientele</u>. Forecasting and analyzing clientele needs; the psychology of the user; initiating user services; development of orientation programs for users; instructing users in reference methods and sources.
[ ]	[ ]	[ ]	44. <u>Literature Searching</u>. Development of current awareness programs, automatic routing systems based on individual profiles of clients; analysis of data.
[ ]	[ ]	[ ]	45. Other:
			HOUSING AND EQUIPMENT
[ ]	[ ]	[ ]	46. <u>Equipment Evaluation, Selection, and Procurement</u>.
[ ]	[ ]	[ ]	47. <u>Library Design and Architecture</u>. Including problems of redesign and remodeling.
[ ]	[ ]	[ ]	48. <u>Planning and Justifying Library Quarters</u>.
[ ]	[ ]	[ ]	49. Other:
			INDEXING AND ABSTRACTING
[ ]	[ ]	[ ]	50. <u>Abstracting and Indexing Services</u>. Principles, practices, and development of abstracting and indexing services; integrating these into the complex of special library operations, with emphasis upon current awareness and the retrospective searching needs of clientele.
[ ]	[ ]	[ ]	51. <u>Content Analysis</u>. Description, analysis and summarization of the intellectual content of information.
[ ]	[ ]	[ ]	52. <u>Theories of Indexing and Information Retrieval</u>. Conceptual aspects of indexing and subject analysis.
[ ]	[ ]	[ ]	53. Other:

APPENDIX A

54. Equipment and Instrumentation.
55. Linguistics and Information Science.
56. Mathematical Techniques for Information Science.
57. The Scope of Information Science. Relationship of information sciences to libraries, information centers, and information networks.
58. Other:

LIBRARIES, GOVERNMENT, AND SOCIETY
59. Current Issues in Librarianship and Information Science.
60. Cybernetics and Society. Implications for libraries and information centers.
61. International Library Services and Resources.
62. Labor Relations and Library Employment.
63. The Library Administrator and Government Policy, Organization and Operation.
64. Library Networks: Interlibrary cooperation at the regional, national, and international levels. Applications of communications technology.
65. Mass Media in Communication. Audience, content, structure, control and effects of mass media in society and their impact on librarianship.
66. Resources and Services of the Federal Library Complex. An orientation through planned on-site visits to selected libraries and information centers.
67. Other:

PUBLICATION
68. Publication in the Library and Information Science Fields. Advanced training in writing, editing, report preparation, layout and design; the individual's responsibility in the dissemination of research findings.
69. Publishing in the Twentieth Century: Book and Non-Book Materials. Survey of publishing industry today; structure of the industry; relations between libraries and publishing; practices in binding and distribution; the copyright controversy.
70. Other:

REFERENCE
71. Development and Maintenance of a Reference Referral Center.
72. Non-Conventional Library Reference Tools. The effective use of the telephone, the authority, the private collector, other libraries, associations, consulates, congressmen, archives, patents, newspaper morgues, commercial catalogs, etc.
73. Organization and Administration of Reference Systems.
74. Search Logic and Tactics.
75. Other:

331

APPENDIX A

PART II. YOUR EDUCATIONAL NEEDS (continued)

WORK-SHOP	COURSE NOW	COURSE LATER	COURSE AREAS
			RESEARCH
[ ]	[ ]	[ ]	76. Operations Research in Library Management.
[ ]	[ ]	[ ]	77. Research Development in Libraries. Survey and impact of recent research findings on library operations; interpretation and application of research findings in other disciplines to the library environment; writing research proposals; management of research groups.
[ ]	[ ]	[ ]	78. Statistical Theory and the Interpretation of Statistical Data for Researching in Libraries and Information Centers.
[ ]	[ ]	[ ]	79. Other:
			SPECIALIZED INFORMATION SOURCES
[ ]	[ ]	[ ]	80. Agricultural Literature and Research.
[ ]	[ ]	[ ]	81. Behavioral Science Literature and Research.
[ ]	[ ]	[ ]	82. Biomedical Literature and Research.
[ ]	[ ]	[ ]	83. Business and Economics Literature and Research.
[ ]	[ ]	[ ]	84. Documents of International Organizations and Foreign Governments.
[ ]	[ ]	[ ]	85. Fine Arts Literature and Research.
[ ]	[ ]	[ ]	86. Legal Literature and Research.
[ ]	[ ]	[ ]	87. Scientific and Technical Literature and Research.
[ ]	[ ]	[ ]	88. Social Science Literature and Research.
[ ]	[ ]	[ ]	89. Technical Report Literature.
[ ]	[ ]	[ ]	90. U.S. Public Documents: Federal, state, and municipal.
[ ]	[ ]	[ ]	91. Other:
			SYSTEMS ANALYSIS
[ ]	[ ]	[ ]	92. Library Management Information Systems.
[ ]	[ ]	[ ]	93. Systems Analysis and Design for Library and Information Center Operations.
[ ]	[ ]	[ ]	94. Systems Analysis in Information Science. Basic concepts of systems applied to the design and analysis of information systems.
[ ]	[ ]	[ ]	95. Other:

96. WOULD YOU ENROLL FOR A ONE YEAR POST-MLS PROGRAM IN LIBRARY SCIENCE?   1.[ ] Yes   2.[ ] No
97. If yes, WOULD CERTAIN CONDITIONS BE NECESSARY FOR YOU TO ENROLL?   1.[ ] Yes   2.[ ] No

APPENDIX A

99. WOULD YOU ENROLL FOR A GRADUATE PROGRAM IN SOME OTHER SUBJECT AREA? 1.[ ] Yes 2.[ ] No
100. If yes, WHAT AREA OR DISCIPLINE?

101. WOULD YOU ENROLL FOR A PH.D. PROGRAM IN LIBRARY SCIENCE? 1.[ ] Yes 2.[ ] No
102. If yes, WOULD CERTAIN CONDITIONS BE NECESSARY FOR YOU TO ENROLL? 1.[ ] Yes 2.[ ] No
103. If yes, WHAT CONDITIONS?

104. WOULD YOU ENROLL FOR A PH.D. PROGRAM IN ANOTHER SUBJECT AREA? 1.[ ] Yes 2.[ ] No
105. If yes, WHAT AREA OR DISCIPLINE?
106. IN ADDITION TO OFFERING COURSES, INSTITUTES, AND WORKSHOPS, IN WHAT OTHER WAYS DO YOU SEE THAT THE LIBRARY SCHOOL COULD HELP YOU IN YOUR PROFESSIONAL DEVELOPMENT?

PART III. SOME INFORMATION ABOUT YOURSELF AND YOUR CAREER

A. Your Present Job

1. WHAT IS THE GRADE OF YOUR PRESENT POSITION? Please check correct grade. If your position is outside the U.S. Civil Service Classification grades, please check the grade level to which it would be equivalent in the Civil Service System.
1.[ ] GS 9; 2.[ ] GS 10; 3.[ ] GS 11; 4.[ ] GS 12; 5.[ ] GS 13; 6.[ ] GS 14; 7. [ ] Other: _____

2. WHAT IS THE TITLE OF YOUR PRESENT POSITION?
3. THE FOLLOWING CATEGORIES ARE USED BY THE U.S. CIVIL SERVICE COMMISSION TO CLASSIFY PROFESSIONAL POSITIONS IN FEDERAL LIBRARIES AND INFORMATION CENTERS. Please check the one classification which best characterizes your present position.

GS 1410--Librarian Series

1.[ ] Librarian (please specify appropriate specialization): _____

2.[ ] Administrative librarian
3.[ ] Supervisory librarian
4.[ ] Library director

GS 1412--Technical Information Services Series

5.[ ] Technical information specialist
6.[ ] Supervisory technical information specialist
7.[ ] Technical information officer (please specify appropriate specialization)

8.[ ] If your position fits none of the classifications listed above, please indicate it here:

APPENDIX A

PART III. SOME INFORMATION ABOUT YOURSELF AND YOUR CAREER (continued)

4. IN WHICH ONE OF THE FOLLOWING TYPES OF LIBRARY ACTIVITY ARE YOU PRIMARILY ENGAGED? Please check only the one box (in Section A, B, C, or D) that indicates your primary responsibility.

A. ADMINISTRATIVE:

1. [ ] Head of library
2. [ ] Assistant or Associate Head
3. [ ] Head of department or division
4. [ ] Head of branch
5. [ ] Head of regional or field library
6. [ ] Other:

OR

B. 7. [ ] SUPERVISORY (responsibility for supervising a number of professional and/or technical positions, but do not have over-all program responsibility).

OR

C. 8. [ ] ONE TO THREE PERSON LIBRARY--general responsibilities

OR

D. PROFESSIONAL SPECIALTY:

- 9. [ ] Abstracting
- 10. [ ] Acquisitions
- 11. [ ] Analyzing source materials
- 12. [ ] Archives
- 13. [ ] Bibliography
- 14. [ ] Cataloging
- 15. [ ] Circulation
- 16. [ ] Classification
- 17. [ ] Clientele services
- 18. [ ] Coordinator
- 19. [ ] Data processing
- 20. [ ] Documents and/or reports
- 21. [ ] Editing and/or writing
- 22. [ ] Indexing
- 23. [ ] Information retrieval
- 24. [ ] Literature searching
- 25. [ ] Non-print materials
- 26. [ ] Personnel
- 27. [ ] Public relations
- 28. [ ] Reference
- 29. [ ] Research
- 30. [ ] Revision
- 31. [ ] Selection of materials
- 32. [ ] Serials
- 33. [ ] Subject specialty: What area(s)?
- 34. [ ] Systems analysis
- 35. [ ] Technical services
- 36. [ ] Terminology control
- 37. [ ] Translation: What language(s)?
- 38. [ ] Other:

5. IS YOUR PRESENT POSITION LOCATED IN:
   1. [ ] Agency headquarters library?
   2. [ ] Regional or field library?
   3. [ ] Branch library?
   4. [ ] Other:

6. APPROXIMATELY WHAT IS THE TOTAL NUMBER OF PEOPLE (professional and non-professional)

APPENDIX A

7. OF THIS NUMBER, APPROXIMATELY HOW MANY EMPLOYEES HAVE A GRADE OF GS-9 OR HIGHER? [   ]

8. APPROXIMATELY WHAT IS THE TOTAL NUMBER OF PEOPLE (professional and non-professional) EMPLOYED IN THE ENTIRE LIBRARY SYSTEM OF WHICH YOUR LIBRARY IS A PART? . . . . [   ]

9. DO YOU SUPERVISE OTHER MEMBERS OF THE LIBRARY STAFF? . . . . 1. [ ] Yes; 2. [ ] No
10. If yes, ALL TOGETHER HOW MANY EMPLOYEES ARE RESPONSIBLE TO YOU? (Please include those you supervise directly and those who report through a chain of command) . . [   ]

11. ARE YOU INVOLVED AT AN ADMINISTRATIVE OR SUPERVISORY LEVEL IN APPLYING ELECTRONIC DATA PROCESSING PROCEDURES? 1. [ ] Yes; 2. [ ] No

WHICH ACTIVITIES IN YOUR LIBRARY ARE AUTOMATED? (Please put a check mark in the box before ALL areas in which your library is now automated or in the process of being automated).

12. [ ] Accounting
13. [ ] Acquisitions
14. [ ] Bibliography production
15. [ ] Book catalog production
16. [ ] Book indexing
17. [ ] Catalog card production
18. [ ] Circulation control
19. [ ] Document information retrieval

20. [ ] Graphic storage of materials
21. [ ] Legislative indexing
22. [ ] Patron control
23. [ ] Personnel records
24. [ ] Reference queries
25. [ ] Report inventory
26. [ ] Selective dissemination

27. [ ] Serial records
28. [ ] Tele-communication devices
29. [ ] Thesauri preparation
30. [ ] Union lists
31. [ ] Other _____

32. WHAT IS THE MINIMUM EXPERIENCE IN LIBRARY OR INFORMATION CENTER ASSIGNMENTS REQUIRED TO PERFORM YOUR JOB? (Please circle approximate number of years).

   None   1   2   3   4   5   6   7   Over 7 Years

33. HOW WELL DOES YOUR JOB UTILIZE YOUR TALENTS? (Please check approximate answer):

   1.[ ] Excellently; 2.[ ] Very well; 3.[ ] Fairly well; 4.[ ] Very little; 5.[ ] Not at all

34. APPROXIMATELY HOW MANY HOURS PER WEEK ARE YOU REQUIRED TO DO AVOIDABLE DETAIL WORK THAT YOU FEEL SHOULD NOT BE PART OF YOUR JOB?
                          [   ] Hours per week

APPENDIX A

PART III. SOME INFORMATION ABOUT YOURSELF AND YOUR CAREER (continued)

B. Your Education

TO GIVE US A PICTURE OF YOUR EDUCATIONAL BACKGROUND, PLEASE COMPLETE THE TABLE BELOW. (Please use a separate line for each degree held and check the box for each line that applies).

TYPE OF STUDY PROGRAM	TITLE OF DEGREE RECEIVED	YEAR PROGRAM COMPLETED	IF PROGRAM NOT COMPLETED Approx. No. of Hours to Date	Last Date Enrolled	AREA OF SPECIALIZATION
35. [ ] Bachelor's (Undergraduate)					
36. [ ] Bachelor's (Undergraduate)					
37. [ ] Bachelor's (graduate degree in Library Science)					
38. [ ] Master's in Library Science					
39. [ ] Master's in information Science					
40. [ ] Doctor's in Library Science					
41. [ ] Doctor's in other subject area					
42. [ ] Post-MLS 6th year program in Library Science					
43. [ ] Certificate or Diploma					
44. [ ] Other courses for Credit					
45. [ ] Non-Credit Courses					
46. [ ] Workshops, Institutes, or Seminars					
47. [ ] Workshops, Institutes, or Seminars					
48. [ ] Other:					

APPENDIX A

49. ARE THERE ANY FORMAL SCIENTIFIC, TECHNICAL, OR PROFESSIONAL COURSES YOU FEEL WOULD HAVE BEEN ESPECIALLY HELPFUL IN YOUR POSITION?   1. [ ] Yes; 2. [ ] No
If yes, Please specify courses or course areas:

50. IN RELATION TO YOUR PRESENT POSITION, ARE THERE ANY ACTIVITIES YOU SHOULD BE ENGAGED IN FOR WHICH YOUR PREVIOUS TRAINING HAS NOT PREPARED YOU?   1. [ ] Yes; 2. [ ] No
If yes, Please specify these activities:

C. Your Experience

DEFINITIONAL NOTE: In this study, the term "professional librarian" includes all librarians, administrators, and other specialists with responsibility in the field of librarianship or information science who have received a Master's degree in Library Science or, before the early 1950's, a Bachelor's degree in Library Science at the graduate level.

BASED ON THIS DEFINITION:

51. HOW MANY YEARS OF PRE-PROFESSIONAL LIBRARY EXPERIENCE DO YOU HAVE? . . . . . [_____] Years

52. HOW MANY YEARS OF PROFESSIONAL LIBRARY EXPERIENCE DO YOU HAVE? . . . . [_____] Years

53. HOW MANY YEARS OF PROFESSIONAL EXPERIENCE HAVE YOU HAD IN YOUR PRESENT ORGANIZATION OR AGENCY LIBRARY? . . . . [_____] Years

54. HOW MANY YEARS HAVE YOU BEEN WORKING IN YOUR PRESENT POSITION? . . . . . . [_____] Years

55. HOW MANY YEARS HAVE YOU WORKED FOR THE FEDERAL GOVERNMENT?
(Exclude uniformed military service if not library related) . . . . [_____] Years

56. IN HOW MANY OTHER LIBRARIES OR INFORMATION CENTERS IN THE FEDERAL GOVERNMENT HAVE YOU HELD PROFESSIONAL POSITIONS? . . . . [_____] Libraries

57. IN HOW MANY LIBRARIES OUTSIDE THE FEDERAL GOVERNMENT HAVE YOU HELD PROFESSIONAL POSITIONS? . . . . [_____] Libraries

APPENDIX A

PART III. SOME INFORMATION ABOUT YOURSELF AND YOUR CAREER (continued)

58. HAVE YOU HAD ANY EXPERIENCE IN AN OCCUPATION OTHER THAN LIBRARIANSHIP? 1. [ ] Yes; 2. [ ] No (If no, skip to question 62).

59. WAS ANY OF YOUR NON-LIBRARY EXPERIENCE AT A PROFESSIONAL, TECHNICAL OR ADMINISTRATIVE LEVEL?
    1. [ ] Yes; 2. [ ] No (If no, skip to question 62).

60. PLEASE SPECIFY THE TYPE OF WORK AND THE OCCUPATIONAL FIELD IN WHICH YOU HAD MOST OF THIS EXPERIENCE (e.g., teaching high school English, programmer for I.B.M.):

61. PLEASE SPECIFY YOUR SECOND PRINCIPAL OCCUPATION PRIOR TO YOUR ENTRY INTO LIBRARIANSHIP (if any):

62. FROM THE TIME THAT YOU ACCEPTED YOUR FIRST PROFESSIONAL POSITION IN A LIBRARY, DID YOU EVER LEAVE LIBRARY WORK FOR A PERIOD OF SIX MONTHS OR MORE?
    1. [ ] Yes; 2. [ ] No   IF YES, WHY? (please check one or more);

    63. [ ] To obtain further education   66. [ ] For military service
    64. [ ] For marriage or family reasons   67. [ ] To travel
    65. [ ] To work in another occupation   68. [ ] Other reason:

BEFORE YOU ACCEPTED YOUR PRESENT POSITION, DID YOU EVER HOLD A PROFESSIONAL POSITION IN: (Please check all those in which you have held professional positions).

    69. [ ] Academic library; 70. [ ] School library; 71. [ ] Special (non-government) library

IN WHICH OF THE ACTIVITIES WHICH CONSTITUTE AN INTEGRAL PART OF YOUR JOB DO YOU FEEL YOU PERFORM WITH THE GREATEST COMPETENCE? PLEASE INDICATE WHY YOU FEEL YOU HAVE ACHIEVED THE GREATEST COMPETENCE IN THESE:

72. I feel that I have probably achieved the greatest competence in _____ because _____

73. I feel that I have probably achieved the next greatest competence in _____ because _____

APPENDIX A

74. Probably the area of my third greatest competence is in
because

IN WHICH OF THE ACTIVITIES WHICH CONSTITUTE AN INTEGRAL PART OF YOUR JOB DO YOU FEEL YOU PERFORM WITH THE LEAST COMPETENCE? PLEASE INDICATE WHY YOU FEEL YOU HAVE ACHIEVED LITTLE COMPETENCE IN THESE AREAS.

75. I feel that I am probably least competent in
because

76. I do not feel very competent, either, in
because

77. Another area in which I do not feel as competent as I would like to be is
because

78. Suppose you were leaving your library or center for another position, and the administration asked you to recommend someone as your replacement. Suppose, further, that you knew your views would weigh heavily in the final decision. Let us assume, further, that you are leaving your present position with great reluctance and that you have great affection for your library hence, you want to see yourself replaced with the type of person most likely to do a top-notch job after you have gone. Also keep in mind the changes that you foresee coming to your library and the necessity of your replacement adapting to these changes.

BASED ON THESE CONSIDERATIONS, WHAT KNOWLEDGE AND WHICH ABILITIES OR SKILLS WOULD YOU CONSIDER MOST IMPORTANT FOR YOUR REPLACEMENT TO HAVE?

Most Important Knowledge   Most Important Abilities and/or Skills

D. Classification Information

79. WHAT IS YOUR AGE? [   ]   80. ARE YOU: 1. [ ] Male;   2. [ ] Female

APPENDIX A

PART IV. LASTLY, YOUR IDEAS AND COMMENTS

● Your comments on job activities:

In spite of the number of job activities listed, it is very possible that there are others which we have overlooked that you may wish to add. Also, any comments you have about the statements as listed would be welcome.

● Your suggestions for courses and curricula:

It is very possible that we have not included courses or areas of study which are very important to you as you plan for your professional development. Further, we may have stated badly a course you need and you may wish to restate it. We would also be interested in your general comments about continuing formal education in a university setting which might help us as we plan for the future.

APPENDIX A

Your Ideas for the Study as a Whole.

We would also appreciate your general or specific recommendations as we proceed with the ultimate objective of curriculum building. After going through this material, is there anything that we have omitted to ask that you feel we should know in order to do a better job for you? This questionnaire represents input from the librarians practicing in the field. Do you have suggestions or advice on other groups we should question or interview, such as supervisors, users, officials in an agency who are served by the library? If some of your ideas seem "way-out," don't hesitate to list them as we want to consider innovative and creative approaches as well as those that are more generally accepted.

This is the end!

Thank you for your help. We look forward to having your reaction to the results of this survey.

Joanne J. Kortendick
Elizabeth W. Stone

Please use the enclosed, self-addressed, reply envelope to return the questionnaire.

APPENDIX B
OUTLINE OF INTERVIEW SCHEDULE WITH
TOP-LEVEL LIBRARY ADMINISTRATORS

SAMPLES OF THE TYPE OF QUESTIONS USED.

1. What competencies do you feel the librarian (fill in type of position about which the interviewee is being queried) needs over and above the formal training that is provided in the typical library school program for the master's degree in order to do his job effectively?

2. What kind of relevant course work do you think might meet the needs for these competencies?

3. If these relevant courses were available in a post-MLS program, would you permit a person in this position to attend classes:
   a. on a part-time basis?
   b. on a full-time basis?
   c. on his own time only?

4. What financial provisions could you provide for the librarians to take relevant courses under the Manpower Training Act or other government legislation?

5. In general, what is your attitude regarding the value of formal course work toward improving performance on the job?

6. How much of the knowledge required to perform the chief librarian's job or the assistant chief librarian's job is "specialized"? In other words, could the librarian learn how to administer the library more effectively by going to a school of business or public administration, or should such advanced training be more advantageously located in the graduate library school which would work into its program interdisciplinary relationships?

7. If the program were based in the library school, do you have recommendations to make concerning the form of the education? (This would include such matters as teaching methods, use of multi-media, use of an interdisciplinary approach, use of a practical approach vs. a theoretical one).

8. What do you feel will be the impact of automation on the job skills and competencies needed for this particular position in the next few years?

APPENDIX B

9. What type of knowledge or skills in automation do you feel should be mastered for this position?

10. How do you think competence in necessary know-how related to automation can best be achieved?
    a. In library school?
    b. In courses in other departments in the university?
    c. In IBM or other computer courses offered by the manufacturer?
    d. In short-term workshops or institutes?
    e. Through on-the-job training
    f. Other ways?
    g. Combination of ways?

11. What courses should be offered in automation at the post-master's level? Specify your idea of what the content of each should cover.

12. How do you feel about the importance of personal traits as related to this particular type of position? Is there anything that can be done about personal traits or characteristics relative to this type of position at a post-master's level?

13. What terminal behavior patterns would you hope the individual would have at the completion of a post-MLS program?

(Workshop Format)
14. How do you value a short-term workshop or institute as a form of continuing education? Who, within the profession, should take the responsibility for such programs?

APPENDIX C: QUESTIONNAIRE TO DETERMINE INTERVIEWEES'
ATTITUDES TOWARD POST-MLS PROGRAMS

Generally how do you view the development of post-MLS programs in library schools? [Please indicate your degree of agreement by checking the boxes to the left.]

Strongly Agree	Mildly Agree	Disagree	No Opinion	
[ ]	[ ]	[ ]	[ ]	I think certain schools should specialize in certain areas.
[ ]	[ ]	[ ]	[ ]	I think that every school having a post-MLS program should try to meet the varied needs of all who wish to come back.
[ ]	[ ]	[ ]	[ ]	I consider such a program important enough that I would let full-time employees attend on a part-time basis.
[ ]	[ ]	[ ]	[ ]	I would be interested, myself, in going back for certain types of training. If checked, please specify type of training: _____
[ ]	[ ]	[ ]	[ ]	I would expect certain terminal behavior patterns from persons who come back after participating in a post-MLS program. If checked, indicate what they would be: _____
[ ]	[ ]	[ ]	[ ]	I think the maximum advantages from a post-MLS program will be obtained only if the person involved has had some experience in a job following the MLS. If checked, how many years should ideally elapse between the MLS and the Post-MLS study? _____
[ ]	[ ]	[ ]	[ ]	I feel the school should offer courses in the library science department, but that they should be highly interdisciplinary in their approach.
[ ]	[ ]	[ ]	[ ]	I feel the school should not try to offer courses relating to course work in other displines, but rather the employee should return to the campus to study in other departments.
[ ]	[ ]	[ ]	[ ]	I feel that updating is done best in the job situation rather than by returning to library school.
[ ]	[ ]	[ ]	[ ]	Courses and training aren't in my mind the answer. Understanding and a developmental type of leadership on the job are much more important for the development of the individual in his job.

APPENDIX E
LIST OF APPENDIX TABLES

Number		Page
I	Distribution of Respondents by Type of Position and Grade Level According to Geographical Regions: 1968	349
II	Profile of Organizational Mobility: Years in the Federal Government: Years in Present Position, and Number of Libraries in which Respondents Have Worked by Type of Position, Grade Level, and Agency: 1968	352
III	Distribution of Reasons for Leaving Library Work by Type of Position and Grade Level: 1968	353
IV	Frequency Count of Respondents Listing Chief Occupations Prior to Entering Professional Librarianship by Type of Position and Grade Level:1968	354
V	Distribution of All 365 Respondents According to Estimated Minimum Library and Information Center Experience Required to Perform Present Job:1968	356
VI	Applicability of Job Inventory: Frequency of Job Items Checked by Respondents by Type of Position:1968	358
VII	Applicability of Job Inventory: Frequency of Job Items Checked by Respondents by Grade Level:1968	360
VIII	Number of Respondents Answering Job Inventory Items According to Time and Importance Applicability:1968	362
IX	Job Activity Items Ranked According to Weighted Time Score by Type of Position: 1968	376
X	Job Activity Items Ranked According to Weighted Time Score by Grade Level:1968	378
XI	Job Activity Items Ranked According to Weighted Importance Score by Type of Position:1968	381
XII	Job Activity Items Ranked According to Weighted Importance Score by Grade Level:1968	383
XIII	Job Activity Items Ranked According to Joint Time/Importance Weighted Score by Type of Position:1968	386
XIV	Job Activity Items Ranked According to Joint Time/Importance Score by Grade Level: 1968	388
XV	Frequency Distribution of Number of Workshops Checked by the Respondents by Type of Position and Grade Level:1968	391
XVI	Frequency Distribution of Number of Courses Checked in Category "Course Now" by the Respondents by Type of Position and Grade Level:1968	392
XVII	Frequency Distribution of Number of Courses Checked in Category "Course Later" by the Respondents by Type of Position and Grade Level:1968	393

APPENDIX E

Number		Page
XVIII	Frequency Distribution of Number of Courses Checked in Categories "Course Now" or "Course Later" by the Respondents by Type of Position and Grade Level:1968	394
XIX	Courses Showing Highest Response Rankings Indicating Interest in "Workshop" by Type of Position:1968	395
XX	Courses Showing Highest Reponse Rankings Indicating Interest in "Workshop" by Grade Level:1968	397
XXI	Courses Showing Highest Response Rankings Indicating Interest in Either "Course Now" or "Course Later" by Grade Level:1968	400
XXII	Frequency of Comments on Courses and Curricula Section of the Questionnaire by Type of Position and Grade Level:1968	403
XXIII	Administrative Skills and Competencies in which Librarians Most Urgently Need Added Training at the Post-MLS Level According to the Free Response Answer of Interviewees: 1969 (N=20)	404

APPENDIX E

APPENDIX TABLE I
DISTRIBUTION OF RESPONDENTS BY TYPE OF POSITION
AND GRADE LEVEL ACCORDING TO GEOGRAPHICAL REGIONS: 1968

States and Regions Where Respondents Are Employed	Type of Position		Grade Level			Total	
	Administrative	Non-Administrative	9	10, 11	12-14	No.	%
New England							
Maine	0	0	0	0	0	0	0.00
New Hampshire	0	0	0	0	0	0	0.00
Massachusetts	2	0	0	1	1	2	0.55
Rhode Island	1	2	2	0	1	3	0.82
Connecticut	0	1	1	0	0	1	0.27
Vermont	0	0	0	0	0	0	0.00
Subtotal	3	3	3	1	2	6	1.64
Middle Atlantic							
New York	12	2	4	4	6	14	3.84
New Jersey	4	0	3	0	1	4	1.10
Pennsylvania	5	1	1	4	1	6	1.64
Subtotal	21	3	8	8	8	24	6.58
East North Central							
Ohio	9	2	3	6	2	11	3.01
Indiana	0	0	0	0	0	0	0.00
Illinois	4	0	1	2	1	4	1.10
Michigan	2	0	1	1	0	2	0.55
Wisconsin	3	0	1	2	0	3	0.82
Subtotal	18	2	6	11	3	20	5.48
West North Central							
Minnesota	2	0	0	1	1	2	0.55
Iowa	1	0	0	1	0	1	0.27
North Dakota	1	0	1	0	0	1	0.27
South Dakota	0	0	0	0	0	0	0.00
Nebraska	1	0	1	0	0	1	0.27
Kansas	0	0	0	0	0	0	0.00
Missouri	3	0	1	1	1	3	0.82
Subtotal	8	0	3	3	2	8	2.18

continued

APPENDIX E

Appendix Table I continued

States and Regions Where Respondents Are Employed	Type of Position		Grade Level			Total	
	Administrative	Non-Administrative	9	10, 11	12-14	No.	%
South Atlantic							
Delaware	0	0	0	0	0	0	0.00
Maryland	12	8	7	5	8	20	5.48
Virginia	10	1	4	4	3	11	3.01
West Virginia	1	0	0	1	0	1	0.27
North Carolina	1	0	0	0	1	1	0.27
South Carolina	1	0	1	0	0	1	0.27
Georgia	4	1	2	2	1	5	1.37
Florida	6	0	5	0	1	6	1.64
Subtotal	35	10	19	12	14	45	12.31
District of Columbia							
Library of Congress	14	59	21	21	31	73	20.00
Other	44	40	14	43	27	84	23.01
Subtotal	58	99	35	64	58	157	43.01
East South Central							
Kentucky	1	0	0	1	0	1	0.27
Tennessee	3	0	1	1	1	3	0.82
Alabama	5	5	4	4	2	10	2.74
Mississippi	0	0	0	0	0	0	0.00
Subtotal	9	5	5	6	3	14	3.83
West South Central							
Arkansas	0	1	1	0	0	1	0.27
Louisiana	4	0	3	1	0	4	1.10
Oklahoma	4	0	2	1	1	4	1.10
Texas	10	1	5	3	3	11	3.01
Subtotal	18	2	11	5	4	20	5.48
Mountain							
Montana	0	0	0	0	0	0	0.00
Idaho	0	0	0	0	0	0	0.00
Wyoming	1	0	1	0	0	1	0.27
Colorado	11	3	5	5	4	14	3.84

APPENDIX E

Appendix Table I continued

States and Regions Where Respondents Are Employed	Type of Position		Grade Level			Total	
	Administrative	Non-Administrative	9	10, 11	12-14	No.	%
Mountain continued							
New Mexico	2	0	0	2	0	2	0.55
Arizona	1	0	0	1	0	1	0.27
Utah	0	0	0	0	0	0	0.00
Nevada	0	0	0	0	0	0	0.00
Subtotal	15	3	6	8	4	18	4.93
Pacific							
Washington	1	0	0	1	0	1	0.27
Oregon	1	0	0	0	1	1	0.27
California	15	8	6	10	7	23	6.30
Alaska	0	0	0	0	0	0	0.00
Hawaii	1	0	0	1	0	1	0.27
Subtotal	18	8	6	12	8	26	7.11
APO							
Atlantic	11	0	7	3	1	11	3.01
Pacific	16	0	6	7	3	16	4.38
Subtotal	27	0	13	10	4	27	7.39
TOTAL	230	135	115	140	110	365	100.00

APPENDIX E

APPENDIX TABLE II
PROFILE OF ORGANIZATIONAL MOBILITY: YEARS IN THE FEDERAL GOVERNMENT: YEARS IN PRESENT POSITION, AND NUMBER OF LIBRARIES IN WHICH RESPONDENTS HAVE WORKED BY TYPE OF POSITION, GRADE LEVEL, AND AGENCY 1968

Category	Average Number of Years Worked for Federal Government	Average Number of Years in Present Position	Average number of libraries in which the respondents have worked inside and outside the Federal government		
			Inside	Outside	Combined
Grades					
GS 9(N=115)	7.09	3.03	1.96	1.30	3.26
GS 10,11(N=140)	12.26	5.63	2.06	1.31	3.37
GS 12-14(N=110)	13.53	5.45	2.10	1.55	3.65
Type of Position					
Administrative (N=230)	13.04	5.90	2.43	1.60	4.03
Non-Administrative (N=135)	7.34	3.37	1.37	0.99	2.36
Agencies					
Library of Congress (N=73)	5.92	1.99	1.18	0.78	1.96
Army (N=52)	13.90	5.25	2.98	1.90	4.88
Navy (N=28)	14.96	6.44	2.48	1.89	4.37
Air Force (N=51)	10.60	4.82	2.55	1.65	4.20
Veterans Administration (N=36)	16.72	10.58	2.14	1.42	3.66
D.C. Public(N=14)	8.21	7.93	1.50	0.64	2.14
Health, Education, and Welfare (N=21)	11.82	5.59	1.82	1.76	3.58
Agriculture(N=15)	9.73	5.33	1.13	1.40	2.53
Other Agencies(N=75)	11.52	3.58	2.08	1.17	3.25
All Together (N=365)	11.00	4.92	2.04	1.38	3.42

APPENDIX E

APPENDIX TABLE III
DISTRIBUTION OF REASONS FOR LEAVING LIBRARY WORK
BY TYPE OF POSITION AND GRADE LEVEL:1968

Reasons for Leaving	Type of Position				Grade Level								Total	
	Administrative		Non-Administrative		9		10,11		12-14					
	No.(N=230)	%	No.(N=135)	%	No.(N=115)	%	No.(N=140)	%	No.(N=110)	%			No.(N=365)	%
For marriage or family	19	32.76	9	45.00	12	52.17	15	44.12	1	4.76			28	35.90
To obtain further education	16	27.59	4	20.00	8	34.78	4	11.76	8	38.10			20	25.64
To work in another field	10	17.24	4	20.00	1	4.35	7	20.59	6	28.57			14	17.95
For military service	10	17.24	0	0.00	2	8.70	3	8.82	5	23.81			10	12.82
To travel	1	1.72	2	10.00	0	0.00	2	5.88	1	4.76			3	3.85
Other Reasons	4	7.89	3	15.00	1	4.35	5	14.71	1	4.76			7	8.97
Total[2]	58	25.22	20	14.81	23	20.00	34	24.29	21	19.09			78	21.37

[1] The table lists the 82 reasons listed by the 78 respondents who gave answers to this question. The percentages are calculated using the total in each category as the base.
[2] Although some respondents gave multiple reasons for leaving, only one per person is added into the total.

APPENDIX E

APPENDIX TABLE IV

FREQUENCY COUNT OF RESPONDENTS LISTING CHIEF OCCUPATIONS PRIOR TO ENTERING PROFESSIONAL LIBRARIANSHIP BY TYPE OF POSITION AND GRADE LEVEL: 1968

Occupation	First Prior Occupation						Second Prior Occupation					
	Type of Position		Grade Level			Total	Type of Position		Grade Level			Total
	Administrative	Non-Administrative	9	10, 11	12-14		Administrative	Non-Administrative	9	10, 11	12-14	
Teaching												
Elementary grades	7	2	3	3	3	9	1	0	1	0	0	1
Junior and senior high school												
Humanities	31	14	18	17	10	45	0	0	0	0	0	0
Sciences	4	2	3	1	2	6	0	1	1	0	0	1
Subtotal	35	16	21	18	12	51	0	1	1	0	0	1
College												
Library Science	2	1	0	0	3	3	1	0	0	0	1	1
All others	5	2	1	3	3	7	1	3	2	2	0	4
Subtotal	7	3	1	3	6	10	2	3	2	2	1	5
Unspecified or more than one category	15	4	7	6	6	19	2	1	1	1	1	3

354

APPENDIX E

Occupation												
Accountant, bookkeeper	1	3	2	1	1	4	2	0	2	0	0	2
Administrator, supervisor	6	1	2	4	1	7	1	1	1	1	1	2
Book selling, publishing	1	0	1	0	0	1	2	1	1	1	1	3
Business	3	2	3	2	0	5	0	1	0	0	1	1
City planning and related work	1	1	1	1	0	2	0	0	0	0	1	0
Economist, economic analyst	1	2	1	1	2	3	0	0	0	0	0	0
Engineer, architect, draftsman	3	2	2	1	3	5	0	0	0	0	0	0
Military officer, unspecified	2	1	1	1	0	3	1	1	1	1	1	2
Minister, missionary	0	1	1	0	0	1	1	0	1	0	0	1
Personnel work	3	3	1	4	1	6	2	1	1	1	1	3
Recreation work	2	3	4	1	0	5	1	1	1	0	0	2
Research assistant	1	3	1	2	1	4	0	0	0	0	0	0
Scientific (chemistry, physics, biology, etc., lab assistants)	4	3	1	1	5	7	1	1	0	1	1	2
Statistical analyst	2	1	0	1	2	3	0	0	0	0	0	0
Systems analyst	1	0	0	1	0	1	0	0	0	0	0	0
Translator	1	0	1	0	0	1	1	1	0	1	0	1
Weather forecaster	1	1	1	0	1	2	0	0	0	0	0	0
Writing, editing, proofreading, journalism	10	3	3	5	5	13	5	0	1	2	2	5
Miscellaneous	4	4	2	2	3	8	7	1	0	6	2	8
Other Occupations -- Subtotal	47	34	28	28	25	81	23	9	9	13	10	32
TOTAL	111	59	60	58	52	170	28	14	14	16	12	42

APPENDIX E

APPEND
DISTRIBUTION OF ALL 365 RESPONDENTS AC
INFORMATION CENTER EXPERIENCE RI

Type of Position Title	No Experience Needed	1	2
Administrators			
Head of Library	2	6	11
Head of Department or Division	1	3	5
Assistant or Associate Head	2	3	3
Head of Regional or Field Library	1	7	7
Head of Branch	1	4	0
Other	1	0	1
Subtotal	8	23	27
Non-Administrators			
Cataloging	11	9	4
Reference	3	9	7
Bibliography	2	3	3
Classification	0	3	0
Coordinator	0	0	1
Systems Analysis	1	0	0
Acquisitions	1	0	1
Documents and/or Reports	1	0	1
Subject Specialty	0	1	0
Technical Services	1	0	0
Other	4	0	3
Subtotal	24	25	20
TOTAL	32	48	47
PERCENTAGE	8.77	13.15	12.

APPENDIX E

TABLE V

...DING TO ESTIMATED MINIMUM LIBRARY AND
...RED TO PERFORM PRESENT JOB: 1968

		Number of Years Needed					Not An-swered	Total
3	4	5	6	7	Over 7			
5	6	16	6	3	9		17	91
9	9	9	4	3	10		13	66
4	0	4	1	0	4		4	25
3	1	1	0	1	1		0	22
4	1	0	0	0	1		2	13
1	1	4	0	1	2		2	13
6	18	34	11	8	27		38	230
3	3	4	0	0	1		5	43
7	1	4	0	0	2		5	38
4	1	2	0	0	0		1	13
0	0	1	0	0	1		1	6
0	1	1	1	0	0		1	5
0	0	1	0	0	0		2	4
4	0	0	0	0	0		0	3
0	0	0	0	0	0		1	3
0	1	0	0	0	0		1	3
0	0	0	0	0	0		2	3
2	2	0	0	0	1		2	14
7	9	13	1	0	5		21	135
3	27	47	12	8	32		59	365
4.52	7.40	12.88	3.29	2.19	8.77		16.16	100.00

357

APPENDIX E

APPENDIX TABLE VI
APPLICABILITY OF JOB INVENTORY: FREQUENCY OF JOB ITEMS CHECKED BY RESPONDENTS BY TYPE OF POSITION:1968

Number of Job Items Checked	Specialized Library Functions			Frequency by Respondent Administrative Functions			All Functions Together		
	Administrative	Non-Administrative	Total	Administrative	Non-Administrative	Total	Administrative	Non-Administrative	Total
0	17	9	26	3	53	56	0	0	0
1	5	8	13	1	10	11	0	3	3
2	2	8	10	1	4	5	0	6	6
3	3	9	12	1	11	12	0	4	4
4	5	11	16	1	2	3	0	5	5
5	6	9	15	2	6	8	0	4	4
6	6	7	13	6	4	10	0	9	9
7	4	6	10	3	2	5	0	9	9
8	6	7	13	3	3	6	1	7	8
9	8	7	15	2	2	4	0	1	1
10	7	5	12	3	5	8	0	5	5
11	7	6	13	3	2	5	0	5	5
12	5	3	8	7	3	10	1	4	5
13	11	2	13	5	3	8	1	4	5
14	6	5	11	4	5	9	3	7	10
15	10	4	14	4	4	8	2	3	5
16	1	4	5	2	1	3	1	5	6
17	4	2	6	4	2	6	2	4	6
18	9	4	13	0	0	0	5	3	8

358

APPENDIX E

21	3	0	3	2	0	2	4	1	5
22	3	3	6	1	0	1	3	1	4
23	6	3	9	4	1	5	1	2	3
24	3	1	4	3	0	3	0	5	5
25	2	0	2	3	1	4	4	2	6
26	4	2	6	4	0	4	1	4	5
27	3	1	4	2	1	3	2	5	7
28	3	0	3	6	0	6	1	2	3
29	7	0	7	1	1	2	3	2	5
30	2	2	4	2	0	2	1	0	1
31	1	1	2	3	0	3	0	0	0
32	4	1	5	2	1	3	6	1	7
33	5	0	5	3	0	3	4	1	5
34	3	0	3	1	2	3	0	1	1
35	1	0	1	4	0	4	3	0	3
36	4	0	4	0	0	0	0	0	0
37	0	0	0	1	0	1	2	0	2
38	3	0	3	5	0	5	5	1	6
39	2	0	2	1	0	1	3	1	4
40 and above	39	0	39	120	3	123	165	12	177
Mean	22.72	9.99	17.99	42.72	6.59	29.36	65.44	16.58	47.35
Median	18.00	8.00	13.00	41.00	3.00	20.00	59.00	14.00	38.00
Standard Deviation	19.41	9.65	17.59	26.78	9.65	28.10	39.95	15.48	41.15
Range	0-105	0-77	0-105	0-109	0-45	0-109	8-192	1-107	1-192

APPENDIX E

APPENDIX TABLE VII
APPLICABILITY OF JOB INVENTORY: FREQUENCY OF JOB ITEMS CHECKED BY RESPONDENTS BY GRADE LEVEL: 1968

Number of Job Items Checked	Frequency by Respondent											
	Specialized Library Functions				Administrative Functions				All Functions Together			
	Grade			Total	Grade			Total	Grade			Total
	9	10,11	12-14		9	10,11	12-14		9	10,11	12-14	
0	2	6	18	26	34	18	4	56	0	0	0	0
1	6	2	5	13	5	4	2	11	2	0	1	3
2	0	5	5	10	2	2	1	5	5	1	0	6
3	2	4	6	12	4	7	1	12	0	4	0	4
4	4	5	7	16	1	2	0	3	2	2	1	5
5	6	4	5	15	4	4	0	8	2	2	0	4
6	5	3	5	13	7	2	1	10	7	2	0	9
7	4	4	2	10	2	1	2	5	4	3	2	9
8	2	8	3	13	4	2	0	6	3	4	1	8
9	4	5	6	15	1	2	1	4	0	1	0	1
10	5	3	4	12	2	3	3	8	4	0	1	5
11	3	3	7	13	1	2	2	5	3	1	1	5
12	2	3	3	8	2	6	2	10	3	2	0	5
13	4	6	3	13	0	4	4	8	1	3	1	5
14	6	4	1	11	1	3	5	9	2	4	4	10
15	3	6	5	14	0	4	4	8	0	3	2	5
16	2	3	0	5	0	2	1	3	2	2	2	6
17	1	3	2	6	0	4	2	6	3	1	2	6
18	5	7	1	13	0	0	0	0	4	2	2	8
19	3	2	5	10	1	0	1	2	3	0	0	3

APPENDIX E

	20	17	2	39	29	40	54	123	46	67	63	176
22	1	3	2	6	0	1	0	1	1	1	2	4
23	3	4	2	9	2	3	0	5	1	0	2	3
24	2	2	0	4	1	1	1	3	1	2	1	5
25	0	2	0	2	0	3	1	4	2	3	2	6
26	3	1	2	6	2	1	1	4	1	4	1	5
27	1	1	2	4	0	2	1	3	0	5	1	7
28	0	2	1	3	1	1	4	6	1	1	2	3
29	2	3	2	7	0	2	0	2	0	4	0	5
30	1	3	0	4	1	0	1	2	1	1	0	1
31	2	0	1	2	0	2	1	3	0	0	0	0
32	0	4	1	5	1	1	1	3	3	3	1	7
33	2	1	2	5	0	2	1	3	2	1	2	5
34	1	1	1	3	1	1	1	3	0	1	0	1
35	0	1	0	1	0	0	3	3	0	2	1	3
36	2	2	0	4	0	0	0	0	0	0	0	0
37	0	0	0	0	2	1	0	1	0	0	2	2
38	2	1	0	3	0	1	2	5	1	2	3	6
39	1	1	0	2	0	0	1	1	2	2	0	4
40 and above	20	17	2	39	29	40	54	123	46	67	63	176
Mean	23.08	19.31	10.48	17.99	30.59	27.39	38.60	29.36	53.67	46.57	49.08	47.35
Median	15	15	8	13	7	17	38	20	24	37	51	38
Standard Deviation	21.69	15.72	10.67	17.59	18.56	27.02	23.85	28.10	47.59	40.65	32.61	41.15
Range	0-105	0-77	0-60	0-105	0-109	0-99	0-103	0-109	1-192	2-153	1-125	1-192

361

APPENDIX E

APPENDI
NUMBER OF RESPONDENT
ACCORDING TO TIME AN

Item Number	Job Item	Mos
1.	Supervise the preparation of all abstracts and/or abstract services	1
2.	Prepare descriptive abstracts	1
3.	Write abstracts of content of materials	1
4.	Evaluate material and state critique in an annotation	1
5.	Make extracts of materials	0
6.	Provide abstracting services through special announcement devices	0
7.	Other: Abstracting	0
8.	Am responsible for the over-all acquisitions program	36
9.	Establish policies for determining acquisitions	10
10.	Establish ordering and checking systems for books	11
11.	Establish ordering and checking systems for reports and/or documents	7
12.	Establish ordering and checking systems for serials	11
13.	Procure books	15
14.	Procure non-book materials	9
15.	Am responsible for acquisitions received by donation or exchange	11
16.	Establish interlibrary loan system	13
17.	Keep financial records and/or accounts for acquisitions	10
18.	Am accountable for keeping record of funds expended	10
19.	Procure materials for the library's document depository	3
20.	Appraise highly specialized and/or rare materials	4
21.	Publish new-acquisitions bulletin	7
22.	Other: Acquisitions	0
23.	Am responsible for the over-all compilation of bibliographies	24
24.	Maintain continuing bibliographies	18
25.	Compile bibliographies in specialized subject areas	24
26.	Produce demand bibliographies upon request	20
27.	Prepare bibliographies using automated methods	6
28.	Other: Bibliography	1
29.	Have over-all responsibility for the cataloging program	38
30.	Have over-all responsibility for the classification program	31
31.	Establish cataloging policies and procedures	15
32.	Establish classification policies and procedures	12
33.	Expand, develop, and improve classification schemes	6
34.	Develop terminology control schemes	2
35.	Classify and/or reclassify books	33
36.	Classify and/or reclassify non-book materials	10
37.	Expand, develop, and improve lists of subject headings	7

APPENDIX E

TABLE VIII
ANSWERING JOB INVENTORY ITEMS
IMPORTANCE APPLICABILITY:1968

Number of Respondents Checking Each Item					Total for Time or Importance[1] and Rank Therefrom[2]		
TIME		IMPORTANCE					
Substantial	Least	Most	Substantial	Least	No.	Rank	%
2	11	1	4	9	14		3.84
4	11	1	7	8	16		4.38
2	11	1	5	8	14		3.84
5	14	1	10	9	20		5.48
1	8	0	2	7	9		2.47
2	4	2	1	3	6		1.64
1	2	0	2	1	3		0.82
73	12	64	52	4	121	(43)	33.15
30	44	28	40	15	84		23.01
25	39	16	37	23	76		20.82
13	36	13	22	21	56		15.34
24	35	15	37	19	71		19.45
30	24	27	31	13	71		19.45
20	39	16	29	25	70		19.18
20	51	16	20	46	82		22.47
26	39	22	32	24	78		21.37
27	20	21	21	14	57		15.62
24	28	24	22	14	62		16.99
2	16	4	6	11	21		5.75
11	21	6	13	17	36		9.86
6	42	11	16	27	55		15.07
2	3	0	2	3	5		1.37
21	43	33	30	25	88		24.11
15	21	20	23	12	55		15.07
39	32	28	45	22	95		26.03
34	54	28	46	35	109		29.86
3	10	6	5	8	19		5.21
1	2	1	1	2	4		1.10
49	29	60	41	17	118	(44)	32.33
38	27	45	34	19	98		26.85
32	39	35	36	16	87		23.84
28	41	31	27	23	81		22.19
11	42	13	19	27	59		16.16
9	23	7	12	15	34		9.32
36	23	42	30	16	88		24.11
19	40	15	23	32	70		19.18
19	49	19	25	31	75		20.55

continued

363

APPENDIX E

Appendix Table VIII continued

Item Number	Job Item	Most
38.	Do descriptive cataloging of books	33
39.	Do descriptive cataloging of non-book materials	12
40.	Do subject cataloging of books	29
41.	Do subject cataloging of non-book materials	12
42.	Work on the production of book catalogs	5
43.	Use reprography for catalog card reproduction	2
44.	Establish and revise filing rules or special codes	3
45.	Maintain cataloging records	4
46.	Revise cataloging and/or classification done by others	21
47.	Catalog and/or classify rare books	2
48.	Catalog and/or classify public documents and technical reports	10
49.	Other: Cataloging and Classification	0
50.	Have over-all responsibility for circulation system	25
51.	Develop circulation systems	6
52.	Circulate holdings on request	6
53.	Circulate holdings using an EAM-based system	0
54.	Circulate holdings using an EDP-based system	1
55.	Circulate interlibrary loan materials	8
56.	Develop procedures for providing photoduplication of materials	3
57.	Route periodicals on request	3
58.	Route pertinent clippings and ephemeral materials	1
59.	Other: Circulation	1
60.	Have over-all responsibility for clientele services	19
61.	Initiate user services	17
62.	Refer clients to sources of information	29
63.	Instruct users in reference methods and information sources	25
64.	Provide research assistance	35
65.	Plan and/or conduct orientation programs for clientele	10
66.	Compile reading lists	8
67.	Other: Clientele Services	0
68.	Supervise the preparation and/or production of all indexes	9
69.	Provide key-word-in-context indexing service	2
70.	Do concept indexing	2
71.	Do coordinated indexing	2
72.	Do citation indexing	1
73.	Do conventional indexing	4
74.	Index data for storage and retrieval	7
75.	Prepare thesauri and/or terminology control schemes	1
76.	Other: Indexing	0
77.	Have over-all responsibility for literature searching program	15

APPENDIX E

umber of Respondents Checking Each Item					Total for Time or Importance[1] and Rank Therefrom[2]		
TIME		IMPORTANCE					
ostantial	Least	Most	Substantial	Least	No.	Rank	%
21	26	37	23	21	81		22.19
11	31	14	14	27	55		15.07
28	26	38	27	19	84		23.01
17	29	17	18	22	58		15.89
3	6	8	2	5	15		4.11
2	8	2	4	6	12		3.29
6	32	5	14	22	41		11.23
23	32	8	30	22	60		16.44
30	32	32	31	20	83		22.74
8	16	5	9	13	27		7.40
21	22	13	22	18	53		14.52
2	2	0	3	1	4		1.10
45	53	44	50	29	123	(40)	33.70
19	22	14	21	13	48		13.15
20	38	18	20	26	64		17.53
1	2	0	1	2	3		0.82
1	2	1	1	2	4		1.10
17	43	18	20	30	68		18.63
8	19	3	12	15	30		8.22
10	36	9	10	30	49		13.42
4	28	4	10	19	33		9.04
0	2	1	0	2	3		0.82
46	30	77	37	12	126	(35)	34.52
31	23	32	28	12	72		19.73
57	48	56	58	22	136	(26)	37.26
45	52	46	49	28	123	(40)	33.70
54	46	61	55	21	137	(24)	37.53
20	47	23	25	30	78		21.37
15	47	17	18	36	71		19.45
0	2	0	1	2	3		0.82
6	14	10	10	10	30		8.22
2	5	3	4	2	9		2.47
4	1	2	4	1	7		1.92
4	1	3	3	1	7		1.92
3	0	1	3	0	4		1.10
11	12	8	14	5	27		7.40
7	5	10	5	4	19		5.21
3	16	7	4	9	20		5.48
0	1	0	0	1	1		0.27
19	25	25	21	13	59		16.16

continued

365

APPENDIX E

Appendix Table VIII continued

Item Number	Job Item	Most
78.	Establish selective dissemination of information program	4
79.	Establish and/or maintain a field-of-interest register for users	4
80.	Match information against field-of-interest profiles	4
81.	Notify users of material that match their profiles	5
82.	Conduct retrospective searches	8
83.	Analyze and evaluate data for users	4
84.	Publish contents of selected periodicals	1
85.	Other: Literature Searching	0
86.	Give over-all supervision to the maintenance of holdings	23
87.	Maintain hardbound holdings	6
88.	Supervise binding of softbound documents	4
89.	Keep serial bindery records	2
90.	Keep non-serial bindery records	1
91.	Store material in microform	1
92.	Provide viewing and printing equipment for microforms	1
93.	Plan a program for updating material	6
94.	Weed out-of-date material by a planned program	9
95.	Other: Maintenance of Holdings	0
96.	Have over-all responsibility for the reference services provided	45
97.	Establish reference service policies	20
98.	Actively answer reference questions	61
99.	Develop and/or maintain a referral reference center	11
100.	Organize systems for quick reference	12
101.	Reference other material pertinent to information under consideration	13
102.	Other: Reference	0
103.	Am responsible for the adequacy and soundness of research activity	14
104.	Research with information	11
105.	Do information scouting using non-print sources	2
106.	Prepare analytical, evaluative state-of-the-art reports	1
107.	Other: Research	0
108.	Have over-all responsibility for operation of selection system	38
109.	Formulate policies for selection	16
110.	Allocate funds between departments, subjects, collections	5
111.	Make final decisions on selection of material for unit or subject area	19
112.	Serve as a selection official for materials purchased centrally for distribution to branch, mobile, extension or regional collections	7
113.	Identify needs of clientele	19

APPENDIX E

|umber of Respondents Checking Each Item					Total for Time or Importance[1] and Rank Therefrom[2]		
TIME		IMPORTANCE					
|bstantial	Least.	Most	Substantial	Least	No.	Rank	%
11	7	5	11	6	22		6.03
0	19	9	13	7	29		7.95
8	13	9	11	6	26		7.12
15	26	15	20	13	48		13.15
15	20	12	23	8	43		11.78
13	10	6	11	10	27		7.40
2	6	1	4	4	9		2.47
1	1	1	0	1	2		0.55
57	37	41	62	14	117	(45)	32.05
24	23	9	32	12	53		14.52
16	23	7	15	20	43		11.78
9	22	6	10	17	33		9.04
2	10	2	5	6	13		3.56
3	15	2	5	11	19		5.21
7	20	3	8	18	29		7.95
20	24	13	25	12	50		13.70
35	47	19	45	26	91		24.93
2	2	0	2	2	4		1.10
59	34	83	39	15	138	(23)	37.81
27	44	44	30	18	92		25.21
77	47	94	68	24	186	(6)	50.96
8	12	15	5	11	31		8.49
20	34	28	22	17	67		18.36
17	19	21	14	14	49		13.42
1	3	2	1	1	4		1.10
16	22	26	16	11	53		14.52
18	10	17	14	10	41		11.23
8	12	6	7	9	22		6.03
2	4	2	2	3	7		1.92
1	1	0	1	1	2		0.55
43.	19	57	35	10	102		27.95
36	34	39	34	14	87		23.84
22	23	15	29	9	53		14.52
40	22	39	31	13	83		22.74
17	8	12	16	5	33		9.04
50	39	50	48	12	110		30.14

continued

367

APPENDIX E

Appendix Table VIII continued

Item Number	Job Item	Most
114.	Make tentative selection of material from reviews, catalogs, lists	27
115.	Prepare lists of materials needed in specific subject areas	12
116.	Decide on number of duplicate copies and on editions	7
117.	Decide on acceptability of gifts	8
118.	Select serials	8
119.	Select non-book materials	9
120.	Make recommendations on selection of materials	17
121.	Other: Selection	0
122.	Have over-all responsibility for my library's translation program	4
123.	Translate material into foreign languages	0
124.	Translate material from foreign languages into English	0
125.	Abstract and translate	0
126.	Extract and translate	0
127.	Other: Translation	0
128.	Integrate library programs with missions of parent organization	29
129.	Establish goals and objectives for the library	23
130.	Forecast new and/or changed demands for service	16
131.	Determine needed programs for the library	19
132.	Direct over-all preparation of the program budget	20
133.	Compute costs of the library's programs and/or activities	14
134.	Compare the cost and effectiveness of feasible alternatives	9
135.	Make budget request decisions	16
136.	Provide analytical studies justifying budget request decisions	13
137.	Prepare a multi-year summary tabulation of library programs in terms of their outputs, costs, and funding for at least 5 years in advance	4
138.	Negotiate with higher management about allocation of funds	15
139.	Prepare material for inclusion in policy statements	7
140.	Recommend policy changes	10
141.	Devise detailed procedures to implement general policy	20
142.	Help develop new programs and/or activities	15
143.	Provide for participation of employees in planning programs	7
144.	Use PERT as an aid in planning	2
145.	Use Operations Research methods as an aid in planning	1
146.	Plan for the installation of mechanized systems	11
147.	Identify and plan research activities	4
148.	Advise on application of research findings	4
149.	Keep informed about the latest relevant research and developments	11
150.	Other: Planning	0

APPENDIX E

Number of Respondents Checking Each Item					Total for Time or Importance[1] and Rank Therefrom[2]		
TIME		IMPORTANCE					
Substantial	Least	Most	Substantial	Least	No.	Rank	%
52	38	45	52	19	117	(45)	32.05
17	22	21	21	8	51		13.97
21	44	16	25	30	72		19.73
19	72	18	27	54	99		27.12
36	39	29	36	18	83		22.74
30	42	23	31	27	81		22.19
35	72	39	45	42	126	(35)	34.52
2	1	1	1	1	3		0.82
1	9	6	1	8	15		4.11
2	4	0	2	4	6		1.64
9	17	2	11	13	26		7.12
0	4	0	0	4	4		1.10
2	2	0	2	2	4		1.10
0	2	0	0	2	2		0.55
54	47	76	38	18	132	(31)	36.16
47	57	67	47	18	132	(31)	36.16
47	66	51	58	24	133	(28)	36.44
59	58	53	63	21	137	(24)	37.53
36	38	50	31	14	95		26.03
24	37	30	29	18	77		21.10
23	30	19	29	16	64		17.53
38	46	42	40	18	100		27.40
29	37	28	34	18	80		21.92
7	16	12	6	11	29		7.95
26	49	38	32	20	90		24.66
28	67	27	45	31	103		28.22
28	102	44	55	42	141	(21)	38.63
39	47	36	48	23	107		29.32
60	69	45	70	31	146	(19)	40.00
18	55	23	32	25	80		21.92
4	9	3	6	7	16		4.38
4	7	1	6	6	13		3.56
15	33	12	25	24	61		16.71
13	19	7	15	15	37		10.14
6	16	7	9	11	27		7.40
33	71	32	54	31	117	(45)	32.05
0	0	0	0	0	0		0.00

continued

APPENDIX E

Appendix Table VIII continued

Item Number	Job Item	
		Mc
151.	Group activities necessary to attain library's objectives	1!
152.	Assign each grouping to a supervisor with authority necessary to manage it	
153.	Allocate personnel to the various activity groupings	
154.	Distribute material resources among the various parts of the library	
155.	Determine line and staff authority relationships	
156.	Prepare and/or update organization charts	
157.	Create and/or maintain a staff manual	
158.	Modify organizational structure to meet changes	
159.	Organize the clerical processing of information	
160.	Sometimes use committees to undertake line or staff functions	
161.	Provide each department with a clear definition of results expected	
162.	Other: Organizing	
163.	Codify personnel philosophy, policies and procedures	
164.	Forecast future staffing needs	1
165.	Recruit additional staff members	
166.	Select personnel	1:
167.	Use probationary period as a testing program before final appointment	
168.	Study and implement the Civil Service Classification Standards	
169.	Prepare position descriptions or analyses	
170.	Develop employee orientation programs	
171.	Determine training needs at each organizational level	
172.	Build training programs	
173.	Serve as an instructor in training programs	
174.	Use some psychological approaches to training, such as sensitivity groups and/or role playing	
175.	Arrange for personnel to go outside agency for training	
176.	Develop and/or implement a system for career development	
177.	Make and/or approve recommendations for promotion	
178.	Nominate employees for awards and/or special recognition	
179.	Make and/or approve recommendations for separation of employees	
180.	Conduct exit interviews	
181.	Make performance appraisals using traditional formal systems	
182.	Make appraisals using "management by objectives" technique	
183.	Provide a feed-back or suggestion system for employees	
184.	Maintain adequate personnel records for all employees	
185.	Participate in meetings with employee associations	

APPENDIX E

Number of Respondents Checking Each Item					Total for Time or Importance[1] and Rank Therefrom[2]		
TIME		IMPORTANCE					
Substantial	Least	Most	Substantial	Least	No.	Rank	%
33	51	33	50	18	101		27.67
23	37	25	28	13	66		18.08
33	54	27	47	20	94		25.75
21	26	8	24	18	50		13.70
23	37	21	24	21	66		18.08
12	60	9	22	45	76		20.82
32	63	27	45	30	102		27.95
25	56	21	41	24	86		23.56
25	42	8	37	25	70		19.18
9	20	6	12	13	31		8.49
26	25	19	26	9	54		14.79
0	1	0	0	1	1		0.27
18	19	15	18	15	48		13.15
27	75	32	46	36	114		31.23
25	55	32	34	24	90		24.66
30	93	55	50	35	140	(22)	38.36
14	57	31	22	25	78		21.37
27	47	26	25	29	81		22.19
48	86	40	56	46	143	(20)	39.18
25	71	31	36	36	103		28.22
15	47	16	27	24	67		18.36
19	41	10	29	23	62		16.99
18	58	14	34	35	83		22.74
8	9	7	5	6	18		4.93
9	58	10	23	36	69		18.90
14	27	10	14	19	43		11.78
26	100	45	54	34	133	(28)	36.44
17	86	35	34	43	112		30.68
7	73	25	16	42	83		22.74
2	33	6	8	22	36		9.86
28	88	27	49	46	122	(42)	33.42
6	9	4	7	5	16		4.38
7	31	3	18	17	38		10.41
19	53	14	33	26	73		20.00
7	27	6	15	15	36		9.86

continued

APPENDIX E

Appendix Table VIII continued

Item Number	Job Item	Mo
186.	Other: Staffing	0
187.	Directly supervise and guide subordinates	72
188.	Assign jobs to subordinates	29
189.	Harmonize individual objectives with library's objectives	17
190.	Train new employees in the performance of their work	23
191.	Check the accuracy of work of subordinates	25
192.	Brief subordinates on immediate and continuing library programs	13
193.	Make decisions without consulting others	24
194.	Make decisions based on consultation with subordinates	12
195.	Give orders to initiate, modify, or stop activities	14
196.	Install operating procedures for new activities and/or programs	15
197.	Give subordinates authority to command or to act in certain areas	6
198.	Review decisions and/or proposals that are made by subordinates	10
199.	Stimulate subordinates toward superior performance and creativity	17
200.	Use "job enrichment" as a means of motivating subordinates	6
201.	Identify and develop potential in subordinates	11
202.	Counsel subordinates about their career development	9
203.	Administer discipline	7
204.	Formulate communication and express it understandably	15
205.	Use the informal organization as a means of communication	8
206.	Give prompt and full attention to all communications received	26
207.	Frame and transmit communications to support organizational objectives	22
208.	Other: Directing	0
209.	Coordinate the activities of separate groups within the library	16
210.	Exchange ideas and reach understandings through direct contact with others in the library who are not my subordinates	10
211.	Hold group meetings with subordinates	8
212.	Participate in developing inter-library cooperative networks	11
213.	Anticipate problems and prevent their occurrence through continuous interchange of information and early and direct contact of all involved	12
214.	Other: Coordinating	0
215.	Establish standards in terms of specific criteria	13
216.	Schedule activities to ensure that deadlines are met	29
217.	Assign priorities for the completion of work	17
218.	Use the budget to monitor progress of activities	9
219.	Solicit and evaluate clientele reactions to library's services	9
220.	Measure performance against standards, schedules, budgets, surveys	9

APPENDIX E

Number of Respondents Checking Each Item					Total for Time or Importance[1] and Rank Therefrom[2]		
TIME		IMPORTANCE					
Substantial	Least	Most	Substantial	Least	No.	Rank	%
0	0	0	0	0	0		0.00
106	49	127	80	22	229	(1)	62.74
77	102	77	92	40	209	(2)	57.26
39	53	38	51	21	110		30.14
88	79	72	85	34	191	(5)	52.33
81	96	65	91	47	203	(3)	55.62
49	86	48	66	35	149	(18)	40.82
69	88	55	82	46	183	(7)	50.14
69	97	41	89	49	179	(8)	49.04
47	114	53	62	61	176	(9)	48.22
53	64	46	59	28	133	(28)	36.44
53	115	56	71	49	176	(9)	48.22
57	95	51	69	44	164	(16)	44.93
61	89	68	63	38	169	(13)	46.30
19	48	20	28	26	74		20.27
47	91	61	58	32	151	(17)	41.37
21	82	33	40	42	115	(49)	31.51
15	104	27	43	56	126	(35)	34.52
50	58	15	55	24	124	(39)	33.97
16	28	11	24	15	50		13.70
82	67	75	60	41	176	(9)	48.22
47	46	45	46	26	117	(45)	32.05
3	2	1	3	1	5		1.37
28	34	31	28	22	81		22.19
39	54	31	46	28	105		28.77
28	77	29	48	38	115	(49)	31.51
25	50	28	35	25	88		24.11
53	64	56	50	24	130	(33)	35.62
0	0	0	0	1	1		0.27
38	53	43	42	20	105		28.77
54	85	76	58	35	169	(13)	46.30
61	92	77	53	42	172	(12)	47.12
15	38	15	18	26	59		16.16
19	77	42	37	27	106		29.04
23	52	22	36	27	85		23.29

continued

APPENDIX E

Appendix Table VIII continued

Item Number	Job Item	M
221.	Correct the deviations from standards that are discovered	
222.	Use statistical analysis and/or special reports as control devices	
223.	Use systems analysis as a means of control	
224.	Use the techniques of work simplification to correct inefficiencies	
225.	Account for the utilization of resources and meeting of goals	
226.	Prepare regular progress reports to higher management	1.
227.	Other: Controlling	
228.	Interpret library programs to key officials, users, special groups	3.
229.	Approve material prepared for public use	
230.	Am responsible for a publication program	
231.	Issue news releases	
232.	Edit drafts of reports, statements and/or technical documents	
233.	Write articles of a professional nature	
234.	Write or dictate at least 25 letters per week	1.
235.	Negotiate with other groups in agency to get goods and/or services	1
236.	Arrange for the services of contractors and/or consultants	
237.	Attend professional meetings and/or conferences	
238.	Other: Representing	
239.	Plan and justify library quarters	1
240.	Determine equipment needed and compute costs	1
241.	Procure equipment needed	1
242.	Manage the use of library space	1
243.	Manage Library's physical maintenance	
244.	Other: Housing	

[1]If the totals are not the same, the larger of the two was taken

APPENDIX E

| Number of Respondents Checking Each Item ||||| Total for Time or Importance[1] and Rank Therefrom[2] |||
| TIME || IMPORTANCE ||| | | |
Substantial	Least	Most	Substantial	Least	No.	Rank	%
22	63	20	37	32	89		24.38
15	37	13	21	23	57		15.62
4	18	6	8	11	25		6.85
26	62	26	39	29	94		25.75
25	28	20	25	15	60		16.44
48	65	45	50	31	126	(35)	34.52
1	0	0	1	0	1		0.27
56	75	86	50	30	166	(15)	45.48
27	44	29	27	23	79		21.64
22	22	22	18	12	52		14.25
4	29	13	16	11	40		10.96
17	29	10	18	22	50		13.70
5	25	6	9	16	31		8.49
19	13	15	24	9	48		13.15
34	35	23	40	17	80		21.92
14	18	9	12	18	39		10.68
29	159	45	77	78	200	(4)	54.79
0	1	0	1	0	1		0.27
35	55	45	40	25	110		30.14
39	72	43	53	34	130	(33)	35.62
21	39	21	31	21	73		20.00
48	71	43	54	37	134	(27)	36.71
29	54	26	34	32	92		25.21
2	0	2	1	0	3		0.82

[2] Ranks for the first fifty job items are given in parentheses

APPENDIX E

APPENDIX TABLE IX
JOB ACTIVITY ITEMS RANKED ACCORDING TO WEIGHTED TIME SCORE BY TYPE OF POSITION:1968

Job Item Number	Job Item	Weighted Time Score	Rank
ADMINISTRATIVE (N=230)			
187.	Directly supervise and guide subordinates	649	1
188.	Assign jobs to subordinates	426	2
206.	Give prompt and full attention to all communications received	408	3
8.	Am responsible for the over-all acquisitions program	403	4
96.	Have over-all responsibility for the reference services provided	401	5
60.	Have over-all responsibility for clientele services	394	6
190.	Train new employees in the performance of their work	381	7
216.	Schedule activities to insure that deadlines are met	372	8
191.	Check the accuracy of work of subordinates	363	9
98.	Actively answer reference questions	359	10
228.	Interpret library programs to key officials, users, special groups	359	10
193.	Make decisions without consulting others	346	12
217.	Assign priorities for the completion of work	335	13
128.	Integrate library programs with missions of parent organization	334	14
108.	Have over-all responsibility for operation of selection system	332	15
199.	Stimulate subordinates toward superior performance and creativity	328	16
29.	Have over-all responsibility for the cataloging program	327	17
194.	Make decisions based on consultation with subordinates	313	18
131.	Determine needed programs for the library	312	19
129.	Establish goals and objectives for the library	307	20
86.	Give over-all supervision to the maintenance of holdings	302	21
50.	Have over-all responsibility for circulation system	294	22
198.	Review decisions and/or proposals that are made by subordinates	290	23
207.	Frame and transmit communications to support organizational objectives	287	24

APPENDIX E

Appendix Table IX continued

Job Item Number	Job Item	Weighted Time Score	Rank
195.	Give orders to initiate, modify, or stop activities	286	25
197.	Give subordinates authority to command or to act in certain areas	286	25
	Mean	265.98*	
	Standard Deviation	192.50	
NON-ADMINISTRATIVE (N=135)			
98.	Actively answer reference questions	224	1
62.	Refer clients to sources of information	142	2
64.	Provide research assistance	139	3
35.	Classify and/or reclassify books	121	4
38.	Do descriptive cataloging of books	120	5
63.	Instruct users in reference methods and information sources	111	6
40.	Do subject cataloging of books	108	7
191.	Check the accuracy of work of subordinates	101	8
25.	Compile bibliographies in specialized subject areas	99	9
120.	Make recommendations on selection of materials	81	10
46.	Revise cataloging and/or classification done by others	79	11
26.	Produce demand bibliographies upon request	78	12
187.	Directly supervise and guide subordinates	78	12
190.	Train new employees in the performance of their work	77	14
48.	Catalog and/or classify public documents and technical reports	76	15
193.	Make decisions without consulting others	69	16
36.	Classify and/or reclassify non-book materials	64	17
37.	Expand, develop, and improve lists of subject headings	63	18
41.	Do subject cataloging of non-book materials	59	19
82.	Conduct retrospective searches	59	19
210.	Exchange ideas and reach understanding through direct contact with others in the library who are not my subordinates	59	19
114.	Make tentative selection of materials from reviews, catalogs, lists	57	22
101.	Reference other material pertinent to information under consideration	54	23
113.	Identify needs of clientele	52	24
199.	Assign jobs to subordinates	52	24
	Mean	37.43*	
	Standard Deviation	45.20	

*These statistics were calculated for all the 223 job items.

APPENDIX TABLE X
JOB ACTIVITY ITEMS RANKED ACCORDING TO WEIGHTED
TIME SCORE BY GRADE LEVEL:1968

Job Item Number	Job Item	Weighted Time Score	Rank
GS 9	(N=115)		
98.	Actively answer reference questions	256	1
187.	Directly supervise and guide subordinates	183	2
29.	Have over-all responsibility for the cataloging program	172	3
60.	Have over-all responsibility for clientele services	171	4
96.	Have over-all responsibility for the reference services provided	168	5
64.	Provide research assistance	165	6
62.	Refer clients to sources of information	155	7
50.	Have over-all responsibility for circulation system system	149	8
191.	Check the accuracy of work of subordinates	144	9
8.	Am responsible for the over-all acquisitions program	143	10
35.	Classify and/or reclassify books	143	10
30.	Have over-all responsibility for the classification program	139	12
114.	Make tentative selection of material from reviews, catalogs, lists	139	12
40.	Do subject cataloging of books	134	14
190.	Train new employees	134	14
188.	Assign jobs to subordinates	133	16
63.	Instruct users in reference methods and information sources	132	17
38.	Do descriptive cataloging of books	131	18
25.	Compile bibliographies in specialized subject areas	115	19
26.	Produce demand bibliographies upon request	113	20
193.	Make decisions without consulting others	113	20
206.	Give prompt and full attention to all communications received	109	22
217.	Assign priorities for the completion of work	107	23
86.	Give over-all supervision to the maintenance of holdings	106	24
	Mean	92.03*	
	Standard Deviation	62.76	
GS 10, 11 (N=140)			
187.	Directly supervise and guide subordinates	291	1
98.	Actively answer reference questions	250	2
190.	Train new employees in the performance of their work	195	3

APPENDIX E

Appendix Table X continued

Job Item Number	Job Item	Weighted Time Score	Rank
191.	Check the accuracy of work of subordinates	195	3
188.	Assign jobs to subordinates	181	5
96.	Have over-all responsibility for the reference services provided	167	6
62.	Refer clients to sources of information	164	7
8.	Am responsible for the over-all acquisitions program	163	8
64.	Provide research assistance	163	8
60.	Have over-all responsibility for clientele services	160	10
193.	Make decisions without consulting others	158	11
216.	Schedule activities to insure that deadlines are met	153	12
228.	Interpret library programs to key officials, users, special groups	150	13
86.	Give over-all supervision to the maintenance of holdings	148	14
206.	Give prompt and full attention to all communications received	148	14
114.	Make tentative selection of material from reviews, catalogs, lists	145	16
108.	Have over-all responsibility for operation of selection system	144	17
128.	Integrate library programs with missions of parent organization	140	18
25.	Compile bibliographies in specialized subject areas	136	19
194.	Make decisions based on consultation with subordinates	135	20
199.	Stimulate subordinates toward superior performance and creativity	128	21
63.	Instruct users in reference methods and information sources	125	22
113.	Identify needs of clientele	124	23
111.	Make final decisions on selection of material for unit or subject area	121	24
217.	Assign priorities for the completion of work	121	24
	Mean	116.32*	
	Standard Deviation	83.49	
GS 12 - 14 (N=110)			
187.	Directly supervise and guide subordinates	253	1
206.	Give prompt and full attention to all communications received	186	2
188.	Assign jobs to subordinates	164	3

continued

APPENDIX E

Appendix Table X continued

Job Item Number	Job Item	Weighted Time Score	Rank
228.	Interpret library programs to key officials, users, special groups	158	4
207.	Frame and transmit communications to support organizational objectives	145	5
142.	Help develop new programs and/or activities	144	6
193.	Make decisions without consulting others	144	6
194.	Make decisions based on consultation with subordinates	142	8
131.	Determine needed programs for the library	135	9
128.	Integrate library programs with missions of parent organization	134	10
216.	Schedule activities to insure that deadlines are met	134	10
217.	Assign priorities for the completion of work	132	12
199.	Stimulate subordinates toward superior performance and creativity	131	13
141.	Devise detailed procedures to implement general policy	130	14
129.	Establish goals and objectives for the library	129	15
190.	Train new employees in the performance of their work	129	15
191.	Check the accuracy of work of subordinates	125	17
195.	Give orders to initiate, modify, or stop activities	125	17
213.	Anticipate problems and prevent their occurence through continuous interchange of information and early and direct contact of all involved	125	17
198.	Review decisions and/or proposals that are made by subordinates	118	20
237.	Attend professional meetings and/or conferences	118	20
130.	Forecast new and/or changed demands for service	117	22
192.	Brief subordinates on immediate and continuing library programs	116	23
196.	Install operating procedures for new activities and/or programs	116	23
140.	Recommend policy changes	113	25
169.	Prepare position descriptions or analyses	113	25
	Mean	95.06*	
	Standard Deviation	88.37	

*These statistics were calculated for all the 223 job items.

APPENDIX E

APPENDIX TABLE XI
JOB ACTIVITY ITEMS RANKED ACCORDING TO WEIGHTED
IMPORTANCE SCORE BY TYPE OF POSITION:1968

Job Item Number	Job Item	Weighted Importance Score	Rank
ADMINISTRATIVE (N=230)			
187.	Directly supervise and guide subordinates	781	1
188.	Assign jobs to subordinates	625	2
216.	Schedule activities to insure that deadlines are met	557	3
217.	Assign priorities for the completion of work	545	4
206.	Give prompt and full attention to all communications received	543	5
228.	Interpret library programs to key officials, users, special groups	540	6
190.	Train new employees in the performance of their work	536	7
199.	Stimulate subordinates toward superior performance and creativity	526	8
191.	Check the accuracy of work of subordinates	518	9
197.	Give subordinates authority to command or to act in certain areas	516	10
96.	Have over-all responsibility for the reference services provided	508	11
128.	Integrate library programs with missions of parent organization	487	12
60.	Have over-all responsibility for clientele services	485	13
129.	Establish goals and objectives for the library	483	14
201.	Identify and develop potential in subordinates	475	15
8.	Am responsible for the over-all acquisitions program	472	16
198.	Review decisions and/or proposals that are made by subordinates	472	16
194.	Make decisions based on consultation with subordinates	468	18
193.	Make decisions without consulting others	467	19
237.	Attend professional meetings and/or conferences	466	20
98.	Actively answer reference questions	457	21
195.	Give orders to initiate, modify, or stop activities	457	21
192.	Brief subordinates on immediate and continuing library programs	451	23
166.	Select personnel	449	24
131.	Determine needed programs for the library	443	25
	Mean	194.25*	
	Standard Deviation	158.43	

continued

APPENDIX E

Appendix Table XI continued

Job Item Number	Job Item	Weighted Importance Score	Rank
NON-ADMINISTRATIVE (N=135)			
98.	Actively answer reference questions	241	1
62.	Refer clients to sources of information	177	2
64.	Provide research assistance	165	3
63.	Instruct users in reference methods and information sources	146	4
35.	Classify and/or reclassify books	131	5
38.	Do descriptive cataloging of books	129	6
191.	Check the accuracy of work of subordinates	127	7
40.	Do subject cataloging of books	121	8
187.	Directly supervise and guide subordinates	116	9
190.	Train new employees in the performance of their work	113	10
120.	Make recommendations on selection of materials	111	11
25.	Compile bibliographies in specialized subject areas	109	12
26.	Prepare demand bibliographies upon request	101	13
193.	Make decisions without consulting others	100	14
37.	Expand, develop, and improve lists of subject headings	92	15
210.	Exchange ideas and reach understandings through direct contact with others in the library who are not my subordinates	91	16
46.	Revise cataloging and/or classification done by others	88	17
114.	Make tentative selection of materials from reviews, catalogs, lists	81	18
82.	Conduct retrospective searches	79	19
113.	Identify needs of clientele	79	19
48.	Catalog and/or classify public documents and technical reports	78	21
188.	Assign jobs to subordinates	76	22
81.	Notify users of material that match their profiles	72	23
228.	Interpret library programs to key officials, users, special groups	70	24
36.	Classify and/or reclassify non-book materials	68	25
237.	Attend professional meetings and/or conferences	68	25
	Mean	26.11*	
	Standard Deviation	35.15	

*These statistics were calculated for all the 223 job items.

APPENDIX E

APPENDIX TABLE XII
JOB ACTIVITY ITEMS RANKED ACCORDING TO WEIGHTED IMPORTANCE SCORE BY GRADE LEVEL:1968

Job Item Number	Job Item	Weighted Importance Score	Rank
GS 9 (N=115)			
98.	Actively answer reference questions	301	1
187.	Directly supervise and guide subordinates	219	2
64.	Provide research assistance	209	3
62.	Refer clients to sources of information	200	4
96.	Have over-all responsibility for the reference services provided	198	5
188.	Assign jobs to subordinates	197	6
191.	Check the accuracy of work of subordinates	192	7
60.	Have over-all responsibility for clientele services	191	8
29.	Have over-all responsibility for the cataloging program	188	9
190.	Train new employees in the performance of their work	180	10
50.	Have over-all responsibility for circulation system	173	11
63.	Instruct users in reference methods and information sources	173	11
114.	Make tentative selection of material from reviews, catalogs, lists	168	13
8.	Am responsible for the over-all acquisitions program	162	14
35.	Classify and/or reclassify books	158	15
217.	Assign priorities for the completion of work	157	16
228.	Interpret library programs to key officials, users, special groups	156	17
40.	Do subject cataloging of books	153	18
216.	Schedule activities to insure that deadlines are met	153	18
30.	Have over-all responsibility for the classification program	147	20
193.	Make decisions without consulting others	145	21
38.	Do descriptive cataloging of books	144	22
113.	Identify needs of clientele	140	23
206.	Give prompt and full attention to all communications received	139	24
26.	Produce demand bibliographies on request	136	25
	Mean	66.23*	
	Standard Deviation	52.46	

continued

APPENDIX E

Appendix Table XII continued

Job Item Number	Job Item	Weighted Importance Score	Rank
GS 10, 11 (N=140)			
187.	Directly supervise and guide subordinates	355	1
98.	Actively answer reference questions	292	2
192.	Brief subordinates on immediate and continuing library programs	283	3
190.	Train new employees in the performance of their work	281	4
188.	Assign jobs to subordinates	266	5
216.	Schedule activities to insure that deadlines are met	229	6
228.	Interpret library programs to key officials, users, special groups	224	7
96.	Have over-all responsibility for the reference service provided	214	8
206.	Give prompt and full attention to all communications received	213	9
217.	Assign priorities for the completion of work	211	10
62.	Refer clients to sources of information	210	11
64.	Provide research assistance	208	12
60.	Have over-all responsibility for clientele services	202	13
128.	Integrate library programs with missions of parent organization	202	13
193.	Make decisions without consulting others	202	13
199.	Stimulate subordinates toward superior performance and creativity	200	16
113.	Identify needs of clientele	198	17
237.	Attend professional meetings and/or conferences	194	18
86.	Give over-all supervision to the maintenance of holdings	192	19
8.	Am responsible for the over-all acquisitions program	190	20
194.	Make decisions based on consultation with subordinates	189	21
201.	Identify and develop potential in subordinates	188	22
114.	Make tentative selection of material from reviews, catalogs, lists	183	23
195.	Give orders to initiate, modify, or stop activities	182	24
63.	Instruct users in reference methods and in information sources	178	25
	Mean	83.50*	
	Standard Deviation	66.88	

APPENDIX E

Appendix Table XII continued

Job Item Number	Job Item	Weighted Importance Score	Rank
GS 12 - 14 (N=110)			
187.	Directly supervise and guide subordinates	323	1
206.	Give prompt and full attention to all communications received	244	2
199.	Stimulate subordinates toward superior performance and creativity	241	3
188.	Assign jobs to subordinates	238	4
228.	Interpret library programs to key officials, users, special groups	230	5
197.	Give subordinates authority to command or to act in certain areas	228	6
198.	Review decisions and/or proposals that are made by subordinates	222	7
193.	Make decisions without consulting others	220	8
201.	Identify and develop potential in subordinates	220	8
237.	Attend professional meetings and/or conferences	219	10
217.	Assign priorities for the completion of work	218	11
194.	Make decisions based on consultation with subordinates	211	12
195.	Give orders to initiate, modify, or stop activities	210	13
216.	Schedule activities to insure that deadlines are met	207	14
138.	Negotiate with higher management about allocation of funds	206	15
213.	Anticipate problems and prevent their occurence through continuous interchange of information and early and direct contact of all involved	206	15
129.	Establish goals and objectives for the library	205	17
142.	Help develop new programs and/or activities	202	18
166.	Select personnel	202	18
128.	Integrate library programs with missions of parent organization	200	20
192.	Brief subordinates on immediate and continuing library programs	197	21
207.	Frame and transmit communications to support organizational objectives	195	22
190.	Train new employees in the performance of their work	188	23
177.	Make and/or approve recommendations for promotion	187	24
131.	Determine needed programs for the library	183	25
	Mean	70.64*	
	Standard Deviation	69.33	

*These statistics were calculated for all the 223 job items.

APPENDIX E

APPENDIX TABLE XIII
JOB ACTIVITY ITEMS RANKED ACCORDING TO JOINT TIME/IMPORTANCE WEIGHTED SCORE BY TYPE OF POSITION: 1968

Job Item Number	Job Item	Joint Time/Importance Weighted Score	Rank
ADMINISTRATIVE (N=230)			
187.	Directly supervise and guide subordinates	3190	1
188.	Assign jobs to subordinates	2617	2
216.	Schedule activities to insure that deadlines are met	2380	3
228.	Interpret library programs to key officials, users, special groups	2285	4
217.	Assign priorities for the completion of work	2247	5
199.	Stimulate subordinates toward superior performance and creativity	2186	6
197.	Give subordinates authority to command or to act in certain areas	2170	7
190.	Train new employees in the performance of their work	2129	8
191.	Check the accuracy of work of subordinates	2119	9
237.	Attend professional meetings and/or conferences	2118	10
206.	Give prompt and full attention to all communications received	2109	11
96.	Have over-all responsibility for the reference services provided	2072	12
60.	Have over-all responsibility for clientele services	2069	13
201.	Identify and develop potential in subordinates	2003	14
129.	Establish goals and objectives for the library	1998	15
195.	Give orders to initiate, modify or stop activities	1976	16
128.	Integrate library programs with missions of parent organization	1973	17
166.	Select personnel	1955	18
198.	Review decisions and/or proposals that are made by subordinates	1950	19
194.	Make decisions based on consultation with subordinates	1941	20
193.	Make decisions without consulting others	1922	21
192.	Brief subordinates on immediate and continuing library programs	1902	22
177.	Make and/or approve recommendations for promotion	1862	23
98.	Actively answer reference questions	1812	24
8.	Am responsible for the over-all acquisitions program	1780	25
	Mean	813.31*	
	Standard Deviation	658.99	

APPENDIX E

Appendix Table XIII continued

Job Item Number	Job Item	Joint Time/Importance Weighted Score	Rank
NON-ADMINISTRATIVE (N=135)			
98.	Actively answer reference questions	1097	1
62.	Refer clients to sources of information	719	2
64.	Provide research assistance	708	3
63.	Instruct users in reference methods and information sources	600	4
38.	Do descriptive cataloging of books	586	5
35.	Classify and/or reclassify books	575	6
40.	Do subject cataloging of books	534	7
191.	Check the accuracy of work of subordinates	493	8
120.	Make recommendations on selection of materials	463	9
25.	Compile bibliographies in specialized subject areas	447	10
187.	Directly supervise and guide subordinates	445	11
190.	Train new employees in the performance of their work	441	12
26.	Produce demand bibliographies upon request	405	13
193.	Make decisions without consulting others	389	14
37.	Expand, develop, and improve lists of subject headings	385	15
46.	Revise cataloging and/or classification done by others	379	16
210.	Exchange ideas and reach understandings through direct contact with others in the library who are not my subordinates	367	17
82.	Conduct retrospective searches	337	18
48.	Catalog and/or classify public documents and technical reports	336	19
113.	Identify needs of clientele	335	20
114.	Make tentative selection of material from reviews, catalogs, lists	332	21
188.	Assign jobs to subordinates	320	22
237.	Attend professional meetings and/or conferences	313	23
81.	Notify users of materials that match their profiles	300	24
228.	Interpret library programs to key officials, users, special groups	299	25
	Mean	113.41*	
	Standard Deviation	148.92	

*These statistics were calculated for all the 223 job items.

APPENDIX E

APPENDIX TABLE XIV
JOB ACTIVITY ITEMS RANKED ACCORDING TO JOINT TIME/ IMPORTANCE SCORE BY GRADE LEVEL:1968

Job Item Number	Job Item	Joint Time/ Importance Score	Rank
GS 9 (N=115)			
98.	Actively answer reference questions	1254	1
188.	Assign jobs to subordinates	883	2
187.	Directly supervise and guide subordinates	879	3
64.	Provide research assistance	867	4
96.	Have over-all responsibility for the reference services provided	828	5
29.	Have over-all responsibility for the cataloging program	814	6
62.	Refer clients to sources of information	809	7
60.	Have over-all responsibility for clientele services	791	8
191.	Check the accuracy of work of subordinates	778	9
63.	Instruct users in reference methods and information sources	734	10
50.	Have over-all responsibility for circulation system	731	11
190.	Train new employees in the performance of their work	720	12
114.	Make tentative selection of material from reviews, catalogs, lists	714	13
216.	Schedule activities to insure that deadlines are met	689	14
217.	Assign priorities for the completion of work	683	15
228.	Interpret library programs to key officials, users, special groups	682	16
35.	Classify and/or reclassify books	679	17
40.	Do subject cataloging of books	650	18
38.	Do descriptive cataloging of books	647	19
8.	Am responsible for the over-all acquisitions program	630	20
30.	Have over-all responsibility for the classification program	625	21
193.	Make decisions without consulting others	607	22
120.	Make recommendations on selection of materials	577	23
237.	Attend professional meetings and/or conferences	573	24
129.	Establish goals and objectives for the library	571	25
	Mean	284.49	
	Standard Deviation	221.58	
GS 10, 11 (N=140)			
187.	Directly supervise and guide subordinates	1411	1
98.	Actively answer reference questions	1210	2

APPENDIX E

Appendix Table XIV continued

Job Item Number	Job Item	Joint Time/Importance Score	Rank
191.	Check the accuracy of work of subordinates	1141	3
190.	Train new employees in the performance of their work	1099	4
188.	Assign jobs to subordinates	1076	5
228.	Interpret library programs to key officials, users, special groups	972	6
216.	Schedule activities to insure that deadlines are met	959	7
237.	Attend professional meetings and/or conferences	908	8
96.	Have over-all responsibility for the reference services provided	900	9
217.	Assign priorities for the completion of work	883	10
60.	Have over-all responsibility for clientele services	876	11
64.	Provide research assistance	873	12
62.	Refer clients to sources of information	858	13
206.	Give prompt and full attention to all communications received	835	14
199.	Stimulate subordinates toward superior performance and creativity	832	15
193.	Make decisions without consulting others	832	15
128.	Integrate library programs with missions of parent organization	806	17
201.	Identify and develop potential in subordinates	788	18
113.	Identify needs of clientele	774	19
195.	Give orders to initiate, modify, or stop activities	774	19
63.	Instruct users in reference methods and information sources	761	21
194.	Make decisions based on consultation with subordinates	751	22
197.	Give subordinates authority to command or to act in certain areas	748	23
86.	Give over-all supervision to the maintenance of holdings	745	24
166.	Select personnel	737	25
	Mean	345.34	
	Standard Deviation	275.08	
GS 12 - 14 (N=110)			
187.	Directly supervise and guide subordinates	1345	1
199.	Stimulate subordinates toward superior performance and creativity	1011	2

continued

389

APPENDIX E

Appendix Table XIV continued

Job Item Number	Job Item	Joint Time/ Importance Score	Rank
197.	Give subordinates authority to command or to act in certain areas	978	3
188.	Assign jobs to subordinates	978	3
237.	Attend professional meetings and/or conferences	950	5
201.	Identify and develop potential in subordinates	948	6
206.	Give prompt and full attention to all communications received	940	7
228.	Interpret library programs to key officials, users, special groups	930	8
140.	Recommend policy changes	927	9
198.	Study and implement the Civil Service Classification Standards	920	10
166.	Select personnel	910	11
195.	Give orders to initiate, modify, or stop activites	909	12
194.	Make decisions based on consultation with subordinates	884	13
216.	Schedule activities to insure that deadlines are met	880	14
193.	Make decisions without consulting others	872	15
192.	Brief subordinates on immediate and continuing library programs	870	16
217.	Assign priorities for the completion of work	848	17
177.	Make and/or approve recommendations for promotion	842	18
128.	Integrate library programs with missions of parent organizations	832	19
213.	Anticipate problems and prevent their occurrence through continuous interchange of information and early and direct contact of all involved	823	20
142.	Help develop new programs and/or activities	810	21
129.	Establish goals and objectives for the library	807	22
207.	Frame and transmit communications to support organizational objectives	763	23
196.	Install operating procedures for new activities and/or programs	756	24
190.	Train new employees in the performance of their work	751	25
	Mean	296.89	
	Standard Deviation	288.59	

*These statistics were calculated for all the 223 job items.

APPENDIX E

APPENDIX TABLE XV
FREQUENCY DISTRIBUTION OF NUMBER OF WORKSHOPS CHECKED BY THE RESPONDENTS BY TYPE OF POSITION AND GRADE LEVEL: 1968

Number of Workshops Checked	Workshop: Frequency by Respondent					Total
	Type of Position		Grade Level			
	Administrative	Non-Administrative	9	10, 11	12-14	
0	59	50	41	36	32	109
1	11	9	5	5	10	20
2	12	13	8	8	9	25
3	9	11	8	6	6	20
4	14	10	5	10	9	24
5	5	3	3	4	1	8
6	10	4	5	3	6	14
7	15	3	6	11	1	18
8	14	2	5	8	3	16
9	7	3	0	7	3	10
10	11	1	1	8	3	12
11	4	4	2	4	2	8
12	5	2	1	2	4	7
13	2	3	1	2	2	5
14	7	3	3	4	3	10
15	3	1	2	1	1	4
16	3	2	2	2	1	5
17	4	1	2	1	2	5
18	4	1	1	3	1	5
19	1	0	0	1	0	1
20	2	1	0	2	1	3
21	2	0	1	1	0	2
22	0	0	0	0	0	0
23	1	0	0	0	1	1
24	3	1	1	1	2	4
25	1	0	0	0	1	1
26	2	1	3	0	0	3
27	0	0	0	0	0	0
28	3	0	1	2	0	3
29	1	2	1	1	1	3
30	0	1	1	0	0	1
31 or above	15	3	6	7	5	18
Total	230	135	115	140	110	365

APPENDIX E

APPENDIX TABLE XVI
FREQUENCY DISTRIBUTION OF NUMBER OF COURSES CHECKED IN CATEGORY "COURSE NOW" BY THE RESPONDENTS BY TYPE OF POSITION AND GRADE LEVEL: 1968

Number of Courses Checked	Course Now: Frequency by Respondent					Total
	Type of Position		Grade Level			
	Administrative	Non-Administrative	9	10, 11	12-14	
0	130	72	68	71	63	202
1	11	7	4	10	4	18
2	13	8	8	4	9	21
3	10	14	8	10	6	24
4	6	4	1	6	3	10
5	6	1	3	0	4	7
6	8	2	3	4	3	10
7	6	1	1	2	4	7
8	4	5	4	5	0	9
9	7	5	1	5	6	12
10	2	2	1	2	1	4
11	2	0	1	1	0	2
12	2	0	0	1	1	2
13	1	3	1	3	0	4
14	0	1	1	0	0	1
15	3	2	1	2	2	5
16	1	4	3	1	1	5
17	4	1	1	3	1	5
18	0	1	0	1	0	1
19	0	1	0	1	0	1
20	0	0	0	0	0	0
21	1	1	1	1	0	2
22	1	0	0	1	0	1
23	0	0	0	0	0	0
24	1	0	0	1	0	1
25	1	0	1	0	0	1
26	2	0	0	1	1	2
27	1	0	0	1	0	1
28	1	0	1	0	0	1
29	1	0	0	1	0	1
30	1	0	1	0	0	1
31 or above	4	0	1	2	1	4
Total	230	135	115	140	110	365

APPENDIX E

APPENDIX TABLE XVII
FREQUENCY DISTRIBUTION OF NUMBER OF COURSES CHECKED IN CATEGORY "COURSE LATER" BY THE RESPONDENTS BY TYPE OF POSITION AND GRADE LEVEL: 1968

Number of Courses Checked	Course Later: Frequency by Respondent					Total
	Type of Position		Grade Level			
	Administrative	Non-Administrative	9	10, 11	12-14	
0	116	64	47	72	61	180
1	12	8	4	9	7	20
2	7	10	4	9	4	17
3	11	5	3	8	5	16
4	14	10	9	7	8	24
5	10	4	3	4	7	14
6	8	4	6	3	3	12
7	5	5	3	4	3	10
8	3	3	3	1	2	6
9	5	4	7	2	0	9
10	3	2	3	0	2	5
11	4	3	3	3	1	7
12	2	3	0	3	2	5
13	2	1	2	1	0	3
14	1	1	1	1	0	2
15	5	2	6	0	1	7
16	5	0	2	1	2	5
17	3	1	2	2	0	4
18	3	1	1	2	1	4
19	3	0	1	1	1	3
20	1	0	1	0	0	1
21	1	0	1	0	0	1
22	0	1	1	0	0	1
23	1	0	0	1	0	1
24	1	0	0	1	0	1
25	1	0	0	1	0	1
26	0	1	0	1	0	1
27	0	0	0	0	0	0
28	1	0	1	0	0	1
29	0	0	0	0	0	0
30	1	0	0	1	0	1
31 or above	1	2	1	2	0	3
Total	230	135	115	140	110	365

APPENDIX E

APPENDIX TABLE XVIII
FREQUENCY DISTRIBUTION OF NUMBER OF COURSES CHECKED IN CATEGORIES "COURSE NOW" OR "COURSE LATER" BY THE RESPONDENTS BY TYPE OF POSITION AND GRADE LEVEL: 1968

Number of Courses Checked	"Course Now" or "Course Later": Frequency by Respondent					Total
	Type of Position		Grade Level			
	Administrative	Non-Administrative	9	10, 11	12-14	
0	91	44	34	56	45	135
1	10	8	3	10	5	18
2	8	9	4	5	8	17
3	9	6	6	6	3	15
4	12	11	8	7	8	23
5	9	3	3	3	6	12
6	10	6	7	5	4	16
7	11	6	3	8	6	17
8	4	4	4	2	2	8
9	7	4	5	4	2	11
10	3	3	2	2	2	6
11	5	4	2	3	4	9
12	1	2	1	1	1	3
13	5	3	5	1	2	8
14	0	2	1	1	0	2
15	5	2	2	2	3	7
16	4	1	3	1	1	5
17	7	2	3	2	4	9
18	4	2	3	2	1	6
19	3	1	1	3	0	4
20	1	0	1	0	0	1
21	4	1	3	2	0	5
22	0	2	1	1	0	2
23	2	1	0	3	0	3
24	2	1	1	2	0	3
25	2	2	1	3	0	4
26	0	0	0	0	0	0
27	2	1	2	0	1	3
28	1	0	1	0	0	1
29	0	2	1	1	0	2
30	2	0	0	1	1	2
31 or above	6	2	4	3	1	8
Total	230	135	115	140	110	365

APPENDIX TABLE XIX
COURSES SHOWING HIGHEST RESPONSE RANKINGS INDICATING INTEREST IN "WORKSHOP" BY TYPE OF POSITION: 1968

Workshop Number	Title of Workshop	Number Checking Workshop	Rank
ADMINISTRATIVE (N=230)			
3.	Current Practices in Acquisition and Selection of Non-Book Materials	65	1
1.	Building and Evaluating Library Collections	64	2
26.	Automation of Library Processes	57	3
66.	Resources and Services of the Federal Library Complex	55	4
40.	Circulation Systems	50	5
5.	Administration Policies and Practices	46	6
8.	General Management	46	6
9.	Human Relations in Library Administration	46	6
15.	Program Planning and Budgeting	46	6
19.	Administration of the Special Federal Library	46	6
59.	Current Issues in Librarianship and Information Science	43	11
64.	Library Networks	43	11
72.	Non-Conventional Library Reference Tools	43	11
2.	Centralized Processing	41	14
12.	Personnel Administration in Libraries	41	14
43.	Information Retrieval for Clientele	41	14
46.	Equipment Evaluation, Selection, and Procurement	40	17
71.	Development and Maintenance of a Reference Referral Center	39	18
13.	Personnel Problems under the Impact of Technological Change: Library Applications	38	19
33.	Cataloging and Classification of Non-Book Materials	38	19
57.	The Scope of Information Science	38	19
6.	Communication Theory and Processes	37	22
41.	Reprography	36	23
48.	Planning and Justifying Library Quarters	36	23
34.	Centralized Cataloging at the National Level	35	25
NON-ADMINISTRATIVE (N=135)			
26.	Automation of Library Processes	26	1
28.	Information Retrieval Systems	25	2
66.	Resources and Services of the Federal Library Complex	22	3

continued

APPENDIX E

Appendix Table XIX continued

Workshop Number	Title of Workshop	Number Checking Workshop	Rank
72.	Non-Conventional Library Reference Tools	22	3
36.	New Advances in Classification Schemes and Cataloging Systems	18	5
43.	Information Retrieval for Clientele	18	5
44.	Literature Searching	18	5
74.	Search Logic and Tactics	18	5
1.	Building and Evaluating Library Collections	16	9
9.	Human Relations in Library Administration	16	9
27.	Information Processing on Computers	16	9
34.	Centralized Cataloging at the National Level	16	9
59.	Current Issues in Librarianship and Information Science	16	9
37.	Recataloging and Reclassification	14	14
69.	Publishing in the Twentieth Century: Book and Non-Book Materials	14	14
8.	General Management	13	16
13.	Personnel Problems Under the Impact of Technological Change: Library Applications	13	16
19.	Administration of the Special Federal Library	13	16
40.	Circulation System	13	16
57.	The Scope of Information Science	13	16
6.	Communication Theory and Processes	12	21
7.	Design of Library Organizations	12	21
71.	Development and Maintenance of a Reference Referral Center	12	21
87.	Scientific and Technical Literature and Research	12	21
3.	Current Practices in Acquisition and Selection of Non-Book Materials	11	25
12.	Personnel Administration in Libraries	11	25
52.	Theories of Indexing and Information Retrieval	11	25
73.	Organization and Administration of Reference Systems	11	25
89.	Technical Report Literature	11	25
90.	U.S. Public Documents	11	25

APPENDIX E

APPENDIX TABLE XX
COURSES SHOWING HIGHEST RESPONSE RANKINGS INDICATING INTEREST IN "WORKSHOP" BY GRADE LEVEL: 1968

Workshop Number	Title of Workshop	Number Checking Workshop	Rank
GS 9 (N=115)			
1.	Building and Evaluating Library Collections	29	1
3.	Current Practices in Acquisitions and Selection of Non-Book Materials	24	2
72.	Non-Conventional Library Reference Tools	23	3
40.	Circulation Systems	23	3
2.	Centralized Processing	22	5
6.	Communication Theory and Processes	20	6
66.	Resources and Services of the Federal Library Complex	20	6
8.	General Management	19	8
9.	Human Relations in Library Administration	19	8
46.	Equipment Evaluation, Selection and Procurement	19	8
41.	Reprography	18	11
43.	Information Retrieval for Clientele	18	11
74.	Search Logic and Tactics	18	11
5.	Administrative Policies and Practices	17	14
12.	Personnel Administration in Libraries	17	14
14.	Policy Formation and Decision-Making in Library Organizations	17	14
28.	Information Retrieval Systems	17	14
37.	Recataloging and Reclassification: Problems and Procedures	17	14
71.	Development and Maintenance of a Reference Referral Center	17	14
19.	Administration of the Special Federal Library	16	20
33.	Cataloging and Classification of Non-Book Materials	16	20
36.	New Advances in Classification Schemes and Cataloging Systems: A Survey	16	20
59.	Current Issues in Librarianship and Information Science	16	20
64.	Library Networks	16	20
7.	Design of Library Organizations	15	25
11.	Management of Records Systems in the Library	15	25
12.	Personnel Administration in Libraries	15	25
26.	Automation of Library Processes	15	25
34.	Centralized Cataloging at the National Level	15	25
44.	Literature Searching	15	25

continued

APPENDIX E

Appendix Table XX continued

Workshop Number	Title of Workshop	Number Checking Workshop	Rank
69.	Publishing in the Twentieth Century	15	25
GS 10, 11 (N=140)			
26.	Automation of Library Processes	37	1
66.	Resources and Services of the Federal Library Complex	36	2
3.	Current Practices in Acquisition and Selection of Non-Book Materials	35	3
72.	Non-Conventional Library Reference Tools	33	4
1.	Building and Evaluating Library Collections	32	5
28.	Information Retrieval Systems	31	6
8.	General Management	28	7
43.	Information Retrieval for Clientele	28	7
59.	Current Issues in Librarianship and Information Science	26	9
9.	Human Relations in Library Administration	26	9
36.	New Advances in Classification Schemes and Cataloging Systems: A Survey	23	11
44.	Literature Searching	23	11
19.	Administration of the Special Federal Library	22	13
27.	Information Processing on Computers	22	13
40.	Circulation Systems	22	13
48.	Planning and Justifying Library Quarters	22	13
87.	Scientific and Technical Literature and Research	21	17
15.	Program Planning and Budgeting	20	18
34.	Centralized Cataloging at the National Level	20	18
46.	Equipment Evaluation, Selection, and Procurement	20	18
57.	The Scope of Information Science	20	18
71.	Development and Maintenance of a Reference Referral Center	20	18
74.	Search Logic and Tactics	20	18
13.	Personnel Problems under the Impact of Technological Change: Library Applications	18	24
33.	Cataloging and Classification of Non-Book Materials	18	24
64.	Library Networks	18	24
73.	Organization and Administration of Reference Systems	18	24
GS 12 - 14 (N=110)			
26.	Automation of Library Processes	31	1

APPENDIX E

Appendix Table XX continued

Workshop Number	Title of Workshop	Number Checking Workshop	Rank
5.	Administration Policies and Practices	22	2
19.	Administration of the Special Federal Library	21	3
66.	Resources and Services of the Federal Library Complex	21	3
12.	Personnel Administration in Libraries	20	5
15.	Program Planning and Budgeting	20	5
1.	Building and Evaluating Library Collections	19	7
9.	Human Relations in Library Administration	19	7
40.	Circulation Systems	19	7
13.	Personnel Problems under the Impact of Technological Change: Library Applications	18	10
57.	The Scope of Information Science	18	10
3.	Current Practices in Acquisition and Selection of Non-Book Materials	17	12
59.	Current Issues in Librarianship and Information Science	17	12
64.	Library Networks	17	12
7.	Design of Library Organizations	16	15
14.	Policy Formation and Decision-Making in Library Organizations	16	15
34.	Centralized Cataloging at the National Level	16	15
92.	Library Management Information Systems	16	15
2.	Centralized Processing	14	19
71.	Development and Maintenance of a Reference Referral Center	14	19
6.	Communication Theory and Processes	13	21
43.	Information Retrieval for Clientele	13	21
8.	General Management	12	23
27.	Information Processing on Computers	12	23
63.	The Library Administrator and Government Policy, Organization and Operation	12	23
76.	Operations Research in Library Management	12	23

APPENDIX E

APPENDIX TABLE XXI
COURSES SHOWING HIGHEST RESPONSE RANKINGS INDICATING INTEREST IN EITHER "COURSE NOW" OR "COURSE LATER" BY GRADE LEVEL: 1968

Course Number	Course Title	Number Checking Either Course Now or Course Later	Rank
GS 9 (N=115)			
26.	Automation of Library Processes	41	1
28.	Information Retrieval Systems	41	1
27.	Information Processing on Computers	34	3
43.	Information Retrieval for Clientele	26	4
15.	Program Planning and Budgeting	23	5
19.	Administration of the Special Federal Library	23	5
73.	Organization and Administration of Reference Systems	22	7
72.	Non-Conventional Library Reference Tools	19	8
5.	Administrative Policies and Practices	18	9
12.	Personnel Administration in Libraries	18	9
36.	New Advances in Classification Schemes and Cataloging Systems: A Survey	18	9
57.	The Scope of Information Science	18	9
74.	Search Logic and Tactics	18	9
7.	Design of Library Organizations	17	14
9.	Human Relations in Library Administration	17	14
13.	Personnel Problems Under the Impract of Technological Change: Library Applications	17	14
44.	Literature Searching	17	14
3.	Current Practices in Acquisition and Selection of Non-Book Materials	16	18
22.	Information Center Administration	16	18
68.	Publication in the Library and Information Science Fields	16	18
71.	Development and Maintenance of a Reference Referral Center	16	18
90.	U.S. Public Documents	16	18
GS 10, 11 (N=140)			
26.	Automation of Library Processes	43	1
28.	Information Retrieval Systems	40	2
27.	Information Processing on Computers	34	3
8.	General Management	29	4
9.	Human Relations in Library Administration	29	4
5.	Administrative Policies and Practices	27	6

APPENDIX E

Appendix Table XXI continued

Course Number	Course Title	Number Checking either Course Now or Course Later	Rank
19.	Administration of the Special Federal Library	27	6
90.	U.S. Public Documents	24	8
12.	Personnel Administration in Libraries	22	9
73.	Organization and Administration of Reference Systems	22	9
93.	Systems Analysis and Design for Library and Information Center Operations	22	9
7.	Design of Library Organizations	21	12
13.	Personnel Problems under the Impact of Technological Change: Library Applications	21	12
43.	Information Retrieval for Clientele	21	12
50.	Abstracting and Indexing Services	21	12
15.	Program Planning and Budgeting	20	16
94.	Systems Analysis in Information Science	20	16
3.	Current Practices in Acquisition and Selection of Non-Book Materials	19	18
30.	Analytical Bibliography	19	18
57.	The Scope of Information Science	19	18
68.	Publication in the Library and Information Science Fields	19	18
GS 12-14 (N=110)			
26.	Automation of Library Processes	35	1
28.	Information Retrieval Systems	35	1
27.	Information Processing on Computers	33	3
5.	Administrative Policies and Practices	17	4
93.	Systems Analysis and Design for Library and Information Center Operations	15	5
19.	Administration of the Special Federal Library	14	6
38.	Subject Representation	13	7
6.	Communication Theory and Processes	12	8
7.	Design of Library Organizations	12	8
9.	Human Relations in Library Administration	12	8
94.	Systems Analysis in Information Science	11	11
74.	Search Logic and Tactics	10	12
15.	Program Planning and Budgeting	9	13
36.	New Advances in Classification Schemes and Cataloging Systems: A Survey	9	13
56.	Mathematical Techniques for Information Science	9	13
78.	Statistical Theory and the Interpretation of Statistical Data for Researching in Libraries and Information Centers	9	13

continued

APPENDIX E

Appendix Table XXI continued

Course Number	Course Title	Number Checking either Course Now or Course Later	Rank
3.	Current Practices in Acquisition and Selection of Non-Book Materials	8	17
8.	General Management	8	17
10.	Innovation and Planned Change in Library Organizations	8	17
12.	Personnel Administration in Libraries	8	17
14.	Policy Formation and Decision-Making in Library Organizations	8	17
43.	Information Retrieval for Clientele	8	17
50.	Abstracting and Indexing Services	8	17
64.	Library Networks	8	17
68.	Publication in the Library and Information Science Fields	8	17
89.	Technical Report Literature	8	17
92.	Library Management Information Systems	8	17

APPENDIX E

APPENDIX TABLE XXII
FREQUENCY OF COMMENTS ON COURSES AND CURRICULA SECTION OF THE QUESTIONNAIRE
BY TYPE OF POSITION AND GRADE LEVEL: 1968

Category of Respondents	Library Science Courses	Non-Library Science Courses	Workshops and Seminars	Work-Study Programs	Doctoral Programs	General Comments	Time, Location, Format of Courses	Attitudes toward Post-MLS Study	Undergraduate Requirements	Study for LS Technician	Total Number of Comments
ADMINISTRATORS											
Library Heads											
GS 9	10	1	2	1	0	3	4	1	0	0	22
GS 10, 11	5	1	2	1	0	4	2	1	1	0	17
GS 12-14	3	1	4	1	2	4	1	2	0	0	18
Subtotal	18	3	8	3	2	11	7	4	1	0	57
Other Administrators											
GS 9	8	3	5	0	0	6	3	2	1	0	28
GS 10, 11	5	5	1	0	0	4	2	2	0	2	21
GS 12-14	8	2	1	0	1	4	3	3	2	1	25
Subtotal	21	10	7	0	1	14	8	7	3	3	74
Total	39	13	15	3	3	25	15	11	4	3	131
NON-ADMINISTRATORS											
GS 9	6	4	0	0	0	6	1	3	0	1	21
GS 10, 11	2	9	2	0	1	2	2	2	2	0	22
GS 12-14	1	2	0	0	0	0	2	1	1	0	7
Subtotal	9	15	2	0	1	8	5	6	3	1	50
ALL RESPONDENTS											
GS 9	24	8	7	1	0	15	8	6	1	1	71
GS 10, 11	12	15	5	1	1	10	6	5	3	2	60
GS 12-14	12	5	5	1	3	8	6	6	3	1	50
TOTAL	48	28	17	3	4	33	20	17	7	4	181

APPENDIX E

APPENDIX TABLE XXIII

ADMINISTRATIVE SKILLS AND COMPETENCIES IN WHICH LIBRARIANS MOST URGENTLY NEED ADDED TRAINING AT THE POST-MLS LEVEL ACCORDING TO THE FREE RESPONSE ANSWERS OF INTERVIEWEES:1969 (N=20)

Frequency of Free Response Comments	Skills or Competencies	Related Major Job Function Category in Questionnaire	Course Number	Related Courses in Questionnaire Course Title
18	Capacity for directing others -- including supervision, interpersonal skills and employee motivation	Directing	9. 12.	Human Relations in Library Administration Personnel Administration
16	Communication Skills	Directing	6.	Communication Theory and Processes
15	Understanding the management process	Planning, organizing, staffing, controlling, etc.	8.	General Management
13	Skill in decision-making	Planning, directing	14.	Policy Formation and Decision Making in Library Organizations
12	Skill in program planning and budgeting	Planning	15.	Program Planning and Budgeting
11	Developing and merchandising user services	Representing	6.	Communication Theory and Processes
10	Innovation: taking the lead in bringing about changes	Planning, controlling	10.	Innovation and Planned Change in Library Organizations
10	Understanding systems design and analysis	Planning, controlling	7.	Design of Library Organizations

404

BIBLIOGRAPHY

This bibliography is designed to help those interested in building a post-master's curriculum. The subdivisions mirror the conclusions and recommendations of the study concerning the form and content of program development. Thus, the interdisciplinary approach recommended is reflected in the sections entitled: "Continuing Education: Other Professions" and "Curriculum Development: Other Professions". The importance of the systems perspective in designing courses and curricula is brought out in "Educational Planning: Multi-Media and Systems Approaches". The necessity for a practical approach, if learning is to be maximized, is documented in "Learning: A Process of Change". As there are signs throughout the study of a certain apathy on the part of the individual librarian and the profession as a whole toward continuing education, signs which indicate the importance of taking motivational factors into consideration in program building, "Continuing Education: Motivational Factors", which is interdisciplinary in content, is included.

Dealing with the content of the program, the sections "Continuing Education: Library and Information Science" and "Curriculum Development: Library and Information Science" seem necessary background for building a program based in the library school, as recommended in the study.

As the greatest demand was for courses in automation and administration, there are sections, interdisciplinary in nature, emphasizing concepts in these areas. If the post-master's program is seen as an important way to upgrade the profession--as presented in this study--data on the manpower situation and the importance of training professional librarians toward the better utilization of the personnel already recruited become exceedingly important; thus, the section on manpower, which also deals with the problems of training the subprofessional to relieve the professional of avoidable detail work.

The respondents to the questionnaire placed great importance on personal characteristics for job success, as did the interviewees, but the findings indicate that different personality characteristics are important at different levels of the hierarchy. Until further research can be done, it would seem advantageous to study some of the personality and attitudinal patterns that have been found characteristic of librarians through previous studies. The interviewees, when asked what terminal behavior patterns they would expect librarians to gain by participating in a post-master's program, gave top priority rating to the librarian's becoming an "agent for change". This concept is highlighted in "Innovation and Change". Finally, there are sections dealing with research concepts and techniques: "Interviewing"; "Questionnaire Sources", which includes references to sample questionnaires of merit; "Job Inventories", philosophy and examples; plus a concluding section on research needs and the importance of research in any upgrading process within a profession.

BIBLIOGRAPHY

CONTINUING EDUCATION: LIBRARY AND INFORMATION SCIENCE

Allen, Lawrence A. <u>An Evaluation of the Community Librarians' Training Courses,</u> with Special Emphasis on the Entire Training Function in the Library Extension Division of the New York State Library. Albany: New York State Library, 1966. (ED 024 406)

Alvarez, Robert S. "Continuing Education for the Public Librarian," <u>California Librarian,</u> 30:177-186, July, 1969.

American Association of School Librarians. Supervisors Section. "Summary Sheet of Responses Received from 'Questionnaire About Continuing Education for School-Library-Media Supervisors' ". Questionnaire published in <u>School Libraries</u>, 18, 53, Summer, 1969.

American Library Association. Association of School Librarians and the National Commission on Teacher Education and Professional Standards. <u>The Teachers' Library.</u> Washington, D.C.: National Education Association, 1966.

American Library Association. Office for Library Education. <u>Continuing Education for Librarians--Conferences, Workshops, and Short Courses 1967-68.</u> Chicago: American Library Association, 1967.

American Library Association. Office for Library Education. <u>Continuing Education for Librarians--Conferences, Workshops, and Short Courses 1968-69.</u> Chicago: American Library Association, 1968.

American Library Association. Office for Library Education. <u>Continuing Education for Librarians--Conferences, Workshops, and Short Courses 1969-1970.</u> Chicago: American Library Association, 1969.

Aspnes, Grieg. "Accreditation: Panel Member No. 3". In: Sarah R. Reed (ed.). <u>Problems of Library School Administration: Report of an Institute, April 14-15, 1965, Washington, D.C.</u> Washington, D.C.: U.S. Office of Education, 1965.

Bentley, B. "Report of an Internship Served in the Abilene (Texas) Public Library, February 1 to August 1, 1960." Unpublished Master's thesis, University of Texas, Austin, 1961.

Bird, J. "The Role of Professional Periodicals in Education for Library and Information Work," <u>Association of Special Libraries and Information Bureaus Proceedings,</u> 8:55-67, 1956.

BIBLIOGRAPHY

Boaz, Martha. "Continuing Education," *Drexel Library Quarterly*, 3:151-157, April, 1967.

──────. "Education A-Go-Go! Continuing..." *California Librarian*, 30:187-190, July, 1969.

──────. "USC Library Education Institute Summary," *Journal of Education for Librarianship*, 2(2):68-76, Fall, 1961.

Boelke, Joanne. *Library Technicians, a Survey of Current Developments.* Washington, D.C.: U.S. Office of Education, 1968. ED 019 530.

Bottle, R. T. "Short Courses on the Use of Specific Subject Literature" In: *Proceedings of International Conference on Education for Scientific Information Work,* London, 1967. The Hague: International Federation for Documentation, 1967, pp. 59-69.

Brodman, Estelle. "Internships as Continuing Education," *Medical Library Association Bulletin,* 48(4):412, October, 1960.

──────ꭥ and others. "Continuing Education of Medical Librarians," *Medical Library Association Bulletin,* 51: 354-383, July, 1963.

Bundy, Mary Lee. "Public Library Administrators View Their Professional Periodicals," *Illinois Libraries,* 43:397-420, June, 1961.

Bundy, Mary Lee and Hilda Womack. "Librarians as Readers," *Illinois Libraries,* 42:427-435, September, 1960.

Burton, Howard A. "Maximum Benefits from a Program for Staff Reading," *College and Research Libraries,* 15:277-280, July, 1954.

Campbell, Boyd P. and Harold A. Williams, comps. *Continuing Education Film Survey, a National Survey of 16 mm Films Prepared for the 1968 NYAPSAE Annual Conference.* Albany, New York: State University of New York, 1968. ED 19-615.

Catholic University of America. Department of Library Science. *Federal Library Resources, Services and Programs.* An Institute for Library Science and Information Science Faculties held June 11-22, 1968, The Catholic University of America, Washington, D.C. (unpublished proceedings).

Connor, John M. "Medical Librarian Trainee Program in a Medical Society Library," *Special Libraries,* 58:428-429, July-August, 1967.

Davis, Richard A. "Continuing Education: Formal and Informal," *Special Libraries,* 58:27-30, January, 1967.

BIBLIOGRAPHY

De Prospo, Ernest R., Jr. and Theodore S. Huang. "Continuing Education for the Library Administrator: His Needs." In: Neal H. Harlow, and others (eds.). <u>Administration and Change: Continuing Education in Library Administration.</u> New Brunswick, New Jersey: Rutgers University Press, 1969, pp. 21-27.

Drexel Institute of Technology. Graduate School of Library Science. <u>How Effective is Education for Librarianship?</u> A digest of the contributions of speakers at the workshop held April 28-30, 1957. Philadelphia. : Drexel Institute of Technology, 1957.

Horn, Andrew H. ["Post-MLS Certificates of Specialization in Library Science at UCLA,"]. Letter in <u>A.B. Bookman's Weekly</u>, 42:1299. October, 1968.

Horn, Francis. "Tomorrow's Targets for University Adult Education." Paper presented at 10th Annual Seminar on Leadership in University Adult Education. Lansing, Michigan: Continuing Education Service, Michigan State University, 1967. (ED 019 536)

Kenney, Louis A. "Continuing Education for Academic Librarians," <u>California Librarian,</u> 30:199-202, July, 1969.

Klassen, Robert. "Institutes for Training in Librarianship: Summer 1969 and Academic Year 1969/1970," <u>Special Libraries,</u> 60:185-189, March, 1969.

Klempner, Irving M. "Information Centers and Continuing Education for Librarianship," <u>Special Libraries,</u> 59 :729-732, November, 1968.

Knox, Margaret Enid. "Professional Development of Reference Librarians in a University Library: A Case Study." Unpublished Doctor's dissertation, University of Illinois, Urbana, 1957.

Knox, Margaret E., and Alan Booth. "Decisions by Scientists and Engineers to Participate in Educational Programs Designed to Increase Scientific Competence." Unpublished nondegree study, National Science Foundation, Washington, D.C., 1966.

Lee, Robert E. <u>Continuing Education for Adults Through the American Public Library, 1833-1964.</u> Chicago: American Library Association, 1966.

Lee, Robert, and others. <u>A Plan for Developing a Regional Program of Continuing Education for Library Personnel in the Western States.</u> Boulder, Colorado: Western Interstate Commission for Higher Education, 1969.

<u>Library School Review.</u> Kansas State Teacher's College, October, 1968.

McJenkin, Virginia. "Continuing Education for School Librarians," <u>ALA Bulletin,</u> 61:272-275, March, 1967.

BIBLIOGRAPHY

Martin, Jess A. "Medical Library Internship at NIH," Medical Library Association Bulletin. 55:207-208, April, 1967.

Martin, R. M. "Report of an Internship Served at the John Crerar Library, February-December, 1954." Unpublished Master's thesis, University of Texas, Austin, 1958.

Meyer, Ursula. "New York's Statewide Continuing Professional Education Program: The Early Stages of Development." Paper presented at the First Annual Staff Development Micro-Workshop, American Library Association Convention, Detroit, Michigan, June 28, 1970.

Monroe, Margaret E. "Variety in Continuing Education," ALA Bulletin, 61:275-278, March, 1967.

"New Program (at Illinois)", Journal of Education for Librarianship, 4:183-4, Winter, 1964.

Phillips, Kathleen. "Training for Federal Librarians," Federal Library Committee Newsletter, 22:7-13, June, 1968.

Reed, Sarah R.(ed.). Continuing Education for Librarians--Conferences, Workshops, and Short Courses, 1966-1967. Washington, D.C.: U. S. Office of Education, 1966.

_____. "The Federal Government and Professional Library Education," ALA Bulletin, 60:163-166, February, 1966.

_____, and Willie P. Toye (eds.). Continuing Education for Librarians--Conferences, Workshops and Short Courses, 1965-1966. Washington, D.C.: U. S. Office of Education, 1965.

Rees, Alan M., and others. Feasibility Study for Continuing Education of Medical Librarians. Interim Report. Cleveland: Case Western Reserve University, 1968.

Richnell, D. T. "University Libraries," Journal of Documentation, 22:291-300, December, 1966.

Rothstein, Samuel. "Nobody's Baby: A Brief Sermon on Continuing Professional Education," Library Journal, 90:2226-2227, May, 1965.

Rowland and Company. The Process of Professional Information Exchange among Science Information Specialists. Final Report. Haddonfield, New Jersey: Rowland and Co., 1967.

Shapiro, Lillian L. "We Must be Doing Something Wrong: Recruiting Young Blood for School Libraries," Library Journal, 92:1992-1994, May, 1967.

Shaw, Ralph R. "Quo Vadis? An Examination of the Librarian's Role in a Democratic Culture," Library Journal, 92:2881-2884, September, 1967.

BIBLIOGRAPHY

"Sixth-Year Degree Offered," Michigan Librarian, 33:27-8, June, 1967.

Special Libraries Association. "Continuing Education for Special Librarianship: Where Do We Go From Here?" Proceedings of a planning session sponsored by the Education Committee held June 2, 1968 in conjunction with the Annual Conference in Los Angeles. (Mimeographed)

Stallman, Esther L. Library Internship: History, Purposes and a Proposal. University of Illinois Library School Occasional papers, No. 37. Urbana,: Library School, University of Illinois, 1954.

_____. The Library Internship Program Maintained for Students in the University of Texas Graduate School of Library Science. Austin : Graduate School of Library Science, University of Texas, 1963.

Stevenson, Grace T. "Training for Growth--the Future for Librarians," ALA Bulletin, 61:278-286, March, 1967.

Stone, C. Walter (ed.). The Professional Education of Media Service Personnel: Recommendations for Training Media Service Personnel for Schools and Colleges. Preliminary Edition. Pittsburgh: Center for Media Studies, University of Pittsburgh, 1964.

Stone, Elizabeth W. "Continuing Education: Avenue to Adventure," School Libraries, 18:37-46, Summer, 1969.

_____. Factors Related to the Professional Development of Librarians. Metuchen, New Jersey: Scarecrow Press, 1969.

Stone, M. H. "Report of an Internship Served at the Enoch Pratt Free Library, Baltimore, September 16, 1957-July 11, 1958," Unpublished Master's thesis, University of Texas, Austin, 1958.

Taube, Mortimer. "Documentation, Information Retrieval, and Other New Techniques," Library Quarterly, 31:90-103, January, 1961.

Troxel, Wilma. "Continuing Education for Medical Librarianship: A Symposium," Medical Library Association Bulletin. 48:404-407, October, 1960.

Tweed, Harrison. "Continuing Legal Education: New Conference to Chart Broader Goals," American Bar Association Journal, 49: 470-474, May, 1963.

Weinbrecht, Ruby Y. "The Junior Librarian," Journal of Education for Librarianship, 3(3):213-226, Winter, 1963.

Williamson, Charles C. Training for Library Service: A Report Prepared for the Carnegie Corporation of New York. New York: Carnegie Corporation, 1923.

BIBLIOGRAPHY

CONTINUING EDUCATION: OTHER PROFESSIONS

Allen, James E., Jr. "The Educational Third Dimension." Paper read to the Galaxy Conference on Adult and Continuing Education, Washington, D.C., December 9, 1969. (Mimeographed)

American Association of School Administrators. In-Service Programs for School Administration. Washington, D.C.: American Association of School Administrators, 1966.

American Psychological Association. Reports of the American Psychological Association's Project on Scientific Information Exchange in Psychology. Vol. I. Washington, D.C.: American Psychological Association, 1963.

Andrews, Kenneth R. "Is Management Training Effective? II. Measurement, Objectives, and Policy," Harvard Business Review, 35:63-72, March-April, 1957.

_____. "Reaction to University Development Programs: as Reported by More than 6,000 Executives who Went back to School," Harvard Business Review, 39:116-134, May-June, 1961.

Anshen, Melvin. "Better Use of Executive Development Programs," Harvard Business Review, 33:67-74, November-December, 1955.

Argyris, Chris. "Executive Development Programs: Some Unresolved Problems," Personnel, 33:33-41, July, 1956.

Barry, F. Gordon, and C.J. Coleman, Jr. "Tougher Program for Management Training," Harvard Business Review, 36:117-125, November-December, 1958.

Blaney, John P., and Douglas McKie. "Knowledge of Conference Objectives and Effect upon Learning," Adult Education Journal, 19(2):98-105, 1969.

Bradford, Leland P. "Toward a Philosophy of Adult Education," Adult Education, 7:83-93, Winter, 1957.

De Solla Price, Derek J. and Donald Beaver. "Collaboration in an Invisible College," American Psychologist, 21(11):1011-1018. November, 1966.

Dill, William R., and others. "Strategies for Self-Education," Harvard Business Review, 43:119-130, November-December, 1965.

Dillman, Beryl R. "Teacher Activities and Professional Growth as Perceived by Physicians, Lawyers, Clergymen and Educators," Journal of Teacher Education, 15:386-392, December, 1964.

BIBLIOGRAPHY

_____. "Teacher Perceptions and Practices in the Development of Responsibility for Professional Growth." Unpublished research paper presented at the American Education Research Association National Annual Convention, Chicago, February 25, 1961.

Doherty, Victor W. "The Carnegie Professional Growth Program: An Experiment in the In-Service Education of Teachers," Journal of Teacher Education, 18:261-268, Fall, 1967.

Dryer, Bernard V. (ed.)."Lifetime Learning for Physicians: Principles, Practices, Proposals," Journal of Medical Education, 37:1-134, June, 1962.

Dubin, Samuel S., and H. LeRoy Marlow. Highlights. A Survey of Continuing Professional Education for Engineers in Pennsylvania. University Park: Pennsylvania State University, 1968.

Dubin, Samuel S., and others. Research Report of Managerial and Supervisory Educational Needs of Business and Industry in Pennsylvania. University Park: Pennsylvania State University, 1967.

_____. Survey Report of Managerial and Supervisory Needs of Business and Industry in Pennsylvania. University Park: Pennsylvania State University, 1967.

_____. The Determination of Supervisory Training Needs of Hospital Personnel -- A Survey of Pennsylvania Hospitals. University Park: Pennsylvania State University, 1965.

DuBois, Edward A.C. The Case for Employee Education. New York: American Management Association, 1967.

Duncan, Margaret. "Making the Special Librarian Special: The Case for Continuing Education," California Librarian, 30:191-198, July, 1969.

Gardner, John W. Excellence: Can We be Equal and Excellent Too? New York: Harper & Row, Publishers, 1961.

_____. Self-Renewal: The Individual and the Innovative Society. New York: Harper & Row, Publishers, 1964.

Green, David E. "An Experiment in Communication: The Information Exchange Group," Science, 143:308-309, January, 1964.

Hall, O. "The Stages of a Medical Career," American Journal of Sociology, 53:327-336, March, 1948.

Hartman, G.W. "The Field Theory of Learning and Its Educational Consequence." In: National Society for the Study of Education. Forty-First Year Book, Part II: The Psychology of Learning. Chicago: University of Chicago Press, 1942, pp. 165-214.

Hewitt, Gordon B. Continuing Education in Pharmacy, A Report. British Columbia: Pharmaceutical Association, Province of British Columbia, 1965. ED 019 545

BIBLIOGRAPHY

Hodges, J.B. "Continuing Education: Why and How," *Education Leadership,* 17:330-346, March, 1960.

Houle, Cyril O. "Education for Adult Leadership," *Adult Education,* 8:3-17, Autumn, 1957.

_____. *The Inquiring Mind.* Madison: The University of Wisconsin Press, 1961.

_____. "The Role of Continuing Education in Current Professional Development," *ALA Bulletin,* 61:259-267, March, 1967.

Jerkedal, Ake. *Top Management Education: An Evaluation Study.* Stockholm: Svenska Tryckeri Bolagen STB AB, 1967.

Kellogg Foundation. *Continuing Education: An Evolving Form of Adult Education.* Battle Creek, Michigan: W.K. Kellogg Foundation, 1959.

Knox, Alan B. "Continuing Legal Education of Nebraska Lawyers." Unpublished nondegree study, Nebraska State Bar Association, Lincoln, 1964.

Kreitlow, Burton W. *Educating the Adult Educator, Part 1: Concepts for the Curriculum.* Madison, Wisc.: University of Wisconsin, 1965. ED 023 969

_____. *Educating the Adult Educator, Part 2: Taxonomy of Needed Research Report.* Madison, Wisc.: University of Wisconsin, 1968. ED 023 031

Kronick, David A. and Alan M. Rees. *Educational Needs in Medical Librarianship and Health Sciences Information.* Cleveland: Case Western Reserve University, 1969.

Lauwerys, J.A. "Definition and Goals of Professional Reading," *Phi Delta Kappan,* 38:365-368, June, 1957.

Lazarus, Charles Y. "Quest for Excellence - A Businessman's Responsibility," *Bulletin of Business Research,* 43(5):1-5. 1968.

Lewin, Kurt. "The Field Theory of Learning." In: National Society for the Study of Education. *Forty-First Year Book, Part II: The Psychology of Learning.* Chicago: University of Chicago Press, 1942., pp. 215-242.

Lindsey, Alfred J. *A Program of Professional Readings for Secondary School English Teachers.* Urbana, Ill.: Illinois State-Wide Curriculum Study Center in the Preparation of Secondary School English Teachers, 1969.

BIBLIOGRAPHY

Liveright, A.A. "Learning Never Ends: A Plan for Continuing Education." In: Alvin C. Eurich. Campus 1980: The Shape of the Future in American Higher Education. New York: Delacorte Press, 1968.

McConnell, T.R., et al. "The University and Professional Education." In: National Society for the Study of Education. Sixty-First Year Book: Education for the Professions. Chicago, University of Chicago Press, 1962, pp. 254-278.

McGrath, Earl J. "The Ideal Education for the Professional Man." In: National Society for the Study of Education. Sixty-First Year Book: Education for the Professions. Chicago: University of Chicago Press, 1962, pp. 281-301.

McMahon, Ernest E., Robert H. Coates, and Alan B. Knox. "Common Concerns: The Position of the Adult Education Association of the U.S.A.," Adult Education Journal, 18:197-213, Spring, 1968.

Mead, Margaret. "Redefinition of Education," National Education Association Journal, 48:15-17, October, 1959.

Mee, John F. Participation in Community Affairs -- The Role of Business and Business Schools. Bloomington: Indiana University, Graduate School of Business, 1968.

Merrell, V. Dallas. An Analysis of University Sponsored Executive Development Programs. Los Angeles, Calif.: University of Southern California, 1965. ED 019 531

Morrow, Evelyn. "Long Range Integrated Programming for Adult Education." Unpublished Doctor's dissertation, University of Chicago, 1957.

Mosher, Frederick C. A Proposed Program of Mid-Career Education for Public Administrators in Metropolitan Areas. A Report of an Ad Hoc Faculty Planning Committee at the University of California, Berkeley, to the National Institute of Public Affairs. Berkeley, Calif.: Institute of Governmental Studies, University of California, 1966.

National Education Association, National Commission on Teacher Education and Professional Standards. The Development of the Career Teacher: Professional Responsibility for Continuing Education. Washington, D.C.: National Education Association, 1964.

National Education Association, National Commission on Teacher Education and Professional Standards. What You Should Know About New Horizons. (A condensation of New Horizons in Teacher Education and Professional Standards.) Washington, D.C.: National Education, 1962.

BIBLIOGRAPHY

National Institute of Mental Health. Training Methodology. Public Health Service Publication 1862. Washington, D.C.: U.S. Government Printing Office, 1969. ED 024 880

Ore, Stanley, H., Jr. "The Development of an Internship Program in Adult Education." Unpublished Master's thesis, University of Wisconsin, Madison, 1964.

Pettit, Maurice L. "What College Graduates Say About Education Courses," The Journal of Teacher Education, 15:378-381, December, 1964.

Projects to Advance Creativity in Education (PACE). A Comprehensive Model for Managing an ESEA Title III Project from Conception to Culmination. Report No. 3. Fairfax, Va.: Fairfax County Public Schools, Virginia Center for Effecting Educational Change, 1968. ED 024 842.

Ranta, Raymond R. "The Professional Status of the Michigan Cooperative Extension Service," Unpublished Doctor's dissertation, University of Wisconsin, Madison, National Agricultural Extension Center for Advanced Study, 1960.

Richards, John R., and others. "Continuing Education Programs in California Higher Education--Delineation of Functions, Coordination, Finance, General Extension Centers." July, 1963. ED 015 713.

Schoenfeld, C. "On Defining Adult Education," School and Society, 81: 69-70, March, 1955.

Singer, Henry A. "ECL--A Dynamic Approach to Group Executive Training," Personnel Journal, 48:372-374, May, 1969.

Slager, Fred C. "What are the Characteristics of an Effective, Professional Growth Program?" Proceedings of the 38th Annual Convention, National Association of Secondary School Principals Bulletin, 38:206-209, April, 1954.

Sloane, Margaret N. "SLA Chapters and Continuing Education." Special Libraries, 58: 24-26, January, 1967.

Spencer, Howard C. "Continuing Liberal Education Through Independent Study," Adult Education, 15:91-95, Winter, 1965.

Stallman, Esther L. Library Internship: History, Purposes and a Proposal. University of Illinois Library School Occasional Papers, No. 37. Urbana, Ill.: University of Illinois, 1954.

_____. The Library Internship Program Maintained for Students in the University of Texas Graduate School of Library Science. Austin, Texas: Graduate School of Library Science, University of Texas, June, 1963.

BIBLIOGRAPHY

Stolz, Robert K. "Executive Development--New Perspective," <u>Harvard Business Review</u>, 44:133-143, May-June, 1966.

Stone, Elizabeth W. "Continuing Education: Avenue to Adventure," <u>School Libraries</u>, 18:37-46, Summer, 1969.

_____. <u>Factors Related to the Professional Development of Librarians</u>. Metuchen, N. J.: Scarecrow Press, 1969.

Stumpf, Felix F. "Continuing Legal Education: Its Role," <u>American Bar Association Journal</u>, 49:248-250, March, 1963.

Swanson, Harold B. "Factors Associated with Motivation Toward Professional Development of County Agricultural Extension Agents in Minnesota," Unpublished Doctor's dissertation, University of Wisconsin, Madison, 1965.

Taylor, Edward B. "An Analysis of the Educational Needs of Nebraska Lawyers in Relation to Career Cycle." Unpublished Doctor's dissertation, University of Nebraska, Lincoln, 1966.

Taylor, Edward B. <u>Relationship Between the Career Changes of Lawyers and their Participation in Continuing Legal Education.</u> Unpublished Doctor's thesis, University of Nebraska, Lincoln, 1967.

Tough, Allen M. "The Teaching Tasks Performed by Adult Self-Teachers." Unpublished Doctor's dissertation, University of Chicago, Chicago, 1965.

The United Presbyterian Church in the United States of America. Temporary Commission on Continuing Education. <u>Report to the 181st General Assembly, San Antonio, Texas, May 1969.</u> Philadelphia, Pa.: Temporary Commission on Continuing Education, 1969.

Weiner, Solomon. "Evaluation of the Professional Trainee Program," <u>Public Personnel Administration,</u> 29:197-206, October, 1968.

BIBLIOGRAPHY

CONTINUING EDUCATION: MOTIVATIONAL FACTORS

Allport, Gordon W. "The Trend in Motivational Theory," American Journal of Orthopsychiatry, 23:107-119, January, 1952.

Anderson, Frederic. "Factors in Motivation to Work Across Three Occupational Levels." Unpublished Doctor's dissertation, University of Utah, Provo, 1961.

Bennis, Warren G., and Edgar H. Schein, eds. Leadership and Motivation: Essays of Douglas McGregor. Cambridge: The Massachusetts Institute of Technology Press, 1966.

Boyd, Robert D. "A Model for the Analysis of Motivation," Adult Education, 16:23-33, Autumn, 1965.

Bray, Douglas W. and Donald L. Grant. "The Assessment Center in the Measurement of Potential for Business Management," Psychological Monographs, No. 625. 80:17, 1966.

Chalupsky, Albert. "Incentive Practices as Viewed by Scientists and Managers of Pharmaceutical Laboratories," Personnel Psychology, 17:385-401, Winter, 1964.

Clark, James V. "Motivation in Work Groups: A Tentative View," Human Organization, 19:199-208, Winter, 1960-1961.

Clegg, Denzil. "The Motivation of County Administrators in the Cooperative Extension Service." Unpublished Doctor's dissertation, University of Wisconsin, Madison, 1963.

Coch, L., and J. R. P. French. "Overcoming Resistance to Change," Human Relations, 1:512-532, August, 1948.

Dill, William R., and others. "How Aspiring Managers Promote their Own Careers: Why do some Young Men in Business Progress Rapidly to Top Management Jobs while Others, with the Same Educational Background, Reach a Stalemate?" California Manage-Review, 2:9-15, Summer, 1960.

Dooley, Bobby J. and William F. White. "Motivational Patterns of a Select Group of Adult Evening College Students," Journal of Educational Research, 57(2):65-66, October, 1968.

Du Bois, Edward A. C. The Case for Employee Education. New York: American Management Association, 1967.

Friedlander, F. "Relationships between the Importance and the Satisfaction of Various Environmental Facts," Journal of Applied Psychology, 49:160-164, June, 1965.

BIBLIOGRAPHY

_____. "Underlying Sources of Job Satisfaction," <u>Journal of Applied Psychology</u>, 47:246-250, August, 1963.

Friedlander, Frank, and Eugene Walton. "Positive and Negative Motivations Toward Work," <u>Administrative Science Quarterly</u>, 9:194-207, September, 1964.

Gellerman, Saul W. <u>Management by Motivation</u>. New York: American Management Association, 1968.

_____. <u>Motivation and Productivity</u>. New York: American Management Association, 1963.

Ginzberg, Eli and John L. Herma. <u>Talent and Performance.</u> New York: Columbia University Press, 1964.

Glaser, Robert, and David J. Klaus. "Proficiency Measurement: Assessing Human Performance." In: Robert M. Gagne, ed. <u>Psychological Principles in System Development.</u> New York: Holt, Rinehart and Winston, 1962, pp. 419-476.

Goodman, Charles H. "Employee Motivation." Paper read at Seminar on Middle Manager Development in Libraries, The Catholic University of America, Washington, D.C., June 17, 1964.

_____. "Target Setting: The New Look in Performance Appraisal." Paper read at DCLA Workshop, The Catholic University of America, Washington, D.C., March 11, 1967.

Haire, Mason. <u>Psychology in Management.</u> 2d. ed. New York: McGraw-Hill Book Co., 1964.

Harper, Dee W. "Some Factors Related to Role Stress and Motivation: A Study in the Sociology of Adult Education." Unpublished Master's thesis, Louisiana State University, Baton Rouge, 1965.

Herzberg, Frederick. "One More Time: How Do You Motivate Employees?" <u>Harvard Business Review</u>, 46:53-61, January-February, 1968.

_____. <u>Work and the Nature of Man</u>. New York: World Publishing Co., 1966.

Herzberg, Frederick, Bernard Mausner, and Barbara Snyderman. <u>The Motivation to Work.</u> 2d. ed. New York: John Wiley and Sons, Inc., 1959.

Hickman, C. Addison. "Managerial Motivation and the Theory of the Firm," <u>The American Economic Review</u>, 45:544-554, May, 1955.

BIBLIOGRAPHY

Hulin, Charles L., and Patricia A. Smith. "An Empirical Investigation of Two Implications of the Two-factor Theory of Job Satisfaction," Journal of Applied Psychology, 51(5):396-402, October, 1967.

Indik, Bernard P. The Motivation to Work, Special Supplement. New Brunswick, N. J.: Rutgers University, 1966. ED 020 316.

Jones, Marshall R., ed. Nebraska Symposium on Motivation. Lincoln, Nebraska: University of Nebraska Press, 1955.

Jones, W. H., and Alan Booth. "Decisions by Scientists and Engineers to Participate in Educational Programs Designed to Increase Scientific Competence." Unpublished nondegree study, National Science Foundation, 1966.

Knapp, Mark L. "Analysis of Motivational Factors of Adults in University and College Adult Speech Education Courses in the Greater Kansas City Area." Unpublished Master's thesis, University of Kansas, Kansas City, 1963.

Knox, Alan B. "Nebraska Adult Interests Study." Unpublished nondegree study, University of Nebraska, Lincoln, 1965.

Konwin, Vern. "A Motivational Approach to Training. Operative Re-Training in the Hosiery Industry," Training and Development Journal, 21:26-31, March, 1967.

Leavitt, Harold J. Managerial Psychology. Chicago: The University of Chicago Press, 1958.

Lewin, Kurt. Resolving Social Conflict. New York: Harper, 1950.

Likert, Rensis. "A Motivational Approach to a Modified Theory of Organization and Management." In: Mason Haire, ed. Modern Organization Theory. New York: John Wiley, 1959, pp. 184-217.

_____. New Patterns of Management. New York: McGraw-Hill Book Co., 1961.

Lindsley, Donald B. "Psychophysiology and Motivation," In: Proceedings of Nebraska Symposium on Motivation: 1957. Lincoln, Nebraska: University of Nebraska Press, 1957.

Locke, Edwin A. What is Job Satisfaction? Washington, D.C.: American Psychological Association, 1968. ED 023 138.

McClelland, David C. The Achievement Motive. New York: Appleton-Century-Crofts, 1953.

_____. The Achieving Society. Princeton, N.J.: Van Nostrand, 1961.

BIBLIOGRAPHY

_____. "Business Drive and National Achievement," <u>Harvard Business Review</u>, 40(4):99, July-August, 1962.

_____. "Money as a Motivator: Some Research Insights," <u>Management Review,</u> 57:23-28, February, 1968.

_____. <u>Studies in Motivation.</u> New York: Appleton-Century-Crofts, 1955.

_____. "Toward a Theory of Motive Acquisition," <u>American Psychologist</u>, 20:321-333, May, 1965.

McClelland, David D., and others. "Obligations to Self and Society in the United States and Germany," <u>Journal of Abnormal and Social Psychology,</u> 61:245-255, March, 1958.

McGregor, Douglas. <u>The Human Side of Enterprise.</u> New York: McGraw-Hill, 1960.

Maslow, Abraham H. <u>Motivation and Personality.</u> New York: Harper and Bros., 1954.

_____. "Theory of Human Motivation," <u>Psychological Review</u>, 50:370-396, July, 1943.

Meyer, Herbert H., and others. "Split Roles in Performance Appraisal," <u>Harvard Business Review</u>, 43:123-129, January-February, 1965.

Meyers, M. Scott. "Who Are Your Motivated Workers?" <u>Harvard Business Review,</u> 42:73-88, January-February, 1964.

Muniz, Peter. "Empathy Training for the Management Development Trainer. Line Duty for Trainers to Give Real Insight," <u>Training and Development Journal,</u> 21:24-28, October, 1967.

Murphy, Gardner. "Social Motivation," In: Gardner Lindzey, ed. <u>Handbook of Social Psychology.</u> Vol. II. Cambridge: Addison-Wesley Publishing Co., 1954.

Myers, Charles A. "Behavioral Sciences for Personnel Managers," <u>Harvard Business Review</u>, 44:154-162, July-August, 1966.

Myers, M. Scott. "Conditions for Manager Motivation," <u>Harvard Business Review,</u> 44:58-71, January-February, 1966.

_____. "How Attitude Surveys Can Help You to Manage. A Results-Oriented Plan from Texas Instruments," <u>Training and Development Journal,</u> 21:34-41, October, 1967.

Nevill, Gale E., Jr. and Martin A. Eisenbell. "Motivating Better Teaching," <u>The Journal of Engineering Education,</u> 58:106, October, 1967.

BIBLIOGRAPHY

Papanestor, William. "A Study of Job Satisfaction as Related to Need Satisfaction Both on the Job and Off the Job." Unpublished Doctor's dissertation, University of Cincinnati, Ohio, 1957.

Porter, Lyman W. and Edward E. Lawler, III. Managerial Attitudes and Performance. Homewood, Ill.: Richard D. Irwin, Inc., 1968.

Preston, James M. "Characteristics of Continuing and Non-continuing Adult Students." Unpublished Doctor's dissertation, University of California, 1957.

Roethlisberger, F. J. "Training Supervisors in Human Relations," Harvard Business Review, 29:47-57, September, 1951.

Schein, Edgar H. Organization Psychology. Englewood Cliffs, N.J.: Prentice-Hall, 1965.

Schreier, Fred T. Human Motivation, Probability, and Meaning. Glencoe, Ill.: Free Press of Glencoe, 1957.

Simon, Herbert A. Administrative Behavior. 2d. ed. New York: Macmillan, 1957.

Smith, Patricia C. and C. J. Cranny. "Psychology of Men at Work," Annual Review of Psychology, 19:467-496, 1968.

Stone, Elizabeth W. "Administrators Fiddle While Employees Burn... or Flee," ALA Bulletin, 63:181-187, February, 1969.

_____. Factors Related to the Professional Development of Librarians. Metuchen, N. J.: Scarecrow Press, 1969.

Wells, Harold C. Achievement Motivation. (Project 662479) Detroit, Michigan: Consortium of Advanced Educational Thinking, 1969.

Wood, Donald A. and William K. LeBold. "The Multivariate Nature of Professional Job Satisfaction." Paper presented at the Annual Conference of the Indiana Manpower Research Association at Purdue University, W. Lafayette, Indiana, November 30, 1967. ED 023 578.

Zeberl, Andrew J. "The Acceptance of Training as Perceived among Volunteers in a Health Agency." Unpublished Doctor's dissertation, University of Michigan, Ann Arbor, 1964.

BIBLIOGRAPHY

CURRICULUM DEVELOPMENT:
ADMINISTRATION

American Association of School Administrators. In-Service Programs for School Administration. Washington, D.C.: American Association of School Administrators, 1966.

_____. Professional Administrators for American Schools. Washington, D.C.: American Association of School Administrators, 1960.

Andrews, Kenneth R. "Is Management Training Effective? I. Evaluation by Managers and Instructors," Harvard Business Review, 35:85-94, January-February, 1957.

_____. "Is Management Training Effective? II. Measurement, Objectives, and Policy," Harvard Business Review, 35:63-72, March-April, 1957.

Argyris, Chris. "T-Groups for Organizational Effectiveness," Harvard Business Review, 42:60-74, March, 1964.

Byrd, Cecil K. "School for Administrators: The Rutgers Carnegie Project," College and Research Libraries, 20:130-133, 153, March, 1959.

Carson, Lettie G. "Remarks at ALTA Meeting, Region VII." Paper read at the American Library Trustee Association Annual Conference, San Francisco, California, June 25, 1967. (Mimeographed.)

Carson, Robert B., ed. Seminar Series for School Administrators: Leadership. Vol. I. Calgary, Alberta: The University of Calgary, 1968.

_____. Seminar Series for School Administrators: Change and Innovation. Vol. II. Calgary, Alberta: The University of Calgary, 1968.

Corson, John J., and R. Shale Paul. Men Near the Top. Baltimore: Johns Hopkins Press, 1966.

Croft, Janice. "The Librarian, A Vital Aide to Management," Sci-Tech News, 22(4):103-105, Winter, 1968.

BIBLIOGRAPHY

Crozier, Michel. "The Present Convergence of Public Administration and Large Private Enterprises, and its Consequences," International Social Science Journal, 20(1):7-16, 1968.

Culbertson, Jack. Differentiated Training for Professors and Educational Administrators. Paper presented to Annual Meeting of the American Educational Research Association. Chicago, Ill., February 8-10, 1968. ED 021 309.

Culbertson, Jack, and Stephen Hencley. Preparing Administrators: New Perspectives. Columbus, Ohio: University Council for Educational Administration, 1962.

DeProspo, Ernest R., Jr. "Contributions of the Political Scientist and Public Administrator to Library Administration." In: Neal Harlow and others, eds. Administration and Change: Continuing Education in Library Administration. New Brunswick, N.J.: Rutgers University Press, 1969, pp. 29-38.

DeProspo, Ernest R., Jr., and Theodore S. Huang. "Continuing Education for the Library Administrator; His Needs." In: Neal Harlow and others, ed. Administration and Change: Continuing Education in Library Administration. New Brunswick, N. J.: Rutgers University Press, 1969, pp. 21-27.

Dimock, Marshall E. "The Administrative Staff College:Executive Development in Government and Industry," American Political Science Review, 50:166-176, March, 1956.

_____. "Executive Development After Ten Years," Public Administration Review, 17:91-97, Spring, 1958.

Dolguchits, L. A. "Pre-Service and In-Service Managerial Training for Industry and Building in the Byclorussian S. S. R.," International Social Science Journal, 20(1):17-27, 1968.

Doughtery, Richard M. "The Scope and Operating Efficiency of Information Centers as Illustrated by the Chemical-Biological Coordination Center of the National Research Center," College and Research Libraries, 25:7-12,20, January, 1964.

Drucker, Peter. Age of Discontinuity: Guidelines to our Changing Society. New York: Harper and Row, 1969.

BIBLIOGRAPHY

Dubin, Samuel S. "Keeping Managers and Supervisors in Local Government Up-To-Date," Public Administration Review, 29: 294-298, May-June, 1969.

Dubin, Samuel, E. Alderman, and H. L. Marlow. Educational Needs of Managers and Supervisors in Cities, Boroughs and Townships in Pennsylvania. University Park: Pennsylvania State University, 1968.

_____. Highlights of a Study on Managerial and Supervisory Educational Needs of Business and Industry in Pennsylvania. University Park: Pennsylvania State University, 1968.

"Educating Executives: Social Science, Self-Study, or Socrates ?" Public Administration Review, 18:275-305, 1958.

Farley, Richard A. "The American Library Executive: An Inquiry Into his Concepts of the Functions of his Office." Unpublished Doctor's dissertation, University of Illinois, Urbana, 1967.

Fayol, Henri. General and Industrial Management. London: Pitman and Sons, 1949.

Ferguson, Lawrence L. "Better Management of Managers' Careers," Harvard Business Review, 44:139-152, March-April, 1966.

Franklin, Robert D. "Personnel Primer: A Topical Index to Library Teamwork," Library Journal, 90:3542-3549, September, 1965.

Frasure, Kenneth. "In-Service Role of Professors of Educational Administration--A National View." Paper presented to an interest group at the National Conference of Professors of Educational Administration in August, 1966. (Mimeographed)

_____. "Perspectives Concerning In-Service Education for Educational Administrators." Albany, N. Y.: Council for Administrative Leadership, 1966.

_____. "Your Leadership Development Program." Paper presented at the Annual Conference of the American Association of School Administrators, Atlantic City, N.J., February, 1968. Washington, D.C.: U. S. Office of Education, 1968. ED 021 330.

Frenckner, T. Paulsson. "Development of Operational Management

BIBLIOGRAPHY

Methods: What Does it Mean for the Education of Managers?" International Social Science Journal, 20(1):29-34, 1968.

Gellerman, Saul W. Motivation and Productivity. New York: American Management Association, 1963.

Gjelsness, Rudolph. "Administrative Organization," Drexel Libarary Quarterly, 3:34-37, January, 1967.

Gleaves, E. S. "More Room at the Top: Librarianship in the Light of Asheim's Proposed Restructure," Southeastern Librarian, 19:64-69, Summer, 1969.

Haire, Mason. "Managing Management Manpower: A Model for Human Resource Development," Business Horizons, 19(4): 23-28, Winter, 1967.

Harlow, Neal, and others, eds. Administration and Change: Continuing Education in Library Administration. New Brunswick: N. J.: Rutgers University Press, 1969.

Hattery, Lowell H. "Organization for a Science Information Service." In: Paul W. Howerton, ed. Information Handling: First Principles. Washington, D.C.: Spartan Books, 1963, pp. 171-181.

Jackson, Terence G., Jr. "The Role of the Information System Executive." In: Paul W. Howerton, ed. Information Handling: First Principles. Washington, D.C.: Spartan Books, 1963, pp. 137-168.

Joeckel, Carleton B., ed. Current Issues in Library Administration: Papers presented before the Library Institute at the University of Chicago, August 1-12, 1938. Chicago: University of Chicago Press, 1939.

Katz, Saul M. Education for Development Administrators: Character, Form, Content and Curriculum. Pittsburgh, Pa.: University of Pittsburgh, 1967.

Kellogg Foundation. Toward Improved School Administration: A Decade of Professional Effort to Heighten Administrative Understanding and Skills. Battle Creek, Michigan: The W. K. Kellogg Foundation, 1961.

BIBLIOGRAPHY

Kittle, Arthur T. "Management Theories in Public Library Administration in the United States, 1925-1955." Unpublished Doctor's dissertation, Columbia University, New York, 1961.

Knox, W. T. "Administration of Technical Information Groups," Industrial and Engineering Chemistry, 51:48A-61A, March, 1959.

Kortendick, James J. "Continuing Education and Library Administration," ALA Bulletin, 61(3):268-271, March, 1967.

_____. "Curriculum: Administration," Drexel Library Quarterly, 3(1):92-103, January, 1967.

_____. "The Supervisor as Leader," Virginia Librarian, 7:56-69, Winter, 1961.

Kortendick, James J., and Elizabeth W. Stone. "Highlights of a Study on Federal Librarians and Post-MLS Education: A Preliminary Report," DC Libraries, 40:71-76, Fall, 1969.

Likert, Rensis. The Human Organization: Its Management and Value. New York: McGraw-Hill, 1967.

Lothrop, Warren C. Management Uses of Research and Development. New York: Harper and Row, 1964.

McGregor, Douglas. The Human Side of Enterprise. New York: McGraw-Hill, 1960.

_____. The Professional Manager. Caroline McGregor and Warren G. Bennis, eds. New York: McGraw-Hill, 1967.

March, J. G. and H. A. Simon. Organizations. New York: Wiley, 1958.

Martin, Lowell A. "Shall Library Schools Teach Administration?" College and Research Libraries, 6:335-340, September, 1945.

Morse, Philip M. Library Effectiveness: A Systems Approach. Cambridge, Mass.: M. I. T. Press, 1968.

BIBLIOGRAPHY

<u>Personnel Administration in State Education Agencies in the Years Ahead.</u> Sacramento, Calif.: California State Department of Education, 1968. ED 025 035.

Piele, Philip. <u>Annotated Bibliography on Educational Administrator Preparation Programs.</u> Eugene, Oregon: Oregon University, October, 1968. ED 023 198.

Powell, Reed M. "Two Approaches to University Management Education," <u>California Management Review,</u> 5:87-104, Spring, 1963.

Randall, Raymond L. and Dick W. Simpson. <u>Science Administration Education and Career Mobility.</u> Summary of Proceedings and Working Papers of the University Federal Agency Conference, November 7-9, 1965. Bloomington, Indiana, Indiana University Institute of Public Administration, 1966. ED 019 563.

Randsepp, Eugene. <u>Managing Creative Scientists and Engineers.</u> New York: Macmillan, 1963.

Ready, William B. "The Rutgers Seminar for Library Administrators," <u>College and Research Libraries,</u> 18:281-283, July, 1957.

Reddin, W. J. "Managing Organizational Change," <u>Personnel Journal,</u> 48:500-504, July, 1969.

Reed, Sarah R., ed. <u>Problems of Library School Administration: Report of an Institute, April 14-15, 1965.</u> Washington, D.C.: U.S. Office of Education, 1965.

Shank, Russell. "Administration Training in Graduate Library Schools," <u>Special Libraries,</u> 58:30-32, January, 1967.

Stahl, O. Glenn. <u>Public Personnel Administration.</u> 5th ed. New York: Harper and Row, 1962.

Stepanek, Joseph E. <u>Managers for Small Industry; an International Study.</u> Glencoe, Ill.: The Free Press, 1960.

Stone, Elizabeth W. <u>An Analysis of the Core Administration Courses of the Library Schools Accredited by the American Library Association.</u> ACRL Microcard Series, No. 138. Rochester, N.Y.: University of Rochester Press, 1962.

BIBLIOGRAPHY

Stone, Elizabeth W. Factors Related to the Professional Development of Librarians. Metuchen, N. J.: Scarecrow Press, 1969.

_____. "Methods and Materials for Teaching Library Administration," Journal of Education for Librarianship, 6:34-42, Summer, 1965.

_____. Training for the Improvement of Library Administration. Monograph of the University of Illinois. Ann Arbor, Michigan: Edwards Brothers, Inc., 1967.

System Development Corporation. "A Centralized Management Information System: The Experience of the 'Largest Organization in the Free World'," SDC Magazine, 11(9):2-16, October, 1968.

System Development Corporation. "Grooming Tomorrow's Managers," SDC Magazine, 13(1):3-15, January, 1970.

Underwood, Willis O. "A Hospital Director's Administrative Profile," Hospital Administration, 8:6-24, Fall, 1963.

University of Maryland. School of Library and Information Service. Library Administrators Development Program, an institute held at Donaldson Brown Center, Port Deposit, Maryland, August 11-23, 1968. (Printed brochure)

Walton, Richard E., and John M. Dutton. "The Management of Interdepartmental Conflict: A Model and Review," Administrative Science Quarterly, 14(1):73-84, March, 1969.

Wasserman, Paul. "Development of Administration in Library Service: Current Status and Future Prospects," College and Research Libraries, 19:283-294, July, 1958.

Wasserman, Paul, and E. Daniel. "Library and Information Center Management." In: Carlos A. Cuadra, ed. Annual Review of Information Science and Technology, Vol. 4. Chicago: Encyclopaedia Britannica, 1969, pp. 405-432.

Whitt, Robert L. Structuring Education for Business Management. Lincoln, Nebraska: Great Plains School District Organization, 1968. ED 020 034.

Zoll, Allen A. Dynamic Management Education. Reading, Mass: Addison-Wesley Publishing Co., 1969.

BIBLIOGRAPHY

CURRICULUM DEVELOPMENT:
AUTOMATION

Association for Educational Data Systems. <u>The Relationship of ADP Training Curriculum and Methodology in the Federal Government.</u> Final Report. Washington, D.C.: U.S. Office of Education, 1968. ED 023 909.

Atherton, Pauline. <u>Development of a Computer-Based Laboratory Program for Library Science Students Using LC/MARC Tapes.</u> Syracuse, New York: Syracuse University, June 1968 to December 1969. EP 011 310.

_____. <u>Second Quarterly Progress Report of Development of a Computer-Based Laboratory Program for Library Science Students Using LC/MARC Tapes.</u> Library Education Experimental Project. Syracuse, New York: Syracuse University, 1968.

Becker, Joseph. "Data Processing Equipment in Libraries: The MEDLARS Project," <u>ALA Bulletin,</u> 58:227-230, March, 1964.

_____. "Systems Analysis--Prelude to Library Data Processing?" <u>ALA Bulletin,</u> 69-293-296, April, 1965.

Becker, Joseph and R. M. Hayes. <u>Information Storage and Retrieval: Tools, Elements, Theories.</u> New York: John Wiley, 1966.

Bright, James R. <u>Automation and Management.</u> Boston, Mass.: Division of Research, Harvard Business School, 1958.

_____. "Does Automation Raise Skill Requirements?" <u>Harvard Business Review,</u> 36:85-98, July-August, 1958.

Bushnell, Don D. and Dwight W. Allen. <u>The Computer in American Education.</u> New York: Wiley and Co., 1967.

Connor, Judith H. "Selective Dissemination of Information: A Review of the Literature and Issues," <u>Library Quarterly,</u> 37:373-391, October, 1967.

Commission on Engineering Education. <u>Computer Sciences in Electrical Engineering.</u> Interim Report. Washington, D.C.: Commission on Engineering Education, 1967. ED 020 128

BIBLIOGRAPHY

Cox, N. S. M., J. D. Dews, and J. L. Dolby. *The Computer and the Library: The Role of the Computer in the Organization and Handling of Information in Libraries.* Newcastle on Tyne, England: University of Newcastle upon Tyne Library, 1966.

Cuadra, Carlos, and others. *Technology and Libraries.* Santa Monica, California: System Development Corporation, 1967. ED 022 481.

Dale, Ernest and L. C. Michelon. "Modern Management Methods." In: Ernest Dale and L. C. Michelon, eds. *Management and the Computer.* Cleveland, Ohio: The World Publishing Co., 1966, pp. 183-196.

Diebold, John. "ADP--The Still Sleeping Giant," *Harvard Business Review,* 42:60-65, September-October, 1965.

Dolby, J. L., V. J. Forsyth, and H. L. Resnikoff. *The Cost of Maintaining and Updating Library Card Catalogs.* Los Altos, Calif.: R & D Consultants Company, 1969.

Evans, Marshall K. and Lou R. Hague. "Master Plan for Information Systems," *Harvard Business Review,* 40:92-103, January-February, 1962.

Federal Council of Science and Technology. Committee on Scientific and Technical Information. *Recommendations for National Document Handling Systems in Science and Technology.* Washington, D. C.: U. S. Government Printing Office, 1965.

_____. *Toward a National Information System: Progress of the United States Government in Scientific and Technical Communication, 1965.* Springfield, Va.:Clearinghouse, U. S. Department of Commerce, 1965.

Flock, L. R., Jr. "Seven Deadly Dangers in EDP," *Harvard Business Review,* 40:88-96, May-June, 1962.

Greenberger, Martin, ed. *Management and the Computer of the Future.* Cambridge, Mass.: M.I.T. Press, 1962.

Griffin, Hillis. "Library Automation and Mechanization." Urbana: University of Illinois, 1969. (A videotape of lectures.)

Hardwick, Arthur L. *The Feasibility of Establishing a Program to Train Computer Programmers Utilizing a Time-Sharing System and Remote Data-Communications Transmission Terminals.* Oklahoma City: Oklahoma State University, 1967.

BIBLIOGRAPHY

Harris, Joann, and others. Computerized Vocational Information System. A Summary of a Project. Villa Park, Ill.: Willowbrook High School, n.d. ED 019 840.

Hayes, Robert M. "Data Processing in the Library School Curriculum," ALA Bulletin, 61:662-669, June, 1967.

Holzbauer, Herbert. "Inhouse ADP Training," Special Libraries, 58:427-428, July-August, 1967.

_____. "Trends in Announcement, Searching and Retrieval Services," Special Libraries, 59:104-106, February, 1968.

Holzbauer, H.W. and E. H. Harris. Technical Report: Library Information Processing Using an On-Line Real-Time Computer System. Poughkeepsie, N. Y.: IBM Systems Development Division, 1966. TR 0011548.

Information Dynamics Corporation. Development Trends in Federal Library and Information Center Automation. Guides for Administrative and Technical Interviews. Bethesda, Maryland: Information Dynamics Corp., 1968. ED 026 096.

Jasinski, Frank J. "Adapting Organization to New Technology," Harvard Business Review, 37:79-83, January-February, 1959.

Kraft, Donald. "A Total Systems Approach to Library Mechanization. Chicago: International Business Machines, 1964.

Kurmey, W. J. "Educational Developments Include Documentation and Automation," Ontario Library Review, 50:237-239, December, 1966.

Lanham, Richard. "Marian the Technologist?" SDC Magazine, 11(10): 2-9, November, 1968.

Library Education Experimental Project (LEEP). Vol.1, March,1969. Syracuse, N. Y.: School of Library Science, Syracuse University.

Mann, Floyd C. and Lawrence K. Williams. "Observations on the Dynamics of a Change to Electronic Data Processing Material," Administrative Science Quarterly, 5:217-256, September, 1960.

BIBLIOGRAPHY

Mathews, Max V., and W. Stanley Brown. "Research Libraries and the New Technology." In: D. M. Knight and E. S. Nourse, eds. Libraries at Large. New York: R. R. Bowker Co., 1969, pp. 265-272.

Morse, Philip M. "The Prospects for Mechanization," College and Research Libraries, 25:115-119, March, 1964.

National Research Council. Committee on Information in the Behavioral Sciences. Communication Systems and Resources in the Behavioral Sciences. Publication 1575. Washington, D.C.: National Academy of Sciences, 1967.

Nicolaus, John J. The Automated Approach to Technical Information Retrieval. Library Applications. Washington, D.C.: U.S. Dept. of the Navy, Bureau of Ships, 1964.

Peterson, Clarence E. Electronic Data Processing in Engineering, Science, and Business: Suggested Techniques for Determining Courses of Study in Vocational and Technical Education Programs. Washington, D.C.: U. S. Office of Education, 1964. ED 013 325.

Salmon, Stephen R., ed. Library Automation: A State of the Art Review. Chicago: American Library Association, 1969.

Schultheiss, Louis A., Don S. Culbertson, and Edward M. Heiliger. Advanced Data Processing in the University Library. Metuchen, N. J.: Scarecrow Press, 1962.

Shera, Jesse H. "Automation Without Fear," ALA Bulletin, 55:787-794, October, 1961.

Simonton, Wesley, ed. Information Retrieval Today. Minneapolis, Minnesota: University of Minnesota, 1963.

"Some Problems and Potentials of Technology as Applied to Library and Information Services." In: D. M. Knight and E. S. Nourse, eds. Libraries at Large. New York: R. R. Bowker Co., 1969, pp. 264-341.

Sultan, Paul and Paul Prasow. The Skill Impact of Automation. Los Angeles, California: University of California, 1964. (Reprint No. 136) ED 020 355.

BIBLIOGRAPHY

Swanson, Don R. "Education and Library Automation." In: Proceedings of Clinic on Library Applications of Data Processing, 1967. Urbana, Ill.: University of Illinois, 1967, pp. 1-7.

Swanson, Rowena, W. Information Entrepreneurship and Education: Prescriptions for Technological Change. Arlington, Va.: U. S. Air Force Office of Scientific Research, 1969. AFOSR 69-0458TR (Mimeographed)

Taube, Mortimer. Computers and Common Sense. New York: Columbia University Press, 1961.

Taylor, Robert S., ed. Planning for Automated Systems in the College Library. Amherst, Mass.: Hampshire College, 1969.

Tell, Bjorn V. "Inclusion of Systems Analysis and Programming in Curricula for Documentalists." In: Proceedings of International Conference on Education for Scientific Information Work, London, 1967. The Hague: International Federation for Documentation, 1967, pp. 207-214.

Thurston, Philip H. "Who Should Control Information Systems?" Harvard Business Review, 40:135-139, November-December 1962.

Turner, Arthur M. "A Researcher Views Human Adjustment to Automation," Advanced Management, 21, May, 1956.

U. S. Office of Education. Computer-based Vocational Guidance Systems. Washington, D.C.: U. S. Government Printing Office, 1969.

U. S. Office of Education. Electronic Data Processing--I. A suggested two-year Post High School Curriculum for Computer Programmers and Business Applications Analysts. Technical Education Program Series No. 4. Washington, D.C.: U. S. Government Printing Office, 1967.

Warheit, I. A. "The Use of Computers in Information Retrieval." In: Wesley Simonton, ed. Information Retrieval Today. Minneapolis, Minnesota: University of Minnesota, 1963, pp. 55-69.

Wasserman, Paul. The Librarian and the Machine. Detroit, Mich.: Gale Publishing Co., 1965.

BIBLIOGRAPHY

CURRICULUM DEVELOPMENT: LIBRARY AND INFORMATION SCIENCE

American Association of Library Schools. Research Committee. Requirements in Addition to the A.B. Degree for Admission to Graduate Study in Library Schools. Chicago: American Association of Library Schools, 1965.

American Society for Information Science. "Report to Members." Schedule and description of annual meeting in Columbus, Ohio, October 22, 1968. Washington, D.C.: American Society for Information Science, 1968.

American Society for Information Science. ASIS-EIS Curriculum Committee. "Model for the Evaluation of Curriculum in Information Science Programs." Prepared for a workshop, 1968.

Asheim, Lester E., ed. The Core of Education for Librarianship: A Report of a Workshop Held under the Auspices of the Graduate Library School of the University of Chicago, August 10-15, 1953. Chicago: American Library Association, 1954.

_____. "Education and Manpower for Librarianship: First Steps Toward a Statement of Policy," ALA Bulletin, 62:1096-1118, October, 1968.

_____. "Education for Librarianship," Library Quarterly, 25:76-90, January, 1955.

_____. "The State of the Accredited Library Schools, 1966-67," Library Quarterly, 38:323-337, October, 1968.

_____. "Statement of Dr. Lester Asheim, Director, Office of Library Education, American Library Association." Paper read to the National Advisory Commission on Libraries, New York City, March 6, 1967.

Ayres, S. F. "Report of an Eleven-Month Internship in the Library of Yale University, July 1959 to June 1960." Unpublished Master's thesis, University of Texas, Austin, 1961.

Baillie, Stuart. "Summer School: A Statistical Look at the Summer Sessions in the Accredited Library Schools," Drexel Library Quarterly, 3:139-150, April, 1967.

BIBLIOGRAPHY

Batty, C. D. "Librarianship by Degree," Library World, 68:155-160, December, 1966.

Belzer, Jack. "Information Science Education: Curriculum Development and Evaluation," American Documentation, 20:323-376, October, 1969.

Bendix, Dorothy, and Arabelle Pennypacker. "Curriculum--Book Selection," Drexel Library Quarterly, 3:72-83, January, 1967.

Bergen, Daniel P. "Educating Librarians for Century 21," Journal of Education for Librarianship, 4 :40-47, Summer, 1963.

_____. "Librarians and the Bipolarization of the Academic Enterprise," College and Research Libraries, 24:467-480, November, 1963.

Berninghausen, David K. "Undergraduate-Graduate Articulation: Crux of the Problem," Journal of Education for Librarianship, 2 219-224, Spring, 1962.

Bonk, Wallace J. "The Core Curriculum and the Reference and Bibliography Courses," Journal of Education for Librarianship, 28-33, Summer, 1961.

Bracken, Marilyn C., and C. W. Shilling. Education and Training of Information Specialists in the U. S.A. Washington, D.C.: Biological Sciences Communication Project, George Washington University, 1966.

_____. Science Information Specialist Training Program: A Progress Report. Washington, D.C.: Biological Sciences Communication Project, George Washington University, 1968.

_____. Survey of Practical Training in Information Science. Washington, D.C.: Biological Sciences Communication Project, George Washington University, 1967.

Broadus, Robert N. "Library Science and Liberal Education," Journal of Education for Librarianship, 7 :203-209, Spring, 1967.

Bromberg, Erik. "Quick Look at Courses on Special Libraries," Special Libraries, 58:22-23, January, 1967.

BIBLIOGRAPHY

Brown, Betty M. "Curriculum--Acquisitions and Cataloging," Drexel Library Quarterly, 3:84-91, January, 1967.

Bundy, Mary Lee. "On Library Education," Maryland Libraries, 32:22-24, Spring, 1966.

Bundy, Mary Lee and Richard Moses. A New Approach to Educational Preparation for Public Library Service. Interim Report. College Park, Md.: University of Maryland, 1969. ED 027 929.

Bundy, Mary Lee and Paul Wasserman. "A Departure in Library Education," Journal of Education for Librarianship, 8:124-132, Fall, 1967.

_____. "Professionalism Reconsidered," College and Research Libraries, 29:5-26, January, 1968.

Bunge, Charles A. "Library Education and Reference Performance," Library Journal, 92:1578-1581, April, 1966.

_____. Professional Education and Reference Efficiency. Urbana, Ill.: University of Illinois, 1967. ED 019 097.

Butler, Pierce. "Librarianship as a Profession," Library Quarterly, 21:234-247, October, 1951.

Carnovsky, Leon. "Accreditation: Panel Member No. 2." In: Sarah R. Reed, ed. Problems of Library School Administration: Report of an Institute, April 14-15, 1965, Washington, D.C. Washington, D.C.: U. S. Office of Education, 1965.

_____. "Changing Patterns in Librarianship: Implications for Library Education," Wilson Library Bulletin, 41:484-491, January, 1967.

_____. "Evaluation and Accreditation of Library Schools." In: Larry E. Bone, ed. Library Education: an International Survey. Champaign, Ill.: University of Illinois, 1968, pp. 131-152.

_____. "Faculty," Drexel Library Quarterly, 3:115-119, January, 1967.

_____. "Graduate and Undergraduate: Problems of Articulation," Journal of Education for Librarianship, 1(1):33-37, Summer, 1960.

BIBLIOGRAPHY

Carroll, Leontine D. "Teachers in A.L.A. Accredited Graduate Library Schools," Journal of Education for Librarianship, 5(3):147-151, Winter, 1965.

Cazen, R. E. "Proposed Doctoral Program in Booktrade Research," Journal of Education for Librarianship, 7:222-231, Spring, 1967.

Center for Documentation and Communication Research. Education for Hospital Library Personnel: Feasibility Study for Continuing Education of Medical Librarians. Interim Report No. 2 and No. 3. Cleveland, Ohio: Case Western Reserve University, 1968.

Chapman, Edward A., John Lubans, Jr., and Paul L. St. Pierre. Library Systems Analysis Guidelines. New York: Wiley, 1970.

Colinese, P. E. "The Education of Librarians and Information Officers: Industrial Information Departments," Journal of Documentation, 22:305-311, December, 1966.

Coughlin, V. L. "Improving Library School Teaching." In: Larry E. Bone, ed. Library Education: an International Survey. Champaign, Ill.: University of Illinois, 1968, pp. 289-316.

Dalton, Jack. "Observations on Advanced Study Programs in the Library Schools of the United States." In: Larry E. Bone, ed. Library Education: an International Survey. Champaign, Ill.: University of Illinois, 1968, pp. 317-328.

Danton, J. Periam. "Doctoral Study in Librarianship in the United States," College and Research Libraries, 20:435-453, November, 1959.

_____. Sixth Year Specialist Programs in Library Education. Berkeley, Calif.: University of California. (Research in progress)

Darling, Richard. "Curriculum--School Library Education," Drexel Library Quarterly, 3:104-107, January, 1967.

Davis, Beatrice. "Admissions," Drexel Library Quarterly, 3:52-58, January, 1967.

Davis, Richard A. "Theses and Dissertations Accepted by Graduate Library Schools: 1966 through December 1967," Library Quarterly, 38:442-452, October, 1968.

BIBLIOGRAPHY

Dearing, G. Bruce. "Critique." In: Sarah R. Reed, ed. Problems of Library School Administration: Report of an Institute, April 14-15, 1965, Washington, D.C. Washington, D.C.: U. S. Office of Education, 1965, pp. 10-12.

Diekhoff, John S. "The Professional School in the University," Journal of Education for Librarianship, 6(2):103-110, Fall, 1965.

"Doctoral Programs at Seven Library Schools," Journal of Education for Librarianship, 8:251-282, Spring, 1968.

Doi, James I. "Critique of Paper No. 4." In: Sarah R. Reed, ed. Problems of Library School Administration: Report of an Institute, April 14-15, 1965, Washington, D.C. Washington, D.C.: U. S. Office of Education, 1965, pp. 46-48.

Donaldson, Mary J. and John F. Harvey. "Library School Instructor Evaluation," College and Research Libraries, 27:470-477, November, 1966.

Donohue, Joseph C. "Librarianship and the Science of Information," American Documentation, 17:120-123, July, 1966.

Downs, Robert B. "Education for Librarianship in the United States and Canada." In: Larry E. Bone, ed. Library Education: an International Survey. Champaign, Ill.: University of Illinois, 1968, pp. 1-20.

Dunkin, Paul. "Good Teaching Methods in Library School Instruction." In: Larry E. Bone, ed. Library Education: an International Survey. Champaign, Ill.: University of Illinois, 1968, pp. 273-288.

Edwards, Dennis G. "The Wandering Wind," Journal of Education for Librarianship, 8(1):3-5, Summer, 1967.

Ennis, Philip H., and H. W. Winger, eds. Seven Questions About the Profession of Librarianship. Proceedings of the 26th Annual Conference of the Graduate School, June 21-23, 1961. Chicago: University of Chicago Press, 1962.

Fagerhaugh, Kenneth F. "Special Libraries," Journal of Education for Librarianship, 3(1):22-24, Summer, 1962.

Farradane, J. E. L. "A Survey of Syllabuses for Education in Information Science." In: Proceedings of International Conference on Education for Scientific Information Work, London, 1967. The Hague, International Federation for Documentation, 1967, pp. 11-16.

Fogarty, John. "Revolution in Our Schools," Library Journal, 92:302-303, January, 1967.

Foster, A. Gordon. "The Ideal Information Scientist." In: Proceedings of International Conference on Education for Scientific Information Work, London, 1967. The Hague, International Federation for Documentation, 1967, pp. 70-72.

Frarey, Carlyle, J. Discussion Group Summary of "How Articulate is Our Articulation," Journal of Education for Librarianship, 4(4):226-230, Spring, 1964.

_____. "Forum on Education for Special Librarianship," Special Libraries, 56:517-519, September, 1965.

_____. "Implications of Present Trends in Technical Services for Library Instruction," Journal of Education for Librarianship, 2(3):132-143, Winter, 1962.

Fryden, Floyd N. "Post-Master's Degree Programs in Some American Library Schools." Unpublished research paper, University of Chicago, Graduate Library School, Chicago, 1968.

Fuller, Muriel L. "What One Library School has Done: A Case Study." In: Guy Garrison, ed. The Changing Role of State Library Consultants. Urbana: University of Illinois, 1968, pp. 75-82.

Gaines, Ervin. "Critique on Public Library Education," Drexel Library Quarterly, 3:202-203, April, 1967.

Galvin, Thomas J. "Teaching Reference through the Case Method," Southeastern Librarian, 16:232-235, Winter, 1966.

Goldstein, Harold. "How Articulate is Our Articulation," Journal of Education for Librarianship, 4(4):218-225, Spring, 1964.

Goldstein, Harold, ed. Library School Teaching Methods: Evaluation of Students. Urbana: University of Illinois, 1967.

BIBLIOGRAPHY

Goldwyn, A. J. "Administration of a University Documentation Center." In: American Documentation Institute. Symposium on Education for Information Science. Washington, D. C.: Spartan Books, 1965, pp. 85-89.

Gull, C. D. "The Challenges of Teaching the Information Sciences," Journal of Education for Librarianship, 6(1):61-64, Summer, 1965.

_____. "Technological Advances in Medical Librarianship: A Symposium: Mechanization: Implications for the Medium-Size Medical Library," Medical Library Association Bulletin, 51:197-210, October, 1963.

Guy, Leonard C. "Teaching the Management of Libraries," Library Association Record, 70:91-95, April, 1968.

Hagan, Helen. "Teaching the Selection of Library Materials: An Institute Summary," Journal of Education for Librarianship, 6(1):19-23, Summer, 1965.

Hall, Anna C. An Analysis of Certain Professional Library Occupations in Relation to Formal Education Objectives. Pittsburgh: Carnegie Library, 1968. ED 021 606.

_____. Selected Educational Objectives for Public Service Librarians: A Taxonomic Approach. Pittsburgh: University of Pittsburgh, 1968.

Hamsher, Mary and and John F. Harvey. "Exemption Tests in Library Education," College and Research Libraries, 30:161-169, March, 1969.

Harlow, Neal R. "Bookman, Information Expert, Documentalist--How Library Schools Meet the Challenge," Special Libraries, 54:503-507, October, 1963.

_____. "The Character and Responsibility of a Graduate School," Library Journal, 93:1869-1875, May, 1968.

_____. "Doctoral Study--Key to What?" College and Research Libraries, 29:483-485, November, 1968.

Harris, Katharine G. "Reference Service Today and Tomorrow: Objectives, Practices, Needs, and Trends," Journal of Education for Librarianship, 3(3):175-187, Winter, 1963.

BIBLIOGRAPHY

Harrison, J. Clement. "Advanced Study: A Midatlantic Point of View." In: Larry E. Bone, ed. Library Education: an International Survey. Champaign, Illinois: University of Illinois, 1968, pp. 329-336.

Hartz, Frederic R. "Curriculum Implications for Training Instructional Materials Center Librarians," Journal of Education for Librarianship, 7(4):232-236, Spring, 1967.

Harvey, John. "Epilogue," Drexel Library Quarterly, 3:216-237, April, 1967.

_____. "The Educational Needs of Special Librarians." Unpublished paper delivered at the 5th Annual IBM Librarians' Conference, White Plains, New York, December 13, 1963.

Harvey, John F., and E. J. Humeston, Jr. "Why Don't the Accredited Library Schools---?" Journal of Education for Librarianship, 1(4):221-224, Spring, 1961.

Havighurst, R. J. "Educational Changes: Their Implications for the Library," ALA Bulletin, 61:537-543, May, 1967.

Havlik, Robert J., and others. Special Libraries, Problems, and Cooperative Potentials; Prepared for the National Advisory Commission on Libraries. Final Report. Washington, D.C.: American Documentation Institute, 1967. ED 022 482.

Hayes, Robert M. "Education for Information Systems Analysis." In: Proceedings of International Conference on Education for Scientific Information Work, London, 1967. The Hague: International Federation for Documentation, 1967, pp. 105-114.

Hines, Theodore C. "Salaries and Academic Training Programs for Information Scientists," Journal of Chemical Documentation, 7:118-120, May, 1967.

Holley, Edward G. "The Library Forum at Urbana," Journal of Education for Librarianship, 2(1):5-8, Summer, 1961.

"How Effective is Education for Librarianship?" A Digest of the Contributions of Speakers at the Library Education Workshop held at Drexel Institute of Technology April 28-30, 1957. Philadelphia, Pa.: Drexel Institute of Technology, Graduate School of Library Science, 1957.

BIBLIOGRAPHY

Hughes, Everett C. "Education for a Profession," Library Quarterly, 31:336-343, October, 1961.

Hummel, Ray O., Jr. "Library Education--What's Missing: Small Fund of Information," Journal of Education for Librarianship, 5 :92, Fall, 1964.

Hunt, Donald. "Recruiting," Drexel Library Quarterly. 3:46-51. January, 1967.

Isabella, Santina M. "Education for Information Center Personnel in ALA Accredited Library Schools of the United States and Canada." Unpublished Master's thesis, Graduate School of Library Science, Drexel Institute of Technology, Philadelphia, 1964.

Jackson, Eugene. "Critique on Special Library Education," Drexel Library Quarterly, 3:211-215, April, 1967.

Jones, W. H. "Report of an Internship Served at the Dallas Public Library." Unpublished Master's thesis, University of Texas, Austin, 1958.

Kee, S. Janice. "Library Development in the States," Journal of Education for Librarianship, 3:24-28, Summer, 1962.

Kirkegaard, Preben. "Recruitment and Selection of Students," In: Larry E. Bone (ed.). Library Education: an International Survey. Urbana: University of Illinois, 1968, pp. 125-130.

Knapp, Patricia B. "The Library-Centered Library School." In: Conference on the Bibliographic Control of Library Science Literature, Albany, 1968. (Preprint)

Kortendick, James J., and Elizabeth W. Stone. "Highlights of a Study on Federal Librarians and Post-MLS Education: A Preliminary Report," DC Libraries, 41:71-76, Fall, 1969.

Lancour, Harold (ed.). Issues in Library Education: A Report on the Conference on Library Education held at Princeton University, Princeton, December 11-12, 1948.

Lee, Calvin B. T. Improving College Teaching. Washington, D.C.: American Council on Education, 1967.

"Library Education," Illinois Libraries, 49:373-379, May, 1967.

BIBLIOGRAPHY

Library School Review, Kansas State Teachers College, October, 1968.

Lieberman, Irving. Education for Health Sciences Librarianship. Proceedings of an Invitational Conference, Seattle, 1967. Seattle: University of Washington, 1968. (ED 015 765)

Lieberman, Myron. "Principles of Education Preparation." In: Larry E. Bone (ed.). Library Education: an International Survey. Urbana: : University of Illinois, 1968, pp. 153-169.

Lilley, Dorothy. "Graduate Education Needed by Information Specialists and the Extent to Which it is Offered in Accredited Library Schools." Unpublished Doctor's dissertation, Columbia University, New York, 1969.

Long, Marie. "Emphasis on Educators." Journal of Education for Librarianship, 5:215-226, Spring, 1965.

Longnecker, Henry C. Staffing an Information Group. Philadelphia: Smith Kline & French Laboratories, 1958. (Unpublished)

Lowrie, Jean E. "Sixth-Year Degree," Library Journal, 92:170, January, 1967.

McCrossan, John. "Education of Librarians Employed in Small Public Libraries," Journal of Education for Librarianship, 7):237-244, Spring, 1967.

_____. Library Science Education and its Relationship to Competence in Adult Book Selection in Public Libraries. Urbana: University of Illinois, 1967. (ED 019 096)

McKinney, Eleanor R. "Another Degree? What For?" School Libraries, 19:19-22, Spring, 1969.

Marco, Guy. "Doctoral Programs in American Library Schools," Journal of Education for Librarianship, 8 :6-13, Summer, 1967.

Melkonian, Albert A. and Joseph C. Donohue. "Study of Information Science Curricula: I. Library Schools," Reprinted from Parameters of Information Science. Washington, D.C.: American Documentation Institute, 1964.

BIBLIOGRAPHY

Merritt, Leroy C. "Doctoral Study in Librarianship--A Supplement," College and Research Libraries, 23:539-540, November, 1962.

Minder, Thomas. "Library Systems Analyst--A Job Description," College and Research Libraries, 27:271-276, July, 1966.

Monroe, Margaret E. "The Core Courses at Wisconsin," Journal of Education for Librarianship, 9(2):116-122, Fall, 1968.

_____. "Graduate Library Education in Space," Journal of Education for Librarianship, 5(1):5-9, Summer, 1964.

Montgomery, Edward B. "Curriculum Implications of Library Dynamics," Journal of Education for Librarianship, 5(2):103-109, Fall, 1964.

Morton, Florrinell F. "Faculty Adequacy." In: Sarah R. Reed, ed. Problems of Library School Administration: Report of an Institute, April 14-15, 1965, Washington, D.C. Washington, D.C.: U.S. Office of Education, 1965, pp. 3-9.

Muller, Robert H. "Critique on University Library Education," Drexel Library Quarterly, 3:204-210, April, 1967.

Munn, Ralph. Conditions and Trends in Education for Librarianship. New York: Carnegie Corporation of New York, 1936.

Myers, Mildred S. "The Constant Target," Journal of Education for Librarianship," 8(2):78-84, Fall, 1967.

Nakata, Yuri Ike. "An Analysis of Various Quantitative Differences Among Library Schols Based on Standards for Accreditation." Unpublished Master's thesis, University of Chicago, Chicago, 1966.

Orne, Jerrold. "Library Education--What's Missing?: Complex Pr Problems," Journal of Education for Librarianship, 5(2):90-91, Fall, 1964.

Osborn, Andrew. "The Doctorate," Drexel Library Quarterly, 3:158-163, April, 1967.

_____. "Elements of a Programme for the Training of Information Scientists." In: Proceedings of International Conference on Education for Scientific Information Work, London, 1967.

The Hague: International Federation for Documentation, 1967, pp. 115-120.

Patterson, Charles D. "The Seminar Method in Library Education," Journal of Education for Librarianship, 8(2):99-105, Fall, 1967.

Piternick, George and Anne Brearley. "Canadian Training of Scientific Information Workers." In: Proceedings of International Conference on Education for Scientific Information Work, London, 1967. The Hague: International Federation for Documentation, 1967, pp. 73-86.

Pope, Elspeth. "You and the Student...Three Views: Dear Dr. Rothstein," Journal of Education for Librarianship, 8(2):65-71, Fall, 1967.

Postell, William D. "Some Practical Thoughts on an Internship Program," Medical Library Association Bulletin, 48:413, October, 1960.

Proctor, Vilma. "MLA Certification: Its Present Problems and Future Development," Bulletin of the Medical Library Association, 55:9-12, January, 1967.

Reece, Ernest. The Task and Training of Librarians. New York: Kings Crown Press, 1949.

Reed, Sarah R., ed. Problems of Library School Administration: Report of an Institute, April 14-15, 1965, Washington, D.C. Washington, D.C.: U. S. Office of Education, 1965.

_____. "Guide to Library Education: Part 1: Trends in Professional Education," Drexel Library Quarterly, 3:1-24, January, 1967.

Rees, Alan M. "The Art of Teaching Information Science." In: American Documentation Institute. Symposium on Education for Information Science. Washington, Spartan Books, 1965, pp. 71-76.

_____. "What We Should Teach Special Librarians," Special Libraries, 58:33-36, January, 1967.

Rees, Alan and Dorothy Riccio. "Curriculum--Information Science," Drexel Library Quarterly, 3:108-114, January, 1967.

BIBLIOGRAPHY

Rees, Alan M. and Dorothy Riccio. "Information Science in Library School Curricula." In: Proceedings of International Conference on Education for Scientific Information Work, London, 1967. The Hague: International Federation for Documentation, 1967, pp. 29-37.

Rees, Alan M. and Tefko Saracevic. "Teaching Documentation at Western Reserve University," Journal of Education for Librarianship, 6(1):8-13, Summer, 1965.

Rockwood, Ruth H. "The Relationship Between the Professional Preparation and Subsequent Types of Library Positions held by a Selected Group of Library School Graduates." Unpublished Doctor's dissertation, Indiana University, Bloomington, September, 1960.

Rothstein, Samuel. "A Forgotten Issue: Practice Work in American Library Education." In: Larry E. Bone, ed. Library Education: an International Survey. Champaign, Ill.: University of Illinois, 1968, pp. 197-222.

Saracevic, Tefko, and Alan M. Rees. "The Impact of Information Science on Library Practice," Library Journal, 93 (19): 4097-4101, November, 1968.

Saunders, Wilfred L. "The Library School in the University Setting." In: Larry E. Bone, ed. Library Education: an International Survey. Champaign, Ill.: University of Illinois, 1968, pp. 73-107.

Schenk, Rachel K. "The Dread and the Terror: Curriculum of 1910," Journal of Education for Librarianship, 1(2):75-80, Fall, 1960.

Schick, F. L., and R. E. Warncke, eds. "The Future of Library Education," Proceedings of an Institute, Cleveland, Ohio, April 25-28, 1962. Journal of Education for Librarianship, 3(1): 3-80, Summer, 1962.

Schlueter, R. A. "Questions and Answers," Journal of Education for Librarianship, 9(2):152-158, Fall, 1968.

Schultz, Claire. "Things They Don't Teach in Library School," Special Libraries, 54: 513, October, 1963.

BIBLIOGRAPHY

Schur, H. "Education and Training for Science Information Work; Cooperation Between University and Industry." In: Proceedings of <u>International Conference on Education for Scientific Information Work, London, 1967.</u> The Hague: International Federation for Documentation, 1967, pp. 227-232.

Selden, William K. "Accreditation: Panel Member No. 1." In: Sarah R. Reed, ed. <u>Problems of Library School Administration: Report of an Institute, April 14-15, 1965, Washington, D.C.</u> Washington, D.C.: U.S. Office of Education, 1965, pp. 59-60.

Sellers, Rose Z. "A Different Drummer: Thoughts on Library Education," <u>Journal of Education for Librarianship,</u> 6(3):151-166, Winter, 1966.

Sharify, Nasser. "The Need for Change in Present Library Science Curricula." In: Larry E. Bone, ed. <u>Library Education: an International Survey.</u> Champaign, Ill.: University of Illinois, 1968, pp. 171-196.

Shera, Jesse H. "The Problem of Finance." In: Sarah R. Reed, ed. <u>Problems of Library School Administration: Report of an Institute, April 14-15, 1965, Washington, D.C.</u> Washington, D.C.: U.S. Office of Education, 1965, pp. 33-45.

_____. "Theory and Technique in Library Education," <u>Library Journal,</u> 85:1736-1739, May, 1960.

_____. "What is Past is Prologue; Beyond 1984," <u>ALA Bulletin,</u> 61:35-47, January, 1967.

Shera, Jesse H., and Margaret E. Eagan. "Review of the Present State of Librarianship and Documentation." In: S. C. Bradford, ed. <u>Documentation.</u> London: Crosby Lockwood and Son, 1953, pp. 11-45.

Sherrod, John. "International Cooperation on Education in Information Science." In: Proceedings of <u>International Conference on Education for Scientific Information Work, London, 1967.</u> The Hague: International Federation for Documentation, 1967, pp. 217-219.

Shilling, Charles W., and Bruce Berman. <u>Science Information Specialist Training Program.</u> A progress report. Washington,

BIBLIOGRAPHY

D. C.: Biological Sciences Communication Project, George Washington University, 1968. ED 019 092.

Shilling, Charles W. and M. C. Bracken. "Survey of Practical Training in Information Work." In: Proceedings of International Conference on Education for Scientific Information Work, London, 1967. The Hague: International Federation for Documentation, 1967, pp. 173-177.

Shores, Louis. "Comparative Library Education: Homework for a National Plan," Journal of Education for Librarianship, 6(4): 231-233, Spring, 1966.

Simonton, Wesley, ed. "Introduction." In: Information Retrieval Today. Minneapolis, Minnesota: University of Minnesota, 1963.

Slamecka, Vladimir. "Graduate Programs in Information Science at the Georgia Institute of Technology," Special Libraries, 59:246-250, April, 1968.

_____. "On the Nature of Information Science and the Responsibility of Institutions of Higher Education." In: American Documentation Institute. Symposium on Education for Information Science. Washington, D.C.: Spartan Books, 1965, pp. 91-93.

Stenstrom, Ralph H. "Some Thoughts on the Future of Library Education," Journal of Education for Librarianship, 4(1):9-14, Summer, 1963.

Stokes, Roy. "The Trading Stamp Mentality," Library Journal, 92: 3595-3600, October, 1967.

Sudar, Dan D. "Three Levels of Library Education," Library Journal, 91:4899-4903, October, 1966.

Swank, Raynard C. "Documentation and Information Science in the Core Library School Curriculum," Special Libraries, 58:40-44, January, 1967.

_____. "The Graduate Library School Curriculum." In: Sarah R. Reed, ed. Problems of Library School Administration: Report of an Institute, April 14-15, 1965, Washington, D.C. Washington, D. C.: U. S. Office of Education, 1965.

BIBLIOGRAPHY

Carr-Saunders, Alexander M., and P. S. Wilson. The Professions. Oxford: Clarendon Press, 1933.

Catholic University of America. The Graduate Curriculum Study. Washington, D.C.: School of Nursing, The Catholic University of America, 1962.

Clark, Burton R. Educating the Expert Society. San Francisco, California: Chandler Publishing Co., 1962.

Cogan, Morris L. "The Problem of Defining a Profession," Annals of the American Academy of Political and Social Scientists, 297:105-111, January, 1955.

Conant, James G. The Education of American Teachers. New York: McGraw-Hill Book Co., 1963.

Cope, Oliver. "The Future of Medical Education," Harpers' Magazine, 235:98-104, October, 1967.

Cope, Oliver and Jerrold Zacharias. Medical Education Reconsidered: Blueprint for Reform. Endicott House Summer Study on Medical Education, 1965. New York: Lippincott, 1966.

Corson, John J. "Equipping Men for Career Growth in the Public Service," Public Administration Review, 23:1-9, May, 1963.

Courtney, E. Wayne. A Conceptual Basis for Developing Common Curricula in Teacher Education Programs for Occupational Education. No. 2, Vol. III. Menomonie, Wisconsin: Stout State University, 1968. ED 022 028.

_____. Implications for the Training of Teachers--Professional Education Preparation and Requirements. Menomonie, Wisc.: Stout State University, 1965.

Crowell, Michael G. "An Experimental Study of the In-Service Preparation of Secondary School English Teachers in Transformational Grammar." Interim Report. Galesburg, Ill.: Knox College, Illinois State-Wide Curriculum Study Center in the Preparation of Secondary School English Teachers, 1969.

Davies, Don. "Professional Standards in Teaching: Moving from Ideas to Action," Journal of Teacher Education, 13:191 ff., June, 1962.

BIBLIOGRAPHY

DeVore, Paul W. Structure and Content Foundations for Curriculum Development. Washington, D.C.: American Industrial Arts Association, 1966.

Diekhoff, John S. "The Professional School in the University," Journal of Education for Librarianship, 6(2):103-110, Fall, 1965.

Doll, Ronald C. Curriculum Improvement: Decision-Making and Process. 2d. ed. Boston: Allyn and Bacon, 1965.

Dressel, Paul I. The Undergraduate Curriculum in Higher Education. Washington, D.C.: Center for Applied Research in Education, 1963.

Drucker, Peter F. "Work and Worker in the Knowledge Society." In: The Age of Discontinuity: Guidelines to our Changing Society. New York: Harper and Row, 1969, pp. 287-310.

Fagan, Edward R. "English Field Theory and General Systems," The Record: The Teachers College Record, 69:733-742, May, 1968.

Ferguson, Bertis F., and others. A Survey of Northeastern State College Industrial Arts Graduates, 1911-1967. Tahlequah, Oklahoma: Northeastern State College, 1967.

Flexner, Abraham. "Is Social Work a Profession?" School and Society, 901-911, June, 1915.

_____. Universities: American, English, German. New York: Oxford University Press, 1930.

Gardner, John W. Excellence: Can We be Equal and Excellent, Too? New York: Harper and Row, 1961.

Goheen, Robert F. "The Teacher in the University," American Scientist, 54(2), 1966.

Goodlad, John I. The Future of Learning and Teaching. Washington, D.C.: National Education Association, 1968.

Haggerty, M. E. The Evaluation of Higher Institutions: The Faculty. Vol. II. Chicago: University of Chicago Press, 1957.

BIBLIOGRAPHY

Swank, Raynard C. "Sixth-Year Curricula and the Education of Library School Faculties," <u>Journal of Education for Librarianship,</u> 8(1):14-19, Summer, 1967.

Sykes, Christa M. "Report of an Internship Served at the Rudolph Matas Medical Library, New Orleans, January 1-June 30, 1956." Unpublished Master's thesis, University of Texas, Austin, 1956.

Tate, Fred A., and James L. Wood. "Libraries and Abstracting and Indexing Services--A Study in Interdependency," <u>Library Trends</u>, 16:353-373, January, 1968.

Taube, Mortimer. "Documentation, Information Retrieval, and other New Techniques," <u>Library Quarterly,</u> 31:90-103, January, 1961.

Taylor, Robert S. <u>Curriculum for the Information Sciences.</u> Report No. 12: Recommended Courses and Curricula. Bethlehem, Pa.: Lehigh University, 1967.

_____. "The Interfaces Between Librarianship and Information Science and Engineering," <u>Special Libraries,</u> 58:45-48, January, 1967.

_____. "Question Negotiation and Information Seeking in Libraries," <u>College and Research Libraries,</u> 29:178-194, May, 1968.

_____. "Toward an Educational Base for the Information Sciences and Information Engineering." In: American Documentation Institute. <u>Symposium on Education for Information Science.</u> Washington, D.C.: Spartan Books, 1965, pp. 77-81.

"Teaching Methods: Pt. 1: Reference and Cataloging; Pt. 2: Government Publications, Documentation, Book Selection, Administration, Adult Education, History of Books and Libraries, Newer Media," <u>Journal of Education for Librarianship,</u> 5:227-258, Spring, 1965; 6:3-68, Summer, 1965.

University of California, Los Angeles, The School of Library Service. <u>Papers, including Guidelines for Professional Schools at UCLA, Development Plan for the School to 1980,</u> November, 1967. (Mimeographed)

University of Maryland. School of Library and Information Services. <u>A Proposal for a Ph.D. Program in Library Science and Informa-</u>

BIBLIOGRAPHY

tion Services. College Park, Md., November, 1968. (Mimeographed)

University of Maryland. School of Library and Information Services. Proposal for a Project "Development of a General Inventory of Library User Services." College Park, Md., January, 1969. (Mimeographed)

University of Pittsburgh. Graduate School of Library and Information Sciences. The Professional Education of Media Service Personnel. Pittsburgh, Pa.: University of Pittsburgh, 1964.

Vainstein, Rose. "What the Library Schools Can Do in the Training and Upgrading of State Library Consultants." In: Guy Garrison, ed. The Changing Role of State Library Consultants. Urbana: University of Illinois, Graduate School of Library Science, 1968, pp. 83-95.

Voight, Melvin J. Scientists' Approach to Information. ACRL Monograph No. 24. Chicago: American Library Association, 1961.

Walker, Richard D. "The Quantity and Content of Masters' Theses Accepted at Library Schools Offering the Doctor's Degree, 1949-1958," Journal of Education for Librarianship, 3:264-279, Spring, 1963.

Wallace, Everett M. and others. Planning for On-The-Job Training of Library Personnel. Santa Monica, Calif.: Systems Development Corporation, 1967. (Technical Memorandum 3762/000/00)

Warncke, Ruth. "The Core Book Selection Course," Journal of Education for Librarianship, 4(4):209-215, Spring, 1964.

_____. "State Libraries, Library Associations and Library Schools: Partners in Library Development," South Dakota Library Bulletin, 51:112-115, October-December, 1965.

Warncke, Ruth, and Richard A. Davis. "Is the Traditional Library School Meeting the Needs of the Profession? Two Viewpoints," Special Libraries, 54:493-496, October, 1963.

Wasserman, Paul. "Trends and Directions in Library Education and Library Practice." Lecture given at Graduate School of Librarianship, University of Denver, Denver, February 21, 1968. (Mimeographed)

BIBLIOGRAPHY

"What's Wrong with Our Library Schools?" Library Journal, 91:1773-1775, April, 1966.

Wheeler, Joseph L. Progress and Problems in Education for Librarianship. New York: Carnegie Corporation, 1946.

White, Lucien W. "Are Library Schools Educating for Librarianship?: The Early Background," Journal of Education for Librarianship, 2(1):8-11, Summer, 1961.

Whitenack, Carolyn. "And the Beat Goes On!," School Libraries, 17:7-9, Spring, 1968.

Wight, Edward A. "Standards and Stature in Librarianship," ALA Bulletin, 55:871-875, November, 1961.

Williamson, Charles C. "Some Present-Day Aspects of Library Training," ALA Bulletin, 13:120-126, July, 1919.

_____. Training for Library Service: A Report Prepared for the Carnegie Corporation of New York. New York: Carnegie Corporation, 1923.

Wilson, Celianna I. "Professional Internship: A Program and a Proposal," Library Journal, 88:2201-2205, June, 1963.

Wilson, Louis R. "Historical Development of Education for Librarianship in the United States," In: Education for Librarianship. Chicago: American Library Association, 1949.

Wood, D. N. and K. P. Barr. "Courses on the Structure and Use of Scientific Literature," Journal of Documentation, 22:22-32, March, 1966.

Wood, R. Kent. "The Changing Face of the Library," Mountain Plains Library Quarterly, 12:3-15, Spring, 1967.

Yenawine, Wayne S. "The Conferences That Were," Journal of Education for Librarianship, 4(4):191-195, Spring, 1964.

Yovits, M.C., "Information Science: Toward the Development of a True Scientific Discipline," American Documentation, 20:376, Oct., 1969.

Zachert, Martha J. "Special Libraries Instruction: The Separate Course," Special Libraries, 58:37-40, January, 1967.

BIBLIOGRAPHY

CURRICULUM DEVELOPMENT:
OTHER PROFESSIONS

Allen, D. W. <u>Micro-Teaching: A Description.</u> Stanford, California: School of Education, Stanford University, 1966. ED 023 314.

American Association of Colleges for Teacher Education. <u>Standards and Evaluative Criteria for the Accreditation of Teacher Education.</u> A Draft of the Proposed New Standards, with Study Guide. Washington, D.C.: American Association of Colleges for Teacher Education, December, 1967.

Arnold, Joseph P. <u>A Study of Recommendations for Technical Education Curricula.</u> Lafayette, Indiana: Purdue University, 1965. ED 016 064.

_____. "Technical Education Curricular Recommendations by Management Representatives of Manufacturing Establishments in Illinois." Unpublished Doctor's dissertation, University of Illinois, Urbana, 1965.

Barzun, Jacques. <u>The House of Intellect.</u> New York: Harper and Row, 1959.

Borg, Walter R. <u>The Minicourse Rationale and Uses in the Inservice Education of Teachers.</u> Berkeley, Calif.: Far West Laboratory for Educational Research and Development, 1968. ED 024 647.

Broudy, Harry S. <u>Building a Philosophy of Education.</u> 2d. ed. Englewood Cliffs, N.J.: Prentice Hall, 1961.

Bruner, Jerome S. <u>The Process of Education.</u> Cambridge, Mass.: Harvard University Press, 1961.

Calkins, Robert D. "Business Education: Goals and Prospects." Paper read before the American Association of Collegiate Schools of Business, Chicago, Illinois, April 30, 1964. (Mimeographed)

_____. "Education for Business--Changing Perspectives and Requirements." Paper read before the International Society of Business Education, New York University, New York, August 25, 1965. (Mimeographed)

BIBLIOGRAPHY

Harrell, Lloyd W. and H. T. Tilley. <u>Continuous Curriculum Development--Rural School: Evaluation Report and Continuation Application.</u> Report No. DPSC-67-4332. Goshen, Indiana: Fairfield Community Schools, 1968. ED 021 665.

Hartmann, George W. "The Field of Learning and its Educational Consequences," In: National Society for the Study of Education. 41st Yearbook, Part II. <u>The Psychology of Learning.</u> Chicago: University of Chicago Press, 1942, pp. 165-214.

Heady, Ferrel, ed. "Higher Education for Public Service," <u>Public Administration Review,</u> 27:292-367, November, 1967.

Heiss, Ann M. <u>The Utilization of the College and University Teacher.</u> Berkeley, California: University of California, 1968. ED 026 002.

Honey, John C. "A Report: Higher Education for Public Service," <u>Public Administration Review,</u> 27:294-321, November, 1967.

Hook, J. N., Paul H. Jacobs, and R. D. Crisp. <u>Illinois State-Wide Curriculum Study Center in the Preparation of Secondary School English Teachers.</u> Final Report. Urbana, Illinois: University of Illinois, 1969.

Jencks, Christopher and David Riesman. <u>The Academic Revolution.</u> New York: Doubleday and Co., 1968.

King, Arthur R., Jr. and J. A. Brownell. <u>The Curriculum and the Disciplines of Knowledge: A Theory of Curriculum Practice.</u> New York: John Wiley and Sons, 1966.

Knowles, Malcolm S. "A General Theory of the Doctorate in Education," <u>Adult Education,</u> 12:136-141, Spring, 1962.

Kohn, Robert D. "The Significance of the Professional Ideal," <u>The Annals,</u> 110:1-5, May, 1922.

Kortendick, James J. "Curriculum:Administration," <u>Drexel Library Quarterly,</u> 3(1):92-103, January, 1967.

BIBLIOGRAPHY

Lee, Calvin B. T. "Knowledge Structure and Curriculum Development," Educational Record, 47:347-360, Summer, 1966.

McGlothlin, William J. The Professional Schools. New York: Center for Applied Research in Education, 1964.

McGrath, Earl J. "The Ideal Education for the Professional Man." In: National Society for the Study of Education. Education for the Professions. 61st Yearbook. Chicago: University of Chicago Press, 1962, pp. 281-301.

_____. The Liberal Arts College and the Emergent Caste System. New York: Columbia University, 1966.

_____, ed. Universal Higher Education. New York: McGraw-Hill, 1966.

Mayhew, Lewis B. The Collegiate Curriculum, An Approach to Analysis. Atlanta, Ga.: Southern Regional Education Board, 1966. ED 014 790.

Miel, Alice. Changing the Curriculum--A Social Process. New York: Appleton-Century-Crofts, 1946.

Mitchell, S. B. Women and the Doctorate. Stillwater, Oklahoma: Oklahoma State University, 1968. ED 024 352.

Mosher, Frederick. Professional Education and the Public Service: An Exploratory Study. Final Report. Berkeley: Center for Research and Development in Higher Education, University of California, 1968. ED 025 220.

National Education Association. National Commission on Teacher Education and Professional Standards. Auxiliary School Personnel. Washington, D.C.: National Education Association, 1967.

National Education Association. National Commission on Teacher Education and Professional Standards. A Position Paper on Teacher Education and Professional Standards. Washington, D.C.: National Education Association, 1963.

National Education Association. National Commission on Teacher Education and Professional Standards. What You Should Know About New Horizons. Washington, D.C.: National Education Association, 1962.

BIBLIOGRAPHY

National League of Nursing. Statement on Nursing Education. New York: National League of Nursing, 1967. ED 020 399.

"New Horizons in Teacher Education and Professional Standards," National Education Association Journal, 50:55-68, January, 1961.

Nichols, Roy F. "A Reconsideration of the Ph.D.," The Graduate Journal, 7:330, Spring, 1967. ED 021 875

Palmer, Dale H. "Situation Factors to be Considered in the Selection Process." Paper given at the Annual Meeting of the American Educational Research Association, February, 1968. ED 019 732.

Pearson, Justus R., Jr. and James Robert Reese. Project Grammar: The Linguistic and Language Preparation of Secondary School Teachers of English. Johnson City, Tennessee: East Tennessee State University, 1969.

Petrof, Barbara G. "The Status of Research Courses," Journal of Education for Librarianship, 8:28-32, Summer, 1967.

Rigby, Avard A. "Education for Whatever Comes." An Address to the State 4-H Leaders' School, Utah State University, Logan, Utah, March 18, 1968. ED 020 046.

Robinson, John and Neil Barnes, eds. New Media and Methods in Industrial Training. London: British Broadcasting Corporation, 1967.

Saylor, J. Galen and William M. Alexander. Curriculum Planning for Modern Schools. New York: Holt, Rinehart and Winston, 1954.

Schill, William J. and Joseph P. Arnold. Curricula Content for Six Technologies, Report of the Bureau of Education Research and the Department of Vocation and Technical Education. Urbana: University of Illinois, 1965.

Schultz, Charles L. The Politics and Economics of Public Spending. Washington, D.C.: The Brookings Institution, 1968.

Sharp, George. Curriculum Development as Re-Education of the Teacher. New York: Columbia University, 1951.

Steinberg, Erwin R., and others. Curriculum Development and Evaluation in English and Social Studies. Pittsburgh, Pa.: Carnegie Institute of Technology, 1964.

BIBLIOGRAPHY

Stone, C. Walter (ed.). *The Professional Education of Media Service Personnel: Recommendations for Training Media Service Personnel for Schools and Colleges.* Preliminary Edition. Pittsburgh: Center for Media Studies, University of Pittsburgh, 1964.

Stone, James C., and Clark N. Robinson. *The Graduate Internship Program in Teacher Education, the First Six Years.* Berkeley : University of California Press, 1965.

Tolley, William P. *American Universities in Transition and the New Role of Adult Education.* Leeds, England: University of Leeds, 1966. (ED 019 556)

Tremonti, Joseph B. *Follow-Up Study of Graduates in the Master of Education Degree Programs at Loyola University, New Orleans, Louisiana.* New Orleans : Loyola University, 1967.

U. S. Office of Education. *Guide to Organized Occupational Curriculums in Higher Education. Graduates: July 1, 1961 through June 30, 1962 and Enrollments: October 1, 1962.* Institutional Data. Prepared by Ken August Brunner. Circular No. 771. Washington, D.C.: Government Printing Office, 1965.

_____. *Occupational Criteria and Preparatory Curriculum Patterns in Technical Education Programs.* Vocational Division Bulletin No. 296. Area Vocational Education Program series No. 4. Washington, D.C.: Government Printing Office, 1965.

_____. *The Post-Doctoral Training Program in Education.* Washington, D.C.: U. S. Office of Education, 1967. ED 021 307.

_____. *A Review of Activities in Federally Aided Programs: Vocational and Technical Education, Fiscal Year 1964.* Washington, D.C.: U. S. Government Printing Office, 1966.

Wagner, C. W. "Organizing for Curriculum Development," *Education,* 82:573-574, 1961-1962.

Weede, Gary D. *Electronic Technician Personnel and Training Needs of Iowa Industries.* Ames: Iowa State University of Science and Technology, 1967. (ED 020 314)

BIBLIOGRAPHY

EDUCATIONAL PLANNING: MULTI-MEDIA AND SYSTEMS
APPROACHES

Adelson, Marvin. "The Systems Approach--A Perspective," SDC Magazine, 9(10):1-10, October, 1966.

Alkin, Marvin C., and William L. Duff, Jr. Some Data Problems in Systems Research (original publisher not given, n.d.) ED 021 324.

Ambry, Edward J., and others. Evaluation for Environmental Education: A Systems Analysis Approach for Self-Evaluation. Mountain Lakes, N.J.: The New Jersey State Council for Environmental Education, 1969.

American Association of Colleges for Teacher Education. Professional Teacher Education II. A Programmed Design Developed by the AACTE Teacher Education and Media Project. Washington, D.C.: American Association of Colleges for Teacher Education, 1968.

_____. Teacher Education and Media--1964: A Selective, Annotated Bibliography. Washington, D.C.: American Association of Colleges for Teacher Education, 1964.

Banathy, Bela H. Instructional Systems. Palo Alto, Calif.: Fearon Publishers, 1969.

Beard, Harry G. A Study of the Meaning of Selected Program Planning Concepts in Vocational Education. Ithaca, New York: Cornell University, 1966.

Berrien, F. Kennedy. General and Social Systems. New Brunswick, N.J.: Rutgers University Press, 1968.

Bertalanfly, Ludwig von. General System Theory. New York: George Braziller, 1968.

Blewett, Evelyn J., ed. Elementary Teacher Training Models. Washington, D.C.: U.S. Office of Education, 1969.

Boulding, Kenneth. The Image: Knowledge in Life and Society. Ann Arbor, Michigan: Ann Arbor Paperbacks, 1961.

Briggs, Leslie J., and others. Instructional Media: A Procedure for the Design of Multi-Media Instruction, A Critical Review of Research and Suggestions for Future Research. Final Report. Pittsburgh, Pennsylvania: American Institutes for Research, 1967.

"Bringing the Campus to the Office," Business Week, 1895:72-73, December 25, 1965.

BIBLIOGRAPHY

Browne, Duffe and Mary H. Smith. The Investigation, Development and Dissemination of Procedures and Techniques Helpful to Inter-institutional Use of Television and Related Media. Atlanta Georgia: Southern Regional Education Board, 1967. ED 021 443.

Case, C. Marston and Stephen C. Clark. A Bibliographic Guide to Operations Analysis of Education. Washington, D.C.: National Center for Educational Statistics, Division of Data Analysis and Dissemination, 1967. ED 025 851.

Cogswell, John F. The Systems Approach as a Heuristic Method in Educational Development--An Application to the Counseling Function. SP Series, SP-720. Santa Monica, California: System Development Corporation, 1962.

Cohen, David M. and Samuel S. Dubin. A Systems Approach to Updating Professional Personnel. Paper presented at the National Seminar on Adult Education Research, Toronto, February 9-11, 1969. University Park: Pennsylvania State University, 1969. ED 025 718.

Cook, Desmond. The Impact of Systems Analysis on Education. Columbus, Ohio: Ohio State University, Educational Research Management Center, 1968. ED 024 145.

_____. PERT Applications in Educational Planning. Columbus, Ohio: School of Education, Ohio State University, 1966. ED 019 751

_____. The Use of Systems Analysis and Management Techniques in Program Planning and Evaluation. Paper presented at the Symposium on the Application of Systems Analysis and Management Techniques to Educational Planning in California, Orange, California, June 12-13, 1967. ED 019 752.

Corrigan, Edmund. "The Instructional Materials Center and the Media Specialist." Catholic Library World, 39:120-122, October, 1967.

Corrigon, Robert E. and Roger A. Kaufman. Why System Engineering? Palo Alto, California: Fearon Publishers, 1965.

Coulson, John E. An Instructional Management System for the Public Schools. Santa Monica, California: System Development Corporation, 1967. (ED 019 885)

Crawford, Meredith P. "Concepts of Training," In: Robert M. Gagne (ed.). Psychological Principles in System Development. New York: Holt, Rinehart & Winston, Inc., 1962.

Culbertson, Jack, and others. The Design and Development of Prototype Instructional Materials for Preparing Educational Administrators. Final Report. Washington, D.C.: U.S. Office of Education, 1968. (ED 019 723)

Cummings, Roy J.,"Removing Intuition from Course Development: Methods at FAA to Prevent Overtraining and Undertraining," Training and Development Journal,10:18-27,January, 1968.

BIBLIOGRAPHY

Egbert, Robert L., and John F. Cogswell. <u>System Design in the Bassett High School</u>. Technical Memorandum TM-1147. Santa Monica, California: System Development Corporation, 1963.

Faegre, Christopher L., and others. <u>Analysis and Evaluation of Present and Future Multi-Media Needs in Higher Education</u>. Silver Spring, Maryland: Communication Research Program, American Institutes for Research, 1968. (ED 024 351)

Finan, John L. "The System Concept as a Principle of Methodological Decision," In: Robert <u>M. Gagné (ed.). Psychological Principles in System Development</u>. New York: Holt, Rinehart & Winston, Inc., 1962, pp. 517-546.

Finn, James D. "A Possible Model for Considering the Use of Media in Higher Education," <u>AV Communication Review</u>, 15:153-157, Summer, 1967.

"For Those who Would Like to Learn More About the Implications of General Systems," <u>International Associations,</u> 22:16-17, January, 1970.

Gagné, Robert M. (ed.). <u>Psychological Principles in System Development</u>. New York: Holt, Rinehart & Winston, Inc., 1962.

_____. "The Analysis of Instructional Objectives for the Design of Instruction". In: <u>Teaching Machines and Programmed Learning II</u>. Washington, D.C.: National Education Association, 1965.

Gagné, Robert M., and Noel E. Paradise. "Abilities and Learning Sets in Knowledge Acquisition," <u>Psychological Monographs: General and Applied,</u> 75:14. Washington, D.C.: American Psychological Association, 1961.

Gagné, Robert M., and others. "Factors in Acquiring Knowledge of a Mathematical Task," <u>Psychological Monographs: General and Applied,</u> 76:7. Washington, D.C.: American Psychological Association, 1961.

Gates, Jesse L., and James W. Altman. <u>Orientation of Educators and Behavioral Scientists to Information Systems</u>. Final Report. Pittsburgh : American Institutes for Research, 1968. (ED 021 601)

Gladmon, William T. "Management Training via Television: The First Four Years at Pittsburgh's WQEX." <u>Training and Development Journal,</u> 21:6-10, May, 1967.

Goldstein, Harold. "The Importance of Newer Media in Library Training and the Education of Professional Personnel." <u>Library Trends</u>, 16:259-265, October, 1967.

Goldstein, Harold, ed. <u>National Conference on the Implications of the New Media for the Teaching of Library Science</u>. Monograph No. 1. Proceedings. Urbana, Ill.: University of Illinois, 1963.

BIBLIOGRAPHY

Greenwood, James W. "Nature and Importance of Systems Education," International Associations, 22:3-5, January, 1970.

Havighurst, Robert J. Developmental Tasks and Education. New York: David McKay, Inc., 1962.

Holton, Gerald, Fletcher Watson, and F. James Rutherford. Harvard Project Physics Progress Report. Papers delivered at the American Association of Physics Teachers Meeting, February, 1967. Cambridge: Harvard Project Physics. 1967. (ED 020 117)

Johnson, Eugene I. The New Media in Public Affairs Education. Prepared for the Task Force on Innovation in Public Affairs. Washington, D.C.: U.S. Office of Education, 1967. ED 022 993.

Joyce, Bruce R. Man, Media, and Machines. Washington, D.C.: National Education Association, 1967.

Kettering, Charles F. The Challenge of Technology: A Symposium on Educational Technology. An IDEA occasional paper. Washington, D.C.: U.S. Office of Education, 1969. ED 021 480.

Knezevich, S. J. The Systems Approach to School Administration: Some Perceptions on the State of the Art in 1967. Paper presented at the U.S. Office of Education Symposium on Operations Analysis of Education, November, 1967. ED 025 853.

Krathwohl, David R., Benjamin S. Bloom, and Bertram B. Masia. Taxonomy of Educational Objectives: The Classification of Educational Goals. Handbook II: Affective Domain. 2d. ed. New York: David McKay Co., 1966.

Kroybill, Edward K. "Evolution of Quality Teaching Programs in Engineering," The Journal of Engineering Education, 58:123, October, 1967. (ED 023 314)

Kuhn, Alfred. The Study of Society: A Unified Approach. Homewood, Illinois: Dorsey Press, 1963.

Lange, Carl J. Developing Programs for Teachers. Professional Paper 20-69. Alexandria, Virginia: Human Resources Research Office, George Washington University, 1969. [ED 033 902]

Leonard, George B. Education and Ecstasy. New York: Delacorte Press, 1968.

Lyman, Helen. The Library Materials Project. Library School Project 348. Madison: Library School, University of Wisconsin, 1969. (Mimeographed)

Mager, Robert F. Preparing Instructional Objectives. Palo Alto, California: Fearon Publishers, Inc., 1962.

BIBLIOGRAPHY

Melching, William H., and others. Deriving, Specifying and Using Instructional Objectives. Professional Paper 10-66. Alexandria, Virginia: The Human Resources Research Office, The George Washington University, 1966.

Moore, Edythe. "Systems Analysis: An Overview," Special Libraries, 58:87-90, February, 1967.

Mueller, Robert. The Science of Art: An Illustrated Study of Creative Cybernetics. New York: The John Day Company, Inc., 1968.

National Education Association. Committee on Educational Finance. Planning for Educational Development in a Planning, Programming, Budgeting System. Washington, D.C.: The National Education Association, 1968.

National Institutes for Mental Health. Training Methodology. Part I: Background Theory and Research. Part II: Planning and Administration. Part III: Instructional Methods and Techniques. Part IV: Audiovisual Theory, Aids, and Equipment. Public Health Service Publication 1862. Washington, D.C.: Government Printing Office, 1969.

New Jersey State Council for Environmental Education and New Jersey Outdoor Education Association. New Jersey Environmental and Outdoor Education Projects. Trenton : New Jersey State Department of Education, 1969.

Ofiesh, Gabriel D. Dial Access Information Retrieval Systems: Guidelines Handbook for Educators. Final Report. Washington, D.C.: The Catholic University of America, July, 1968.

_____. Educational Technology: Past, Present, and Prospects. (In process)

_____. "The New Education and the Learning Industry," Educational Leadership, 26:760-763, May, 1969.

Oklahoma State University. Educational Planning for an Emerging Occupation: A Summary Report of a Research Project in Electromechanical Technology. Stillwater, Okla.:Oklahoma State University, 1966. ED 023 812.

O'Toole, John F., Jr. "Systems Analysis: A Rational Approach to Decision-Making in Education," SDC Magazine, 8:1-16, July, 1965.

Paulson, Casper F., Jr. An Examination of the Structure and Effectiveness of Slide-Tapes Produced by Rational Analysis and Self-Sequencing Techniques. Final Report, Office of Education Project No. 5-0952. Monmouth, Oregon: Teaching Research Division, Oregon State System of Higher Education, 1967.

BIBLIOGRAPHY

Payne, John G. "Videotape Recording for Management Training: A Report from Western Electric on How to Use Television," Training and Development Journal, 21:18-25, April, 1967.

Perlberg, Arye, and David C. O'Bryan. The Use of Video-Tape Recording and Micro-Teaching Techniques to Improve Instruction on the Higher Education Level. Urbana, Illinois: University of Illinois, 1968. ED 023 314.

Pfeiffer, John. New Look at Education: Systems Analysis in Our Schools and Colleges. Poughkeepsie, New York: Odyssey Press, 1968.

Piele, Philip. Planning Systems in Education. Eugene, Oregon: Oregon University, 1969. ED 025 855.

Pletsch, Douglas H. Communication Concepts for Adult Educators: Paper presented at the National Seminar on Adult Education Research at Toronto, Canada, February 9-11, 1969. ED 025 727.

Polya, George. How to Solve It. Garden City, N.Y.: Doubleday, 1957.

Pomeroy, E. C. "Introduction." In: W. Schueler, and others (eds.). Teacher Education and the New Media. Washington, D.C.: American Association of Colleges for Teacher Education, 1967. (ED 023 314)

Poorman, Lawrence E. "A Comparative Study of the Effectiveness of a Multi-Media Systems Approach to Harvard Project Physics with Traditional Approaches to Harvard Project Physics." Unpublished dissertation, Indiana University, Bloomington, 1967.

Porter, Elias H. Manpower Development: A System Training Concept. New York: Harper & Row, Publishers, 1964.

Preparation of Educational Planners for California (PEP). Symposium on the Application of System Analysis and Management Techniques to Educational Planning in California. Orange, California: Chapman College, 1967. (ED 023 181)

Reisman, Arnold, ed. Engineering: A Look Inward and a Reach Outward. Proceedings of the Symposium. Milwaukee: University of Wisconsin, 1967.

Ripley, Kathryn J. PERT as a Management Tool for Educators. Columbus : Ohio State University, Educational Research Management Center, 1968. (ED 023 368)

Rogers, Carl R. Freedom to Learn. Columbus: Charles E. Merrill Publishing Co., 1969.

BIBLIOGRAPHY

_____. "The Facilitation of Significant Learning," In: Laurence Siegel (ed.). Instruction: Some Contemporary Viewpoints. San Francisco: Chandler Publishing Co., 1967.

Rossi, Peter H., and Bruce J. Biddle (eds.). The New Media and Education. Garden City, New York: Doubleday & Company, Inc. (Anchor), 1967.

Ryans, David G. "A Model of Instruction Based on Information System Concepts," In: Curriculum Research Institute. Theories of Instruction. Washington, D.C.: Association for Supervision and Curriculum Development, 1965.

Schalock, H. Del. Appendix A. - A First Approximation to a Taxonomy of Learner Outcome. Portland, Oregon: Northwest Regional Educational Laboratory, 1968. (ED 026 306)

_____. A Competency Based Field Centered Systems Approach to Elementary Teacher Education: Overview and Specifications. Vol. 1. Final Report. Washington, D.C.: Office of Education, 1968. (ED 026 305)

Scheueler, H., C. S. Lesser, and A. L. Bobbins. Teacher Education and the New Media. Washington, D.C.: American Association of Colleges for Teacher Education, 1967. (ED 023 314)

Schramm, Wilbur. "Instructional Television: Promise and Opportunity," Monographic Service, 4:1-23, January, 1967. (ED 019 848)

Seiler, John A. Systems Analysis in Organizational Behavior. Homewood, Illinois: Richard D. Irwin, Inc., 1967.

Shaw, Malcolm. "Television in Management Development: Pros and Cons of a Rapidly Growing Training Method," Training and Development Journal, 21:2-8, February, 1967.

Siebert, Fred S. An Analysis of University Policy Statements on Instructional Recordings and Their Re-Use. Stanford: ERIC Clearinghouse at Stanford University, 1968. (ED 023 310)

Siegel, Laurence. "Integration and Reactions," In: Laurence Siegel (ed.). Instruction: Some Contemporary Viewpoints. San Francisco, Chandler Publishing Co., 1967.

Sizemore, Glen. An Investigation of the Effects of Pre-Set, Post-Set and No-Set on the Amount of Factual Knowledge Retained from Viewing an Educational Film. Tahlequah, Oklahoma: Division of Education and Psychology, Northeastern State College, 1967.

Slavens, Thomas P. "Films for Teaching," Journal of Education for Librarianship, 9:149-151, Fall, 1968.

BIBLIOGRAPHY

Smietana, Walter. <u>Training Elementary and Secondary Student Teachers to Utilize Technology: A Feasibility Study.</u> Final Report. Elmhurst, Illinois: Elmhurst College, 1969.

Smith, Robert G., Jr. <u>The Design of Instructional Systems.</u> Technical Report 66-18. Alexandria, Virginia: Human Resources Research Office, George Washington University, 1966.

_____. <u>The Development of Training Objectives.</u> Alexandria, Virginia: Human Resources Research Office, George Washington University, 1964.

Snow, Richard E., and Gabriel Salomon. <u>Aptitudes and Instruction Media.</u> Technical Report No. 3. Stanford : Stanford University, 1968. (ED 023 295)

Society for General Systems Research. <u>Yearbook of the Society for General Systems Research.</u> Washington, D.C.: The Society for General Systems Research, [n.d.].

Southern Methodist University Institute of Technology. <u>Talkback Television at the SMU Institute of Technology.</u> A brochure published by the SMU Institute of Technology, 1968.

Spurr, Stephen H. "New Degrees for College Teachers." In: <u>Current Issues in Higher Education, 1967: In Search of Leaders.</u> Washington, D.C.: American Association for Higher Education, 1967. ED 020 200.

Stevens, Rolland E. "Instruction on Microforms: Its Place in the Library School," <u>Journal of Education for Librarianship,</u> 6(2): 133-136, Fall, 1965.

Stock, Gary, and George Cranford. <u>Attitudes toward Educational Television.</u> Project Report No. 4. Plattsburgh, New York: Office of Institutional Research, State University College, 1967.

Stolurow, Lawrence M. <u>Some Educational Problems and Prospects of a Systems Approach to Instruction.</u> Technical Report No. 2. Urbana, Ill.: Training Research Laboratory, University of Illinois, 1964.

"The Systems Approach," <u>Audiovisual Instruction</u>, 10, May, 1965.

Thornton, James W., Jr., and James W. Brown. <u>New Media and College Teaching.</u> Washington, D.C.: National Education Association, 1968.

Totten, Herman L. "An Analysis and Evaluation of the Use of Educational Media in the Teaching of Library Science in Accredited American Graduate Library Schools." Unpublished Doctor's dissertation, University of Oklahoma, Norman, 1966.

BIBLIOGRAPHY

Trow, William C. Teacher and Technology: New Designs for Learning. New York: Appleton-Century-Crofts, 1963.

U. S. Department of Agriculture Graduate Schools. Faculty Handbook, Part II: Improving Teaching. Washington, D. C.: U. S. Department of Agriculture Graduate Schools, 1967. ED 024 854.

U. S. Department of Health, Education and Welfare. Research and Development: Advances in Education. Washington, D. C.: U. S. Government Printing Office, 1968.

University of Pittsburgh. Graduate School of Library and Information Sciences. The Professional Education of Media Service Personnel: Recommendations for Training Media Service Personnel for Schools and Colleges. Preliminary edition. Pittsburgh: University of Pittsburgh, 1964.

Verdium, John R. Conceptual Models in Teacher Education. Washington, D.C.: The American Association of Colleges of Teacher Education, 1967. ED 023 314.

Walruth, Donald C. "A Systems Approach to the Training Program," Training in Business and Industry, 2(1):22-24, January-February, 1965.

Wasserman, Paul, "Toward a Methodology for the Formulation of Objectives in Public Libraries: An Empirical Analysis." Unpublished Doctor's dissertation, University of Michigan, Ann Arbor, 1961.

Welch, Wayne W. Harvard Project Physics Research and Evaluation Bibliography. Cambridge, Mass.: Harvard Project Physics. Harvard University, 1968. ED 025 424.

Williams, Gareth L. "Towards a National Educational Planning Model." Paper prepared for the Symposium on Operations Analysis of Education, National Center for Educational Statistics, U. S. Office of Education, Washington, D.C., November 19-22, 1967. ED 021 311.

BIBLIOGRAPHY

FEDERAL LIBRARIES:
GENERAL REFERENCE SOURCES FOR PROJECT

Aines, Andrew A. "The Promise of National Information Systems," Library Trends, 16:410-418, January, 1968.

American Library Association. Library Education Division. Financial Assistance for Library Education: Academic Year 1969-70. Chicago: American Library Association, 1968.

Ash, Lee, ed. Who's Who in Library Service: A Biographical Directory of Professional Librarians in the United States and Canada. 4th ed. New York: Shoe String Press, 1966.

Cuadra, Carlos A., ed. Annual Review of Information Science and Technology, Vols. 1-4. Chicago: Encyclopaedia Britannica, 1966-1969.

Evans, Luther H., and others. Federal Departmental Libraries. Washington, D.C.: Brookings Institution, 1963.

Federal Council for Science and Technology. Committee on Scientific and Technical Information. Directory of Federally Supported Information Analysis Centers. Springfield, Va.: Clearinghouse, U.S. Department of Commerce, 1968.

Federal Library Committee. Newsletter, Vol. 1- , 1965- Washington, D.C.: Federal Library Committee.

_____. The Federal Library Mission: A Statement of Principles and Guidelines. Washington, D.C.: The Federal Library Committee, 1966.

_____. Roster of Federal Libraries by Agency. Washington, D.C.: U.S. Library of Congress, 1968. (Mimeographed)

_____. Roster of Federal Libraries: Alphabetically by State and City. Washington, D.C.: U.S. Library of Congress, 1967. (Mimeographed)

_____. Task Force on Automation. Summary Reconnaissance Paper on Trends Toward Library Automation

Based on an Initial Analysis of the Literature. Prepared by the Staff of the Technical Information Exchange of the Center for Computer Sciences and Technology, National Bureau of Standards. Washington, D.C.: Federal Library Committee, 1968. (Multilithed)

Herner, Saul. A Brief Guide to Sources of Scientific and Technical Information. Washington, D.C.: Information Resources Press, 1969.

Howard, Paul. "The Federal Library Committee: Progress and Prospects," DC Libraries, 40(1):12-16, Winter, 1969.

Klempner, Irving M. National Documentation Center Abstracting and Indexing Services and the Diffusion of Results from Government-Sponsored Research. New York: Scarecrow Press, 1968.

Knight, Douglas M. and E. Shepley Nourse, eds. Libraries at Large: Tradition, Innovation, and the National Interest. New York: R. R. Bowker Co., 1969.

Knight, Douglas M. Library Services for the Nation's Needs, Toward Fulfillment of a National Policy. Report of the National Advisory Commission on Libraries. Final Report. Washington, D.C.: U. S. Office of Education, 1968. ED 020 446.

Kruzas, Anthony T., ed. Directory of Special Libraries and Information Centers. Detroit, Michigan: Gale Research Co., 1963.

Leach, Richard H. "A Broad Look at the Federal Government and Libraries." In: D. M. Knight and E. S. Nourse, eds. Libraries at Large. New York: R. R. Bowker Co., 1969, pp. 346-398.

Machlup, Fritz. The Production and Distribution of Knowledge in the United States. Princeton, New Jersey: Princeton University Press, 1962.

National Science Foundation. Federal Funds for Research, Development, and Other Scientific Activities. Washington, D.C.: U. S. Government Printing Office, 1966.

_____. Nonconventional Scientific and Technical Information Systems in Current Use. NSF 66-24, No. 4. Washington, D.C.: U. S. Government Printing Office, 1966.

BIBLIOGRAPHY

Nimer, Gilda. "Professions and Professionalism: A Bibliographic Overview." In: <u>Newsletter.</u> University of Maryland, Manpower Research Project. Issue No. 2. July, 1968.

Nourse, E. Shepley. "Areas of Inadequacy in Serving Multiple Needs." In: D. M. Knight, and E. S. Nourse (eds.) <u>Libraries at Large: Tradition, Innovation and the National Interest.</u> New York: R. R. Bowker, 1969, pp. 161-167.

Painter, Ann F. <u>The Role of the Library in Relation to Other Information Activities: A State-of-the-Art Review.</u> TISA Project Report No. 23. Washington, D.C.: U.S. Department of the Army, 1968.

Schick, Frank L. <u>Survey of Special Libraries Serving the Federal Government.</u> Washington, D.C.: National Center for Educational Statistics, U. S. Department of Health, Education and Welfare, 1968.

Simpson, G. S., Jr. "Scientific Information Centers in the United States," <u>American Documentation,</u> 13:43-57, January, 1962.

Strauss, Lucille J., and others. <u>Scientific and Technical Libraries.</u> New York: Interscience Publishers, 1964.

U. S. Atomic Energy Commission. <u>Directory of USAEC Specialized Information and Data Centers.</u> Oak Ridge, Tennessee, U.S. Atomic Energy Commission, 1967.

U.S. Library of Congress. <u>Library and Reference Facilities in the Area of the District of Columbia.</u> Washington, D.C.: Government Printing Office, 1966.

U.S. Office of Education. <u>Financial Aid for Higher Education.</u> Washington, D.C.: Government Printing Office, 1968.

U.S. President's Science Advisory Committee. <u>Science, Government and Information: The Responsibilities of the Technical Community and the Government in the Transfer of Information.</u> Washington, D.C.: Government Printing Office, 1963.

University of Minnesota. ERIC Clearinghouse for Library and Information Sciences. <u>Library Surveys and Development Plans: An Annotated Bibliography.</u> Bibliography Series No. 3. Minneapolis: ERIC Clearinghouse for Library and Information Sciences, University of Minnesota, 1969.

BIBLIOGRAPHY

INNOVATION AND CHANGE

Belasco, James A. "Training as a Change Agent: A Constructive Evaluation." Unpublished Doctor's dissertation, Cornell University, Ithaca, 1967. ED 024 888.

Bickert, Roderick. Selected Organizational Values and Characteristics of Innovative and Non-Innovative School Systems. Iowa City: Iowa University, 1968. ED 019 745.

Butts, David P. and Chester E. Raun. A Study in Teacher Attitude Change. Austin, Texas: Science Education Center, The University of Texas, 1967. ED 021 806.

Caven, William J. "Designing a Set of Guidelines for Dynamic Planned Change." In: Operation PEP Symposium on the Application of Systems Analysis Management Techniques to Educational Planning in California. Washington, D.C.: U. S. Office of Education, 1967, pp. 198-207.

Coleman, James, E. Katz and H. Menzel. "The Diffusion of an Innovation Among Physicians," Sociometry, 20:253-270, December, 1957.

Estes, Nolan. "The Need for Programs of Planned Change in Education." In: Operation PEP Symposium on the Application of Systems Analysis Management Techniques to Educational Planning in California. Washington, D.C.: U. S. Office of Education, 1967. pp. 1-10.

Evans, Richard K. and K. Leppman. Resistance to Innovation in Higher Education. San Francisco: Jossey-Bass, Inc., 1967.

Kurland, Norman D. and Richard I. Miller, comps. Selected and Annotated Bibliography on the Processes of Change. New York: New York State Education Department, 1966. ED 023 025.

Lionberger, Herbert F. Adoption of New Ideas and Practices. Ames, Iowa: The Iowa State University Press, 1960.

Lippitt, J. Watson and B. Westley. The Dynamics of Planned Change. New York: Harcourt-Brace, 1958.

BIBLIOGRAPHY

Lorenz, John G. "The Challenge of Change," *PNLA Quarterly*, 29:7-15, October, 1964.

Marcum, R. Laverne. *Organizational Climate and the Adoption of Educational Innovation*. Logan, Utah: Utah State University, 1968. ED 023 158.

Martin, Warren B. *The Development of Innovation: Making Reality Change*. Berkeley, California: Center for Research and Development in Higher Education, University of California, 1968. ED 026 004.

Miller, Richard. "The Role of Educational Leadership in Implementing Educational Change." In: *Operation PEP Symposium on the Application of Systems Analysis and Management Techniques to Educational Planning in California*. Washington, D.C.: U.S. Office of Education, 1967, pp. 32-41.

Moore, Leo B. "How to Manage Improvement," *Harvard Business Review*, 36(4):75-84, July-August, 1958.

Rogers, Everett M. "Developing a Strategy for Planned Change." In: *Operation PEP Symposium on the Application of Systems Analysis and Management Techniques to Educational Planning in California*. Washington, D.C.: U.S. Office of Education, 1967.

Schwab, Bernard, comp. *Libraries in Transition: Responses to Change*. Madison: Wisconsin Library Association, 1968. ED 023 440.

Shuck, Lester E. "Planning for Policy Development." In: *Operation PEP Symposium on the Application of Systems Analysis and Management Techniques to Educational Planning in California*. Washington, D.C.: U.S. Office of Education, 1967, pp. 88-99.

Stuart, Michael and Charles Dudley. *Bibliography on Organization and Innovation*. Eugene, Oregon: University of Oregon, 1967. ED 019 722.

Trump, J. Lloyd. "Basic Changes Needed to Serve Individuals Better," *Educational Forum*, 26:93-101, November, 1961.

Venn, Grant. "Educational Implications of Technological Change." A report to the Annual Convention of the Department of Rural Education, Detroit, Michigan, October 6-9, 1963. ED 020 060.

BIBLIOGRAPHY

INTERVIEWING TECHNIQUES

American Psychological Association. *The American Psychological Association's Project on Scientific Information Exchange in Psychology.* Vol. 2. Washington, D.C.: American Psychological Association, 1965.

Anderson, R.C. "Guided Interview as an Evaluative Instrument," *Journal of Educational Research*, 48:203-209, November, 1954.

Argyris, Chris. *Understanding Organization Behavior.* Homewood, Illinois: Dorsey Press, 1960.

Arnold, Joseph P. *A Study of Recommendations for Technical Educational Curricula.* Final Report. West Lafayette, Indiana: Purdue University, 1965. ED 016 064.

Becker, H.S. "A Note on Interviewing Tactics," *Human Organization,* 13 :31-32, 1954.

Bingham, W.V.D. and others. *How to Interview.* 4th rev. ed. New York: Harper & Bros., 1959.

Bunge, Charles A. *Professional Education and Reference Efficiency.* Research Series No. 11. Urbana: Library Research Center, University of Illinois, 1967. ED 019 097

Cannell, Charles F., and Morris Axelrod. "The Respondents Reports on the Interview," *American Journal of Sociology,* 62:177-181, September, 1956.

Cannell, Charles F., and R.L. Kahn. "The Collection of Data by Interviewing." In: L. Festinger and D. Katz (eds.). *Research Methods in the Behavioral Sciences.* New York: Dryden Press, 1953, pp. 327-380.

Corson, John J., and R. Shale Paul. *Men Near the Top: Filling Key Posts in the Federal Service.* Baltimore: The Johns Hopkins Press, 1966.

Dohrenwend, Barbara Snell, and Stephen A. Richardson. "A Use of Leading Questions in Research Interviewing," *Human Organization,* 23(:76-77, Spring, 1964.

Fisher, Waldo E. *The Interview--A Multi-Purpose Leadership Tool.* Circular No. 34. Pasadena, Calif.: California Institute of Technology, 1966.

Froehlich, Clifford P. and John G. Darley. *Studying Students.* Chicago: Science Research Associates, Inc., 1952.

BIBLIOGRAPHY

Gergen, Kenneth J. and Kurt W. Back. "Communication in the Interview and the Disengaged Respondent," *Public Opinion Quarterly*, 30(3):385-398, Fall, 1966.

Gibson, Frank K. and Brett W. Hawkins. "Research Note: Interviews Versus Questionnaires," *American Behavioral Scientist*, 12(1): NS9-NS16, September-October, 1968.

Haberman, Paul W. and Jill Sheinberg. "Education Reported in Interviews: An Aspect of Survey Content Error," *Public Opinion Quarterly*, 30(2):295-301, Summer, 1966.

Hall, Anna C. *Selected Educational Objectives for Public Service Librarians: A Taxonomic Approach.* Pittsburgh: University of Pittsburgh, 1968.

Hyman, Herbert H. *Interviewing in Social Research.* Chicago, Ill.: University of Chicago Press, 1954.

Jackson, Robert M. and J. W. M. Rothney. "A Comparative Study of the Mailed Questionnaire and the Interview in Follow-Up Studies," *Personnel and Guidance Journal*, 569-571, March, 1961.

Kahn, Robert L. and Charles F. Cannell. *The Dynamics of Interviewing: Theory, Technique and Cases.* New York: Wiley, 1958.

Kornhauser, A. and P. B. Sheatsley. "Questionnaire Construction and Interview Procedure." In: C. Selltiz, and others, eds. *Research Methods in Social Relations.* New York: Holt, 1959, pp. 574-587.

Lazarsfeld, P. F. "The Controversy Over Detailed Interviews--An Offer for Negotiation," *Public Opinion Quarterly*, 8:39-60, 1944.

Levin, H. "Influence of Fullness of Interview on the Reliability, Discriminability, and Validity of Interview Judgments," *Journal of Consulting Psychology*, 18(4):303-306, August, 1954.

Maccoby, Eleanor and N. Maccoby. "The Interview: A Tool of Social Science." In: G. Lindzey, ed., *Handbook of Social Psychology.* Cambridge, Mass.: Addison-Wesley, 1954, pp. 448-487.

McDonagh, Edward D., and A. Leon Rosenblum. "A Comparison of Mailed Questionnaires and Subsequent Structured Interviews," *Public Opinion Quarterly*, 29(1):131-136, Spring, 1965.

Morrison, Denton E. "A Boxing System for Interview Schedules," *American Sociological Review*, 23:83-84, February, 1958.

Parker, Clyde A., E. Wayne Wright, and Selby G. Clark. "Questions Concerning the Interview as a Research Technique," *Journal of Educational Research*, 51:215-221, November, 1957.

BIBLIOGRAPHY

Richardson, Stephen A., Barbara S. Dohrenwend, and David Klein. <u>Interviewing: Its Forms and Functions.</u> New York: Basic Books, 1965.

Roethlisberger, F. J., and W. J. Dickson. <u>Management and the Worker.</u> Cambridge: Harvard University Press, 1941, pp. 189-191.

Rogers, Carl B. <u>Counseling and Psychotherapy.</u> Boston: Houghton Mifflin, 1942.

_____. "The Non-Directive Method as a Technique for Social Research," <u>American Journal of Sociology,</u> 50:179-181, 1945.

Schill, William J. and Joseph P. Arnold. <u>Curricula Content in Six Technologies.</u> Report of the Bureau of Educational Research and the Department of Vocational and Technical Education, College of Education, University of Illinois. Urbana, Ill.: University of Illinois, 1965.

Schuman, Howard. "The Random Probe: A Technique of Evaluating the Validity of Closed Questions," <u>American Sociological Review,</u> 31(2):218-222, April, 1966.

Slocum, W. L., L. T. Empey, and H. S. Swanson. "Increasing Response to Questionnaires and Structured Interviews," <u>American Sociological Review</u>, 21:221-225, 1956.

Smith, Robert G., Jr. <u>The Development of Training Objectives.</u> Alexandria, Virginia: The Human Resources Research Office, George Washington University, June, 1964.

Vaughn, Charles L. and William A. Reynolds. "Reliability of Personal Interview Data," <u>Journal of Applied Psychology,</u> 35:61-63, February, 1951.

Webb, Eugene J. <u>Unobtrusive Measures: Nonreactive Research in the Social Sciences.</u> Chicago, Ill.: Rand McNally, 1966.

BIBLIOGRAPHY

LEARNING: A PROCESS OF CHANGE

Abbatiello, Aurelius A. "An Objective Evaluation of Attitude Change in Training, a Before and After Study of Twelve Stimuli in a Supervisory Program," Training and Development Journal, 21:23-24, November, 1967.

Air University. Academic Instructor and Allied Officer School. AIAOS Additions to Principles and Techniques of Instruction. Maxwell Air Force Base, Alabama: Air University, 1967. ED 024 876.

Anderson, Richard C., and others, eds. Current Research on Instruction. Englewood Cliffs, New Jersey: Prentice-Hall, 1969.

Demak, Leonard S., coordinator. Behavior Modification, New Ideas in Michigan Education. Detroit, Michigan: Statewide Dissemination Service, 1969.

Dworkin, Leo, coordinator. Learning Disabilities Reconsidered. A Report of the Wayne County Committee for the Study of Children with Learning Disabilities, 1967-69. Detroit, Michigan: Consortium of Advanced Educational Thinking, 1969.

Eastern Regional Institute for Education. Improving Process-Oriented Education. Syracuse, N. Y.: Eastern Regional Institute for Education, n.d.

Gagne, Robert M. The Conditions of Learning. New York: Holt, Rinehart and Winston, 1965.

_____. "A System Approach to Adult Learning." In: K. W. Wientge and others, eds. Psychological Research in Classroom Learning. St. Louis, Mo.: Washington University, 1967, pp. 6-21.

Gagne, Robert M. and R. C. Bolles. "A Review of Factors in Learning Efficiency." In: E. Galanter, ed. Automated Teaching. New New York: Wiley, 1959.

Hilgard, E. R. Theories of Learning. 2d. ed. New York: Appleton-Century-Crofts, 1956.

"How to Enhance Individuality in Learning," The Report of an International Seminar sponsored by The National Association of

Secondary School Principals and The Institute for Development of Educational Activities (I/D/E/A/). Melbourne, Florida: Informational Services Division, IDEA, 1968.

Kase, Donald H. "Developing a Need Assessment Program," In: Operation PEP Symposium on the Application of Systems Analysis and Management Techniques to Educational Planning in California. Washington, D.C.: U. S. Office of Education, 1967.

Kingsley, H. L. and R. Garry. The Nature and Conditions of Learning. 2d. ed. Englewood Cliffs, N. J.: Prentice-Hall, 1957.

Lewin, Kurt. "Field Theory and Learning." In: National Society for the Study of Education. The Psychology of Learning. 41st Yearbook, Part II. Chicago: University of Chicago Press, 1942, pp. 215-242.

McGeoch, J. S. and A. L. Irion. The Psychology of Human Learning. 2d. ed. New York: Longmans, 1952.

McKeachie, Wilbert N. The Learning Process as Applied to Short-Term Learning Situations. Conference proceedings, National University Extension Association, Purdue University, Lafayette, April 23-27, 1965. ED 019 532.

Mager, Robert F. Developing Attitude Toward Learning. Palo Alto, Calif.: Fearon Publishers, 1968.

_____. Preparing Instructional Objectives. Palo Alto, Calif.: Fearon Publishers, 1962.

National Education Association. National Association for Public School Adult Education. When You're Teaching Adults. Washington, D. C.: National Education Association, 1959.

Osborn, Alex F. Applied Imagination. New York: Scribner's, 1953.

Schrock, Robert W. "A Clearinghouse for Creativity," Ohio School Boards Association Journal, 12:2, February, 1968. ED 020 037.

Snow, Richard E. and Gabriel Salomon. Aptitudes and Instructional Media, Project on Individual Differences in Learning Ability as a Function of Instructional Variables. Technical Report No. 3. Stanford, Calif.: Stanford University, 1968. ED 023 295.

BIBLIOGRAPHY

Taft, Martin I. "Design for Education: A Systems Approach." In: J. A. Reisman, ed. Engineering: A Look Inward and a Reach Outward. Madison: University of Wisconsin, 1967, pp. 41-60.

Tough, Allen M. Why Adults Learn, a Study of the Major Reasons for Beginning and Continuing a Learning Project. Toronto, Canada: Ontario Institute for Studies in Education, 1968. ED 025 688.

Trow, William C. Teacher and Technology: New Designs for Learning. New York: Appleton-Century-Crofts, 1963.

U. S. Department of Health, Education and Welfare. Research and Development: Advances in Education. Washington, D.C.: U. S. Government Printing Office, 1968.

Watson, Eugene R. "Interpersonal Changes Through Immediate Feedback Approaches," Adult Education Journal, 19:251-267, Summer, 1969.

Wientge, King M., Philip H. DuBois, and Harry Gaffney, eds. Psychological Research in Classroom Learning. St. Louis, Mo.: School of Continuing Education, Washington University, 1967. ED 017 793.

Zahn, Jane. "Some Adult Attitudes Affecting Learning: Powerlessness, Conflicting Needs and Role Transition," Adult Education Journal, 19(2):91-97, 1969.

BIBLIOGRAPHY

MANPOWER

American Library Association. <u>National Inventory of Library Needs.</u>
Chicago: American Library Association, 1965.

Asheim, Lester, ed. <u>Library Manpower Needs and Utilization.</u>
Chicago: American Library Association, 1967. ED 027 903.

Asheim, Lester. "Manpower: A Call for Action," <u>Library Journal</u>,
92:1795-1797, May, 1967.

Auerbach Corporation. <u>A Study of Manpower Requirements for Technical Information Support Personnel.</u> Study for Office of Manpower, Automation and Training, U. S. Department of Labor. Philadelphia, Pa.: Auerbach Corporation, 1964.

Battelle Memorial Institute. <u>A Survey of Science-Information Manpower in Engineering and the Natural Sciences.</u> Final Report. Columbus, Ohio: Battelle Memorial Institute, 1966.

Bernard, Jessie S. <u>Academic Women.</u> University Park, Pa.: Pennsylvania State University Press, 1964.

Boaz, Martha. "More Than Deliberate Speed," <u>ALA Bulletin</u>, 60: 286-288, March, 1966.

Boelke, Joanne. <u>Library Technicians--A Survey of Current Developments.</u> Review Series No. 1. Minneapolis: ERIC Clearinghouse for Library and Information Science, University of Minnesota, 1968.

Bolino, August C. "Trends in Library Manpower," <u>Wilson Library Bulletin,</u> 43(3):269-278, November, 1968.

Case, Robert N. <u>School Library Manpower Project</u>. Chicago: American Library Association, 1968- (In progress)

Drennan, Henry T. and R. L. Darling. <u>Library Manpower: Occupational Characteristics of Public and School Librarians.</u> Washington, D.C.: U. S. Government Printing Office, 1966. Also ED 017 299.

Drennan, Henry, and Sarah Reed. "Library Manpower," <u>ALA Bulletin,</u> 67:958-960, September, 1967.

Duchac, Kenneth F. "Manpower: A Proposal," <u>Library Journal,</u> 92:1797-1798, May, 1967.

Edwards, A. P. J. "National Survey of Staff Employed on Scientific and Technical Information Work," <u>Journal of Documentation,</u> 22:210-244, September, 1966.

BIBLIOGRAPHY

Federal Council of Science and Technology. Committee on Scientific and Technical Information. <u>Recommendations for National Document Handling Systems in Science and Technology</u>, Appendix A, Vol. II, November, 1965. Springfield, Va.: Clearinghouse, U. S. Dept. of Commerce.

Finkler, Norman. "Maryland's Manpower Shortage," <u>Library Journal</u>, 93:3745-3746, October, 1968.

Frarey, Carlyle. "Placement," <u>Drexel Library Quarterly</u>, 3:167-175, April, 1967.

Gaver, Mary V. "Masters of the Raging Book?" <u>ALA Bulletin</u>, 60: 794-799, 802-805, September, 1966.

Ginzberg, Eli, and Carol A. Brown. <u>Manpower for Library Services</u>. New York: Conservation of Human Resources Project, Columbia University, 1967. ED 023 408.

Harlow, Neal. "News of the New Founde Worlde--What's New in the Education of Librarians?" <u>Library Journal</u>, 88:2189-2193, June, 1963.

_____. "Misused Librarians," <u>Library Journal</u>, 90:1597-1599, April, 1965.

Havens, Shirley. "ALA Conference: Manpower--The Big Show," <u>Library Journal</u>, 92:2713-2719, August, 1967.

Hyslop, Carol. <u>Manpower Planning and Utilization in the Federal Government</u>. Washington, D.C.: U. S. Civil Service Commission, June, 1963.

Lester, Richard. <u>Manpower Planning in a Free Society</u>. Princeton, N. J.: Princeton University Press, 1965.

"Manpower and the Library Profession," <u>Wilson Library Bulletin</u>, 41:793-822, April, 1967.

Marshall, John. "Search for Status," <u>Library Journal</u>, 91:5556-5563, November, 1966.

"Minimum Professional Personnel and Staffing Standards for Maryland's Public Library Systems," <u>Maryland Libraries</u>, 34:7-12, Summer, 1968; <u>Library Journal</u>, 93:3747-3749, October, 1968.

National Advisory Council on Education Professions Development. <u>Second Annual Report</u>. Washington, D.C.: National Advisory Council on Education Professions Development, 1969.

BIBLIOGRAPHY

National Education Association. National Commission on Teacher Education and Professional Standards. <u>What We Need to Know About Educational Manpower: Research Priorities and Implications.</u> Washington, D.C.: U. S. Department of Health, Education and Welfare, 1968. ED 013 778.

National Education Association. Research Division. "School Library Personnel, Task Analysis Survey," <u>American Libraries,</u> 1(2): 176-177, February, 1970.

National Manpower Council. <u>Manpower Policies for a Democratic Society.</u> New York: Columbia University Press, 1965.

Reed, Mary M. "A Pilot Program on Occupational Trends and Career Planning," <u>ALA Bulletin,</u> 59:1006-1009, December, 1965.

Reed, Sarah R. "Library Manpower--Realism, Relevancy, and Requirements," <u>Journal of Education for Librarianship,</u> 7:43-47, Summer, 1966.

Schick, Frank L. "Manpower Shortage and Library Education," <u>Journal of Education for Librarianship,</u> 3(1):37-40, Summer, 1962.

_____. "Professional Library Manpower," <u>ALA Bulletin,</u> 58:315, 317, April, 1964.

Shera, Jesse H. "The Propaedeutic of the New Librarianship." In: Wesley Simonton, ed. University of Minnesota Center for Continuation Study. <u>Information Retrieval Today.</u> Minneapolis, Minnesota: University of Minnesota, 1963.

Simpson, Martha. "Placement Systems in Library Schools," <u>Journal of Education for Librarianship,</u> 1(4):217-220, Spring, 1961.

Taylor, Nettie B. "The Professional Personnel and Staffing Standards Report--A Constructive Dissent," <u>Maryland Libraries,</u> 34:13-15, Summer, 1968; <u>Library Journal,</u> 93:3750-3751, October, 1968.

Totaro, Joseph V., ed. <u>Women in College and University Teaching: A Symposium on Staff Needs and Opportunities in Higher Education.</u> Madison: University of Wisconsin, School of Education, 1965.

U. S. Civil Service Commission. Bureau of Manpower Information Systems. <u>Occupations of Federal White-Collar Workers.</u> Pamphlet SM 56-7, Washington, D.C.: U. S. Civil Service Commission, 1967.

U.S. Department of Labor. <u>Manpower Report of the President, and A Report on Manpower Requirements, Resources--Utilization, and Training by the U. S. Department of Labor.</u> Washington, D. C.: U. S. Government Printing Office, 1968.

481

BIBLIOGRAPHY

U. S. Department of Labor. Library. Manpower Projections: Selected References. Washington, D.C.: U. S. Department of Labor, November, 1966, updated through April, 1967. (Mimeographed)

U. S. Women's Bureau. 1965 Handbook on Women Workers. Bulletin No. 290. Washington, D.C.: U. S. Women's Bureau, 1965.

University of Wisconsin. Library School. Professional Librarians: An Inventory of Personnel and Personnel Needs in Wisconsin in College, University, School, Public and Special Libraries. Madison: University of Wisconsin Library School, 1965.

Ward, Patricia L. Women and Librarianship. London: The Library Association, 1966.

Warncke, Ruth. "Careers in Librarianship," ALA Bulletin, 60:806-808, September, 1966.

Wasserman, Paul. "Elements in a Manpower Blueprint--Library Personnel for the 1970's," ALA Bulletin, 63:581-599, May, 1969.

Wasserman, Paul, and Mary Lee Bundy. "Manpower Blueprint," Library Journal, 92:197-200, January, 1967.

_____. "Manpower for the Library and Information Professions in the 1970's: An Inquiry into Fundamental Problems." Unpublished proposal for the U. S. Department of Labor, Office of Manpower, Automation, and Training. School of Library and Information Service, University of Maryland, College Park, 1966. (Mimeographed)

_____. A Program of Research into the Identification of Manpower Requirements, the Educational Preparation and the Utilization of Manpower in the Library and Information Professions. Final Report, Phase I. College Park: University of Maryland, 1969. ED 023 938.

Wayne State University Libraries. Survey of the Status of Academic Librarians (January, 1966). Detroit, Michigan: Wayne State University Libraries, 1966. (Mimeographed)

BIBLIOGRAPHY

PERSONAL CHARACTERISTICS

Aceto, Vincent J. *An Exploratory Study of the Occupation of Teacher of Librarianship.* Cleveland: Western Reserve University, June 1967 to June 1968. EP 010 851.

Alvarez, Robert S. "Qualifications of Heads of Libraries in Cities of over 10,000 Population in the Seven North-Central States." Unpublished Doctor's dissertation, University of Chicago, Chicago, 1939.

Arnold, Margaret J. "Library Education--What's Missing? Select the Students," *Journal of Education for Librarianship,* 5(2):92, Fall, 1964.

Ballard, Robert M. "A Job History of the Atlanta University School of Library Service Graduates, 1948-1959." Unpublished Master's thesis, School of Library Service, Atlanta University, Atlanta, 1961.

Beggs, James J. *Personality Shift in Women at a Choice Point in Middle Life.* Eugene: Oregon University, 1967. (University Microfilms #68-3968) ED 024 853.

Bergen, Daniel P. "Librarians and the Bipolarization of the Academic Enterprise," *College and Research Libraries,* 24:467-480, November, 1963.

Blankenship, W. C. "Head Librarians" How Many Men? How Many Women?" *College and Research Libraries,* 28:41-48, January, 1967.

_____. "Library School Deans: A Superficial Profile," *Journal of Education for Librarianship,* 8:20-27, Summer, 1967.

Caldwell, John. "Degrees Held by Head Librarians of Colleges and Universities," *College and Research Libraries,* 22:227-228, May, 1962.

Carlson, William H. "The Junior Librarian and the Administrator," *Journal of Education for Librarianship,* 3(3):227-235, Winter, 1963.

BIBLIOGRAPHY

Clayton, Howard. An Investigation of Personality Characteristics Among Library Students at One Midwestern University. Final Report. Brockport, N.Y.: State University of New York, 1968.

Cohan, Leonard and Kenneth Craven. Science Information Personnel: The New Profession of Information Combining Science, Librarianship, and Foreign Language. New York: Modern Language Association of America, 1960. ED 013 365.

Colley, Louise A. "Relationship of Ego Development to Re-Creation." Unpublished Doctor's dissertation, University of Wisconsin, Madison, 1965.

Danton, J. Periam, and LeRoy C. Merritt. Characteristics of the Graduates of the University of California School of Librarianship. University of Illinois Library School Occasional Paper, No. 22. Urbana: University of Illinois, 1951.

Douglass, Robert R. "The Personality of the Librarian." Unpublished Doctor's dissertation, University of Chicago, Chicago, 1957.

Dow, June B. "Characteristics of Non-Credit University Extension Students." Unpublished Doctor's dissertation, University of California, Berkeley, 1965.

Drennan, Henry T. and Richard L. Darling. Library Manpower: Occupational Characteristics of Public and School Librarians. Washington, D.C.: U. S. Government Printing Office, 1966.

Giles, Fleetwood, Jr. "Texas Librarians: A Study Based on Who's Who in Library Service, 3d ed., 1955." Unpublished Master's thesis, Graduate School, University of Texas, Austin, 1958.

Harlow, Neal. "Misused Librarians," Library Journal, 90:1597-1599, April, 1965.

_____. Personnel for Research Libraries--Qualifications, Responsibilities, and Use. New Brunswick, N.J.: Rutgers University, January 1969 to December 1969. EP 011 532.

Harmon, Glynn. "Research Problem Sensitivity: A Professional Recruitment Criterion," College and Research Libraries, 28 (6): 375-381, November, 1967.

BIBLIOGRAPHY

Harvey, John F. "The Educational Needs of Special Librarians." Unpublished paper delivered at the 5th Annual IBM Librarians' Conference, White Plains, New York, December 13, 1963.

_____. The Librarian's Career: A Study in Mobility. ACRL Microcard Series No. 85. Rochester, N. Y.: University of Rochester Press, 1957.

Korb, George M. "'Successful' Librarians as Revealed in Who's Who in America," Wilson Library Bulletin, 20:603-604, 607, April, 1946.

Kraus, Joe W. "The Qualifications of University Librarians, 1948 and 1933," College and Research Libraries, 11:66-72, January, 1950.

Leathers, Chester. "Educational Backgrounds, Professional Experience, Role Conceptions and Career Aspirations of Conference Coordinators." Unpublished Master's thesis, University of Chicago, Chicago, 1965.

Lilley, Dorothy. "Graduate Education Needed by Information Specialists and the Extent to Which it is Offered in Accredited Library Schools." Unpublished Doctor's dissertation, Columbia University, New York, 1969.

Longnecker, Henry C. "Staffing an Information Group." Unpublished paper. Philadelphia, Pennsylvania: Smith Kline and French Laboratories, 1958.

Morrison, Perry D. The Career of the Academic Librarian: A Study of the Social Origins, Educational Attainments, Vocational Experience, and Personality Characteristics of a Group of American Academic Librarians. ACRL Monograph No. 29. Chicago: American Library Association, 1968.

_____. "The Personality of the Academic Librarian," College and Research Libraries, 24:365-368, September, 1963.

Muller, Robert H. "The Research Mind in Library Education and Practice," Library Journal, 92:1126-1129, March, 1967.

Parr, Mary Y. "Whatever Happened to the Class of 1962?" College and Research Libraries, 28:208-216, May, 1967.

BIBLIOGRAPHY

Parr, Mary Y. and Marilyn Filderman. "Some Characteristics of Successful Alumni," College and Research Libraries, 27:225-226, 238-239, May, 1966.

Penland, Patrick R. "Image of Public Library Adult Education as Reflected in the Opinions of Public Library Supervisory Staff Members in the Public Libraries of Michigan Serving Population over 25,000." Unpublished Doctor's dissertation, University of Michigan, Ann Arbor, 1960.

Pollard, Frances M. "Characteristics of Negro College Chief Librarians." Unpublished Master's thesis, Western Reserve University, Cleveland, 1963.

Porter, Lyman W. and Mildred M. Henry. "Job Attitudes in Management: V. Perceptions of the Importance of Certain Personality Traits as a Function of Job Level," Journal of Applied Psychology, 48(1):31-36, February, 1964.

_____. "Job Attitudes in Management: VI. Perceptions of the Importance of Certain Personality Traits as a Function of Line Versus Staff Type of Job," Journal of Applied Psychology, 48(5):305-309, October, 1964.

Reagan, Agnes L. "A Study of Certain Factors in Institutions of Higher Education which Influence Students to Become Librarians." Unpublished Doctor's dissertation, University of Illinois, Urbana, 1957.

Reaves, Alice C. "A Study of the Graduate Students who Received Master's Degrees from the School of Library Science, University of North Carolina, 1953-1962." Unpublished Master's thesis, University of North Carolina, Chapel Hill, 1964.

Robinson, Charles W. "Library Education--What's Missing? A Realistic and Mature Selection Process," Journal of Education for Librarianship, 5(2):87-90, Fall, 1964.

Schiller, Anita R. Characteristics of Professional Personnel in College and University Libraries. Urbana, Ill.: Library Research Center, University of Illinois, 1968. ED 020 766.

Schultz, Claire. "Things They Don't Teach in Library School," Special Libraries, 54:513, October, 1963.

BIBLIOGRAPHY

Shera, Jesse H. "The Propaedeutic of the New Librarianship." In: Wesley Simonton (ed.). <u>Information Retrieval Today</u>. Minneapolis: University of Minnesota, 1963.

Shores, Louis. "The Library-College Librarian," <u>Tennessee Librarian,</u> 19:140-145, Summer, 1967.

_____. "Students," <u>Drexel Library Quarterly</u>, 3:59-64, January, 1967.

Simmons, Gloria M. "A Study of Professional Librarians in the Southwestern Region of the United States as Indicated in <u>Who's Who in Library Service, 1955."</u> Unpublished Master's thesis, School of Library Service, Atlanta University, Atlanta

Special Libraries Association, Illinois Chapter, Membership and Recruitment Committee. <u>Age Survey of Special Librarians in the Land of Lincoln.</u> Chicago: Special Libraries Association, 1965.

Stonecipher, Charles L. "Characteristics of Adults Who Utilize University Educational Activities in Columbia County, Wisconsin." Unpublished Master's thesis, University of Wisconsin, Madison, 1964.

Taylor, Gerry M. "Vocational Interests of Male Librarians in the United States." Unpublished Master's thesis, University of Texas, Austin, 1955.

Thomas, Mary Ellen. "A Study of the Graduates of the School of Library Science, University of North Carolina, 1951-1957; An Analysis of the Careers in Librarianship of Recipients of the Bachelor of Science in Library Science." Unpublished Master's thesis, School of Library Science, University of North Carolina, Chapel Hill, 1964.

BIBLIOGRAPHY

QUESTIONNAIRE:
SOURCES USED FOR FORMULATION OF INSTRUMENT

Alvarez, Robert S. "Qualifications of Heads of Libraries in Cities of over 10,000 Population in the Seven North-Central States." Unpublished Doctor's dissertation, Graduate Library School, University of Chicago, Chicago, 1939.

Andrews, Kenneth R. "Is Management Training Effective? I. Evaluation by Managers and Instructors," Harvard Business Review, 35:85-94, January-February, 1957.

_____. "Is Management Training Effective? II. Measurement, Objectives, and Policy," Harvard Business Review, 35:63-72, March-April, 1957.

_____. "Reaction to University Development Programs: As Reported by more than 6,000 Executives who went back to School," Harvard Business Review, 39:116-134, May-June, 1961.

Arnold, Joseph P. "A Study of Recommendations for Technical Education Curricula." Lafayette, Indiana: Purdue University, 1965. ED 016 064.

Barry, F. Gordon, and C. J. Coleman, Jr. "Tougher Program for Management Training," Harvard Business Review, 36:117-125, November-December, 1958.

Bloom, Benjamin S., and others. Taxonomy of Educational Objectives: The Classification of Educational Goals. Handbook I: Cognitive Domain. 10th ed. New York,: David McKay Co., 1966.

Bracken, Marilyn. Survey of Texts and Instructional Material Used in Information Science Programs. Washington, D.C.: George Washington University, 1967.

Bracken, Marilyn C. and C. W. Shilling. Education and Training of Information Specialists in the U.S.A. A Report prepared for the Biological Sciences Communication Project. Washington, D.C.: George Washington University, 1966.

_____. Survey of Practical Training in Information Science. Washington, D.C.: Biological Sciences Communication Project, George Washington University, 1967. Grant Number 1 TL LM 101-01A1.

BIBLIOGRAPHY

Bundy, Mary Lee. "Factors Influencing Public Library Use," Wilson Library Bulletin, 42:371-382, December, 1967.

Coch, L. and J. R. P. French. "Overcoming Resistance to Change," Human Relations, 1:512-532, August, 1948.

Cornell, Francis G. "Sample Surveys in Education." Review of Educational Research, 24(5):359-373, December, 1954.

Deming, W. Edwards, "On Errors in Surveys," American Sociological Review, 9:359-369, 1944.

Douglass, Robert R. "The Personality of the Librarian." Unpublished Doctor's dissertation, Graduate Library School, University of Chicago, 1957.

Eckland, Bruce K. "Effects of Prodding to Increase Mail-Back Returns," Journal of Applied Psychology, 49:165-169, June, 1965.

Edwards, Allen L. Statistical Analysis for Students in Psychology and Education. New York: Rinehart and Co., 1946.

Flanagan, John C. "Data Processing in Large-Scale Research Projects," Harvard Educational Review, 31(3):250-256, Summer, 1961.

Fryden, Floyd N. "Post-Master's Degree Programs in Some American Library Schools." Unpublished research paper, Graduate Library School, University of Chicago, Chicago, 1968.

Good, Carter V. Essentials of Educational Research: Methodology and Design. New York: Appleton-Century-Crofts, 1966.

Guilford, Jay P. Fundamental Statistics in Psychology and Education. 3d. ed. New York: McGraw-Hill, 1956.

Heberle, Rudolf. "On the Use of Questionnaires in Research: Open Letter to a Graduate Student," American Sociological Review, 16:549, 1951.

Hyman, Herbert. Survey Design and Analysis. Glencoe, Ill.: Free Press of Glencoe, 1955.

Knox, Margaret E. "For Every Reference Librarian--A Development Program," Southeastern Librarian, 11:303-310, Winter, 1961.

BIBLIOGRAPHY

Leigh, Robert D. The Public Library in the United States: The General Report of the Public Library Inquiry. New York: Columbia University Press, 1950.

Levine, Sol, and Gerald Gordon. "Maximizing Returns on Mail Questionnaires," Public Opinion Quarterly, 22:568-575, Winter, 1958-1959.

Maxwell, Albert E. Analyzing Qualitative Data. New York: Wiley, 1961.

Morrison, Perry D. The Career of the Academic Librarian: A Study of the Social Origins, Educational Attainments, Vocational Experience, and Personality Characteristics of a Group of American Academic Librarians. ACRL Monograph No. 29. Chicago: American Library Association, 1969.

Oppenheim, A. N. Questionnaire Design and Attitude Measurement. New York: Basic Books, Inc., 1966.

Professional Librarians: An Inventory of Personnel and Personnel Needs in Wisconsin in College, University, School, Public and Special Libraries. Madison: University of Wisconsin Library School, 1965.

Reagan, Agnes L. "A Study of Certain Factors in Institutions of Higher Education which Influence Students to Become Librarians." Unpublished Doctor's dissertation, University of Illinois, Urbana, 1957.

Reece, Ernest. The Task and Training of Librarians : Report of a Field Investigation. New York: Kings Crown Press, 1949.

Reuss, Carl F. "Differences Between Persons Responding and Not Responding to a Mailed Questionnaire," American Sociological Review, 8:433-438, 1943.

Rothstein, Samuel. "Nobody's Baby: A Brief Sermon on Continuing Professional Education," Library Journal, 2226-2227, May, 1965.

Scates, Douglas E. and A. Y. Scates. "Developing a Depth Questionnaire to Explore Motivation and Likelihood of Action," Educational and Psychological Measurement, 12:620-631, 1952.

BIBLIOGRAPHY

Schilling, Charles W. and Bruce Berman. <u>Science Information Specialist Training Program: A Progress Report</u>. Washington, D.C.: Biological Science Communication Project, George Washington University, 1968.

School Library Manpower Project. "School Library Manpower Project: A Vital New Study," <u>School Libraries</u>, 18:45-47, Fall, 1968.

"The School's Executive Development Programs: The Advanced Management Program; Objectives of Training for Top and Middle Managers and what Makes Program Tick," <u>Harvard Business School Bulletin,</u> 41: 7-9, May-June, 1965.

Selltiz, Claire, and others. <u>Research Methods in Social Relations</u>. Rev. 1 vol. ed. New York: Holt, Rinehart and Winston, 1959.

Shuttleworth, F. "Sample Errors Involved in Incomplete Returns to Mail Questionnaires," <u>Journal of Applied Psychology,</u> 25:588-591, 1941.

Slocum, W. L., L. T. Empey, and H. S. Swanson. "Increasing Response to Questionnaires and Structured Interviews," <u>American Sociological Review</u>, 21:221-225, 1956.

Snedecor, George W. "On the Design of Sampling Investigations," <u>American Statisticians,</u> 2(6):6-9, 13, December, 1948.

Spurr, William A., L. S. Kellogg, and J. H. Smith. <u>Business and Economic Statistics</u>. New York: Richard D. Irwin, 1961.

Strout, Donald E. and R. B. Strout. "Salaries Stronger, More Positions," <u>Library Journal,</u> 82:1597-1604, June, 1957.

_____. "The Story is the Same," <u>Library Journal</u>, 87:2323-2329, April, 1962.

Suchman, Edward A., and Boyd McCandless. "IV. General Research Techniques. Who Answers Questionnaires?" <u>Journal of Applied Psychology,</u> 24:758-769, 1940.

Toops, H. A. "Questionnaire." In: W. S. Monroe, ed. <u>Encyclopedia of Educational Research</u>. New York: Macmillan, 1941.

Wasserman, Paul. "Development of Administration in Library Service Current Status and Future Prospects," <u>College and Research Libraries,</u> 19:283-294, July, 1958.

BIBLIOGRAPHY

Wasserman, Paul. The Librarian and the Machine. Detroit: Gale Publishing Co., 1965.

"We Should Use the Best Evidence," [Editorial comment] Educational Research Bulletin, 39:44, 56,

Webb, Eugene J., and others. Unobtrusive Measures: Nonreactive Research in the Social Sciences. Chicago: Rand McNally & Co., 1966.

Wheeler, Joseph L. Progress and Problems in Education for Librianship. New York: Carnegie Corp., 1946.

Williamson, Charles C. "Some Present-Day Aspects of Library Training," Bulletin of the American Library Association, 13: 120-126, July, 1919.

Worcester, Robert M. "Association Survey Report," Association Management, 14-16, May, 1966.

Questionnaire Samples

Aceto, Vincent J. "A Study of the Occupation of Teacher of Librarianship," School of Library Science, State University of New York at Albany, 1967. (In progress)

Drennan, Henry T., and Richard L. Darling. Library Manpower: Occupational Characteristics of Public and School Librarians. Washington, D.C.: Government Printing Office, 1966.

Friedlander, Frank. Two Questionnaires, Two Analyses of Variance Tables, and Two Multiple Range Test Tables. ADI-8027. Washington, D.C.:American Documentation Institute, [n.d.].

Gross, Edward, and P. V. Grambsch. "Academic Administrators and University Goals: A Study of the Center for Academic Administration Research, University of Minnesota." Minneapolis·Center for Academic Administration Research, University of Minnesota, 1965.

Johnson, James A. A National Survey of Student Teaching Programs. Washington, D.C.:U.S. Office of Education, 1968.

Knox, Alan B. "Continuing Legal Education of Nebraska Lawyers." Unpublished nondegree study, Nebraska State Bar Association, Lincoln, 1964.

BIBLIOGRAPHY

Knox, Alan B. "Nebraska Adult Interests Study." Unpublished non-degree study, Adult Education Research, University of Nebraska, Lincoln, 1965.

Kortendick, James J. The Library in Priestly Formation: A Study of Libraries in the Roman Catholic Major Seminaries and Religious Houses of Formation in the United States. Washington, D.C.: The Catholic University of America, 1963.

McCreedy, Sister Mary Lucille. "Questionnaire for Students in Graduate Library Schools and Students in Selected Undergraduate Library Science Departments." Unpublished questionnaire used in preparation for a Doctor's dissertation, School of Library Service, Columbia University, New York, 1963.

_____. "The Selection of School Librarianship as a Career." Unpublished Doctor's dissertation, School of Library Service, Columbia University, New York, 1964.

Myers, M. Scott. "Management Attitude Questionnaire." Unpublished questionnaire developed at Texas Instruments Inc., Dallas, Texas, 1964.

National Science Foundation and Center for Applied Linguistics. "National Register of Scientific and Technical Personnel in the Field of Linguistics and Allied Specialties." Washington, D.C.: Center for Applied Linguistics, 1966.

Passow, A. Harry. Washington D.C. Teacher Study. Bureau of Applied Social Research, Columbia University, New York, 1967.

Schiller, Anita. "Survey of Professional Personnel in College and University Libraries." Urbana: Library Research Center, University of Illinois, 1967.

Stone, Elizabeth W. "A Study of Some Factors Related to the Professional Development of Librarians." Doctor's dissertation, American University, Washington, D.C., 1968.

Survey of Information Processing Personnel conducted by the American Federation of Information Processing Societies (AFIPS), The Data Processing Management Association (DPMA), and the Numerical Control Society (NCS). Washington, D.C.: AFIPS, 1968.

BIBLIOGRAPHY

Swanson, Harold B. "Factors Associated with Motivation Toward Professional Development of County Agricultural Extension Agents in Minnesota." Unpublished Doctor's dissertation, University of Wisconsin, Madison, 1965.

Taylor, Edward B. "An Analysis of the Educational Needs of Nebraska Lawyers in Relation to Career Cycle." Unpublished Doctor's dissertation, University of Nebraska, Lincoln, 1966.

Thomas, Mary E. " A Study of the Graduates of the School of Library Science, University of North Carolina, 1951-1957; An Analysis of the Careers in Librarianship of Recipients of the Bachelor of Science in Library Science." Unpublished Master's dissertation, University of North Carolina, Chapel Hill, 1964.

Tough, Allen M. "The Teaching Tasks Performed by Adult Self-Teachers." Unpublished Doctor's dissertation, University of Chicago, Chicago, 1965.

University of Southern California. School of Library Science. "Alumni Personnel Questionnaire." Unpublished questionnaire, University of Southern California, Los Angeles, 1965.

_____. "Library Rating of Recent Graduates of the School of Library Science, University of Southern California." Unpublished questionnaire from the School of Library Science, University of Southern California, Los Angeles, 1965.

White, Rodney. The Cornell Study of the Hospital Administrator. Ithaca: Sloan Institute of Hospital Administration, Graduate School of Business and Public Administration, Cornell University, [n.d.].

Zeberl, Andrew J. "The Acceptance of Training as Perceived Among Volunteers in a Health Agency." Unpublished Doctor's dissertation, University of Michigan, Ann Arbor, 1964.

BIBLIOGRAPHY

QUESTIONNAIRE:
JOB INVENTORIES

Bernstein, Marver H. The Job of the Federal Executive. Washington, D. C.: The Brookings Institution, 1958.

Bryan, Alice I. The Public Librarian. New York: Columbia University Press, 1952.

Carlson, Sune. Executive Behaviour: A Study of the Work Load and the Working Methods of Managing Directors. Stockholm: C.A. Stromberg Aktiebolag Publ., 1951.

Corson, John J. and R. Shale Paul. Men Near the Top: Filling Key Posts in the Federal Service. Baltimore: The Johns Hopkins Press, 1966.

Curnow, Geoffrey Ross. "The Dimensions of Executive Work in the U. S. Federal Career Civil Service: A Factor Analytic Study." Unpublished Doctor's dissertation, Cornell University, Ithaca, 1967.

Educational Testing Service. "Appendix B.: Selected 'Job-Elements' from a Check List with the Job Dimensions Project." In: Assessing Managerial Potential: Report of a Seminar. Ann Arbor, Michigan: The Foundation for Research on Human Behavior, 1958.

Finn, Robert Howard. "A Factor Analysis of Selected Job Characteristics." Unpublished Doctor's dissertation, Purdue University, Lafayette, 1954.

Foundation for Research on Human Behavior. Assessing Managerial Potential. Report of a Seminar. Ann Arbor, Michigan: Foundation for Research on Human Behavior, 1958.

Friedlander, Frank. "Job Characteristics as Satisfiers and Dissatisfiers," Journal of Applied Psychology, 48:388-392, December. 1964.

Hemphill, John. Dimensions of Executive Positions. Research Monograph No. 98. Columbus, Ohio: Bureau of Business Research, The Ohio State University, 1960.

BIBLIOGRAPHY

Howard, Paul. "Library Staff Manuals and a Theory of Library Management." Unpublished Master's dissertation, Department of Library Science, University of Chicago, 1939.

Koontz, Harold and Cyril O'Donnell. Principles of Management: An Analysis of Managerial Functions. 4th ed. New York: McGraw-Hill Book Company, 1968.

Lundy, James L. "An Analysis of Work Sampling in the Study of Management Job Activity." Unpublished Doctor's dissertation, University of Minnesota, Minneapolis, 1957.

McLennan, Kenneth. "The Manager and His Job Skills," Academy of Management Journal, 10(3):235-245, September, 1967.

Mahoney, Thomas A., Thomas H. Jerdoe, and Stephen J. Carroll. Development of Managerial Performance: A Research Approach. Cincinnati: South-Western, 1963.

Meltzer, Morton. The Information Center: Management's Hidden Asset. New York: American Management Association, 1967.

Morsh, Joseph E., M. Joyce Giorgia, and Joseph M. Madden. A Job Analysis of a Complex Utilization Field: The R & D Management Officer. Lackland Air Force Base, Texas: Air Force Systems Company, 1965.

National Education Association. Research Division. School Library Personnel Task Analysis Survey. School Library Manpower Project. Chicago: American Library Association, 1969.

Peterson, Clarence E. Electronic Data Processing in Engineering Science, and Business: Suggested Techniques for Determining Courses of Study in Vocational and Technical Education Programs. Washington, D.C.: U. S. Office of Education, 1964. ED 013 325.

Phillips, Kathleen. "Training for Federal Librarians," Federal Library Committee Newsletter, 21:7-13, June, 1968.

Porter, Lyman W. and Edward E. Lawler, III. Managerial Attitudes and Performance. Irwin-Dorsey Series in Behavioral Science. Homewood, Ill.: Richard D. Irwin, Inc., 1968.

BIBLIOGRAPHY

Rushforth, Norman B. "A Comparison of Sample Correlation Matrices and a Multivariate Analysis of Job Concepts of Selected Industrial Executive Groups." Unpublished Doctor's dissertation, Cornell University, Ithaca, 1961.

Saunders, David R. Use of an Objective Method to Determine Engineering Job Families that will Apply in Several Companies. Princeton, N. J.; Educational Testing Service, 1954.

Scheips, Charles D. "A Pattern Analysis of Job Requirement Factors for a Sample of Jobs." Unpublished Doctor's dissertation, Purdue University, Lafayette, 1954.

Schick, Frank. Survey of Special Libraries Serving the Federal Government. Washington, D.C.: National Center for Educational Statistics, U. S. Department of Health, Education, and Welfare, 1968.

Scientific American. The Big Business Executive, 1964: A Study of His Social and Educational Background. New York: Scientific American, 1965.

Smith, Robert G., Jr. Controlling the Quality of Training. Technical Report 65-6. Alexandria, Va.: Human Resources Research Office, George Washington University, 1965.

_____. The Design of Instructional Systems. Technical Report 66-18. Alexandria, Va.: Human Resources Research Office, George Washington University, 1966.

_____. The Development of Training Objectives. Alexandria, Va.: Human Resources Research Office, George Washington University, 1965.

Stogdill, Ralph. A Predictive Study of Administrative Work Patterns. Columbus: Ohio State University, 1956.

Stogdill, Ralph and Carroll L. Shartle. Methods in the Study of Administrative Leadership. Columbus: Ohio State University, 1955.

Stogdill, Ralph, and others. Patterns of Administrative Performance. Columbus: Ohio State University, 1956.

BIBLIOGRAPHY

Stone, Elizabeth W. Training for the Improvement of Library Administrators. Monograph of the University of Illinois. Ann Arbor, Michigan: Edwards Brothers, Inc., 1967.

Teller, James D. and William B. Camm. Studies of Air Force Executives: I. Pretesting a Task Inventory for Executives (TIE) of the U. S. Air Force. Research Report 62-4. Directorate of Civilian Personnel Headquarters, U. S. Air Force, 1962.

———. Studies of Air Force Executives: II. Pretesting a Task Inventory for Executives (TIE) of the U. S. Air Force. Research Report 63-2. Directorate of Civilian Personnel Headquarters, U. S. Air Force, 1963.

U. S. Civil Service Commission. Federal Employment Characteristics and Requirements. Personnel Bibliography, No. 12. Washington, D. C.: U. S. Civil Service Commission, 1964.

———. Position-Classification Standards, Transmittal Sheet No. 62. Personnel Management Series GS-201. Washington, D.C.: U. S. Civil Service Commission, June, 1967.

———. Position-Classification Standards, Transmittal Sheet No. 60. Technical Information Services Series GS-1412. Washington, D.C.: U. S. Civil Service Commission, February, 1966.

———. Civil Service Handbook X-118: Qualification Standards for White Collar Positions Under the General Schedule, Transmittal Sheet No. 108. Washington, D.C.: U. S. Civil Service Commission, July, 1967.

Underwood, Willis O. "A Hospital Director's Administrative Profile," Hospital Administration, 8:6-24, Fall, 1963.

Wallace, Everett M. and others. Planning for On-The-Job Training of Library Personnel. Santa Monica, Calif.: Systems Development Corporation, 1967.

Warner, W. L., Paul P. Van Riper, and others. The American Federal Executive. New Haven: Yale University Press, 1963.

Wasserman, Paul and Mary Lee Bundy. Manpower for the Library and Information Professions in the 1970's: An Inquiry into Fundamental Problems. College Park, Md.: University of Maryland, 1966.

BIBLIOGRAPHY

RESEARCH:
STATUS AND NEEDS IN CONTINUING EDUCATION

American Library Association. Commission on Library Education. "A Report from the Commission on a National Plan for Library Education." ALA Bulletin, 61:419-422 April 1967.

Association of American Library Schools. Committee on Research, Advisory Eds. "Research in Librarianship," Library Trends, 6 103-253, October, 1957.

Beveridge, W. I. B. The Art of Scientific Investigation. 3d. ed. New York: Random House, Inc. (Vintage Books), 1967.

Brunner, Edmund de S., and others. An Overview of Adult Education Research. Washington, D.C.: Adult Education Association, 1959.

Cole, Dorothy E. "Research Literature of Librarianship: Some Thoughts on Bibliographical Control," Journal of Education for Librarianship, 7 :220-221, Spring, 1967.

Cook, Desmond L. An Overview of Management Science in Educational Research. A paper presented at a Symposium on Management Science in Educational Research, 15th International Meeting of the Institute of Management Science, Cleveland, Ohio, September 11-13, 1968. (ED 025 002.)

Courtney, E. Wayne. Research Needs in Vocational-Technical Education. Menomonie : Wisconsin State Board of Vocational Technology and Adult Education, Stout State University, 1966. (ED 020 410)

Cross, K. Patricia. "When Will Research Improve Education?" The Research Reporter, 2:1-4, 1967. (ED 025 206)

Garrison, Guy. "Research in Librarianship," Libri, 13:206-214, 1963.

_____ (ed.). "Research Methods in Librarianship," Library Trends, 13 : 3-149, July, 1964.

Gaver, Mary. "Is Anyone Listening? Significant Research Studies for Practicing Librarians," Wilson Library Bulletin, 43:764-772, April, 1969.

BIBLIOGRAPHY

Goldhor, Herbert. "A Plea for a Program of Research in Librarianship," ALA Bulletin, 56:44-46, January, 1962.

_____. "Preparation of a Manual for the Conduct of Research in Librarianship." Urbana: University of Illinois, June 1967 to August, 1968. EP 010 938.

Goldhor, Herbert, ed. Research Methods in Librarianship: Measurement and Evaluation. Papers presented at a conference conducted by the University of Illinois. Monograph series No. 8. Urbana: Graduate School of Library Science, University of Illinois, 1968.

Gomersall, Earl R. and M. Scott Myers. "Breakthrough in On-The-Job Training," Harvard Business Review, 44:62-72, July-August, 1966.

Hertz, David B. The Theory and Practice of Industrial Research. New York: McGraw-Hill, 1950.

Jahoda, Gerald. "Correlative Indexing Systems for the Control of Research Records." Unpublished Doctor's dissertation, School of Library Service, Columbia University, New York, 1960.

Jesse, William H. and Ann E. Mitchell. "Professional Staff Opportunities for Study and Research," College and Research Libraries, 29:87-100, March, 1968.

"A Kaleidoscopic View of Library Research," Wilson Library Bulletin, 41:896-949, May, 1967.

Krug, J. "Writing Research Proposals," ALA Bulletin, 61:1314-1318, December, 1967.

Lancour, Harold. "Research," Drexel Library Quarterly, 3:164-166, April, 1967.

Logsdon, Richard H. "The Need for Research in the Library Field," College and Research Libraries, 22:363-365, September, 1961.

Lothrop, Warren C. Management Uses of Research and Development. New York: Harper and Row, 1964.

McConnell, T. R. Research or Development: A Reconciliation. Bloomington, Indiana: Phi Delta Kappa International, 1967.

BIBLIOGRAPHY

McCrossan, John. "How to Get a Grant for Library Research," *ALA Bulletin*, 62:722-732, June, 1968.

McMullen, Haynes. "The Place of Research in Library Schools." In: Larry E. Bone, ed. *Library Education: An International Survey.* Champaign, Ill.: University of Illinois. 1968, pp. 345-372.

Maxwell, Albert E. *Analyzing Qualitative Data.* New York: Wiley, 1961.

Mial, Dorothy. *Special Project to Train Action Researchers and Trainers of Action Research Collaborators.* Final Report. Washington, D.C.: National Training Labs. Inst. for Applied Behavioral Science, 1967. ED 021 783.

Mosher, Frederick C. *Professional Education and the Public Service: An Exploratory Study.* Final Report. Berkeley, California: Center for Research and Development in Higher Education, University of California at Berkeley, 1968. ED 025 220; also listed as ED 023 971.

Muller, Robert H. "Research Approach to University Library Problems," *College and Research Libraries,* 24:199-203. May, 1963.

_____. "The Research Mind in Library Education and Practice," *Library Journal,* 92:1126-1129, March, 1967.

Parker, Edwin B., David A. Lingwood, and William J. Paisley. *Communication and Research Productivity in an Interdisciplinary Behavioral Science Research Area.* A Report of the Institute for Communication Research. Stanford, Calif.: Stanford University Institute for Communication Research, 1968.

Petrof, Barbara G. "The Status of Research Courses," *Journal of Education for Librarianship*, 81:28-32, Summer, 1967.

Reagan, Agnes L. "Needed Research in Education for Librarianship," *ALA Bulletin,* 56:333-334, April, 1962.

Reece, Ernest J. "Research in Education for Librarianship, 1957-63," *American Library Association, Education Division Newsletter,* 53:10-20, March, 1965.

BIBLIOGRAPHY

Reed, Sarah R. "Library Education Report," Journal of Education for Librarianship, 5(3):201-204, Winter, 1965.

Research in Education. Washington, D.C.: U. S. Office of Education, 1966-

Rubenstein, Arthur H. "Timing and Form of Researchers' Needs for Technical Information," Journal of Chemical Documentation, 2:28-31, January, 1962.

Saracevic, Tefko. Linking Research and Teaching. Cleveland, Ohio: Western Reserve University, 1967.

Saunders, W. L. "The Establishment of Priorities." In: Research into Library Services in Higher Education. 1968, pp. 22-26.

Schick, Frank L., and others. "Library Science Research Needs," Journal of Education for Librarianship, 3:280-291, Spring, 1963.

Schoenfeldt, Lyle F. Program for Training in Computer and Multivariate Applications to Educational Research. Pittsburgh, Pa.: American Institutes for Research, 1967.   ED 021 791.

Selltiz, Claire, and others. Research Methods in Social Relations. Rev. ed. New York: Holt, Rinehart and Winston, 1959.

Shera, Jesse H. "Darwin, Bacon, and Research in Librarianship," Library Trends, 13:141-149, July, 1964.

Silk, Leonard S. The Research Revolution. New York: McGraw-Hill, 1960.

Walker, Richard D. "Research Methods--A Selected Bibliography," Journal of Education for Librarianship, 7(4):210-219, Spring, 1967.

Wallace, Everett. Research and Development of On-The-Job Training Courses for Library Personnel. Santa Monica, Calif.: Systems Development Corporation.

Wasserman, Paul. "Research Frontiers," Library Journal, 86:2409-2416, July, 1961.

BIBLIOGRAPHY

Webb, Eugene J. Unobtrusive Measures: Nonreactive Research in the Social Sciences. Chicago, Ill.: Rand McNally, 1966.

Wendt, Paul. "New Library Materials and Technology for Instruction and Research," Library Trends, 16:197-210, October, 1967.

Whatley, H. A. "Research for Librarians: Elementary Stages," Research in Librarianship, 2:17-20, January, 1968.

Whitlock, Gerald H. "Research Information Sources in Training. A Comprehensive Survey of Present and Planned Resources," Training and Development Journal, 21:2-8, November, 1967.

Williamson, Charles C. "The Place of Research in Library Service," Library Quarterly, 1:1-17, 1931.

"Winning a Research Bid: Tips on Proposal Writing," American Education, 4:30, May, 1968.

Woodworth, Mary L. The Identification and Examination of Areas of Needed Research in School Librarianship. Final Report. Madison: University of Wisconsin, 1967. ED 018 243.

Zim, Herbert S. "Science: The Process of Discovering New Facts," Drexel Library Quarterly, 5(3):135-143, July, 1969.

Z
668
K665

FEB 24 1972